A Haunted Mind

Inside the Dark, Twisted World of H.P. Lovecraft

Dr. Bob Curran

Illustrated by Ian Daniels

New Page BOOKS

A Division of
The Career Press, Inc.
Pompton Plains, NJ

A HAUNTED MIND
EDITED AND TYPESET BY GINA TALUCCI
Cover design by Jeff Piasky
Cover and interior artwork by Ian Daniels
Printed in the U.S.A.

To order this title, please call toll-free 1-800-CAREER-1 (NJ and Canada: 201-848-0310) to order using VISA or MasterCard, or for further information on books from Career Press.

The Career Press, Inc.
220 West Parkway, Unit 12
Pompton Plains, NJ 07444
www.careerpress.com
www.newpagebooks.com

Library of Congress Cataloging-in-Publication Data
Curran, Bob.
    A haunted mind : inside the dark, twisted world of H.P. Lovecraft / by Bob Curran ; illustrated by Ian Daniels.
                        p. cm.
    Includes index.
    ISBN 978-1-60163-219-7 -- ISBN 978-1-60163-596-9 (ebook)
    Lovecraft, H. P. (Howard Phillips), 1890-1937--Criticism and interpretation.
    2. Horror tales, American--History and criticism. I. Daniels, Ian. II. Title.

PS3523.O833Z586 2012
813'.52--dc23

                                                            2012013736

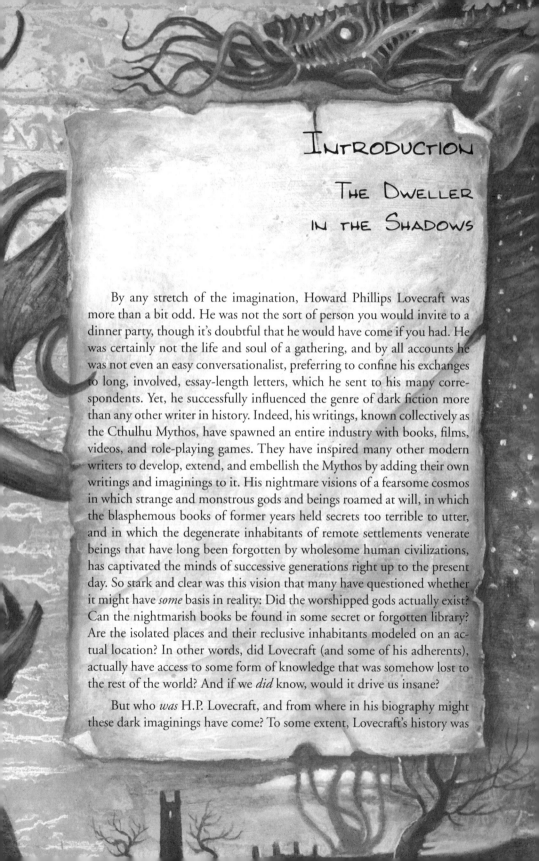

Introduction

The Dweller in the Shadows

By any stretch of the imagination, Howard Phillips Lovecraft was more than a bit odd. He was not the sort of person you would invite to a dinner party, though it's doubtful that he would have come if you had. He was certainly not the life and soul of a gathering, and by all accounts he was not even an easy conversationalist, preferring to confine his exchanges to long, involved, essay-length letters, which he sent to his many correspondents. Yet, he successfully influenced the genre of dark fiction more than any other writer in history. Indeed, his writings, known collectively as the Cthulhu Mythos, have spawned an entire industry with books, films, videos, and role-playing games. They have inspired many other modern writers to develop, extend, and embellish the Mythos by adding their own writings and imaginings to it. His nightmare visions of a fearsome cosmos in which strange and monstrous gods and beings roamed at will, in which the blasphemous books of former years held secrets too terrible to utter, and in which the degenerate inhabitants of remote settlements venerate beings that have long been forgotten by wholesome human civilizations, has captivated the minds of successive generations right up to the present day. So stark and clear was this vision that many have questioned whether it might have *some* basis in reality: Did the worshipped gods actually exist? Can the nightmarish books be found in some secret or forgotten library? Are the isolated places and their reclusive inhabitants modeled on an actual location? In other words, did Lovecraft (and some of his adherents), actually have access to some form of knowledge that was somehow lost to the rest of the world? And if we *did* know, would it drive us insane?

But who *was* H.P. Lovecraft, and from where in his biography might these dark imaginings have come? To some extent, Lovecraft's history was one of privilege, its roots dug deep in old New England aristocracy and gentility, a world away from the squalid and crumbling cabins of the inbred folk in the Rhode Island hills that he sometimes wrote about. It was also, to some extent, a protected up-bringing, in which his immediate family shielded the growing boy from the supposed horrors and demands of the rapidly changing world of the early 1900s. Subsequently, this left him strange and withdrawn, and not terribly proficient at making or sustaining face-to-face personal relationships.

He was born at 9 a.m. on August 20th, 1890, at the family home of 194 Angell Street, Providence, Rhode Island. (The house was later renumbered as 454 and then torn down in 1961.) His father, Winfield Scott Lovecraft (1853–1898), was a commercial traveler for Gorham and Company, silversmiths of Providence. But it was his mother, the neurotic, headstrong, and emotionally unstable Sarah Susan Phillips (1857–1921) who made the biggest impact on his developmental years. Susie, as she was known, had married beneath her station—she came from an old Providence family who could trace their origins back to the Colonial founding fathers. Prior to becoming a traveling salesman, Winfield had been a lowly blacksmith during the 1870s and was incapable of giving her the life that she expected as part of the prestigious Phillips family. Winfield's father, George Lovecraft (1814–1895), lived in Mount Vernon, New York, where he had been a harness-maker and accumulated no real fortune that he could pass on to his son. By contrast, Howard's maternal grandfather was the wealthy industrialist Whipple Van Buren Phillips, who later on became a surrogate father to Howard.

There may have been a great deal of discord in the Phillips family regarding the marriage. Although generations of the Phillips family had been married in Providence, Susie married Winfield at St. Paul's Episcopal Church in Boston, Massachusetts. In his essay entitled "The Parents of Howard Phillips Lovecraft" in *Epicure of the Terrible* (Schultz and Joshi, 1991), Kenneth F. Faig suggests that the wedding may have taken place against the wishes of Susie's parents and sisters.

After Howard's birth, Susie did not stay long in Providence and returned to Dorchester. Early in 1892, the couple vacationed in Dudley, Massachusetts, with Susie's friend, Miss Ella Sweeney. Sweeney later recalled that Susie didn't enjoy the holiday, because she fretted so much about Howard. When he was upstairs, Susie was incredibly agitated downstairs thinking that someone or *something* would get into the house and molest or injure her infant son. As time passed, she convinced herself that Howard was incredibly delicate, and the slightest exertion might prove grievous.

Later in 1892, the Lovecrafts were forced to give up their rented house in Dorchester and move to a cheaper apartment in the Auburndale suburb of Boston. This move brought them into contact with an eccentric landlady, the poetess Louise Imogen Guiney. Miss Guiney lived in the same house as the Lovecrafts along with her mother, and the two ladies took the young Howard under their wings. Louise had a number of soirees and trained Howard in the memorization of verse, so that he could entertain her guests with long recitals of complicated poetic works. She also instilled in him an abiding love of books and letters, as literary figures came and went through Miss Guiney's rooms. (Lovecraft later claimed that he remembered sitting on the knee of Oliver Wendell Holmes.) The attention given to the young boy by such figures gave him an overwhelming air of self-importance, which cut him off from other boys his age in the surrounding area.

This cosseted literary world was about to change, however. In April 1893, in a hotel room in Chicago, Winfield Lovecraft went mad. After attending a sales convention in the city, he retired to his room only to wake in the middle of the night screaming that his wife was being assaulted in the room above. Susie, of course, was in Massachusetts. Winfield was restrained for his own protection and on April 25th, he was committed to the Butler Hospital in Providence.

Howard was 2 years old at the time of his father's institutionalization, and his life was about to change dramatically. Faced with abject poverty—Winfield had little savings—and without any real prospects of her own, Susie was forced to return to Providence, which brought Howard under the influence of his powerful grandfather, Whipple Phillips.

Whipple Phillips was what we would today call "a self-made man." After his father's death in 1848, Whipple purchased a general store. The store prospered and, in 1853, Whipple married his first cousin Robie Place, who brought with her a fairly substantial dowry. Using this and the earnings of the store, Whipple bought the entire village of Coffin's Corner in western Rhode Island, which he renamed "Greene" in 1859. By this time he was a Freemason and even built a large Masonic Hall in the village. His Masonic connections were a successful acquisition, and he served as a representative for Coventry in the Rhode Island General Assembly between 1720 and 1722, becoming one of the most influential men in the state. In 1873, he sold all his interests in Greene and transferred what was now a thriving property business to Providence, eventually building himself a three-story house on Angell Street. Today, the house he built would not be considered a mansion, but in the confines of developing Providence it was rather grand. Lovecraft would refer to it years later in a 1916 letter to Rheinhart Klein, one of his correspondents, as "one of the handsomest residences in the city."

Shortly after the move to Providence, Howard received a package of books from his paternal grandfather, George Lovecraft. This represented the entire Lovecraft family library and was the only gift that he ever received from his father's side of the family. Whipple Phillips also boasted an extensive library, and from these tomes the literary education that Howard received from Louise Imogen Guiney began to bear fruit, as he started to read voraciously as soon as he was.

The house immediately beside Howard's was occupied by the Phillips's coachman, an Irishman named Kelly, who lived in the upper part of the house with his wife. Kelly was a renowned storyteller, as well as something of an engineer, and he befriended the young boy, telling him wonderful stories and helping him construct a play railway on a vacant lot nearby. He also built a playhouse for Howard, which he called "The Engine House"; Howard and Kelly even constructed a toy engine from an old boiler mounted on a small trolley. Kelly was well known by many of the children in the district, and a number of them gathered around the lot to play. However, by 1900 Whipple Phillips was facing a slight dip in his fortunes, and had to release the coachman from his employ. The children drifted away, but Lovecraft continued to lay alone in the now-abandoned Engine House.

When he did play with some of the other children, he built a make-believe Alaskan village, which he called New Anvik. It was supposedly a settlement of white colonists and was fortified against Indian attack. The name was derived from an 1895 children's novel called *Snow-shoes and Sledges* by Kirk Monroe. It was the imaginary world of most young boys, but Lovecraft clung to it longer than most. There were whispers among some of the other children that he hadn't really grown up and was still playing childish games. However, Lovecraft sunk deeper and deeper into his own imagination, something that would help him as a writer in later years. New Anvik was, perhaps, the first step in the creation of his own worlds and cosmos.

By 3 years old, he had already learned to read *Grimm's Fairy Tales* on his own; by age 4, he could read most books with ease. In 1895, he read *Arabian Nights,* a book that had a monumental effect on him. It became one of his favorites, and it would inspire in him a fascination for all things Arabian. As he got older, he began to decorate his room with furnishing that had an Arabian look to them, and when he played he dressed himself in a winding sheet, and took to calling himself Abdul Alhazred. Where the exotic name came from is unknown, but it eventually became the name of the writer attached to the famed but blasphemous *Al-Azif* (later becoming the abhorred *Necronomicon*). In a 1924 letter to the editor of *Weird Tales* (Edwin Baird), Lovecraft claimed that he had come up with the name and had used it to pass himself off as "a devout Mohommedan" in order to surreptitiously obtain some Arab pottery and objet d'art for his room. In 1932, however, in a letter to writer Robert E. Howard, he suggested that he heard the name from the family lawyer and friend, Albert Baker. The moniker eventually became the name of the mad prophet of Sana'a in Yemen, whose mind had been blasted by the horrors that he'd seen.

Coupled with his interest in all things Arabian was his growing fascination with Greek mythology. In 1896, he began reading a version of Homer's *Odyssey*. The version he read was simplified, but it gave Howard a taste for the bizarre and the fantastic. His aunt, Lillian Phillips, also gave him a copy of Thomas Bulfinch's *Stories of Gods and Heroes*. This moved his interests from the deserts of Arabia to the groves of Greece. Intrigued by the Greek text he also became interested in collecting plaster reproductions of the classical gods and goddesses, which now lined his room just as the Arabian artifacts had. He started visiting the classical art museums of Providence to look at Greek art showing representations of the ancient gods. He also changed his imaginary name from Abdul Alhazred to Lucius Valerius Messala.

By 1896, he had already started composing original works of poetry and short sections of text. He also started to think that he was something of a young prodigy, although his writings were nowhere near those to whom he compared himself, such as Edgar Allen Poe and Nathaniel Hawthorne. During the time of his initial writings, he started to connect with all things English. This may have arisen from his own lineage, which he traced back to the founding of Bay Colony, Massachusetts, in 1630. The Phillips family had come from England around that time, and even though they weren't in the same social class, the Lovecraft family had come from established English stock as well. Indeed, he frequently boasted that he was only several generations removed from being English. He began to read the works of English writers—particular the Gothic ones—such as Horace Walpole, Matthew Lewis, and Ann Radcliffe, which were filled with spectral visitations, walking skeletons, abandoned houses, and mad relatives. This period of writers had a great affect on him; he would remain an Anglophile for the rest of his life.

Whipple Phillips encouraged Howard's learning interests by lending him more and more books from his own library, along with obtaining some from bookstores all over America. Lovecraft imitated all that he read and this habit would be repeated throughout his career. Two writers in particular impressed him greatly, and he strove to imitate their styles and their ideas. The first was Edgar Allen Poe, who he discovered in 1898, which turned out to be a very traumatic year for him. On July 19th, Lovecraft's father died of paralytic dementia, the third and final stage of syphilis. As a result, Howard buried himself in Poe's literature as a way to cope.

The second writer that appealed to Lovecraft was an Irish author by the name of Edward John Moreton Drax Plunkett, the 18th Baron of Dunsany. Lovecraft was especially drawn to *A Dreamer's Tales*. However, his interest in Poe and Dunsany led Lovecraft down dark paths, and his writing took on Gothic aspects. The foundations of his eerie cosmology were already being laid.

Years later on March 28th, 1904, Whipple Phillips suddenly died of a cerebral hemorrhage. Howard was 13 years old when he witnessed his grandfather's death, and would later describe it as "the worst day of my life." After Whipple's death, the family met to hear the will. They were dismayed to hear that Whipple's fortune had been far less than they had imagined. According to S.T. Joshi in *A Dreamer and Visionary* (2001), Lovecraft only received $1,500, along with his grandfather's gun collection (most of which he gave away). Furthermore, a decision was made that the house on Angell Street should be sold in order to meet expenses. Susie's two sisters—Lillian and Annie—were married and out of the house, so Susie reluctantly agreed to move in to the ground floor of a much smaller house on 598 Angell Street. Although the apartment had five rooms and she had access to the attic and cellar for storage, it was a step down in the world for the Lovecrafts. Howard solemnly promised his mother that he would become famous and earn enough money to re-buy the Phillips property, a promise he never came close to fulfilling.

The most notable result of the declining family circumstances was the reaction of former friends and neighbors. According to Joshi there is evidence that Lovecraft's neighbors and playmates thought him "a bit odd," but these were dismissed as eccentricities or as the result of a cosseted upbringing. Such toleration was made easier by thinking that Lovecraft might one day inherit his grandfather's fortune and remember those to whom he had been friendly. Those who had formerly tolerated him now began to openly mock and shun him.

In the fall of 1904, he entered Hope Street High School in Providence. Formal education for Lovecraft was something of an ordeal. During his enrollment at the Slater Avenue primary school years earlier, his attendance was erratic at best. His problem was not one of intellect; he had no difficulty coping academically, and excelled at reading, writing, and general studies. When he did attend, he argued with the teachers and refused to do what he was told. There was little doubt that he was spoiled at home and clearly expected the same sort of treatment in school. In the end, Susie removed him and he received a primary education at home. High school, however, was another matter.

For someone who assumed affected speech, had eccentric interests, put on airs of superiority, and often made bizarre facial grimaces, school was a difficult place. The other teenagers called him "Lovey" and bullied him physically, mentally, and emotionally. Because of his aversion to popular forms of music and dancing and his lack of interest in women, rumors circulated that he was homosexual. He had no girlfriends and his odd mannerisms kept him apart from all of his classmates.

The argument as to whether Lovecraft had homosexual tendencies has been prevalent for many years. Throughout his life he maintained a strong outward hostility toward homosexuality, however, he had a number of homosexual friends and acquaintances throughout his life. It may be that he was asexual rather than sexual, and that he was untroubled by any erotic tendencies. In the end, he treated his schoolmates with a lofty disdain and took to spying on them, saying that he was observing them as an anthropologist might observe animals of a lower order. This, of course, didn't make him very popular among them, either.

As far as academic studies went, Lovecraft didn't fare all that badly during his first year at Hope Street, though there was an incident completely unrelated to his studies that may have determined his academic career. Around the end of 1904, a black cat that Lovecraft had raised went mysteriously missing. Despite the lack of evidence, Lovecraft suspected that some of the other teenagers might have lured it away and killed it; the possible loss of his pet traumatized him. He withdrew from the school in 1905, citing the reasons that he had used at Slater Avenue: a nervous condition and a weak constitution. The real reason may have been his difficulty with and dislike for his fellow students. He took to wandering about the streets at night talking to himself and stopping at lighted windows to peer in and frighten small children. He also took up astronomy with a vengeance and began writing articles on the subject for local papers.

He stayed out of school for the entire 1905 academic year, not resuming his studies until the fall of 1906. Once again, he proved an able scholar, but his missing year had left him a little behind. He kept his distance from his fellow students even though his newspaper articles had earned him a kind of grudging respect—they nicknamed him "the Professor." He worked hard enough to scrape by a passing grade in his mathematics class, although his arts grades were excellent. He left school for good in 1907 and, years later, he claimed that he had achieved a high school diploma; the reality was that he had dropped out without completing his schooling. Although he had hoped at one point to go to Brown University where he could study astronomy, the reality was that this door was now closed to him.

After high school his life entered a curious phase that brought him to the very brink of suicide. Until around 1918, he seems to have more or less withdrawn from human society, becoming something of a hermit and recluse. He received no visitors and made no attempt to contact anybody; he saw no one except his mother.

In order to make himself slightly different and perhaps fit in with the characters that he'd created for himself (Abdul Alhazred, Lucius Valerius Messala, and so on), Howard worked on his many facial grimaces. However, as time went on, this became more or less involuntary and spasmodic, and he found that he couldn't control them. They persisted through his teenage years, but went dormant later in life.

During his teenage years, Lovecraft considered ending it all several times. Perhaps faced with the same black moods, another teenager might have found a temporary solace in either alcohol or sex, but Lovecraft abhorred alcohol and sex was not really an option. He had, of course, discovered sex only in a theoretical sense, largely by reading books in his grandfather's library. He found the idea of the human reproductive process both vulgar and extremely unpleasant. In many ways this was a confirmation of humanity's animalistic nature from which he felt quite divorced. In a letter to J. Vernon Shea in February 1934 he stated:

THE WHOLE MATTER WAS REDUCED TO A PROSAIC MECHANISM—A MECHANISM WHICH I RATHER DESPISED OR AT LEAST THOUGHT NON-GLAMOROUS BECAUSE OF ITS PURELY ANIMAL NATURE AND SEPARATION FROM SUCH THINGS AS INTELLECT AND BEAUTY—ALL THE DRAMA WAS TAKEN OUT OF IT.

In his attempt to repress any sexual desires (and it may be that sex simply did not interest him), Lovecraft seemed to withdraw even more from his peers. He became fearful of various conditions, one of which was wide-open spaces. This fear would later manifest itself in some of his writings that involved vast subterranean caverns and limitless gulfs between worlds. The darkness that was starting to infest his mind was slowly taking shape.

At this point in his life, several of his works had been published. Although he was the author of several prose pieces—for example, the short story *The Alchemist* (written in 1908)—much of his writing concentrated on poetic works. His first poem,

Providence in the Year 2000, which he described as a "satire," was published in the *Evening Bulletin* on March 4th, 1912, when Lovecraft was 21. The 62-line work ridicules a group of Providence Italians living in the Federal Hill area regarding their attempt to change a street name from Atwell's Avenue to the grander-sounding Columbus Avenue. The poem provoked protests from the Italian community, but few paid much attention, least of all Lovecraft. In April of that same year, he penned another poem with racist overtones called *New England Fallen*. In 1913, he penned another "satire" entitled *The Creation of Niggers*, the language of which was extremely racist:

> TH'OLYMPIAN HOST CONCEIV'D A CLEVER PLAN,
> A BEAST THEY WROUGHT IN SEMI-HUMAN FIGURE,
> FILLED IT WITH VICE AND CALLED THE THING A NIGGER.

Of course, such sentiments would not be tolerated today. Perhaps it was the perception of himself and his family as the inheritors of the puree English stock that engendered in Lovecraft a deep-rooted racism and bigotry.

Around this time, he started to attack the work of other writers who had a negative viewpoint of him and his writing. A favorite target was a writer named Fred Jackson, who wrote romantic love stories for a magazine called *The Argosy*. Lovecraft cited them as "quaint Queen Anne prose." His mockery was rooted in the assumption that Jackson's stories were taking up space in the magazine, which could be used for Lovecraft's science fiction stories instead. *The Argosy* published a letter from Lovecraft in its September issue. Jackson, however, had a number of fans, many of whom were outraged by what they saw as a sneering, unwarranted attack on their favorite writer. They wrote several letters in his defense, all of which were published. In fact, a gentleman named John Russell replied with a humorous verse at Lovecraft's expense. Lovecraft was incensed and replied with a 44-line satire based on Alexander Pope's *Dunciad*. He implied that Russell was little more than an unlettered barbarian. It was published in the magazine in January 1914, and provoked even more outrage among readers. Lovecraft responded with more scathing letters that attacked the intellect of his critics; the correspondence went back and forth until the editor of *The Argosy* informed Lovecraft that he would publish no more of his letters, as they were generating too many complaints among his readers and taking up too much space in the magazine. However, this did not stop him from using a couple of Jackson's stories as a template for some of his later works—most notably a romantic dream-based tale called "The Green Meadow," which was eventually a template for "Beyond the Wall of Sleep" in 1919.

The literary jousting with his critics had an unexpected and beneficial outcome for Lovecraft. One of *The Argosy's* readers was a gentleman named Edward F. Daas from Milwaukee, Wisconsin. Daas was the president of the United Amateur Press Association and editor of its magazine, *The United Amateur*. The Association was a collection of amateur writers who wished to see their work published and did so by paying for the work to go into print. Daas set up an in-person meeting with Lovecraft in order to extend an invitation to join the UAPA. At first, Lovecraft was reluctant to become involved; he viewed the prospect of having his work lumped in amidst the scribblings of amateurs with disdain. However, he had little else to do with his time, and on April 16th, 1914, he joined the UAPA.

Although he had been reluctant to join, this enclosed world appealed to Lovecraft. Perhaps it was the sheer narrowness of the environment in which he found himself; maybe it was the fact that he could correspond with the other writers without ever having to meet them face to face. Commentators such as Donald Tyson have suggested that at this point in life, Lovecraft was beginning to view himself primarily as an English gentleman. Such figures, in his view, amused themselves with various pastimes such as writing but, because they were wealthy, it was not writing for profit. Writing for money was viewed as a low profession and a betrayal of intellectual ideals. So the idea of writing for free may have appealed to Lovecraft's aesthetic sensibilities, playing into the idea that he was indeed an intellectual gentleman.

He published his first article in *The United Amateur* in January 1915, but by April of that year he was publishing his own periodical, *The Conservative*, which he circulated to other UAPA members. He now attended some of the UAPA's meetings, and was elected Chairman of the Department of Public Criticism, a rather grand title. In July, he was elected as the organization's first vice president, and in 1917, he served as its president. He would eventually become official editor of *The United Amateur*.

Despite his obvious enthusiasm for the organisation and its publication, Lovecraft was not the most loyal of members. He still considered himself to be a superior writer, but, despite his prestigious position, others were submitting work that was getting published and praised above his own. He left the UAPA in 1917 and joined a rival writers' group called the National Amateur Press Association. He later claimed that the sole reason for his defection was to bring the two groups closer, but it's more likely because he thought his high intellect and work were not being fully appreciated.

At this time, his bigoted view of racial groups other than his own was more prevalent and, as a result, would haunt his fiction for the rest of his life. To those who knew him, he was both friendly and urbane, and his views were only expressed subtly in his work. In this respect he appeared to be a mass of contradictions; he was fiercely anti-Semitic, yet one of his best friends during adulthood, Samuel Loveman, was Jewish. Lovecraft also married a Jewish woman named Sonia H. Greene. In his magazine *The Conservative* (which had strong right-wing views), he complained about immigrants—Italians, Poles, Irish, and others—entering the country in terms that would not be far removed from the perspectives of Adolph Hitler. He saw racial purity (which was being corrupted by such immigrants) as something to be cherished by Americans. Presumably, he was referring to a white, Anglo-Saxon race that had come from England. In a 1917 issue of *The Conservative*, he wrote:

RACE PREJUDICE IS A GIFT OF NATURE, INTENDED TO PRESERVE IN PURITY THE VARIOUS DIVISION S OF MANKIND WHICH THE AGES HAVE EVOLVED.

This perspective fed into his fiction: the degenerate worshippers of dark and evil gods would be wizened foreigners—people who were not "racially pure," and whose ways were strange and different.

This was a time when America was establishing an identity for itself in the world, so Lovecraft's narrow, xenophobic ideas must have seemed off-kilter with the times. Many writers were extremely tolerant of the always-changing society, and his self-centered world view must have seemed odd to the majority of them. However, they could not readily dismiss his intellect. Although he often had a supercilious air about him, he always seemed ready to aid those who asked him for literary help. As long as he kept those with whom he actually associated to a limited number and they were willing to overlook his oddness, he was reasonably personable company. Indeed, he almost seemed to revel in the fact that he was outside the bounds of normal society and did not actively seek out friendships of any sort. He was the outsider only looking into the "normal" world when he saw fit. It was the ideal vantage point from which he could create an entire and separate cosmos.

As he started to carve out a place for himself in society, his mother's mental health deteriorated. In January of 1919 Susie suffered a nervous breakdown, coupled with severe abdominal pains. (Her mental health had been deteriorating since 1916, though Lovecraft was afraid to admit it. For three years, she had been experiencing hallucinations in which she saw terrible creatures coming and going through their apartment, some of which would later figure into his works.) Lovecraft contacted his Aunt Lillian who suggested that his mother come and stay with her until she got well. However, no such invitation was made to Lovecraft, even though at the age of 30 he couldn't look after himself for long periods of time. It was suggested that he go to live with his Aunt Annie, who was his mother's younger sister. However, he refused to leave his apartment, so as a compromise Annie came to stay with him, despite being married and having her own life. This was the first time that he and his mother had ever been apart, and he was terrified without anyone to cosset him. His aunt arrived and immediately Lovecraft was against having anyone strange in the apartment—he couldn't eat or get out of bed for any long period of time. In the end, his response to Annie's presence was one of his periodic "breakdowns" in which he shut himself in his room and refused to speak to her.

Susie's health did not improve, and on March 13th, Lillian said that she could no longer take care of her; she committed Susie to the Butler Hospital where Lovecraft's father had died. In all the time she was there—another two years—he would not enter the building to see her, but met her in the hospital grounds, convinced that if he entered the place he would never come out.

The shock of having his mother committed was almost too much for Lovecraft. Even though he was now in his 30s, his mother had always provided for him and looked after him, so he never had to face the world. He never even had to look for a job, and could afford to scribble while her meagre monies kept him afloat. He did the only thing he could do: he withdrew from the world and retreated into his work. It was at this time that he began to write and revise some of the tales he had written earlier. However, without Susie's income his financial situation became more and more precarious, and he was forced to think the unthinkable: asking for payment for his writings.

Therefore, throughout 1920 and 1921, Lovecraft wrote extensively, but received no money for his works. His financial position grew steadily worse and his Aunt Annie found it almost impossible to stay with him for any period of time. But then he had an unexpected stroke of luck. A man named George Julian Houtain started up a small professional fiction magazine early in 1921. Entitled *Home Brew*, it was to be a collection of various sorts of fiction and, remembering that Lovecraft had written a number of horror stories, Houtain approached him to write for the first issue. In return, he would pay him $5 per story. Given Lovecraft's precarious financial position, he couldn't refuse it. His first story for the magazine was "Herbert West—Reanimator," which he based on Mary Shelley's *Frankenstein*. He continued the story as a series, beginning in September 1921 and finishing around mid-June of 1922.

Inspired by this, he sold "The Lurking Fear" to *Home Brew* in 1922, and it was published in parts like a serial, starting in 1923. Despite payment, Lovecraft thought that the magazine was far beneath his real talents—characterizing it as "a vile rag," as it contained both romantic stories and fairly salty humor. Although he accepted the money, Lovecraft virulently denigrated the publication behind Houtain's back. However, in 1923, he passed by a newsstand; a new magazine called *Weird Tales* was on display and Lovecraft purchased a copy. Lovecraft liked what he read, as well as the choice of stories. He decided to write for this new publication and submitted five of his stories to the editor, Edwin Baird. The cover letter that he enclosed with the stories amused Baird so much that he published it in the letter section of the September 1923 issue as an example of how not to write such a letter. Lovecraft suggested that the magazine should be flattered that he had bothered to write, spoke about himself and his own personal tastes, and talked down to Baird in a high-handed tone. Lovecraft told Baird how he disapproved of commercial writing and that he was only submitting these stories because friends had urged him to. Rejection was therefore unimportant to him; if Baird were to read the first two stories and didn't like them, he could ignore the other three. And if Baird were to publish them, he would only consent to it provided there were no editorial changes. The slightest tinkering with the prose, down to colons and semicolons, would cause the work to get withdrawn. In conclusion, he told Baird that he quite liked *Weird Tales* as a magazine, even if the stories in it were "too commercial" and lacked imagination.

Faced with such a cover letter, most editors would have simply thrown the stories in the bin without a glance, but Baird was in a good mood when he read it and actually found it very amusing. He replied to Lovecraft, telling him to retype the stories in double spacing and resubmit them. This would make them easier to edit should he decide to use them. Lovecraft was stung by the suggestion that his work might be edited. By this time, however, his finances were in such dire straits that he could not really refuse any prospect of a sale. As a compromise, he retyped only "Dagon" and resubmitted it. It appeared in the October 1923 issue of the magazine; Four others followed, and from then on *Weird Tales* became Lovecraft's main market for his fiction Not only did Baird publish the fiction that Lovecraft sent, but Baird also sent him stories from other writers for him to revise. Far from a simple ghostwriter, Lovecraft began to redesign the tales so that the readers could sense his influence; some of the stories were more his work than that of the original writer.

As a magazine, *Weird Tales* started off well, but after a while sales decreased and the publication began to struggle. Initially, Baird bought almost everything that Lovecraft sent him—he liked the style of writing and the dark images—but as the magazine faltered, he became more hesitant. With *Weird Tales* now deeply in debt, the publisher, J.C. Henneberger, sacked Baird and employed a new editor, Farnsworth Wright.

Wright was far less tolerant of Lovecraft. He was not as enamored with his style as Baird had been, and preferred to give work to Robert E. Howard, who had a more gritty style, and it's thought that he didn't particularly like Lovecraft personally. As an amateur writer, Wright had been the focus of Lovecraft's most withering scorn and criticism. Now that he was editor of Lovecraft's main market, he took the opportunity to get revenge. He forced Lovecraft to revise and resubmit his stories in ways that Lovecraft found personally demeaning and abhorrent. He suspected that Lovecraft's financial position was so precarious that he couldn't refuse. He took it upon himself to change and edit some of the works without consulting Lovecraft, and he also rejected some of his submissions, including "The Shadow over Innsmouth" and *At the Mountains of Madness,* telling Lovecraft that they were not up to the magazine's high standards.

Wright must also have taken a particular and vicious delight in telling Lovecraft that his stories were not all that popular among both the readership and other writers. Wright criticized that Lovecraft's stories were too "samey" and conventional—a criticism that Lovecraft had previously aimed at Wright. Lovecraft's baroque style was based around a number of elements and seldom varied. He became lost in the descriptions of Oriental palaces and exotic fortresses in an effort to mirror Dunsany. He further wished to show off his knowledge of esoteric things such as witchcraft, magic, and demonology (and there is no doubt that he had read extensively about these), and often went into long and convoluted explanations on these subjects. Moreover, many of his settings were quite similar to one another and were all suggestive of an academic, bookish interest such as shadowy libraries, falling colonial houses, lost cities, shunned graveyards, forgotten churches, and mausoleums. Many of them followed similar themes as well: a haunted and ghastly inheritance that was hinted at in dreams and visions, and shadowy families in the thrall of ancient gods. A few of these stories might be enough to stimulate the public appetite, but as Lovecraft turned them out, many of his readers became bored with the similarity and academic slant of the tales. They much preferred the earthier, more swashbuckling adventures of Conan and Solomon Kane, or the works of writers such as Robert Bloch, whom many said was a far better storyteller than Lovecraft (although Bloch later acknowledged his debt to Lovecraft and borrowed some of his themes).

Because of the history between Wright and Lovecraft, it must have given Wright a great deal of pleasure to inform Lovecraft of his dwindling popularity. Many readers had taken a great dislike to his stories and demanded that more modern writers get space in the magazine. Although these were not printed, they influenced Farnsworth Wright's view, and he began to reject more and more of Lovecraft's submissions.

Lovecraft steadfastly refused to modernize any of his stories. Although other writers such as August Derleth suggested that he should introduce the concepts of sex and money to his fiction, not one reference to either subject ever appeared. In many respects, his fiction reflected the concerns of his own narrow world: the notions of inheritance, a quasi-mystical Eastern location, and a Gothic verboseness. His stories made absolutely no attempt at serious characterization and the figures in them simply became ciphers of his own neuroses and simple cardboard cut-outs.

Under Farnsworth Wright's strict editorial policies, *Weird Tales* thrived and began to increase its circulation once again. Its success also spawned a number of other imitators in the pulp fiction market, some of whom flourished only briefly, but also some of whom made their mark. Many of these helped to shape fictional tastes and establish a fan base for the work of their writers. Magazines such as *Unknown*, *Science Wonder Stories*, *Planet Stories*, *Astonishing Stories*, and *Astounding Stories* began to appear, offering a whole new gallery of imaginative authors such as Ray Bradbury, Philip K. Dick, Edgar Rice Burroughs, and Seabury Quinn to the horror and science fiction fields.

Had he been willing to compromise and accept new ideas, Lovecraft could have made both a reputation and a sizeable income from such a boom in pulp fiction. Instead, he stuck to his artistic principles and only did "hack work" because of his dire financial circumstances. For example, later in his career he wrote two stories for Zealia Bishop—"The Mound" and "The Curse of Yig"—which are considered classics, even though, as he mentioned in a letter to Robert E. Howard, he found the act of writing them "abhorrent" and "demeaning."

However, the stories in many of the new magazines took on a much different slant than Lovecraft's staid fiction. Rather than concentrating on Gothic fiction many moved into the areas of high adventure and hard-nosed science-fiction, and the titles, such as Planet Stories, Stirring Science Stories, and Fantastic Novels, reflected this. They dealt with lusty heroes on lost or forgotten continents and valiant spacemen battling on unknown worlds. Lovecraft's tales seemed out of tune with the trend, so to make his writing more appealing he began to shift his cosmos from a theologically centered Universe to a largely scientific one. His gods and entities, while still retaining their eeriness and horror, now became alien beings whose malign purposes were being acted out on earth. Even with these alterations, his style did not change and he still retained many of the themes that pleased his readers. It is those styles and themes that make him popular today, turning some of his stories (rejected during his career) into horror classics.

In 1921, his mother Susie passed away at Butler Hospital, which threw Lovecraft into a suicidal depression, both restricting and liberating him at the same time. No longer could he rely on his mother to look after him, but at the same time he was free of her influence. He had seldom ventured too far beyond Providence while she was alive, but now he started traveling to writers' conferences in various parts of America and meeting people with whom he had corresponded through letters. But there was another agenda: Lovecraft felt unable to look after himself and he needed a strong and determined woman to replace Susie. His Aunt Lillian moved in with him as a short-term solution, but even with her as a guardian, Lovecraft still took trips and made visits.

Later in 1921, Lovecraft attended a convention in Boston. Also attending was a vivacious and forceful widow from New York named Sonia Haft Greene, who was introduced to Lovecraft by his friend Rheinhart Kleiner. Sonia Greene was a well-paid executive in the retail clothing trade and she was also interested in amateur horror fiction. She was Jewish, born with the name Sonia Shafirkin, near Kiev in the Ukraine. She migrated with her mother and brother to Liverpool, England, sometime around 1890, and then to New York in 1892. In 1899 she married Samuel Seckendorff, and a year later bore him a son who died after only three months. In 1902, the couple had a daughter named Florence Carol.

Worried about anti-Semitism in New York, Seckendorff changed his name to Greene and his family did likewise. However, the marriage was not a happy one, and in 1916 Samuel Greene committed suicide. After that, Sonia went straight into business, becoming a clothing buyer for a Manhattan store. She soon reached the executive level of the firm and became a reasonably wealthy woman. At the time she was introduced to Lovecraft, she was older than him by almost seven years and had an adult daughter. Although he followed no formal religion, Lovecraft was by birth a Baptist and this made his interest in a member of the Jewish faith religiously unsuitable for him. But, Sonia was strong-willed and had money. She was known to dispense largesse to her friends and fellow writers, such as expensive meals, taxis to and from venues, and quality books as presents. These were all the things that Lovecraft associated with his own station in life and, despite his own extreme anti-Semitism, he found her fascinating.

Some have commented that, for Lovecraft, it was "love at first dollar." Sonia had already financed two issues of a magazine called *The Rainbow* in which Lovecraft's writings were featured, so he may have also seen her as a financial opportunity to self-publish more of his work.

On September 21st, 1921, Sonia Greene arrived in Providence and stayed there for two days at the rather opulent Crown Hotel where she received Lovecraft and some other literary friends. He took her to his home and introduced her to his Aunt, who was shocked but favorably surprised. After the meeting, the couple then returned to the hotel where Lovecraft enjoyed an expensive meal, paid for by Sonia.

A number of meetings subsequently took place between them throughout the next 18 months. When he visited her, he didn't stay in a hotel, but in the fashionable

Parkside Avenue area of Brooklyn. He also met Sonia's daughter Florence, and the distaste between the two of them was immediate and mutual. Lovecraft would later write to a friend, Maurice Moe, that he thought Florence was "overly spoilt" and had a "hard-boiled visage."

In order to get Lovecraft to herself, Sonia suggested that they holiday in the seaside town of Magnolia, Massachusetts. Lovecraft agreed to go, provided Sonia would pay all his expenses, which she did. They traveled to Magnolia on June 26th, ostensibly for a sight-seeing trip, but there is little doubt that, in Sonia's mind, it was a romantic interlude. On the first night, when Sonia attempted to kiss him on the lips, she claimed he went pure white and almost fainted. He informed her that this was the first time that he had been kissed by anyone other than a relative and that it was shocking. Lovecraft wrote to Maurice Moe stating that he had "set boundaries" in the relationship. Most of the trip was spent working on a short story that he reworked for Sonia called "The Invisible Monster," which was published in *Weird Tales* in 1923. It was later reworked as "The Horror at Martin's Beach." As with so many other "collaborations," the original author was soon eased out and the work became Lovecraft's own.

By now, Sonia had her heart set on winning Lovecraft. The relationship continued to develop throughout the winter of 1923 and into 1924 when Sonia announced that it was time for them to marry. Supposedly, he formally proposed while on a trip to Marblehead, Massachusetts, where the couple supposedly consummated their relationship. However, this is doubtful, as Lovecraft was more entranced with the architecture of the quaint old town rather than relations with his new partner. Indeed, he always abhorred sex, and it's thought that he engaged in it (if at all) only before getting back to studying the architecture, which he would describe as "the climactic moment of his entire life."

They were married on March 3rd, 1924, at St. Paul's Church in New York. He had left Providence the day before (his train fare to New York was paid by Sonia), without telling his aunts, and set off to his wedding. The church was one of the oldest in New York and Lovecraft insisted that this was where he wished to be married in order to give a sense of history to the occasion. Following the wedding, the couple honeymooned in Philadelphia at Sonia's expense. They traveled by train, but had to divert to Providence station in order to pick up a manuscript that Lovecraft accidentally left there. The manuscript was a draft of "Under the Pyramids," which he was ghost-writing for Harry Houdini. It was eventually published by *Weird Tales* as "Imprisoned with the Pharaohs" in 1924. Instead of enjoying his nuptials, he rented a typewriter and typed up the text as Sonia dictated from handwritten copy.

After the honeymoon, they resided in Sonia's apartment. Florence moved out immediately, refusing to share the place with Lovecraft, which created a rift between mother and daughter.

After getting established with Sonia, Lovecraft soon gathered together a number of amateur writers, which he called the Kalem Club (the surnames of the founding members began with the letter K, L, or M) and they gathered in a local hostelry to discuss the possibility of publishing something. Nothing was ever agreed upon and as soon as Lovecraft left New York, the group fell apart. He wandered around New York, meeting up with some of his friends, coming home at all hours of the morning, and sleeping most of the day. Meanwhile, Sonia paid all of his bills, cooked for him, and paid for lavish meals at the finest New York hotels. For Lovecraft, it was the ideal existence, but it was not to last.

His period with Sonia was probably his most prolific time in which he penned stories such as "Hypnos," "What the Moon Brings," "The Hound," and "The Lurking Fear" for *Weird Tales*. Just before his marriage, the owner of *Weird Tales* had put him in touch with another writer from Providence named Clifford Martin Eddy, Jr., and the two began to collaborate on stories. Their most famous tale was "The Loved Dead," which was published in the magazine in October 1924. Most of the story was Lovecraft's, but the hints of necrophilia contained within it were so offensive that many of the readers were outraged, and the authorities in Indiana tried to have the magazine banned. Lovecraft revelled in the notoriety, as it gave him some status among his literary associates. Nevertheless, his stories still attracted a following and Lovecraft was offered an editorial position with *Weird Tales*. This would have guaranteed Lovecraft a steady income, but he turned it down because he would have to travel to Chicago and might have to look after himself there—something he was not prepared to do.

Soon after Lovecraft's job offer, Sonia lost her job at the clothing store, but was determined to go in to business on her own. She opened a hat shop in Manhattan and poured a good deal of her capital into it, much against Lovecraft's advice. The shop turned out to be a total failure, only lasting a few months. Suddenly, his privileged lifestyle was threatened, and he urged Sonia to find work elsewhere. Eventually, she found new employment at a department store in Cincinnati, which meant leaving Lovecraft to fend for himself.

For a while, he did nothing except live on the money that Sonia had left him. Either too hopeless or too lazy to find work, he spent the first half of 1924 wandering around New York, sightseeing, meeting friends, or writing ("The Shunned House" was written during this period). Even so, Sonia could no longer afford the lavish apartment and Lovecraft had to move out. He rented a room at a seedy and decaying brownstone at 169 Clinton Street in Red Hook, New Jersey, which was about all his meagre salary could afford. For Lovecraft, this was a tremendous step down in the world, as he had to share the house with a number of immigrants whose customs and cooking smells both alarmed and sickened him. Moreover, the landlady seemed to have a grudge against him, especially when he was slow in paying his rent. Relations became so strained between Lovecraft and his landlady that she refused to turn on the heat in his rooms until the rent was paid. This may have led to the composition of one of his better-known stories, "Cool Air." It was at this time that he also penned "The Horror at Red Hook," based loosely around the house in which he was living.

In Cincinnati, Sonia was admitted to a hospital to be tested for a stomach condition. As a result, she lost her job at the department store. Desperate, she wrote to Lovecraft asking him to come and stay with her; he steadfastly refused to offer her the support that she needed. In 1925, she returned to New York, but did not go back to Lovecraft, preferring to stay with a female friend in Saratoga Springs instead. Apart from a couple of half-hearted attempts at reconciliation, the marriage was more or less over.

His finances were now in a desperate state. The nearest he came to any actual employment was as a salesman with the Creditors' National Clearing House, which involved going to see businessmen about investing in the agency. The work was on commission only, and Lovecraft was fired in less than a week without earning a single penny. In the end, he gave up trying to find a job and, in 1925, was forced to write to his aunts in Providence for money, and there is little doubt that he was on the verge of a depression and was frequently thinking of suicide. However, his spirits may have lifted slightly when he managed to get a paying position through his friend James Morton in March of 1926. His job was hand-addressing envelopes for a catalog club; for addressing 10,000 catalogues a week he received $17.50. This, together with the money that he received from his aunts, and the occasional check from *Weird Tales*, kept him afloat, but it was not an ideal situation.

His aunts were, however, worried about his state of mind, and were frightened that he might indeed commit suicide (he had taken to walking with a little bottle of poison in his pocket), as were some of his friends. Morton tried to get him a job at the Paterson Museum in New Jersey, but this came to nothing; Lovecraft didn't even bother showing up for the interview. In the end, his aunts convinced him to return to Providence; they rented the lower level of a house located at 10 Barnes Street near Brown University. Knowing that he could not look after himself, his Aunt Lillian rented the room above him.

Hearing that he had returned to Providence, Sonia made one last-ditch attempt to save their marriage. At first, Lovecraft didn't see her, but sent his aunts instead. Having lived off of Sonia's money in the good times, he seems to have felt no compunction in abandoning her when the circumstances changed. She left defeated and humiliated and, during the next two years, she and Lovecraft saw very little of each other. The couple divorced in 1929 on the grounds that Sonia had been unfaithful to Lovecraft. It was conducted under the fairly liberal divorce laws of Rhode Island and he took little part in it, leaving its execution up to his Aunt Lillian. Though for some reason he never signed the final papers, so the divorce never actually went through.

With Sonia gone from his life, Lovecraft breathed a sigh of relief and sank back into his pampered torpor. His Aunt Lillian now looked after him and provided him with money when he needed it. Ironically, he was now sinking back into the lifestyle with which he was most comfortable—that of a genteel man who only interacted with the world around him when he felt like it, and who had sufficient monies to maintain such a lifestyle choice.

Much of his interaction with others was carried out through voluminous correspondence. Anyone who called to see him in person, even for the most social reasons, was greeted with a closed door as Lovecraft pretended to be out. If anything, Lovecraft became more difficult to access as time went on. He told his Aunt Lillian that no matter how well-meaning visitors were, they simply got on his nerves and he wouldn't see them.

The only person who could see him during this period was a young man named Frank Belknap Long, the son of a prosperous dentist who had become interested in writing while attending college. The two had met face to face in April 1922 when Long was just 21, but they had corresponded for two years previously when Long had joined the UAPA and Lovecraft had shown an intense interest in him. Long would later become one of the foremost pulp writers of his day.

Lovecraft became obsessed with Long, calling him "my kid protégé" and "little Belknap." He continually wrote him complex letters to which Long responded, and even incorporated elements from Long's fiction into his own, an example being the Hounds of Tindalos in "The Whisperer in Darkness." This obsession with younger men would manifest itself again in his curious relationship with Robert Haywood Barlow who first contacted him in 1931. At the time, Barlow was just 13 years old and lived in DeLand, Florida. He was interested in becoming a writer of weird fiction, however, in his letter, he didn't disclose his true age, and Lovecraft assumed that Barlow was an adult. In 1934, he traveled to Florida only to discover that the person with whom he'd been communicating was in fact a teenager. Far from being angered or upset by the discovery, Lovecraft took to the boy just as he'd taken to Long. He received a warm welcome from Barlow's parents and was invited to stay with them. Lovecraft stayed at Barlow's house from the beginning of May until late June 1931. The relationship led to the suspicion that, in the latter stages of his life, Lovecraft was something of a sexual predator, obsessed with young men and boys. However, there is absolutely nothing to suggest that this was the case or that Lovecraft had explicit homosexual tendencies toward Barlow. Lovecraft also made two extended visits to Florida in 1934 and 1935, and Barlow stayed for two months in Lovecraft's house in 1936.

Among some of Lovecraft's other notable correspondents was the enigmatic Clark Ashton Smith (who had a background just as strange and not all that far removed from Lovecraft). Through Lovecraft's intervention, he was approached by Farnsworth Wright, who printed several of his poems in *Weird Tales*. When he wrote some of the Mythos tales, Smith added a certain ethereal quality that fit in well with the Dreamworld tales that Lovecraft was. However, some of the stories that Lovecraft inspired were either rejected or heavily censored by Farnsworth Wright, much to both Smith and Lovecraft's frustration.

A more "earthy" writer than either Clark or Lovecraft, and one with whom Lovecraft formed a long and enduring friendship, was Robert Ervin Howard. He was a great admirer of Lovecraft's work and the two began to communicate when Robert wrote to Farnsworth Wright praising Lovecraft's "Rats in the Walls," which had been reprinted in *Weird Tales* in June 1930 (it was first printed in March 1924).

Both Smith and Howard added immensely to Lovecraft's work—particularly in the area of allegedly forbidden books. Smith added an occult text called the *Book of Eibon* (*Livre d'Eibon* in French and *Liber Invonis* in Latin), from which he quotes in his story "Ubbo-Sathla." Howard also contributed one of the Mythos's most famous books outside of the *Necronomicon* called *Unaussprechlicen Kulten* (roughly translated as *Nameless Cults*). Although Howard introduced this book in his story *Children of the Night*, Lovecraft seized upon the opportunity and attempted to introduce it into his own work under the German title *Ungenenete Heidenthume*, which all of his correspondents immediately disliked. (American writer August Derleth eventually reverted it back to the original German title.)

These correspondents built upon the basic Mythos through their letters to Lovecraft, and the result was an organic product of many writers and imaginations coming together. For Lovecraft, this was once again an immensely fruitful period. Many of the themes that he had developed earlier in his career now flourished into full-fledged stories, which were published by *Weird Tales* and a number of other magazines. During this time, he produced the final draft of the story that would give its name to the entire Mythos: "The Call of the Cthulhu," which was originally published in 1928. He was also working on a number of collaborations, most notably with Zealia Bishop, Hazel Heald, and Duane Rimmel. And despite being something of a recluse, he used what meagre monies he had to finance journeys to various parts of America to see various writers. In 1930, he traveled to Quebec City about which he wrote *A Description of the Town of Quebeck*, composed from the point of view of an 18th-century traveling Englishman (hence the spelling).

At this point in his writing career, the emphasis of Lovecraft's fictional work began to change slightly. Perhaps in response to a growing trend in the pulps, he was now producing stories that were a unique blend of both horror and science fiction, producing some of what is now regarded as his best work. During this period of time, he produced *At the Mountains of Madness* and "The Thing on the Doorstep," both now regarded as classics. Interestingly, *At the Mountains of Madness* was originally rejected by Farnsworth Wright, who still delighted in revising and rejecting Lovecraft's work and, as a result, it wasn't published until 1936, when *Astounding Stories* bought it for $350. Around the same time, Lovecraft's correspondent Donald Wandrei sold "The Shadow out of Time" to the same publication for $280, which was written between 1934 and 1935, but not published until 1936.

Amid all of the career success, he returned from a trip to New Orleans in July of 1932 to find that his Aunt Lillian had been ill; she would die two days later. Although distraught about her death, Lovecraft wondered who would look after him and loan him money when he needed it. He approached the younger of his two aunts, Annie, and asked if she could help. At the time, she was separated from her husband and lived less than a mile away; she volunteered to help when she could, but less than six months later, it was clear that Lovecraft (now in his 40s) couldn't look after himself at all.

In May 1933, he moved to the upper apartment of a yellow clapboard Colonial house known as the Samuel B. Mumford House at 66 College Street, just behind the John Hay Library attached to Brown University. Aunt Annie got him the apartment through some contacts that she had, and she moved in with him to look after his needs.

After the move, he started to grow more distant with his friends, even those to whom he had written for a number of years. The world of pulp horror fiction was changing, and his views were now becoming slightly dated. In 1936, he persuaded a publisher named William Crawford, who published a small magazine called *Marvel Tales*, to publish "The Shadow over Innsmouth" as a small book. Four hundred copies of the book were published, but Lovecraft was unsatisfied with it due to the number of errors and spelling mistakes. As a result, the book sold about 150 copies, which was a massive loss for the publisher. That same year, Robert Howard committed suicide, which had a great affect on him. His works were now being criticized, and Lovecraft did not respond well to it. For example, his friend and correspondent August Derleth had so severely criticized his "The Dreams in the Witch House," leading Lovecraft to assert that his fictional days were most probably over.

With no other profession to fall back on, the threat of abject poverty reared its head. He now talked frequently about "taking the cyanide route," as he feared that poverty would force him to sell his cherished possessions, which had been with him since childhood. He dressed in second-hand clothes, which were long out of date, and ate sparingly. For some time, he had experienced intense stomach cramping, and this new lifestyle was only making it worse. Alarmed, his Aunt Annie finally persuaded him to see a doctor. Alas, growing in his lower intestines was a cancer that would kill him in just over a year.

Despite the pain, he continued to write, making final adjustments to "The Haunter of the Dark," which would be the last story published under his own name in *Weird Tales* in December 1936. He also worked on some collaborations but, desperately aware of his precarious financial situation, he simply wrote for what money he could at the moment. Though he was exhausted, he began working on the revision of a textbook entitled *Well Bred Speech* for the educationalist Tillery Renshaw, who had promised him roughly $300 for his work. When he was finished, the text was such a mess that he was only paid $100.

Throughout the month of February 1937, he spent most of his time in bed, scarcely able to write at all. In March of 1937, a second specialist confirmed what was already known: the cancer was too advanced and was inoperable. Lovecraft, never one to fight against anything, quietly sank under the ravages of the condition and, on March 10th, was admitted to the Brown Memorial Hospital in Providence. He died on the morning of March 15th at the age of 46.

His funeral was held in Providence's Swan Point Cemetery where the Phillips family had a plot. Only four mourners showed up—his Aunt Annie, one of her friends who came to look after her, and one of his second cousins and his friend who came along out of curiosity.

Through neglect and inability to organize (he was used to others doing it for him), he had left his affairs in a complex mess. According to a will that had been signed in 1912, he left his entire estate to his Aunt Annie. Legally, this would have made her the owner of all his written work, but in a separate document he had also made Robert Barlow "literary executor" of his estate. Lovecraft had also signed an agreement with August Derleth that gave him rights to part of Lovecraft's estate, namely a collection of stories that Derleth intended to publish as a book.

Barlow's handling of Lovecraft's work was remarkably cavalier. He gathered up some of the papers and took them with him to Kansas where he was attending the Kansas City Art Institute; others he left behind, and others he simply lost. This flagrant carelessness angered Derleth, Clark Ashton Smith, and Donald Wandrei, not only because of his attitude toward the work, but also for Barlow's alleged bullying toward Lovecraft's aunt. Whether this was true or not, it created disputes between a number of those who had been associated with Lovecraft. In 1938, Barlow sought to rid himself of any obligation he might have had to Lovecraft by dividing his papers between Derleth and the Brown University Library, where they were put in a private collection. In June 1938, he placed the rest in a small book published by the Futile Press in California entitled *H.P. Lovecraft's Commonplace Book*. This was simply a collection of jottings and story ideas set out in the form of a notebook. It did not sell very well, but more or less marked the end of Barlow's interest in Lovecraft.

Derleth, on the other hand, was determined to make some money off of Lovecraft's tales. However, he couldn't find a publisher for them, so both Derleth and Donald Wandrei decided to publish the stories themselves. In 1939, a book entitled *The Outsider and Others* (a title Lovecraft had allegedly chosen himself) became the first publication of the new publishing house. The print run was 1,268 copies, and it was a commemorative hardcover that contained 36 of his stories and one essay called "Supernatural Horror in Literature." The edition sold slowly and steadily.

Following the death of his Aunt Annie in 1941, her nephew's library was handed to a local bookseller for auction. Among the books were manuscripts, unfinished letters, and various papers that had been ignored by Barlow and disregarded by his elderly aunt. Indeed, Annie had instructed that they be burned and had them placed in front of a furnace ready for destruction. The bookseller bought these and later offered them to Brown University where they became part of the Lovecraft collection.

However, Derleth now had legal hold on the bulk of Lovecraft's stories. In her will, Annie reverted the royalty rights on *The Outsider and Others* back to him. From this position of strength he began to gain control of Lovecraft's writing. *The Outsider and Others* sold mainly among Lovecraft's friends and writing colleagues and sales were incredibly slow. Therefore, Derleth decided to publish other works—including his own—in an attempt to boost profits. In 1941, Derleth published a book of his own horror stories, some written in a vaguely Lovecraftian style, entitled *Someone in the Dark*, and the following year he published some of the stories of Clark Ashton

Smith in a book called *Out of Space and Time*. At the same time, he and Wandrei began to work on a collection of Lovecraft's voluminous correspondence. They contacted those to whom Lovecraft had written, gathered together as many of the letters as they could, and had them professionally typed up before returning them to the original correspondents. He originally intended to reproduce them in a single volume, but the letters were so long and detailed that this proved impossible.

The second book of fiction—written by Derleth—sold better than the first collection, and this prompted him to publish more. By now he had managed to acquire several more of Lovecraft's stories as well as some outlines to others. He also had several fragments of stories that Lovecraft had begun and then abandoned. In 1943, he published a second hardcover collection of the tales entitled *Beyond the Wall of Sleep* but, stung by the lack of interest in the original anthology, he only printed about 1,000 copies. This contained two novellas, *The Case of Charles Dexter Ward* and *The Dream-Quest of Unknown Kadath*, along with some of his poetry and some revised tales.

Derleth also had notes for proposed stories that Lovecraft had considered writing. He could also create a fair impression of Lovecraft's method and style of storytelling. Many of the themes in Lovecraft's tales were rather formulaic, written around shadowed heredity, blasphemous books, inbred folks, and suspicious immigrants. Although Derleth shared none of Lovecraft's paranoia, he could still do a fair copy of the content and style of his work. He began to write stories, passing some of them off as Lovecraft's own, in a series that he called the "Cthulhu Mythos." He claimed that Lovecraft had encouraged him to follow this practice during the final years of his life. For this he received a great deal of criticism from some of Lovecraft's correspondents who denied that this was what the writer would have wished. Whatever the reason, he continued to write pastiches in Lovecraft's style, some of which he sold to various magazines, including *Weird Tales*.

In 1977, a collection was launched among fans to raise a memorial stone to Lovecraft in Swan Point Cemetery. A motto was approved by the city council that simply says "I Am Providence," which was considered to be a fitting tribute for a great writer and a son of the area.

Some commentators such as Daniel Harms have argued that Lovecraft did not initially set out to create an entire connected cosmology populated by fearsome gods or alien beings. Such a cosmos emerged out of his narrow world view, his neuroses, and his prejudices. He claimed that it came out of his nightmares and dreams, and it was only much later that he realized he was evolving the kind of unified cosmology that has come to characterize his work. It probably reveals more about his fears and his own self-absorption than it does about anything else. He did not even coin the term *Cthulhu Mythos*; that was the brainchild of August Derleth, and was used to refer to the corpus of Lovecraft's work.

Although Lovecraft laid the foundations of the Mythos, it was up to other writers to interpret, develop, and expand upon his original vision. There seems to be little doubt that his visions served as an inspiration for a host of writers, particularly those with whom he corresponded and to whom he explained his nightmare world. The idea of arcane gods, terrible books, and haunted locations struck a chord with other writers of horror and fantasy, and they immersed themselves in the fearful Universe that Lovecraft had created. They added entities, books, and places, linking them into his basic template, and created new and imaginative levels of horror. However, many of these lack the sheer *alienness* of the original fiction, and with the exception of one or two writings, seem slightly more insipid. This is probably because the horror arose out of Lovecraft's own sense of personal alienation and from his utter disgust both for himself and for those around him. It was an easy task, then, to count the people and places around him as nothing when set in the cosmic frame. Thus, there is little character development in any of his stories—the individuals simply serve as relatively colorless foils for the cosmic activity.

Nowadays, some Lovecraft aficionados suggest that he may have had access to occult knowledge that is somehow denied to the rest of us. It is perhaps fashionable to think of him poring over ancient and blasphemous texts and incorporating fragments of them into his tales. Although Lovecraft was well read, there is little evidence to suggest that this was the case. He was familiar with myth and folklore—particularly the tales from Egyptian and Arabic mythology—but he appears to have only a fairly superficial knowledge and understanding of them. He was a kind of folkloric magpie, lifting references to certain mythological elements here and there, and incorporating them into some sort of literary cycle. For instance, he may have taken beliefs concerning an ancient Assyrian queen and merged them with ancient English and European lore to create the entity Shub-Niggurath. Into this he also incorporated elements of djinn lore from the Middle East. As in the case of the daemon-sultan Azathoth, he seems to change the nature of the entity during the course of his tales from some monstrous supernatural figure to a seething mass of nuclear energy. This combining of different folklore elements in no way diminishes Lovecraft's power or skill as a storyteller, but it does not appear to suggest access to a clandestine body of arcane lore.

There is little doubt that his influence lives on. What Derleth referred to as the "Cthulhu Mythos" has grown and expanded, and is now an important part of horror fiction and the horror industry. Yet as a person, H.P. Lovecraft could not be counted as "normal" in any accepted social sense. He was cosseted, selfish, and something of a sponger who placed his own needs far above others. He was emotionally stunted and was not even a good or trustworthy friend. His vision was narrow, inhibited, and formulaic. And yet, his influence on the horror genre has been immense. Indeed, his very failings as a person have arguably been his strengths as a visionary and writer. He established a vision of such intensity that it inspired others to an extent that no other writer has been able to achieve. Rather than being consigned to history and largely forgotten, as he thought he would be, he has prodded the imaginations of and given untold pleasure to thousands of devotees across the world. There is a renewed interest in Lovecraft's work, so perhaps now is a good time to take a look beyond the man, and probe into the folkloric and other influences that inspired him. It is a journey that will take us into some strange places throughout history—maybe stranger than even Lovecraft imagined.

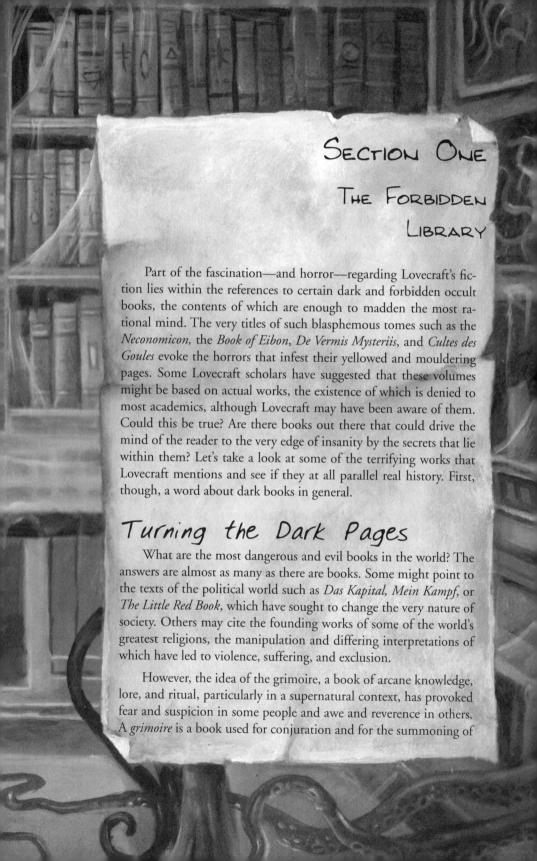

Part of the fascination—and horror—regarding Lovecraft's fiction lies within the references to certain dark and forbidden occult books, the contents of which are enough to madden the most rational mind. The very titles of such blasphemous tomes such as the *Neconomicon*, the *Book of Eibon*, *De Vermis Mysteriis*, and *Cultes des Goules* evoke the horrors that infest their yellowed and mouldering pages. Some Lovecraft scholars have suggested that these volumes might be based on actual works, the existence of which is denied to most academics, although Lovecraft may have been aware of them. Could this be true? Are there books out there that could drive the mind of the reader to the very edge of insanity by the secrets that lie within them? Let's take a look at some of the terrifying works that Lovecraft mentions and see if they at all parallel real history. First, though, a word about dark books in general.

Turning the Dark Pages

What are the most dangerous and evil books in the world? The answers are almost as many as there are books. Some might point to the texts of the political world such as *Das Kapital*, *Mein Kampf*, or *The Little Red Book*, which have sought to change the very nature of society. Others may cite the founding works of some of the world's greatest religions, the manipulation and differing interpretations of which have led to violence, suffering, and exclusion.

However, the idea of the grimoire, a book of arcane knowledge, lore, and ritual, particularly in a supernatural context, has provoked fear and suspicion in some people and awe and reverence in others. A *grimoire* is a book used for conjuration and for the summoning of spirits; it is also a repository of ancient lore and a book of protection against evil and witchcraft, as it shows how to make charms and talismans that ward away evil. However, not all books of magic are grimoires; some magical texts are concerned with the use of natural herbs or alchemical explorations rather than the summoning of spirits or arcane beings. The derivation of the word *grimoire* is unknown, although it might come from the French word *grammaire*, which originally meant "book" in Latin and implied great age and sagacity. Some of these grimoires were not about magic and sorcery at all, but concerned themselves with religious and theological matters. It is only in the 19th century, with a rising interest in the occult among the more educated tiers of society, that the word took on dark and sinister connotations.

Such books came into existence because of a general desire to retain certain knowledge that had been passed down orally by recording it in a physical form. According to historian Matthew Dickie, such an imperative stretched back as far as the second millennium B.C., and they existed within the Babylonian Empire. From there, written (as opposed to oral) magic spread across the Middle East to Europe and across the Atlantic to America. A number of volumes also contained mathematical grids and unfamiliar designs, which only added to their air of secrecy and mystery. Also, the size and venerable appearance of the tome might give it an air of ancient authority. In fact, some of the books were thought to be magical, and were dipped in water to produce a "medicine" to cure ailments. For example, the seventh-century *Book of Durrow*, an illuminated manuscript of certain gospels, was repeatedly dunked in a well by farmers during the 17th century in order to provide a cure for sick animals.

Many of the early secret books originated in the Far and Middle East, but were brought into the Mediterranean and Western worlds along caravan routes from Persia, Egypt, and further east. Many of these were books of magic, some were parts of the Bible, and others were chemical and mathematical expositions. A few even contained references to ancient religions and rituals for summoning old gods. Although we refer to them as "books," some were no more than passages written on pieces of paper, others were scrolls, and some were large, bound volumes. Many were hand-written and possibly copied from other tomes.

Because these books were cross-fertilizations of Middle Eastern intellectual thought and Westernised Christian perceptions, many of them were concerned with religious thinking from Islamic, Judaistic, and Christian perspectives, scientific and mathematical matters, and astronomy. Also, the language in which they were written was important—any tome written in Greek or Persian *had* to be magical in nature.

On the same note, early Jewish, Islamic, and Christian traditions had been influenced by Babylonian myths, and these suggested that some of these texts had been handed down from a time before the Flood. Although some of them were ascribed to Adam or to Cain, many medieval scholars suggested that the true author of the works was Enoch, the great-grandfather of Noah. It was he, they said, who had actually invented writing and books. Other sources state that the angel Raziel gave a book directly to Noah, which Noah kept in a golden chest that he brought onto the Ark and subsequently bequeathed to his son Shem. This was later transcribed into a work entitled *The Treatise of Shem*, which circulated in Europe around the end of the first century A.D.

However, both of Noah's sons, Shem and Ham, were associated with the books of magic. By interacting with demons and renegade angels, Ham learned their secrets, writing them down on tablets of stone and burying them just before the Flood. They were later found and secretly retained by some of the early Hebrews. Herbert de Losinga, first Bishop of Norwich, believed that these secret tablets were retained within the Ark of the Covenant. The 12th-century scholar Michael Scot declared that Zoroaster was Shem, and Ham had invented the arts of divination and other magical arts with the help of demons. Ham then passed on the knowledge to his son Canaan, who wrote it down in 30 separate volumes, which were burned shortly after he was killed in battle. However, several copies of the books were reputedly made. According to Judaic tradition, Ham was the father of all Egyptians, therefore, the copies were passed into the hands of Egyptian sorcerers.

Later, a clear distinction was made in Jewish circles between "portents and miracles" and "base magic," the latter having its origins in Egypt. Here, magic had been learned from demons and "corrupt angels" who had shown men the arts of astrology, necromancy, and other dubious sciences. In the medieval period, Moses was considered more as an Egyptian than an Israelite and heir to the magical traditions of that land. Indeed, his name became associated with all types of magic that supposedly emanated from Egypt.

Ancient Egyptian magic also centered on a mysterious figure known as Hermes Trismegistus, the inventor of mathematics and a powerful magician. In fact, it is not certain that he was one single individual. In Islamic lore, he is three separate men— the first being Enoch, who carved his magical treatise on the wall of a temple that survived the Flood; the second was an Egyptian or Chaldean magician who lived after the Flood and who taught Pythagoras; and the third was a great Egyptian physician who lived many centuries later and wrote several books on healing and on various poisons. In fact, the name *Trismegistus* can mean "thrice great," but it might also mean the "sum of three parts." However, there seems to be little doubt that he/they wrote a vast number of books on magic and healing. The third-century B.C. Egyptian historian Manetho stated that he/they had written at least 36,525 volumes, many of which became lost. However, after his death, it was discovered that he ascribed the authorship of such texts as *The Book of Sothis* (a dubious chronicle of the Egyptian kings) to Trismegistus, whom he claimed had written it before the Flood. However, it dealt with Egyptian royalty, which existed only *after* the Flood, so it casts doubt on both it and a number of other similarly ascribed works. Some medieval scholars stated that many of these texts had not been written by Trismegistus at all, but by another ancient mage named Toc (or Toz) the Greek. (Some said that Toz was one of the incarnations of Trismegistus.) Nevertheless, Toz's unnamed volume surfaced again in a Latin version during the 17th century under the title *A Commentary by Toz Graecus, a Philosopher of Great Name*. This claimed to be a distillation of Solomon's wisdom, which the monarch had written down in a series of scrolls for his son Rehoboam. This was discovered by Toz, who was unable to understand the ancient language until an angel revealed it to him. However, the original text supposedly disappeared and Mankind was left with Toz's transcription only.

This brings into focus King Solomon, who was also closely associated with many of the early magical texts. According to historians, Solomon had a special relationship with the Israelite god Yahweh, who, according to legend, asked for great wisdom far beyond that of mortal men. Part of this knowledge was the control of demons and spirits, which he instructed to build the temple in Jerusalem. The Jewish historian Josephus alleged that the monarch may have written up to 3,000 books, most of which were magical treatises. Many of them concerned exorcism and the curing of illness (in the medieval mind, illness and demon-possession were linked), as well as the understanding of the language of birds and animals. The first actual magical book directly attributed to him appears to be the *Testament of Solomon*, which was written in Greek somewhere in Babylonia or Egypt during the first five centuries A.D. This book consisted of a number of papyri containing magical symbols and alleged spells, and may not have been attributed to the king originally.

The *Testament* is a story about the construction of the Jerusalem Temple and how demons impeded some of Solomon's favorite masons in their work. Thanks to his great knowledge, the monarch was able to summon the Archangel Michael and between them they constructed a magical ring inscribed with arcane and very powerful symbols. Through the power of this ring, 36 of the troublesome demons were compelled to appear before Solomon and to identify themselves. He also forced them to tell him the full extent of their powers and how these could be controlled. Using his infinite knowledge and skills, Solomon was able to drive some of the demons into clay jars and kept them in a place where they could do no harm; others he put to work on the building of the Temple and various other tasks. Solomon would later lose all his supernatural wisdom and powers through lying with a foreign woman (the Queen of Sheba). Sometime during the medieval period, the *Testament* was copied from papyri into a book with various annotations by the scribe regarding the explanation of and various forms of the exorcisms within the text.

During the 12th and 13th centuries, in major European cities such as Cologne and Paris, almost a dozen books bearing his name were in circulation. Several would remain in existence until the early 1500s, the most notable being the *Almandal*, a series of invocations to summon angels and instructions for them to do one's bidding.

Because he was considered to be a good and wise king, many of the books attributed to Solomon dealt mostly with benevolent magic. Even so, the circulation of such books was ferociously condemned by the Church. However, the most notorious of all the works attributed to Solomon was the *Clavicula Salomonis*, or the *Key of Solomon*. The earliest versions of this work were written in Greek around the 15th century and bore the title *The Magical Treatise of Solomon*, also known as *The Little Key of the Whole Art of Hygromancy Found by Several Craftsmen and the Holy Prophet Solomon*. There seem to be a number of versions of this book, all of them dating from around the later medieval period, all varying slightly. They do, however, contain a number of similar spells for drawing down an "Angel of Darkness" and for advancing one's personal rather than spiritual circumstances. It might truly be considered a grimoire or book of dark magic.

The last quasi-biblical figures come from the time of the New Testament: Jesus and Simon Magus. Among the early Christians, Simon became the embodiment of all evil, and is usually portrayed as a magician of the darkest kind. He is said, for instance, to have used semen, parts of infants, and menstrual blood in his charms and incantations. This image was compounded by the rise of a formidable cult in Asia Minor, generally known as the Simonian Gnostics, which flourished throughout the third century A.D. The cult was largely Hellenistic in tone, although it took its principles from early Mosaic literature, which portrayed God as a devouring fire. It may be that the theology and ritual, which was supposedly associated with cult members seeking to obtain the divine gnosis of their deity, outraged more orthodox churchman who declared them and their writings as heretic. This sect was allegedly founded by Simon Magus. Whereas Jesus used his powers to relieve suffering, heal sickness, and guide the righteous, Simon Magus was the consummate evil magician that used his powers for material gain, greed, and base desires. He is also credited with bringing evil magic into the world and teaching some of the most malignant sorcerers their arts.

The Later Grimoires

Whereas the early magical books had owed their authorship to biblical and quasi-biblical figures, the later books did not. They also did not concern themselves solely on calling down Divine or angelic intervention on disciplines such as the arts or sciences, or with the pursuit of pure knowledge and enlightenment. And although many were transcribed and maybe even written by monks, scholars, and popes, most concerned themselves with material things, such as the discovery of treasure, the acquisition of wealth, the gaining of love, and the satisfaction of love or lust.

The connections between the books and their authors also became more tenuous. Without any form of religious or biblical framework, such books were attributed to individuals at random. An example of this is *The Sworn Book of Honorius*, which appeared in the first half of the 13th century. It was initially attributed to the fourth-century emperor Honorius. However, the authorship later shifted to a Greek mathematician who lived in Alexandria at the time. The book was a hotchpotch of prayers and symbols held together by gibberish and convoluted instructions, which were written in both Hebrew and Babylonian. By following these, the adherent could discover treasure, see visions of other worlds, and gain great fame and status. According to popular legend, it originated from a gathering of the world's Masters of Magic in A.D. 811. The mages instructed Honorius to write down their proceedings into one text, of which three copies were made. Whether such a convocation took place is extremely doubtful, but the book was enough to inflame the passions of the Church, who may have seen its very existence as a radical challenge to its authority. Nevertheless, the book circulated secretly and further copies were made.

It resurfaced around 1600, but by now the authorship of the work had changed. Books were circulating in Paris bearing the title *Grimoire du Pape Honorius*, transferring authorship from a Greek mathematician to an Italian Pope named Honorius III. Although a good and kindly man, his name became associated with dark things. The book was widely used in the emerging occult circles of the Renaissance and, although there were many versions of it, it still bore the name of Horonius.

However, Honorius was not the only pontiff to have his name associated with a work of dark magic. Pope Leo III supposedly penned such a tome, as did Pope Formosus. For the latter, a book detailing the construction of a *speculum vitae* (a magical mirror) into which a demon could be lured and trapped, was still circulating in the late 1600s and into the 1700s. An overtly political pontiff, his body was later exhumed by one of his successors, Stephen VI, and placed on trial in the hideous Cadaver Synod where it was accused of a number of crimes and sorcery.

The growing tide of Protestantism mixed with the machinations of Papal enemies within the Church often led to a number of popes being accused of witchcraft. Pope Sylvester II was accused of being able to summon up spirits from the lowest pits of hell to do his bidding. Although a Frenchman, he supposedly studied necromancy in Toledo, Spain, under Arab masters. From them, he stole one of the books to which he appended his own name. This supposedly had been a diabolic work, which contained necromantic incantations and Arabic arithmetical formulae. Another pope who amended a grimoire was Boniface VIII. Boniface was an unlikeable, irascible, and manipulative man who was greatly disliked by many. Even after his death, he was still denounced as a sorcerer who had practiced demonic magic in secret.

Although these slurs against the papacy were perhaps nothing more than the fevered imaginations of the reformers, dark books were still circulating. The first thing to realize is that the Catholic Church probably *did* have a hand in their creation and that, although the Protestants devised fantastic and dubious accusations against them, some of the medieval and early modern clergy actually did practice and write down various forms of "magic." It must also be realized that it was churchmen who had both the understanding and the necessary writing skills to compose such volumes. Therefore, monasteries were the largest repositories of such works, and many held collections of forbidden texts. St. Augustine's Abbey in Canterbury, England, for instance, held a collection more than 30 such volumes. An abbey at Mortemer in Normandy allegedly held more than 20, and the Abbey of St. Columcille's Seat at Magilligan in North Derry, boasted an impressive Druid library, which had been the property of the Irish exorcist St. Ambrose O'Coffey. A rather extensive collection of books on witchcraft and sorcery was held in England by Friar John Erghome of York, and subsequently became part of the library of the Austin Friars. Although closed in monastic libraries, such texts were consulted by various people—those from other monasteries, scholars, clerks, and copyists—and gradually both portions and copies of them began to filter out into the wider world.

However, it was not only saints and popes who penned terrible grimoires. Around the mid-16th and 17th centuries a book began to circulate in some parts of Europe, particularly in Germany. Its origins lay not in Egypt or the Middle East, but far to the north in Iceland.

Iceland had always been familiar with dark folklore. It was considered to be a grim and brooding place, constantly wrapped in dark magic. It was here, according to legend, that secret institutions called Black Schools flourished. The acolytes learned the dark arts from the lips of grim masters, many of whom were churchmen. This was no Hogwarts, for the secrets taught here were of a blasphemous nature and were merely taught for evil purposes. Iceland was also the home of the *ffolkynngisfolk* (wise, cunning folk who performed magical acts using shamanistic traditions), who kept strange old ways very much alive.

The late 1400s and early 1500s saw massive social upheaval in Iceland as Lutheran Protestantism uprooted Catholicism, and those who practiced Catholicism became equated with witches. Witchcraft trials were rife within the country as neighbor accused neighbor, providing a climate in which ideas concerning books of dark magic and necromancy could flourish.

One of these was allegedly the *Raudskinna* or *Red Skin*, which found its way to Germany. This was supposedly the work of Gottskálk grimmi Nikulásson, Bishop of Hólar, between 1496 and 1520. Gottskálk was supposedly a zealous Catholic, and upheld and enforced the edicts of his church against the rising Lutheran tide. Naturally, the Lutherans accused him of all sorts of wickedness and diabolism, one of which was the *Raudskinna*. Allegedly obtained by Gottskálk from the *ffolkynngisfolk*, this was a collection of spells containing magic that went beyond the time of the Vikings. It has sections on what was described as "stave magic"—sheets of magical stave-like symbols, which are used in sorcerous charms. This form of magic was peculiar to Iceland, and was cited in many of the Icelandic witch trials of the 1600s.

Also originating in the frozen lands was the *Galdrabok,* which generated a fair amount of interest in European circles. This circulated throughout Europe starting at the beginning of the 16th century, and was a collection of at least 47 different spells and incantations. Some Lutherans attempted to link its origin to Gottskálk, although it was generally agreed that it had come out of the Icelandic Black Schools. There were supposedly four authors—three Icelandic mages and one Dane—who worked from the Icelandic material. It contained evocations to quasi-Christian entities as well as to older Norse gods; it also contained stave magic and instructions for the construction of amulets to bind demons. In the herbal section, it gave detailed spells to cause flatulence, ease the pain of childbirth and headaches, and help with insomnia. Others involved conjurations designed to get women into bed. It was the usual rag-bag of herbal lore, local superstition, and clandestine pseudo-magical gibberish, but it appealed to the popular minds and was classed as something strange and demonic, which only a true scholar or sorcerer would have in his or her possession.

It was in Germany, however, that books of magic really took off at the end of the 16th century. In many of the major cities, pamphlets and collections of work known as *teufelsbucher* (Devil's books) were all the rage—not only among the educated and austere literati, but among some of the lower orders as well. Although these were largely penned by Protestants as religious propaganda, they were immensely popular and had an effect on German culture. In their pages, the majority of them depicted various forms of a demon or devil and the ways in which they could lead sinners astray. They contained a number of stories, some of which were extremely humorous, no doubt adding to their appeal. It is thought that the story of Faust, the doctor who sold his soul to the Devil, was one of the stories contained in these texts. Indeed, one pamphlet that appeared in 1553—"Der Zauber Teuffel" ("The Devil of Magic")—contained an illustration of a woodcut, depicting a sorcerer raising up a demon, clearly inspired by the Faustian tale.

One of the most important occult philosophers of the Renaissance age was also of German influence. Heinrich Cornelius Agrippa von Nettesheim, or Cornelius Agrippa as he came to be known, traveled extensively and served in the military, but also studied at the Universities of both Paris and Cologne. During a military expedition to Italy, he became fascinated with the work of Johannes Trithemius, a German Benedictine abbot who had experimented with drawing benign spirits into crystals. Using ancient medieval texts, Trithemius produced a book entitled *Steganographia* (Secret Writing), written around 1499, but it only appeared in printed form in 1606. Contained within this work, Trithemius declared that there was an occult code that would enable communication with certain spirits and angels. Cornelius Agrippa was greatly taken with this and worked hard to "decode" the work, dedicating his own writings on the subject—*De Occulta Philosophia,* or *Three Books of Occult Philosophy*—to Trithemius. This was a work of celestial and ceremonial magic, designed for communication with angels, along with sections from the Kabbalah concerning dialogue between the material and spiritual worlds. Although written around 1510, the book did not appear in any finalized form until a version appeared in Antwerp in 1533. The Church was outraged, drawing attention to the inclusion of sections on alchemy and the Kabbalah as "blasphemous sciences," and condemned the work in its entirety, including the "damnedable arts" of geometry and arithmetic.

A Germanic contemporary of Agrippa, the stunningly named Phillipus Aureolus Theophrastus Bombastus von Hohenheim, who was thankfully better known as Paracelsus, was another major influence at the time. He was a Swiss physician who was interested in medicine, alchemy, astrology, and celestial magic. Very few of his writings were published during his lifetime, but some of them turned up in bundles after his death and were hugely influential among collectors and early scientists.

In their texts both Agrippa and Paracelsus made frequent denunciations of what they called "vain magic"—an attempt to use magic for malicious or selfish purposes. Magic, they argued, should be seen as a higher art form. Agrippa, it was said, regularly consorted with demons and kept a familiar in the shape of a great black dog. Paracelsus dealt regularly with witches and with sorcerers of the blackest kind. Therefore, anyone who read their blasphemous books would be automatically damned.

One book in particular stood out from the masses because of the darkness of its tone and its sinister subject matter. It was attributed to Agrippa, although it almost certainly was not written by him. *The Fourth Book of Occult Philosophy* appeared in Marburg, Germany, in 1553, although amended copies would also appear in Basle about six or seven years later. This indeed was a true grimoire, and according to the Church, it was incontrovertible proof that Agrippa and Paracelsus were deeply involved in the diabolic arts. This only served to make copies circulate more quickly all across Europe in a variety of languages.

The first English edition appeared in 1653 and was published in Cambridge by the physician-astrologer Robert Turner. It is possible that some editions of *The Fourth Book of Occult Philosophy* included little more than folk remedies. They may also have included bits and pieces of old tales and snippets of local folklore, but the main body of the book concerned itself with the summoning of demons and "unclean angels." The text circulated widely, albeit with various amendments, and spawned many similar volumes written by what might be called "hedge magicians" (magicians of a lower order), as the distinctions between magic and science became even more blurred, and a "magical fever" gripped Europe and the West.

Although many of these terrible books were circulating in Europe during the 17th and early 18th centuries, America was not immune from their influence. As migration of the New World quickened its pace, the magical texts traveled with the immigrants. During the early 19th century groups of German farmers began to settle across Pennsylvania; these were composed mainly of the Amish and Mennonites. Although deeply religious, they also carried their own beliefs in the supernatural and in witchcraft which, to some extent, colored their world view. The word *hex* (taken from the German word *hexe* meaning "witch") began to creep into the language and was now taken to mean a spell or charm. Although much of their tradition was oral, there was some publishing of charms and protections in what became known as *Himmelsbrief* (*Celestial Letters*), which were scraps of localized wisdom, ballads, and medical advice all wrapped up in esoteric and quasi-religious language. These, it was said, came directly from the lips of angels who revealed them in dreams, and were in no way connected with witchcraft.

The first actual "charm book" or "spell book" designed for the consumption of settlers was printed in German in Germantown, Pennsylvania, around 1793. It was a small, 28-page volume entitled *Der Freund in der Noth, oder Geheime Sympathetische Wissenschaft*; it was a book of information for farmers concerning crops and veterinary matters. However, it also contained a number of charms and hexes as well as a "magical preface," which stated that some of the contents were taken from "ancient Spanish manuscripts." The booklet proved incredibly popular and prompted the publication of another "friend"—*Der lange verborgene Freund* (*The Long Secreted Friend* or more popularly *The Long Lost Friend*), which was published in Reading, Pennsylvania, in 1824. Already a number of such books were starting to appear among the German-speaking community there where they were known as "pow-wows."

The man behind *The Long Lost Friend* was John George Hohman, a German immigrant who had sailed to America from Hamburg in October 1802. In 1811, he published a Himmelsbrief, which he brought with him from Europe. Although little more than a pamphlet, the publication was snatched up and Hohman expanded his business and turned his attention to more occult matters. Around 1820, he put together a collection of the pow-wows and hexes that he'd picked up from the houses he'd visited, and published them in a small booklet. However, rather than magic and charms, these were "true and Christian instructions for everyone," according to the preface of the book. Indeed, many of the charms were not American at all, but had been taken from a work known as the *Romanus-Büchlein*, a part of the Pious Gertrude Books, which had been circulating among German Catholics during the 17th and 18th centuries. At the time of publication, Hohman was supplementing his printing business by acting as a healer, and had performed several notable medical "miracles." Confident from these successes, Hohman began to publish a number of occult treatises including a version of the Jewish Apocrypha, several veterinary cures, and a version of the Wandering Jew. Among these was *Pow-Wows* or, *The Long Lost Friend*. Its pages not only provided charms, but also practical help mingled with herbal lore, all written in a way that common people could understand. The book was hugely popular and several editions were printed throughout the next couple of decades. In 1842, Hohman also printed *Egyptische Geheimnisse* as a follow-up to *The Long Lost Friend*. This was a compilation of folk remedies and hexes, and was just as popular, establishing Hohman in the occult community of America. An awkwardly translated English version of *The Long Lost Friend* appeared in 1846 making the book "the first home-made American grimoire." Even though Hohman died shortly after the printing, better translated versions of the work appeared throughout the years. Around the beginning of the 20th century, a version bore the title *John George Hohman's Pow-Wows*. Indeed, just to own a copy served as a measure of protection against evil, so sometimes copies were held by one person within a family or one person in a community who consulted its pages and gained a reputation as a "wise person."

If *The Long Lost Friend* was seen as a holy collection of charms and remedies, the same could not be said of *The Sixth and Seventh Books of Moses*. Written in German and printed by an unknown publisher in Elizabethville, Pennsylvania, in the 1860s, a later English edition appeared in New York in the 1880s. Unlike *The Long Lost Friend,* which concerned itself with charms and protections, the Moses books—brought together in one volume—dealt with bewitchings, curses, the construction of talismans, and other potent spells. The volume was an essential tool for any hex doctor across the central or southern states, and it is thought that it was used as a reference well into the 20th century. The books were supposedly a distillation of "Egyptian magic" and their contents were attributed to scrolls penned by Moses. Couched in quasi-mystical language, it was supposedly translated from a forgotten Samaritan tongue, which only added to its supposed antiquity and mystery. This, in most people's eyes, was a true grimoire of the darkest kind.

Individual publishers, inspired by the success of the Germanic books, looked back into the magical traditions of other settlers for fresh text. The most fruitful was the Scandinavian tradition, taking their lead from the works of Gottskálk Nikulásson. The first black book of Nordic magic was published by John Anderson in Chicago in 1870. The main magical work that he printed was a large volume entitled *Oldtidens Sortebog* (printed in 1892), which was supposedly based on several Nordic tomes including some writings by Gottskálk and texts emanating from the Icelandic Black Schools. It was supposed to include incantations to induce the *mundklem* (the stealing of the breath) and instructions to make the *nabrok* (Finnish breeches), a ghastly spell for finding treasure using the lower portions of a corpse. In his preface, Anderson added all sorts of fantastic stories as to the book's origin. He claimed that it was written by a beautiful 14th-century Mexican nun who was held in a dungeon by a debauched cleric. In prison, she was visited by an angel who revealed certain mystical things to her; desperate to preserve this wisdom, she wrote it in her own blood on several pieces of torn clothing. These secrets eventually found their way into the possession of a Danish knight and sorcerer who copied them into a book, which he buried in a golden casket. It lay hidden in a field until a peasant ploughing the land uncovered it and gave it to some academics who, in turn, passed it to Anderson.

The book was supposedly written in code with a key to the work signed by "Cyprianus" (allegedly the name of the nun), which stated that the formulae therein had to be repeated backward. Despite its alleged fearsome reputation when translated, the *Oldtidens* contained little more than the usual charms for healing, finding lost property, inciting love, and detecting thieves. In some versions, however, it's thought that there had been additions that hinted at the raising of spirits, but in general there was little of the diabolical "Black Magic" with which the book became associated.

In England, however, a magical revolution was also stirring. A man named Samuel Liddell Mathers befriended one of his neighbors, Frederick Holland, who was a member of the Freemasons. In 1882, the pair was admitted to the circle of English Rosicrucians. It was around this time that Mathers began to develop a new persona for himself. This was the title of Count McGregor of Glenstrae, which he claimed had been given to his ancestor by Louis XV of France. Mathers moved to London where he published a number of books on the occult and ancient sorcery. In 1888, he published his first work, *The Qabbalah Unveiled*, together with a 17th-century Latin treatise and a work on the Tarot. However, the following year, he published what would become his opus by putting together the first English print edition of the *Key of Solomon*.

In 1890, Mathers was employed as a curator of the then private Horriman Museum. This allowed him to study many occult works and, four years later, he moved to Paris to continued his researches. There, he became fascinated by one volume called *The Sacred Book of Abra-Melin the Mage*, which was handwritten at the end of the 18th century. This was apparently the translation of a script written in Hebrew around 1458 by a Kabbalist named Abra-Melin. The knowledge was extremely detailed, having been culled from many parts of Europe in which the mage had traveled, including the court of the English king Henry VI. Abra-Melin eventually settled in Wurzburg, Germany, where he became the embodiment of ancient Jewish magic. Mathers readily believed this tale and was ready to accept Abra-Melin as the authentic voice of ancient Kabbalistic magic. He also believed that *The Sacred Book* was the unadulterated wisdom of the ages, much "purer" than the *Key of Solomon*. He printed an English version of the original text, which was popular outside of his small occult circles in London and Paris, and became a "classic" of occult literature.

Meanwhile, Arthur Edward Waite, slightly better known than Mathers, had already established himself as a reasonably successful author. He began churning out a number of books on so-called "occult studies," but refused to put his name on them. These included the *Handbook of Cartomancy*, which was largely reviled by occultists and was little more than a piece of florid hackwork. His next work, *Devil Worship in France*, published in 1896, was an expose of supposed Satanists and fake occultists and drew a great deal of praise, especially in academic circles. The journal *American*

Anthropologist declared it an excellent piece of anthropological work, which should be read by all those who wished to seriously study occultism from a scientific viewpoint.

In 1898, he published his most significant work: *The Book of Black Magic and Pacts*. This work provided extracts from many earlier grimoires with references to practical magic. Although the book was designed as a practical manual for occultists and would-be magicians, Waite was no practical sorcerer. Nevertheless, his book contained instructions for the construction of various talismans with numerous transcriptions of prayers, exorcisms, invocations, and spells. However, the book did not sell all that well, so Waite made little profit from it, and there was much opposition to its publication. However, a cheaper edition of the book, *The Book of Ceremonial Magic*, did much better.

Both Waite and Mathers were members of the Hermetic Order of the Golden Dawn, a 19th-century organization devoted to the exploration of occultism and the practice of ritual magic, however, the organization was riddled with factionalism and petty jealousies. Mathers, who considered himself something of an arch-mage, assumed an arrogant and dictatorial position. Waite, by contrast, tried obliquely to nudge it toward a more Christian mysticism. He warned against a new and rising member of the organization—a self-proclaimed magician named Aleister Crowley—who had been inspired by reading Waite's *Book of Black Magic*. Crowley would go on to become a cruel, egotistical, and amoral magician, who was described as the wickedest man in the world. He had published *The Lesser Key of Solomon* together with documentation relating to the rituals of the Golden Dawn in an occult journal that he'd founded. They revealed a hotchpotch of materials and ceremonies, some borrowed from ancient sources, some obviously made up. The age of the great grimoires was already passing, and from now on they would be confined to libraries and colleges.

It was against this backdrop of ancient grimoires and books of magic that Lovecraft began to write his own tales and books. Similar to some of the alleged grimoires, his books were a mixture of medieval witch lore and pre-human knowledge and, as such, they were often central to the plots of the tales. Other writers who followed Lovecraft created their own Cthulhu Mythos fiction and their own awful books, adding to a forbidden library of blasphemous literature. It is into this library of horrors that we now delve, in order to examine some of the terrible books themselves.

THE NECRONOMICON

Perhaps no book in the entire Cthulhu Mythos is as celebrated (or cursed) as the blasphemous *Necronomicon*—a Latin translation of a foul text known as the *Kitab Al-Azif,* which originated in the Middle East. It was supposedly written around A.D. 730 by the mad Arab demonologist Abdul Alhazred. The fictitious writer was another product of Lovecraft's mind, influenced by the small amount of Middle Eastern history that he knew, even though the name is not grammatically correct in Arabic. Since the *Kitab Al-Azif* first appeared in Lovecraft's tale "The Hound" (written in 1922 and published in *Weird Tales* in 1924), it has been extensively written about and modern versions of it have been printed to satisfy fan appetites. Of course, these are not actual grimoires; they have been created from the imaginations of writers and publishers for a specific market. There are, however, rumors that such a book did exist, and that Lovecraft had access to it. Other stories say that it was based on another book of which Lovecraft might have been aware.

According to author Daniel Harms, the book was probably inspired by the work of the Roman writer Marcus Manilius, who lived in the first century A.D. He was known as both a poet and an astrologer, and is credited as the author of *Astronomica,* a five-volume astronomical poem. According to Lovecraft scholar S.T. Joshi, Lovecraft was definitely familiar with Manilius's work, as he quoted from it in an amateur astronomy column that he wrote for the *Asheville Gazette-News* in 1915. In "The Hound," the *Necronomicon* is not yet the horror that it eventually becomes.

Although the exact nature of the *Necronomicon* was not specified in "The Hound," its context is certainly set in "The Festival" (written in 1923 and published in 1925). In this story, the protagonist visits an ancestral home in the snowy town of Kingsport, which exerts a sinister hold over him when he learns that four of his kinsmen were hanged for witchcraft there in 1692. His destination becomes the home of an old, mute gentleman who may be more than he seems. In a musty room within this old gentleman's house, a pile of "hoary and moldy" tomes sit on a table. The titles include *Saducismus Triumphatus* by Joseph Glanvill, the *Daemonolatreia* of Regimius, and a Latin version of the *Necronomicon* translated by Olaus Wormius. The first two of these books are real, the last is not. Glanvill's book confirms the existence of witches and deals in part with Swedish witchcraft cases, whereas the *Daemonolatreia* is a compendium of alleged demonic matters relating to the trial of European witches. The context of the *Necronomicon* is a witch book that deals with ancient and forbidden lore and, according to Lovecraft, is worse than any other volume in that terrible pile.

Lovecraft states that the book was compiled around A.D. 730 in Sana'a (the current capital of Yemen) by a wandering poet and scholar named Abdul Alhazred. The choice of Sana'a may not have been an arbitrary one, because the city is one of the oldest continuously inhabited places in the world with a history dating back more than 2,500 years. Far from being a "crazed poet," Alhazred may have been a well-traveled man who visited the ruins of Babylon Fortress and Memphis in Egypt. It is here that Lovecraft's initial image of an urbane and measured researcher appears to break down slightly, for the title that he gives to the book is the *Kitab Al-Azif*. In ancient Arabia, the term *Al-Azif* was used by the *kahina* to describe the insect-like buzzing voices of the djinn with whom they communicated. Prolonged exposure to such buzzing was enough to drive any rational human insane. Therefore, many of the *kahina* were usually considered to be mad and issued many of their prophesies in rambling verse. Although the title *Al-Azif* has been used by countless Lovecraft aficionados to refer to the original work, Lovecraft uses it only once in a revision of Adolphe de Castro's *The Last Test*. Nevertheless, Alhazred is portrayed as a rambling madman, transcribing terrible knowledge that he learned from the djinn in the wilderness. Some writers claim that during his travels he had visited Irem, City of the Pillars, which had been built by the djinn. According to Iraqi scholar Ibn Khallikan, the horror of the knowledge that Alhazred sought to share with a wider world was confirmed when, in A.D. 738, he was torn to pieces by invisible forces in a corner of the marketplace in Damascus. The book, however, survived.

Besides Alhazred's texts, it is thought that Lovecraft may have had knowledge of another book, on which his work may have been based. Southern Jordan is home to a remote valley that boasts a spectacular rocky outcropping lying about 60 kilometers east of Aqaba known as Wadi Rum, or Valley of the Moon. It is perhaps the largest wadi in all of Jordan and contains traces of human habitation from around the third or fourth century.

Many people believe the wadi to be a mystical place. Local legends state that there was once a great city here—a fortress built by the djinn in the days before King Solomon ruled Israel in the second half of the 10th century B.C. Local muquarribun, Ghost Priests who still live among the Bedouin of the region, claim that in a local cave lie several cylinders in which a number of scrolls known as *The Whispers of Angels* are stored.

Written by the djinn, the knowledge that they contain supposedly dates from just before the formation of the earth, and concerns old pre-Islamic gods who dwelt at that time. They also revealed spells and incantations that could affect the very nature of reality itself. The incantations were used to create an earthly paradise in which the gods relaxed before the coming of Mankind, and the book reveals how animals and men were created, as well as instructions for the manipulation of our very reality.

Another legend states that the scrolls contain words of power used by Allah in the creation of the world, which were written down by djinn who secretly overheard them. The muquarribun claim that some of their kind have access to and can read at least part of these scrolls, but not all of them.

Although the Ghost Priests of the Bedouin claimed sole knowledge of *The Whispers of Angels*, the Al Sulaba, the Lost Shamans of the Arabian Peninsula, also claimed to be the true guardians of such arcane texts. Little is known about this strange group; recently they seem to have vanished into the desert or may have completely died out. Even when they were first mentioned in 1853 by the explorer Sir Richard Burton (who referred to them as *Khlawiyah*, a name derived from *khala* meaning "wilderness") they appear to have been small in number and nomadic by nature. Among some of the other Bedouin groups they were classed as great magicians who were directly in touch with ancient gods and djinn out in the desert. They carried with them the ancient text of *The Whispers of Angels*, which they claimed came from a place known as Majlis al-Jinn—the Congregation of the Spirits—a mysterious cavern on the Selma Plateau in Oman. The text was supposedly passed down in a number of lacquered wooden boxes, which the nomads carried away with them. Significantly, the Al Sulaba are also associated with the city of Sana'a, which is where Abdul Alhazred allegedly penned the *Necronomicon*.

According to journalist George Hay, the great Arab philosopher Al-Kindi is also a possible contender for producing the text. Al-Kindi was the first of the peripatetic Arab philosophers, earning the title "father of Islamic philosophy." He is credited with melding ancient Greek and Middle Eastern philosophy and wrote on a whole range of subjects including mathematics, astrology, astronomy, meteorology, earthquakes, sword-making, and religious matters. One of his books, *The Essence of the Soul*, although dealing with religion and philosophy, also contained sections on magic; Hay claims this was the forerunner of the *Necronomicon*.

As for the *Al-Azif*, Lovecraft claims the formal translation into Greek was carried out by the fictional scholar Theodorus Philetas of Constantinople in A.D. 950. Lovecraft states that Theodorus found the *Kitab Al-Azif* in the Imperial Library, and set about translating and renaming it the *Necronomicon*. Lovecraft confidently asserted that the translation meant "an image of the laws of the dead" but, as writer Robert M. Price has pointed out, it can be translated in a number of ways: "the book of dead names," "knower of the laws of the dead," or simply "laws of the dead." Claiming that Lovecraft's Greek etymology is unsound, S.T. Joshi says that the title actually means "book considering the dead," perhaps simply referring to a manual of classification.

According to the writer Dennis Detwiller, around A.D. 1,000, the Greek *Necronomicon* was translated back into Arabic by philosopher and healer Ibn Sina under the title *Kitab al-Majmu* (*The Book of Collections*). The *Kitab al-Majmu* is not printed in the conventional way, but is passed down among them in handwritten form between what they describe as an "Initiated Master" and "Apprentice." The Alawites have a mystical reputation and some Islamic clerics declare that they are not Muslims at all. Little is known about their holy books, although they seem to be pretty standard historical and religious texts and certainly not the *Necronomicon*.

However, despite the translation back to Arabic, the Greek translation was still popular, and in 1050 it came to the attention of Michael I Cerularius, a theologian noted for his strong views. It is said that Michael was so shocked by what he had heard about the book that he ordered all copies to be gathered up and burned along with all known copies of the *Kitab Al-Azif*. However, Michael was not thorough in his destruction of the terrible work, for a copy or two survived. According to some sources, a copy of *Al-Azif* was found somewhere in Jerusalem by a Crusader knight around 1099, and it was brought to the Comte de Champagne, a student of the occult, who set his knights to guard it. The book would later form the basis for a French version of the *Necronomicon,* and in the early 13th century, several French copies circulated in a number of French monasteries including Mortemer Abbey in Normandy and the monasteries of St. Hilaire and St. Martin du Canigou in Languedoc. In all of these holy houses, the copies were held in secret, and were not spoken about in the outside world.

Although Greek, French, and Belgian variations of the *Necronomicon* existed, the edition to which most people refer is a 1228 Latin translation by one of Lovecraft's fictional characters, a Danish monk named Olaus Wormius. The name Olaus Wormius emerges again in connection with another version of the *Necronomicon* in 1487. This time, Olaus Wormius is a monk in Catholic Spain, and is a secretary to Tomas de Torquemada, a senior official in the Inquisition.

Both of these versions of Olaus Wormius were based on a Danish physician named Ole Worm (1588–1655). Something of a perpetual student, he obtained degrees from the University of Marburg in Germany (1605) and the University of Basel in Switzerland (1611), holding a doctorate in medicine. His contribution to modern medicine lies in the naming of bones in the cranium, which are known today as Wormian bones. He also acted as a court physician to King Christian IV of Denmark, advising the Monarch on various contagions that had broken out in the country. This urbane and learned Protestant physician seems very far removed from the Lovecraftian creation of Olaus Wormius, who translated the blasphemous Greek text of the *Necronomicon* in far-away Spain.

According to Lovecraft, the fictional Wormius sent a printed copy of the translated text to Johannes Trithemius, Abbot of the Schottenklöster in Wurzburg, Germany. Trithemius was a learned cryptologist and occult scholar who, in 1499, produced a book entitled *Steganographia,* which was allegedly about magic. Although he had published a number of books on the occult, Trithemius was shocked and alarmed at the content of Wormius's book, and reported it to the church officials, who had Wormius seized and burned at the stake as a witch. (The real Ole Worm died at home.)

Despite all this suppression, copies of the *Necronomicon* continued to circulate. The most famous was the black-letter text, which was a direct printing of Wormius's earlier text that had been printed in Germany around 1400. Lovecraft says that the book had now been placed on the Vatican's *Index Librorum Prohibitorum* (The List of Banned Books). Unfortunately, the *Index* did not actually exist at this time and was only introduced in 1559 by Pope Paul IV. Therefore, Lovecraft's knowledge of Vatican history seems slightly suspect. It is quite possible that other lists of banned literature may have existed, but many of these related to religious heresies or those which directly challenged the views of the Church.

Despite having a place on the list, copies of the book still continued to circulate; more French editions appeared, along with Russian and Italian versions. In fact, Leonardo da Vinci reputedly possessed a copy of the book, and a copy was also translated by the Spanish writer Miguel de Cervantes (author of *Don Quixote*). However, one of the copies made around this time was of special interest: Around 1586, the most comprehensive and accurate English translation of the *Necronomicon* was written by a mysterious but well-known individual named Dr. John Dee.

Dee was an enigmatic figure in 16th-century society who straddled the worlds of science and magic as they gradually became distinct from each other. Always interested in both science and the occult (particularly in astrology) Dee was arrested for treason in 1555 because he allegedly cast the horoscopes of Queen Mary I and Princess Elizabeth (later Elizabeth I), which showed the Queen in an unfavorable light and doomed to an early death. He appeared before the Parliamentary Star Chamber and exonerated himself, but he was placed under the supervision of a number of Catholic bishops anyway. This led to continual rumors of magic and necromancy, which would follow him for the rest of his life. When Mary died in 1558, Dee found some favor with her successor, her half-sister Elizabeth, and become her consultant regarding astrological and scientific matters. He put forward proposals for the creation of an early English empire, as well as extending English claims in the New World.

While on a visit to Prague, he visited the court of the Holy Roman Emperor Rudolf II. According to some accounts, Dee supposedly came across a copy of the *Necronomicon*. Others say that he found Olaus Wormius's translation at the castle of a Transylvanian noble, although there is no mention of a trip to the country in any of Dee's own diaries. A third story stated that Dee acquired the book from his questionable associate, the spirit-medium Edward Kelley. Kelley allegedly purchased it in Prague from a Jewish mystic and Kabbalist named Jacob Eliezer—the so-called "Black Rabbi," who fled to the city from Italy to avoid charges of necromancy.

Regardless of where he obtained the Latin version of the *Necronomicon*, Dee supposedly started to work on the English translation in 1586. According to journalist George Hay, there are two dates for the printing of the work: One is recorded as 1585 in Haarlem, Holland. The other is 1571 in Antwerp. Daniel Harms, however, dismisses both accounts, saying that the English translation was undertaken from 1586 onward, and that the text was never printed but kept in a handwritten form only. Dee died in 1608 or 1609, and if he possessed a copy of the *Necronomicon* no one knows what happened to it. He did, however, leave several mysterious volumes including the *Book of Soyga*, which was a Latin treatise on magic and the mystic arts written sometime before the 16th century. It contained Kabbalistic tables as well as incantations for the summoning of various angels—the angel Uriel in particular. After Dee's death, it was deemed lost, but was found again in 1994 and is now in the Bodleian Library at the University of Oxford.

In his *Guide to the Cthulhu Cult,* Fred Pelton mentions another copy of the Wormius volume written by Baron Frederick I of Sussex under the title *Cultus Maleficarum,* more commonly known as *The Sussex Manuscript.* This is, Pelton says, a confused and barely intelligible version, and is not considered to be reliable. However, it should be noted that Sussex was never a Barony, so the book that Pelton produced as evidence was probably written by Pelton himself. Although August Derleth considered publishing it, and made reference to it in some of his stories, this idea was eventually abandoned. Lovecraft scholars suggest that Dee's translation is probably the most complete and reliable version in English.

Although vehemently suppressed, versions of the *Necronomicon* were starting to appear in many languages besides English at this time. A reference to yet another copy appeared in a work entitled *My Understanding of the Great Book,* by a German scholar named Joachim Kindler. The copy surfaced in the city of Buda in 1641, and he says it was written in the Gothic tongue (a language spoken by the ancient Germanic tribes), although other writers dispute this and say that it was written in a form of proto-Turkish. Kindler gives the first real clues—apart from scattered quotations—as to the overall content of the abhorred volume. The translation, he claims, "offers proofs logickal and glorious" of the "stellar numbers, potentiated objecks, signs and passes, probatories, phylacteries, and craftsmanly artes." In other words, the *Necronomicon* could be viewed as a grimoire in the conventional sense.

Throughout the succeeding centuries, various copies and sections of the *Necronomicon* surfaced in several parts of the world, most notably in America where a number of English variations appeared among some of the remote New England communities. Several of these copies had been passed down through the generations of families as heirlooms. According to tradition, many of these families were living in remote areas such as Rhode Island and Vermont, and were lacking in formal education, but they possessed an arcane knowledge that they obtained from the book and others like it. For example, according to Lovecraft's own *The Case of Charles Dexter Ward,* a 1771 raid on a farmhouse near Providence, Rhode Island, supposedly uncovered a copy belonging to a degenerate branch of the Curwen family. Subsequent writers have suggested that certain raiders took this book and made copies of it, which then found their way into the hands of certain antiquarians in the area. One of these was allegedly a relative of Lovecraft.

According to Keith Herber in *Arkham Unveiled*, somewhere between 1895 and 1900, Henry Armitage, head librarian at Lovecraft's fictional Miskatonic University (clearly modeled on Brown University, not far from Lovecraft's own house), purchased a copy of the *Necronomicon* from Whipple Phillips, Lovecraft's grandfather. This is perhaps the first time the book was directly linked with the family of the Mythos author. Lovecraft fans claim the book is at Brown University, but is only available to certain scholars.

Other writers have attempted to link the deadly book with actual places, documents, and historical events. For instance, a copy of the *Necronomicon* was apparently donated to Harvard University by the estate of an antiquary who perished on the RMS *Titanic*; the occultist Aleister Crowley supposedly published a copy in 1916; in 1928, a copy was found in Russia in a secret library of Ivan the Terrible; eventually it found its way into the hands of Joseph Stalin before World War II. But among all of these is one document that may be more plausible than any other.

The Voynich Manuscript

The most famous (and authentic) text that is most closely associated with the *Necronomicon* is the Voynich Manuscript. Some Lovecraft scholars have argued that is a partial copy of the *Necronomicon* couched in a cipher that only the "initiated" can read.

The manuscript takes its name from the Polish-born book-dealer and bibliophile Wilfrid Voynich, who bought it at a villa in central Italy in 1912. Until today, no one has been able to decipher the text in which it is written. The book is heavily illustrated, but even the profuse and lavish pictures make little sense without the accompanying text to guide the reader. There have been many theories about the book: It is a secret text used by French Cathars. It is a "polyglot tongue" comprising Old High German, Middle Dutch, and Old French used to cover the writings of a secret Egyptian cult. It is a constructed encrypted language used for conveying state and political secrets. And, of course, some say that it contains portions of the *Necronomicon*.

The text is comprised of about 240 vellum pages, most of which are illustrated. Several pages appear to be missing; what has become of these is unknown. Originally, it was thought that the book was some sort of herbal guide since many of the pages portray plants and similar vegetation; however, most of the growths that are depicted are unknown. In 2009, the University of Arizona performed an advanced carbon dating exercise on one of the vellum pages. The results placed the material originating between 1404 and 1438. In addition, the McCrone Research Institute in Chicago dated the ink that was used to around the same period.

Between the leaves of the manuscript was a letter dated from 1666, which stated that the book had once belonged to the Holy Roman Emperor Rudolf II and that it was being passed from Jan Marek Marci to Athanasius Kircher. Marci was the court physician to the Holy Roman Emperors and Rector of the University of Prague. Kircher, a German Jesuit scholar and philosopher, was also associated with medicine, but it was languages and ciphers that fascinated him most. In 1666, Kircher was a teacher at Collegio Romano in Rome and had just published an Egyptian Coptic dictionary; he also deciphered certain Egyptian hieroglyphs.

In 1639, Kircher received one of two letters from Georg Baresch, a scientist and alchemist living in Prague. The manuscript had come into Baresch's possession and, being a scholar, he had tried to translate it, imagining it to be some kind of early herbal guide. However, he was stumped by the encrypted text and wrote to Kircher, sending him a sample of the script and asking him to help. Whether or not Kircher replied is uncertain, but when Baresch died, the manuscript passed into the hands of Jan Marek Marci, who took over the task of getting it translated and wrote to Kircher again.

The manuscript's history becomes somewhat murky at this point, but it seems to have been part of the library at the Collegio Romano. It probably remained there until Victor Emmanuel II declared himself the king of Italy and annexed the Papal States. As Italian troops closed in, much of the College's library was transferred into private hands in order to protect it. The manuscript became the personal property of Peter Beckx, who may have taken it to the Villa Mondragone. After his death, his library was bought by the Roman Society of Jesus and partly moved back to Rome, though it is thought that the mysterious volume stayed in Frascati.

In 1912, the Collegio Romano found itself in financial difficulties and was persuaded to sell off some of its books. Along with the Manuscript, Voynich bought approximately 30 others. When he died, the book passed into the hands of his widow Ethel, who bequeathed the volume to her friend, Miss Anne Nill, when she passed away in 1960. In turn, she sold the book to another book dealer, Hans P. Kraus. Unable to find a buyer for it, Kraus donated it to Yale University in 1969. Today, it lies in the University's Beinecke Rare Book and Manuscript Library as item MS 408.

Of course, some have suggested that the entire manuscript was a hoax, either perpetrated by Voynich and his wife (who were both revolutionaries), or by someone else. They dismiss the 1666 letters to Kircher saying that, although they are probably genuine, they do not refer *specifically* to the book. In fact, there is a theory that the discovery of the letter actually *inspired* Voynich to fabricate the book. Some historians say the volume was actually a joke by a scholar named Jacobus Sinapius. Sinapius was an extremely learned man who worked as a physician at the Court of Rudolf II and wrote extensively on medical and botanical matters. In his latter years, he was Curator of the Emperor's Botanical Gardens and was considered to be something of an expert on plants and herbs. He was, however, also known for his clever jests and teases.

On the contrary, Voynich claimed that by using certain chemicals on the vellum, he detected the faint signature of "Jacobj a Tepenence," which he thought *might* be Jakob Horcicky of Tepenec. This has led to speculation that Jacobus was the author of the manuscript, but others say this it was just a forgery by Voynich. Another scholar, Andreas Mueller, had once played a joke on Kircher by sending him a scroll in an unintelligible language explaining that it had been found in Egypt and asked for a translation.

In his book *The Curse of the Voynich,* Nick Pelling makes the suggestion that the manuscript was written by a Florentine architect named Antonio di Pietro Averlino and that the book was used as a method for moving military and engineering secrets through the Ottoman Empire. He asserts that much of the material contained in the work is fake, designed to divert the Ottoman cryptographers. Pelling and several computer experts have shown how easy it is to create an almost-indecipherable language using certain mathematical formula, which would have been known at the time. Indeed, similar books have been created throughout the years by enterprising cryptographers, all of them done simply as exercises in the construction of ciphers.

So where does that leave the *Necronomicon* in relation to the Voynich Manuscript? Perhaps it is the sheer *mysteriousness* of the text that has contributed to the belief that there are elements of the shunned book within its pages. Was the author familiar with the dark Alhazred text enough to incorporate it into his creation? Until we know exactly *who* the author was and why the book was written we cannot even begin to speculate.

The *Necronomicon* is, arguably, one of Lovecraft's most famous creations and its fearsome reputation has reverberated all through the Cthulhu Mythos. Does such a terrible book truly exist? We can't really say for sure, but if it does, perhaps the quest for it is just as intriguing as the discovery of the tome itself.

The Forbidden Library
De Vermis Mysteriis

Of all the arcane books in the Mythos library, *De Vermis Mysteriis* lies second to the dreaded *Necronomicon* in terms of blasphemy and terror. The tome is a grimoire in the conventional sense, but sections of it also link the entities of the Mythos with ancient Egyptian gods and mythology. With spells and rituals designed to summon entities from beyond the stars, *De Vermis Mysteriis* makes such a connection possible. Divided into 16 chapters, the book deals with magical aspects such as familiars, elementals, divination, and the Philosopher's Stone. Of particular interest to many Lovecraftian scholars is the section on Saracen magic and the tales concerning an ancient entity known as Byatis, which eventually formed the basis for the Berkeley Toad.

De Vermis Mysteriis was not actually created by Lovecraft, but by the writer Robert Bloch, though it was mentioned in correspondences between the two. Lovecraft was always happy to use the creations of those with whom he corresponded, so there are certainly references to it throughout Lovecraft's writings.

In one of the correspondences, Lovecraft suggested that Bloch call the book *De Vermis Mysteriis* instead of *The Mysteries of the Worm*, and he even gave him a passage for the book:

Tibi, magnum Innominandum, signa stellarum nigrarum et bufaniformis Sadoquae sigillum.
(To you, the great Not-to-be-Named, signs of the black stars, and the seal of the toad-shaped Tsathoggua.)

After much discussion between the Lovecraft and Bloch, it first appeared in a short story entitled "The Shambler from the Stars," published in *Weird Tales* in September 1935. In it, a friend of the protagonist, Robert Harrison Blake, reads one of the spells aloud and summons a star vampire from the Outer Void, which tears him apart.

The book is largely a hotchpotch of spells, incantations, and lore. Part of it concerns the fictional author Ludvig Prinn and his travels in the Middle East, the mages whom he encountered, and what he learned from them. These details form the main core of the work, although there are many conventional spells and snatches of information that may have been added later by others. Some of these are summoning spells, used to drawing down djinn and efreet together with other entities. Of course, there are connections into the Mythos within its pages, such as tales of Byatis or the lore of the worm-wizards of Irem (which gives the book its name), as well as references to invisible beings that dwell out beyond the stars.

However, it is the section on Saracen magic that is of most interest. This is the knowledge that Ludvig Prinn supposedly accumulated in Egypt and it deals with the links between the Mythos entities and the near-forgotten deities of that country. In particular, Prinn discloses the true nature of the crocodile-headed god Sebek, and divulges certain secrets of the deity known as Thoth, god of knowledge. It is said that some of the descriptions in this chapter can drive the mind of a rational man to the very edge of insanity. It is no small wonder that the volume created a stir in both the Catholic and emergent Protestant churches of the 1500s.

The suggestion has been made that Ludvig Prinn was born to a Flemish couple in Constantinople, though some writers like Harry Davey suggest that he might have been born near Ghent, Belgium. Prinn was incredibly reticent to speak of where he was born, but before he was burned at the stake, he boasted of having attained a miraculous age. At the time of his death in 1542, Prinn suggests he was even older than he appeared. For example, he claimed to be the only survivor of the ill-fated Ninth Crusade in 1271 and 1272.

Several centuries after Prinn had been burned at the stake, a reference to a "gentleman retainer" named Ludwig Prinn was found among the records of the forces of Montserrat. This is curious, as Montserrat played little part in the Ninth Crusade. If Prinn *had* been captured by the Saracens, it was more likely to be in the disastrous Seventh Crusade (1248–1254). Later commentators, such as Keith Herber, have suggested that this was most probably a Crusader ancestor, but even that explanation is suspect. Interestingly, a writer named Emerald Hammer has connected him to the Teutonic Knights. This may have given Prinn access to certain Templar secrets allegedly brought back to Europe from the Holy Land. Although the two Orders were markedly different, their objectives were the same, and it may be that Prinn was a part of this enterprise rather than actually fighting in the Crusade.

According to Prinn, he was captured by the Saracens and taken to Syria where he spent some time as a slave. According to Bloch, he acquired a great deal of arcane knowledge from the wizards and wonder workers while in Syria. Bloch also make a crucial connection between Prinn and Egypt (this allows him to make comparisons between Mythos deities, lore, and Egyptian tradition), though how he traveled there is unknown. He writes that there are "legends amongst the Libyan dervishes concerning the old seer's deeds in Alexandria." Sometime during his time in Syria, Prinn abandoned Christianity and adopted the ways of the Muslims. Daniel Harms suggests that he may have spent some time as a captive of Syrian warlocks in a mountain range in the lower Orontes Valley in Syria. According to Harms, Prinn spoke with the priests of the Black Pharaoh Nephren-Ka and dwelt for a time in the ruins of the city of Chorazin by the Sea of Galilee.

What became of Prinn thereafter seems largely unknown. Professor Richard Stanley suggested that he spent it wandering among the various Bedouin tribes of the deserts, eventually visiting Irem, City of Pillars, allegedly in Southern Jordan, which had been built by the djinn in the time of King Solomon. Writer Emerald Hammer states that for about 200 years, there were reports of him all over the Middle East. Hammer estimates that Prinn returned to Europe around the end of the 14th century, but the date is not known for sure. He also could have returned to the land of his supposed birth in the Flemish lowlands. According to Harms, he initially settled somewhere between Ghent and Bruges, and finally in a forest near Brussels. There, he took up habitation in a pre-Christian tomb deep in the woodlands where he lived for years as an eccentric hermit. Rumors concerning him circulated in the locality. It was said, for instance, that he was a sorcerer and necromancer, and that he carried on hideous and dreadful magical experiments. Eventually, such rumors reached the ears of the Roman Inquisition. Generally speaking, the Inquisition around Brussels was relatively lenient when compared to other such institutions. However, around the mid-16th century, the Roman ecclesiastical area of Tournai was coming under increasing pressure from expanding Protestantism and decided to taken a tougher line against heretics. Prinn was also accused of teaching "Islamist heresies" to those who came to visit him, and this could not be tolerated. It was also a time when the Catholic Church feared the rise of witchcraft, allegations of which were perhaps stirred by Protestant sympathizers. With all of these factors working against Prinn, he was arrested in 1540.

When he came before the Court of the Bishop of Tournai, Ludvig Prinn denied nothing. He confessed to being an incredible age, which had been brought about, he claimed, by the magics of the Middle East where some hermits had lived for thousands of years. He further agreed that he had been visited by invisible companions and star servants, and spoke of "greater mysteries than those of which the feeble imaginings of the Church could conceive." The Bishop now had an example to enforce Church discipline and discourage heresies (Protestant, Islamic, or other) and sentenced Prinn to be burnt at the stake as a witch and a heretic. On the orders of the Bishop, officers of the Inquisition allegedly went to his crypt-house and removed certain things there, most of which were destroyed later on. Although tortured and ordered to recant, Prinn still maintained that everything was true, and while in prison awaiting execution, he penned De Vermis Mysteriis. Somehow, in the dead of that night in 1542, just before his execution, he managed to smuggle it from his cell and release it into the world.

A day later, Prinn was burned at the stake. It is said that before the flames reached him he cried out in a tongue that no one understood. The smoke from the pyre began to thicken and darken and form strange shapes as the flames rose up. All who witnessed his death crossed themselves. Ludvig Prinn was dead, but his book lived on.

Roughly three years after Prinn's death, *De Vermis Mysteriis* appeared in printed form. Roughly 40 folio copies were printed in Cologne, Germany, in the original Latin and black-letter text. They may have been printed on the presses of Eucharius Cervicornus (an early and well-known Cologne printer), and were distributed by some of his agents. Declaring it to be an Islamic and sorcerous text, the Church immediately seized as many copies as it could and destroyed them. Fifteen copies are thought to have survived.

As previously discussed, an attempt was also made to translate Prinn's work into English. This task was carried out by Dr. John Dee and Edward Kelley, and their version was printed in London in 1573; it relied heavily on the German black-letter text. Kelley and Dee may have also made further additions to Prinn's work, inserting portions on how to command a ghost, how to create a scrying glass or window, and how to create a zombie. However, this version is badly translated in parts and appears incomplete.

Centuries later, a slightly better English version entitled *Mysteries of the Worm* was produced in 1821 by Charles Leggett. The edition was privately printed by an unknown press, and though it relied heavily on the old black-letter German text, it seems to be a much better translation than the Kelley edition. It is not known how many copies were printed, but it is thought that there were less than 20. What became of these is largely unknown, but one of them is in the British Library's Restricted Books Section and can only be viewed by private arrangement and in connection with academic study.

In the mid-1800s, a curious document appeared in rural England that was thought to be a section of *De Vermis Mysteriis* translated into English. The text dealt with Saracen rituals and was printed as a single monograph. No author is given for this work, although the translator is thought to have been an English rural Anglican clergyman, so the writing has been credited to "Clergyman X." Akin to the other English translations it contained elements from the German black-letter edition, although it has been suggested that portions of it may come from some other source. Although no copies of this monograph now exist (it may have had an extremely small printing and distribution) a fairly extensive footnote concerning it is to be found in Reverend Jennings's *Curiosities of English Literature* (1903).

Another printing of this book can be found in the Huntingdon Library in California; this copy may have been printed around the mid-1800s using an original Latin text. There was also a complete volume privately printed by the Starry Wisdom Press in Providence, Rhode Island, but the date of the printing is not known. The British Museum possesses roughly half a Latin text of the book, although it is in extremely poor condition and is not available for viewing. According to writer Ramsey Campbell, another copy was kept in the Brichester University Library in England, but the building burned down in the 1960s and no one knows what became of the book.

As late as the 1930s rumors of *De Vermis Mysteriis* emerged again, reportedly in the possession of the famous German explorer Hermann Van Dultz. Originally from an old German/Dutch family, Van Dultz was widely traveled and therefore built up a secret library of curious and esoteric books. A grouping within the developing Nazi Germany called the Ahnenerbe (a Nazi think tank that included Heinrich Himmler, Herman Wirth, and Richard Walther Darre) demanded access to this library particularly to study *De Vermis Mysteriis*. Although a German patriot, Van Dultz refused to grant such access—he maintained that there were things contained in the book that Mankind was certainly not meant to know. For his stubbornness, he was arrested and sent to a prison camp near the Polish border where he died during World War II. Since Van Dultz lived in Dresden, it was assumed that his library was destroyed in the bombing of the city in February 1945. This, however, may not have been the case, because several of the books that he supposedly possessed have recently turned up in Russia. The remnants of Van Dultz's library is supposed to be in the hands of the estate of his former student Heinrich Hassler, who is currently and secretly selling it off.

According to some, the text that Van Dultz owned is an original manuscript, although whether it is the one that was written in prison by Ludvig Prinn is open to question. Although we have no evidence, it is possible that several manuscript copies were made for various reasons in the 1550s and this may be one of those. It might even be a manuscript copy of the German black-letter text (several handwritten copies were allegedly made of that as well). In the occult world, some people wait with baited breath to see what emerges.

Byatis and the Berkeley Toad

As previously discussed, one of the central elements in *De Vermis Mysteriis* is the figure of the "serpent-bearded Byatis," a creature that Ramsey Campbell connects to the old English folktale of the Berkeley Toad. He is first mentioned in Bloch's *The Shambler from the Stars* in 1935. It is thought that Prinn witnessed the secret worship of this deity somewhere in Egypt. In the Mythos, he is classed among the Great Old Ones: ultra-powerful alien beings who have been on Earth since the earliest times and who have had an influence on ancient history and the development of Mankind. However, according to Mythos lore, they are subject to certain restrictions and can be commanded by certain individuals using the correct incantations or rituals. Byatis appears in the guise of a one-eyed, multi-colored, shimmering amphibian or as a great and jewelled spider. It also displays a proboscis, crab-like pincers, and a row of tentacles beneath its mouth. Byatis can sometimes be represented by a glowering male face with a beard of writhing tentacles hanging down. It has the power to hyp-notise those whom it chooses to prey upon, and each victim that it devours adds to its strength and power.

The entity had been brought to Earth in an ancient time by a primal people known as the Deep Ones who still exist in certain remote locations on the planet (see *Innsmouth* later in the book). Whether they are a form of proto-human or not is a debateable point, for they physically resemble something that is somewhere between humanoid and fish. They are bachtrian in nature, with bulging eyes, gills, and webbed hands and feet—looking more like great frogs than humans. It is thought that they may communicate telepathically, although they have also been known to speak in harsh croaking voices. Some have argued that they came to Earth from another world along with the great Cthulhu, and eventually evolved enough to be capable of surviv-ing in water—particularly in the oceans of Earth. The species is an immortal one, only dying through acts of violence. It was they who brought Byatis to our planet as an object of worship, and these actions were carried on into later centuries by the serpent men of Valusia and by the people of the lost continent of Mu in the Pacific Ocean.

It is said that the cult of Byatis was strongest in pre-Roman Britain where the entity was equated with a fertility god. Roman legions occupying the Severn Valley had found Byatis (or some representation thereof) behind an ancient carved stone door in an abandoned pagan camp. The were so horrified by what the found that they resealed the door, securing it with a five-pointed star (a form of protection against the Old Ones) before marking the place as somewhere no Roman should go.

However, the protection was weak, and from time to time Byatis would break free from the prison and terrify the surrounding countryside in various guises. Such incidents have found their way into local English folklore, a concept that English writers such as Ramsey Campbell have been keen to exploit. The most famous of these tales is the story of the terrible Berkeley Toad.

In the chancel of St. Mary's Church in Berkeley, Gloucestershire, there is a carv-ing of a huge toad adorning the tomb of the Berkeley family. Beneath it are the carv-ings of the heads of two small children. According to a local legend, a monstrous toad emerged from a nearby swamp and ate two of the children belonging to the family. But the church is not the only place that such a carving may be found, for in the

Morning Room of nearby Berkeley Castle (which was the seat of the family) there is a similar carving of the Toad that lives in the Castle dungeon. A collection of notes and stories complied by James Herbert Cooke, land steward to the Berkeley estate in the 19th century, took his notes from another steward, John Smyth of Nibley. Citing Smyth's words in the original English he states:

OUT OF A DUNGEON IN THE LIKENESS OF A DEEPE, BROAD WELL GOINGE STEEPLY DOWN IN THE MIDDLE OF THE DUNGEON CHAMBER IN THE SAID KEEPE, WAS (SO TRA-DITION TELLS) DRAWN FORTH A TOAD, IN THE TIME OF KINGE HENRY THE SEVENTH, OF INCREDIBLE BIGGNES, WHICH IN THE DEEPE DRY DUST IN THE BOTTOM THEREOF HAD DOUBTLESSE LIVED THERE DIVERS HUNDREDS OF YEARES; WHOSE PORTRAITURE IN JUST DIMENSION AS IT WAS THEN TO ME AFFIRMED BY DIVERSE AGED PERSONS I SAW, ABOUT 48 YEARES AGONE, DRAWNE IN COLOURS UPON THE DOORE OF THE GREAT HALL AND UPON THE UTTER SIDE OF THE STONE PORCH LEADINGE INTO THAT HALL, SINCE BY PARGETTORS OR POINTERS OF THAT WALLWAHED OUT OR OUTWORNE WITH TIME, WHICH IN BREDTH WAS MORE THAN A FOOT, NEERE 16 INCHES, AND IN LENGTH MORE. OF WHICH MONSTROUS AND OUTGROWNE BEASTE, THE INHABITANTS OF THIS TOWNE, AND IN THE NEIGHBOUR VILLAGES ROUND ABOUT FABLE MANY STRANGE AND INCREDIBLE WONDERS; MAKING THE GREATNES OF THIS TOAD MORE THAN WOULD FILL A PECK, YEA, I HAVE HEARD SOME, WHO LOOKED TO HAVE BELIEFE, SAY FROM THE REPORT OF THEIR FATHERS AND GRANDFATHERS THAT IT WOULD HAVE FILLED A BUSHEL OR STRIKE, AND TO HAVE BEEN MANY YEARES FED WITH FLESH AND GARBAGE FROM THE BUTCHERS; BUT THIS IS ALL THE TRUETH I KNOWE OR DARE BELIEVE.

Whether or not the Berkeley Toad existed, descriptions of both it and its activities vary from story to story. Some tales say that it went on a rampage through the country, devouring people; others say that it was no more than "a wonder" and "a marvel," and was extremely quiet so long as it was fed; others claim it was the very embodiment of the Devil. As Smyth said: "Everie man's beliefe is left to himself and I knowe what myself thinketh thereof, and of the like, bee it a lye or a trueth, it was generally believed."

Nevertheless, the legend of the Toad expanded and grew more and more fanciful throughout the years. During the 1600s, the tale became strongly associated with witchcraft in the area—the Toad being the physical embodiment of dark forces. Author Ramsey Campbell takes this legend and weaves it into his Mythos tale *The Room in the Castle*. (It was initially printed in 1964 and reprinted in 1985.) In this tale, an 18th-century warlock named Sir Gilbert Morley lived in a castle beyond Severnford, and draws Byatis into his cellar; he then used the entity to wreak havoc on the surrounding countryside. Eventually, Byatis turns on the warlock and kills him. This, Campbell assets, is the basis for the Berkeley Toad legend.

The legend is certainly an old one, and may even pre-date the Berkeley connections, so it *might* reflect some sort of toad-like god that was once worshipped in parts of prehistoric Britain. It certainly is well ingrained into the psyche of the region, as it is now possible to buy representations of the Toad, both in glass and metal, made by various craftsmen. The Berkley Toad is still a potent symbol in English folklore.

The other incarnation of Byatis also shows up in classical mythology as the face of Poseidon, the Greek god of the sea. This god supposedly rose from the waves with a beard of deadly sea-serpents about his face as a symbol of his power. Bloch referred to Byatis as "the god of forgetfulness," and stated that he was worshipped by the Greeks under the name Hypnos, although the two would seem to have a quite different appearance. Prinn seems to have witnessed the worship of the god somewhere in Egypt, and his descriptions of the ritual surrounding it features heavily in his section on Saracen magic.

Inspirations for De Vermis Mysteriis

Is it possible that Ludvig Prinn could have lived for hundreds of years as he claimed? And if so, could this strange longevity be as a result of some of the spells or incantations contained within *De Vermis Mysteriis?* Perhaps the idea of an immortal man arises out of the scriptures. Christian variations of the concept appear in Matthew 16:28 when Jesus says, "Verily I say unto you. There are some standing here which shall not taste of death until they see the Son of Man coming in His Kingdom." According to this passage, some of the faithful might be immortal, or at least live for an extremely long time, possibly even until the Second Coming.

In the late 11th and 12th centuries it was widely believed that St. Peter, one of Jesus' disciples, had never died. It was the Church's theory that Jesus would not allow His favorite disciple to die until the Second Coming. Old Testament scholars also drew attention to Methuselah, the son of Enoch, who had supposedly lived until he was 969 years old and died just before the Flood. Methuselah also appears in Judaistic lore as one of those who urged Mankind to return to Jehovah's laws in the years before the world was flooded.

The Wandering Jew

The most common immortal figure to emerge in the medieval period, however, was the Wandering Jew, who appeared during the 12th or 13th centuries. His story began when he taunted Jesus on His way to the Crucifixion, and because of his actions, he was cursed to walk the earth until Christ returned for the Second Coming.

The belief in the Wandering Jew was given fresh impetus by the chronicler Roger of Wendover, a monk at the Abbey of St. Albans around the year 1228, in his *Flores Historiarum*, in which he reported that an Armenian monk had met the immortal man. The Wandering Jew confessed to the monk that he had taunted Jesus on His way to the Cross. The man's real name, according to Roger's account, was given as Cartaphilius.

Roger's story was picked up by other medieval writers; the notion of the damned, sinful Jew ceaselessly wandering without hope of rest until the coming of Christ, struck a chord within the medieval Christian mind. And the image persisted with alleged sightings of the wanderer from Hamburg in the 16th century to New York and Philadelphia in the 19th and 20th centuries. The notion of the immortal man living and moving among us had become an important image. So much so that he has passed into popular literature.

For example, the Wandering Jew is mentioned in Geoffrey Chaucer's "The Pardoner's Tale," one of his famous *Canterbury Tales*. There are also references to him in a number of pamphlets and plays written throughout the late 1500s and early 1600s. However, the legend really came into its own with Charles Maturin's *Melmoth the Wanderer* with its depiction of the immortal, damned traveler who laughs at and mocks human misfortune and their misfortune of mortality.

Even today, the idea of the Wandering Jew still turns up from time to time in our fiction. In most cases, the immortal simply yearns for death, which is denied to him. Could Ludvig Prinn have been one of those people, and if so did he use *De Vermis Mysteriis* to extend his existence?

The Philosopher's Stone and the Emerald Tablet

Throughout the Middle Ages, as science began to separate itself from sorcery, two great mythical quests taxed the minds of scientists and alchemists; for many of them, finding the Philosopher's Stone and decoding the Emerald Tablet became the twin "Holy Grails" of early scientific endeavor. In the West, both had religious connotations, as they were part of a Divine Knowledge revealed by God to men. In the 17th century, the antiquary and politician Elias Ashmole argued that the origin of the Stone went all the way back to the time of Adam, when its secrets were passed down from God into the Garden. The origin of the Emerald Tablet was similar, although there were those who said it was firmly rooted in the foul and ungodly magical practices of Islam.

The Philosopher's Stone was the perfect element and it had miraculous powers. For example, it could turn base metals—iron, lead, and so on—into gold simply by being mixed with them. A tiny portion of it, consumed in a goblet of water, could confer countless added years upon the drinker. The Arabian chemist Jabir al-Hayyan thought that if the basic elements were rearranged using some other factor, then the transmutation *might* be possible. Other Middle Eastern alchemists suggested that such a transforming factor would have to be very pure, so it might have other properties, such as the conferment of longevity on an individual.

Alchemist and philosopher Albertus Magnus of Cologne discovered the secret to the Stone and passed it on to his pupil, St. Thomas Aquinas, who held on to the formula for many years before destroying it. Other alchemists also sought the Stone; the most famous of these was Nicholas Flamel. Supposedly he was born around 1418, however, there is no record of Flamel's death, so was assumed that he had the formula for the Philosopher's Stone as well.

While the Philosopher's Stone is something of a legend, the Emerald Tablet or "Secret of Secrets" has its own allure. The oldest known source for the Tablet is an old Arabic book called the *Kitab sirr al-asrar*, which was a book by an unknown author, purporting to give advice to local Islamic rulers. It was translated from the original Arabic into Latin under the title *Secretum Secretorum* by John of Seville around 1140, and it became a source for many medieval alchemists. However, one of the "secrets" that the Tablet contained was an invocation that would extend human life beyond its natural span.

The life-increasing properties of both the Philosopher's Stone and the Emerald Tablet may belong in the realm of legend and fable—or do they? Have certain individuals found some way of extending their lifespans to an incredible length either by using alchemical means, and could this person be the template for the figure of Ludvig Prinn?

The Comte de St. Germain

Few figures in history are as mysterious as the Comte de St. Germain. Although not much is known about him, he was described by writer Voltaire as "A man who knows everything and who never dies." The Comte had also been portrayed as a courtier, alchemist, adventurer, charlatan, musician, and inventor. He is also linked with mysticism, occultism, secret societies, and Black Magic.

According to Germain's own account of his life, he had been an alchemist in the Middle East when he stumbled upon some sort of elixir that had made him immortal. He had advised Jesus, he had known Alexander the Great, he had been in Rome when it burned, and he had fought against Attila. He also traveled to England where he entertained the salons of the time with his fine violin playing and stories.

St. Germain now set out for France and was in Paris during the mid-1740s. There he contrived to gain the attention and favor of the king's mistress, Madame de Pompadour, and through her found favor with the king as well. Indeed, Louis was so taken with him that in 1749, he made him a French diplomat in charge of a number of missions. Despite this, the Comte continued to play extensively in the French salons and wrote several musical pieces, as well as a number of books on alchemy while living in France.

In 1779, he traveled to Schleswig, Germany, where he visited Prince Charles of Hesse-Kassel. The Prince had a deep interest in mysticism and occultism and, having heard so much about the Comte, he wanted to meet him in person. The Comte was very impressive and convinced the Prince that he had invented a new and "magical" method of dying and coloring cloth, which he would develop if only he could find the right financial backer. The Prince set the Comte up in an abandoned factory and supplied the Comte with all the cloth and chemicals that he needed. During this time, the Prince claimed that the Comte had revealed to him that he was actually the son of Frances II Rákóczi and that he was a Transylvanian prince. He also revealed that even though he claimed he would live forever, this wasn't true, and that he had acquired much of his formidable knowledge through reading ancient books. The Prince also stated that St. Germain was in fact 88 years old when he arrived in Schleswig.

The Comte allegedly died on February 27th, 1784, at the residence in the factory in Eckernforde. Afterward, his factory was turned in to a hospital.

Nevertheless, there are those who insist that the Comte did not die and that his death and funeral were staged to allow him to move somewhere else. There are those who insist that he is alive somewhere in the world today. Some have even claimed to have met him in America during the early 1920s. Could the enigmatic Comte be the inspiration for the long-lived Ludvig? Or could there be somebody else?

The Dweller in the Catacomb

A late 1400s/early 1500s story out of Germany may be a better inspiration for the "crazed old Ludvig Prinn" than any other.

According to legend, deep in the forests of Southern Bavaria lay the catacombs of a Roman fortress or early Church, where a strange tenant resided. No one knows exactly where Heinrich Kroll came from—some say he was a teacher in one of the German monasteries; other said that he was a military man who had fought during the Landshut War of Succession. The woods where he lived were badly haunted, as were the catacombs in which he set up his home. Kroll seems to have been a fairly learned man and something of an alchemist. Where he had honed his alchemical talents is unknown, but it was said he was exceptionally proficient in the ways of sorcery and poisoning, and was consulted by nobility of the area concerning the feuds that still rumbled on after the War.

His isolation, his odd ways, and his queer interests all added to a sinister perception. However, he may have been nothing more than a penniless soldier who had taken up residence in the ruin because he had no other choice. Nevertheless, Kroll used his location the way Prinn used his star servants. Kroll engaged in alchemic work that was detrimental to those who lived around him, and these sorcerous beings helped him. People with grudges against their neighbors may have consulted with him to cast curses or to prepare poisons for them. At times too, the Devil was said to appear in the ruins, and the dark recluse supposedly worshipped him in those remote forest depths.

What became of Heinrich Kroll is unknown. He simply vanishes from the pages of folklore and legend; it is possible that he might have died in his lonely hovel or perhaps, like Ludvig Prinn, he was arrested and executed as part of the witch hunts that swept through parts of Germany in the 1500s and 1600s.

The Black Hag

Heinrich Kroll was not the only weird hermit who enjoyed such a sinister reputation. The ruins of Old St. Katherine's Augustinian Convent, Monisternagalliaghduff, Shanagolden in County Limerick, hold another grim story. Founded in 1298, St. Katherine's was one of the largest religious houses in that area of Limerick. But by the end of the 1400s it was dissolved by direct order of the pope, as he said that the nuns there were practicing witchcraft. The Abbess, however, continued to live within the deteriorating convent. She became known in the locality as "the Black Abbess" or "the Black Hag," and was regularly consulted by people of the countryside who required her sorcerous services. She was often seen in the old fairy raths and earthworks late in the evening, gathering herbs for her potions and spells.

Her end was as dramatic as her life had been. A passing peddler called at the Old Abbey only to find her stone dead and seated in a great chair in the ruined cloister (now referred to as "The Black Hag's Cell"). No one knows exactly where in the grounds her body is buried, but it is said that her ghost still haunts the tumbled stones of Old St. Katherine's Abbey. Perhaps, like Heinrich Kroll, she was just an unfortunate soul, reduced to living in the ruins of an ancient building, or maybe she was something more.

So what are we to make of *De Vermis Mysteriis?* Is it a horrific grimoire that contains ancient secrets and the links between medieval magic and the gods of Egypt?

Was it compiled by a man who lived for hundreds of years? Does it therefore hold the key to longevity? Or were the stories of Comte de St. Germain, Heinrich Kroll, or the Black Hag the *real* source of Ludvig Prinn and his infernal tome? Does the book—or something like it—actually exist as Lovecraft suggested? If it does then we had better be wary, for such dread knowledge can threaten our very perceptions of reality!

Of the three books in the Mythos creations, the *Book of Eibon* (or *Liber Ivonis*) stands strong alongside the *Necronomicon* and *De Vermis Mysteriis.* It is certainly one of the oldest as its creation dates back to a time before recorded history. Although there is some debate as to who actually created it within Mythos fiction (whether it was Lovecraft or Clark Ashton Smith) is a matter of debate among Cthulhu purists, but within the context of the Cthulhu writings there can be no doubt of the book's malign influence. In his short story "Ubbo-Sathla," Smith writes:

> THE BOOK OF EIBON, THAT STRANGEST AND RAREST OF OCCULT VOLUMES...IS SAID TO HAVE COME DOWN THROUGH A SERIES OF MANIFOLD TRANSLATIONS FROM A PRE-HISTORIC ORIGINAL WRITTEN IN THE LOST TONGUE OF HYPERBOREA.

According to this, Clark asserts that the Book is unspeakably ancient and that it dates back to a fabled land. What are the origins of such a dangerous tome? Does it really date back to a prehistoric time?

The beginnings of the *Book of Eibon* are shrouded in mystery, although generally speaking, its authorship is often attributed to Eibon, a wizard of primal Hyperborea who was one of the most powerful magicians of the vanished land. According to the Book, Eibon was born in the town of Iqqua. When he was very young, his father committed a crime that caused the Elk-Priests of the god Y'houndeh to drive his family out of Iqqua. Now orphaned, he was found and taken in by the wizard Zylac, who made him his apprentice. Eibon studied ancient pre-human sorceries, learning of the blasphemous toad-god Tsathoggua and the primal entity Ubbo-Sathla, from which all things had come. He proved to be an able pupil and after Zylac's untimely demise he set forth through the cities, towns, and villages of Hyperborea teaching and performing feats of magic. Eventually, he settled down in a tower on the peninsula of Mhu Thulan to study and work. There, he worshipped Tsathoggua and learned the magics of the furry hominids that had inhabited Hyperborea before man. He was reputedly charged with heresy by a rival magician, Murghi, but managed to escape through a mystical doorway that led to the planet Saturn, where he became worshipped as a god. He is said to now inhabit the Dreamlands.

There is also a suggestion that Eibon may have destroyed himself (or been destroyed) through his magic arts since, in some variations, the manuscript of his work was allegedly found in the ruins of his shattered tower. However, in a forward to the book, Eibon's disciple, Cyron of Vanaad, tells of how Eibon left him the manuscript and how he, Cyron, arranged it into some sequential order. The text was then passed down from teachers to pupils, with occasional notes and explanations added to Eibon's original text. The Book was frequently copied by those who had been given the task.

Unfortunately, many of these copies perished with the destruction of Hyperborea in the Great Ice Age, but several survived and were passed among the early humans in the emerging civilizations of Zobna and Lomar. Unable to fully read the Hyperborean script, the humanoid people made imperfect copies of the book—some on metal cylinders, which have been subsequently lost. When these civilizations fell, the Book was given to Atlantis by a secret cult that was dedicated to Eibon's teachings. On Atlantis, the Book was secretly venerated in hidden temples and may have been in some way related to the *Pnakotic Manuscripts* (see later in the section). The majority of the Atlantean copies of the Book were destroyed, but during the Hyborian Age other copies had been made in Brythunia (a Hyborian kingdom) and these did survive.

After Atlantis, the *Book of Eibon* passed into the classical and medieval ages. The first route was through Egypt, where some Lovecraftian scholars such as Daniel Harms have argued that several hieroglyphic copies of the Atlantean versions appeared. These are referred to by Harms as the "Kishite recension," and may have been copied by the priests at Sarnath from an original Atlantean scroll. From this Egyptian edition, a Punic translation was also made by the Syro-Phoenician scholar Imilcar Narba around 1600 B.C. This, in turn, may have been the basis for the ninth-century Latin translation by C. Philippus Faber, which is the main source of later texts. It was also the basis for the Latin *Liber Ivonis* version that was printed in Rome in 1662 (though it is believed that only six copies were made).

A second route into the early world was through a mysterious race known as the Averones. Supposedly, these were survivors from the destruction of Atlantis who had fled to Europe, bringing a version of the *Book of Eibon* with them. It is argued that this version was carved into stone tablets that they carried in several caskets. They would eventually settle in an area of France that would later become Averoigne, and they would continue to use the tablets in their secret rituals, just as they had done back in Atlantis. Allegedly, at least one of these tablets in the original language existed until the early 14th century. Throughout the years, copies of this version made their way to Ireland where they became part of the libraries of remote monasteries; rumor has it they can still be found there today.

In the early 13th century, a French alchemist and Black Magician named Gaspard du Nord of Averoigne supposedly translated part of the text into French, naming it *Livre d'Ivon*. Du Nord was a pupil of the dark wizard Natharire, who lived in the city of Voynes, and it is said that du Nord was aided in the translation by a Greek text that Natharire might have owned. In some traditions, du Nord used a local variation of the *Book of Eibon* that had been held in a village near the city since the time of the Averones.

An English version of the book also exists, dating back to the early 1600s. The translation was carried out by an unknown scholar. Eighteen copies of this version were made, and although they could still exist, they are riddled with errors and are not to be trusted.

Other copies and versions do exist, and some of them have made their way to America, possibly through Dutch involvement. In the mid-1500s the Van der Heyl family established themselves on the Eastern coast in advance of the developing New Netherlands era. In his story "The Diary of Alonzo Typer" (published in *Weird Tales* 1938), Lovecraft refers to some text in the form of two diaries written between 1560 and 1580 by Claes Van der Heyl, which make reference to the *Book of Eibon*. It is possible that the Dutch family held a copy of the book (they were rumored to be alchemists and sorcerers during the 17th century).

In "The Man of Stone" (published in *Wonder Stories* October 1932), Lovecraft also mentions a Dutch family with the last name van Kuaran—descendents from Nicholas van Kuaran, who was hanged in Wijtgaart in 1587 on allegations that he was a sorcerer. Upon burning his house, the soldiers never got his copy of the *Book of Eibon*; his grandson William van Kuaran brought it over when he came to Rensselaerwick and later crossed the river of Espous.

Regarding the text of the *Book of Eibon*, history's accounts are often confused and contradictory. It is suggested that at least part of the main text was copied by Eibon for an earlier work known as *The Book of K'Yog*, which was a book of ritual dealing with the worship of Tsathoggua. It reveals how the entity was brought to Earth from its home on Yuggoth by an unspecified aquatic race (possibly the Deep Ones). This copy is supplemented with tales of Eibon's youth and his magical experiments. He also gives details of his journeys to the distant world of Shaggai and to the Vale of Pnath (located in the Dreamlands). There are also spells for controlling horrors such as the Green Decay and dholes.

The Green Decay is a fearsome incantation that can turn anyone or anything into a pile of mold. The spell involves the creation of a bronze image of the victim, which is then buried with various curses being spoken above its "grave." However, the spell is extremely slow-acting and the degenerative process is lengthy, so many wizards dislike it as a weapon. It features heavily in Stephen Sennit's story *The Green Decay* (2002).

Dholes or Doles are small, white wormlike creatures with a ravening mouth at one end. From such a cavity, the dhole can spit out vast quantities of a mucus-like substance that completely engulfs its victim. The dhole can then devour it at leisure. Dholes are usually only encountered in the Vale of Pnath in the Dreamlands, but they might also be found residing in ossuaries (containers for holding bones and dead matter) in the Underworld.

Dholes can be extremely dangerous in large numbers, as they can eat through anything including the material and rock of a world. They tunnel through the world leaving it uninhabitable—something they have done with many worlds across the Universe, including Yaddith, which was once the home world of Shub-Niggurath. The infants of the species can take up residence in human bodies, their waste products conferring great age on the individuals concerned. Indeed, it is believed that they can stop a host's aging process indefinitely provided that the host can obtain suitable narcotics to stop the dhole growing inside. A number of Egyptian pharaohs supposedly attained extreme longevity in this way. Therefore, control of these creatures might give an individual great power and the *Book of Eibon* is said to contain a formula for bringing these beings to Earth and bending them to an individual's will.

The idea of the dholes may come from a writer whom Lovecraft greatly admired named Arthur Machen. Machen made a passing reference to a "dol" in his short story *The White People* (originally printed in *Horlick's Magazine* in 1904 and later in Machen's collection *The House of Souls* in 1906). In this tale, dols are mysterious creatures that are grouped with nymphs and voolas. Inspired by this, Lovecraft created a work called Dhol Chants, part of which was first mentioned in "The Horror in the Museum" (published in *Weird Tales* in 1933). Frank Belknap Long used the term "doel" in his story *The Hounds of Tindalos* using a correct Welsh spelling. (In some Welsh folklore "doels" are mischievous and sometimes malignant sprites.) However, August Derleth misread this and referred to them as dholes, which other writers repeated in their stories. They are linked to certain incantations within the Book as is Rlim Shaikorth, a creature from beyond the edges of the Solar System.

Rlim Shaikorth often appears as a massive worm-like being with a face, the eyes of which continually drip blood. It was called to Earth in the great days of Hyperborea and settled in the citadel of Yiklith in the far north (according to Lin Carter in his reworking of Clark Ashton's Smith's *Light From the Pole* published in 1980) from which it traveled as it blasted all the lands with freezing ice and snow. The cold that it generated killed off most of the life that it encountered. Only certain powerful mages were saved, so only they might worship the entity. Was this the Great Ice Age in which many kingdoms were lost? The cold ended when Yiklith melted away, although what happened to Rlim Shaikorth is unknown. The *Book of Eibon* suggests that it may have been captured by Aphroom Zhah, a fire entity that dwelt among the ice mountains somewhere at the North Pole.

Hyperborea

For Lovecraft's friend and correspondent Robert E. Howard, Hyperborea was a distant place that existed long ago. It was a world perpetually locked in winter—a place of eternal cold and solitude. It was a place of empty, frozen plains and deep snow-filled valleys though which a harsh wind continually whistled. Its only inhabitants were ferocious tribes of fur-clad warriors who eked out a violent existence among the glaciers.

For the ancient Greeks, Hyperborea was the furthest point in the world that they could imagine, but for different reasons. The name of the country ("the land behind the Boreas or North Wind") suggested desolation and bleakness to them. It was a country of unending black rock where the people lived in almost perpetual darkness and experienced an utterly wretched existence. Yet, for some, the place was suggestive of an earthly paradise where no one had to work and the inhabitants lived in splendid towns and cities.

Its location was also a matter of some dispute. For some Greeks, it lay very far north beyond the lands of the Scythian kingdoms (currently Kazakhstan, Belarus, and Georgia). For other Greeks, Hyperborea did not lie in the north at all. Like Lovecraft, perhaps they believed it as a great island continent located somewhere beyond the Pillars of Hercules in the North Atlantic. The philosopher Plato believed this version, and declared that Hyperborea had been visited by the great Carthaginian explorer Hanno the Navigator around 570 B.C. Hanno had spent much of his time mapping out the coastline of North Africa, but traveled further south and west. It was on one of those journeys that he allegedly visited Hyperborea. He claimed that it had already been colonized and small kingdoms had been established there. These kingdoms traded with ports in Morocco and the Iberian Peninsula. Other explorers disagreed and located the continent slightly further north. Around 325 B.C., according to Pliny the Elder, a Greek explorer named Pytheas of Massila had sailed through the Pillars of Hercules following a course that took him well north of Ireland. After many days, he made landfall on the coast of an unknown continent where the climate was warm and much different than the harsh conditions all around it. Pytheas named the land Thule (which others have claimed as Hyperborea) where the peaceful inhabitants were fully aware of the Greeks and their gods, and spent much of their time organizing great festivals honoring such deities. From his descriptions, many Greeks assumed that these were Celtic people, which caused some, including the philosopher Aristotle, to suggest that this was where the Druids came from and where they learned the "mysteries" of their religion. It is possible that Pytheas had visited the Outer Hebrides, an island chain off the northern Scottish coast, and had mistaken the Celtic peoples for the mythical Hyperboreans.

Around 55 B.C. the Greek historian Diodorus Siculus spoke of a large island far beyond the Pillars of Hercules, which was only slightly larger than Sicily. Here was a large temple dedicated to the moon where holy men worshipped and called down strange deities. The temple that Diodorus describes may have been the impressive stone circle at Callenish on the island of Lewis in the Hebrides, which was supposedly raised by a proto-Celtic people and may have been dedicated to both sun and moon worship. Although Diodorus had never been there, he probably relied on an earlier work written by the Greek geographer Hecataeus of Miletus around 300 B.C. Hecataeus had mentioned an island no bigger than Sicily lying somewhere in the northern seas.

However, some Greeks suggested it was a part of Thrace (parts of Turkey, Greece, and Bulgaria); some placed it on the other side of the Black Sea while others still placed it in a warm valley in the Ural Mountains. Although Pliny the Elder attempted to resolve the issue by talking about various climactic zones, many Greeks remained unconvinced. Moreover, Hyperborea had shrunk from a mighty continent to the size of a large island in the public's perception.

But what sort of people lived there? Were they anything like the sorcerers of whom Lovecraft spoke? And could it be possible that textual material resembling the the *Book of Eibon* could come from such a place? According to Greek texts, the remoteness of their country did not stop them from dealing with places such as Athens, Delos, and Delphi, which were all centers of Greek culture. Indeed, one of the earliest references to the Hyperborians comes from the Greek scholar Hesiod in 700 B.C. Later, writers such as Herodotus and Cicero also mention them. All speak of a cultured race that was extremely fit and athletic; Cicero states that many of them lived to be more than 1,000 years old. They were extremely wealthy, possessing gold that they confiscated in wars and large treasures left by former races. Although they traded with other peoples, they refused to be drawn into their politics or wars, although Greek heroes Perseus and Theseus had visited their land and found them extremely able warriors. They were a very old race, according to those who encountered them, with a wealth of tradition behind them, but it is doubtful that they were sorcerers.

According to Hanno the Navigator, they resembled the people who would later become known as the Moors, inhabiting much of the North African coast and parts of Spain and Portugal. They were reputedly dark-skinned people, but lighter skinned than the Africans who lived further south and smaller than many Europeans.

But once again there is some conflict and confusion with their appearance. According to Pliny the Elder they were giants with extremely pale skin and fair or red hair, perhaps suggestive of a more Nordic origin. They were extremely civilized, living in cities and towns while trading with nearby lands and people. They were, however, extremely secretive, particularly in matters of religion. Although they were placid, they could be quickly roused to anger at the slightest transgression of their laws.

Legends concerning Hyperborea have been used to explain the diverse races that are scattered about the Mediterranean and Atlantic areas. The most popular of all these "explanations" concerned the original inhabitants of the Canary Islands who were known as "Gaunche" or "Gaunchinet." The name actually comes from a mixture of ancient linguistic sources—*Guan* meaning "man" and *Chinet* representing the island of Tenerife (one of the Canary Islands). When first discovered by European explorers during the medieval period, the people of the Canaries were considered relatively primitive, not having advanced far beyond the Stone Age. There were, however, suggestions that the Islands had been previously inhabited by another more advanced race. The Gaunches claimed that they descended from these peoples and some have declared that this previous race was Hyperborean. Hanno claimed that he found them almost completely uninhabited, but he also claimed that he found extensive ruins there as evidence of previous cities. The Gaunches, he said, had migrated from North Africa and knew very little about who had built these ruined dwellings. Other explorations claimed that they were living among fallen dwellings that they could not possibly have built themselves. Were these the ruins of the Hyperborean cities of which Lovecraft wrote?

Pliny the Elder points to a curious tongue that was spoken by the islanders, which was extremely distinctive from any that he knew. Finally, some of the Gaunche were allowed to marry into Spanish society, which more or less eliminated their culture altogether, including their language. It is completely possible that those civilizations could have been responsible for such literature as the *Book of Eibon*.

However, the Gaunches were not the only race that emerged from ancient Hyperborea; the Aryans also came from the ancient land. The word *Aryan* may come from a mingling of Persian and Vedic Sanskrit and means "spiritual or noble." It was first used to describe a culture that had sprung up in ancient Iran, which contained elements of both early Persian and Indian thinking. The term "Aryan race" was used around the early 20th century linking a number of linguistic groupings, although it's not clear of these peoples actually saw themselves as one race. The idea suggested a common ancestry and a common point of origin that some people saw as Hyperborea or Thule. Scientific evidence, mainly involving cranial measurements, was brought forward to suggest that a tall, fair-haired, pale-skinned race spread out from a certain point (Hyperborea) and into Europe and some lands north of Scandinavia. Others argued that the Aryan race had originated in a temperate valley in the Caucasus Mountains in Southern Russia (which had been the real location of Hyperborea) and from this idea the word *Caucasian* would emerge.

The writer and theosophist H.P. Blavatsky added to the idea under the direction of her "Secret Masters" in Tibet. In her book *The Secret Doctrine* (published in 1888), she declared that Hyperborea had indeed existed and that it was the home of the second of her "root races." This gave a kind of "occult edge" to the idea and suggested that the land had been home to ancient and mystical secrets long forgotten.

The French anthropologist Joseph Deneker added yet another twist to the idea of Aryanism. It was he who coined the term *Nordique* to refer to a white-skinned, fair haired race that had come into Europe. This became the basis of the theory of Nordic-Aryanism. Occultists claimed that they had come from Hyperborea, but the idea had taken on a more political significance. Aryanism had taken on the significance of a "Master Race" that had settled in parts of Germany. They were "the purest race of Earth." Such theories were widely accepted throughout Europe in the era following the First World War, but it the mid-20th century they took on a much more sinister tone.

In 1918, a German occultist named Rudolf von Sebottendorf founded the Thule Society, which was an occult and folklore society. The "folklore" element of the group, however, concerned itself with a highly romanticized view of German history. Much of it was devoted to the view that Germans were descendants from an Aryan people who had come from Hyperborea or Thule. The pure Germans were the perfect race and the true inheritors of ancient knowledge

One important group that took an interest in Von Sebottendorf's work was the the National Socialist German Workers' Party or NSDAP. The so-called "mystics" in the Party viewed the blonde-haired, blue-eyed Hyperboreans as a form of "ubermenschen" (supermen) and the German people as their descendants, thus constituting a "Master Race." They took Ultima Thule to be the capital of Hyperborea and the country to be the epitome of all ancient civilizations. They confidently asserted that the Hyperboreans held wonderful and mystical secrets that the world had long forgotten, but which could be relearned. The Nazi leader, Adolph Hitler, was especially in favor of such ideas, as they matched his own views regarding racial superiority.

Partly because of its association with the Nazis, interest in Hyperborea began to die away during the 1960s/70s. It now had a racist tinge, so perhaps it is easy to see how Lovecraft (with his own rather racist views) would be attracted to the concept. However, Hyperborea was not the only ancient civilization that might have produced copies of the *Book of Eibon*.

Atlantis

Almost everybody knows the story of how the mighty island kingdom of Atlantis was swallowed up by the sea. Indeed, even in the 20th century, the idea of a technologically and intellectually advanced culture being overwhelmed by natural forces intrigued the general imagination and prompted much speculation. Atlantis was seen as an ancient superpower dominating prehistoric times, which was destroyed by a series of volcanic explosions. But could such a fantastic realm actually have existed, and did it produce any literature which might be comparable to the *Book of Eibon?*

There is actually little reference to Atlantis in ancient texts, but one mention of it is particularly significant, mainly because of the person who wrote it. The scholar Plato specifically names the island-continent and states that it lies far to the west of Greece past the Straits of Gibraltar. According to the description, Atlantis was a relatively advanced civilization and an incredibly aggressive one, boasting a significant naval prowess that had established a presence in both Europe and in parts of Africa roughly 8,000 years before Plato was writing. The country had made war on the developing city-state of Athens, but after a fierce conflict they were eventually defeated and driven back beyond the rim of the Mediterranean. Shortly afterward, the entire continent was destroyed in what Plato describes as "a single day and night of misfortune." All that remained of the once-proud continent of Atlantis, says Plato, was a mudbank.

Plato's reference to Atlantis occurs in a set of literature known as the *Dialogues*. These dialogues were a set of "conversations" between historical and/or imaginary characters and centered around philosophical topics and moral problems often concerning the nature of the Universe and Man's place within it. The reference to Atlantis appears in what are known as the *Conjoined Dialogues*, which were written around 360 B.C. Two characters named Criteas and Timeaus consider the nature of the Cosmos and how this may have determined the direction and fate of ancient civilizations. A greater part of it is taken up with Plato's musings on the perfect society, but Criteas actually names Atlantis, comparing it rather unfavorably to some of Plato's own theories. The Republic that Plato envisaged, mused Criteas, is probably as near perfection as a society can attain, whereas Atlantis was the very antithesis of this. Claiming that his information comes from a trip to Egypt by the Greek poet and lawmaker Solon, Criteas goes on to speak of a powerful seafaring nation that raided the Mediterranean in order to obtain slaves. In Sais, Egypt, Solon met a priest who showed him a series of papyri scrolls; they detailed the early history of Athens and its war against Atlantis.

According to the priest, the gods had divided up the world between them, and a large portion of land was given to the sea-god Poseidon. This landmass was Atlantis. Poseidon handed this land to his son Atlas, making him Atlantis's first king. To Atlas's twin brother Gadeius, Poseidon gave the outer limits of the island, lying toward the Pillars of Hercules, as well as some of its sections to several of his other children.

Apart from Plato, however, no other ancient scholars make reference to Atlantis, so we must rely on his account for any detail of this civilization. Indeed, there is much to suggest that many other ancient men thought Plato's account was entirely fictitious. Since Plato's time, many have thought that the scholar was "confused" and simply mistook some other catastrophe in the ancient Greek world for the destruction of Atlantis.

And of course, an element of mystic knowledge was added in 1888 by H.P. Blavatsky. Similar to Hyperborea, Blavatsky saw Atlantis as one of the sites for her "Root Races" and published an account of the civilization in her work *The Secret Doctrine*. As Atlantean society had evolved, she stated it had become "spiritually wise" and the beings of Atlantis were knowledgeable, mystical, and compassionate. This is at odds with Plato's account of them as vicious and militaristic slave-traders. Nevertheless, it was Blavatsky's idea that took hold and the idea of an advanced, philanthropic, erudite, and totally mystical civilization based in Atlantis was born.

Influences for The Book of Eibon
The Book of Dzyan

Blavatsky's *The Secret Doctrine* also contained the *Book of Dzyan*. Lovecraft was well aware of this tome and has used a slightly modified version of it in his stories, for example, in "The Haunter of the Dark" (published in Weird Tales in 1936). These stanzas could have been a major influence when creating the *Book of Eibon.*

According to the Lovecraftian tradition, the *Book of Dzyan* originated on the planet Venus from which the Lords of Venus brought the first six chapters of it to Earth and revealed it to humans. It was written in the lost Senzar language of Atlantis, but the Venusians taught humans the tongue and, in return, humankind venerated the book in the now-lost city of Shamballah.

Chinese traders discovered the oldest known copy of the *Book of Dzyan* in a cave—a copy that was written in Chinese, Sanskrit, and characters of another unknown language. The contents of the book actually remain a mystery. Part of it seems to be a conventional grimoire, sealing with incantations surrounding the mystical Seal of Solomon, and other portions deal with the Elder Sign as well as incantations to ward off ancient evil.

Lovecraft's description of the Book is based in part on Madam Blavatsky's assertions. While traveling in 1875, Blavatsky claimed she saw an ancient text in a remote monastery in Tibet. Being a great Adept, she was permitted to study this text, which was composed of a number of stanzas that eventually formed her book *The Secret Doctrine.* This text was named Dyhana, which Blavatsky rendered as Dzyan. She claimed that the stanzas were the mystical records of "a race unknown to ethnology" and was written in a "tongue absent from the nomenclature of languages and dialects with which philology is acquainted." This tongue was Senzar, a mystical form of Sanskrit that might have come from Atlantis. Although she called it (as did Lovecraft) the *Book of Dzyan* could this *really* have been the basis for the *Book of Eibon?* It is a book written by a lost race, possibly from either Hyperborea or Atlantis, which discloses mystical things around the origins of our world. Blavatsky also claimed that the *Book of Dzyan* belonged to a set of Tibetan esoteric scriptures known as *The Thirty-Five Folios of Kiu-Te* of which it was the first set of Seven Secret Commentaries.

The Druid Library and the Iron Book

In the middle of 1186, a lone monk approached the Abbey of St. Columcille's Seat in Magilligan in North Derry, Northern Ireland. The monk had come to the holy house to die and would do so before the following spring was out. However, among his possessions were a vast number of scrolls and a huge collection of parchments bound in iron. St. Ambrose O'Coffey was a noted Irish exorcist and demonologist, and in his travels he had gathered a number of very ancient texts, which dated from the time of the druids in Ireland and long before. They concerned "spirits of the air" and other ghastly beings that had lived in the world. Among these terrible manuscripts was the Iron Book of Skeld, which was the record of a prehistoric race living far to the north (the settlement of Skeld lies in one of the most northerly points of the British Isles). This race had "commerce" with the spirit world and records of the links were found within the pages of the Iron Book. This knowledge was so blasphemous that only iron could contain it and metal covers had been wrought especially for it. In some accounts, the outer bindings were embossed with a grim and brooding face, like that of some stern and ancient deity. How St. Ambrose had come by the Book is unknown, but it is suspected that he traveled in the Western Isles of Scotland and might have obtained it there. It was said to have come from a land far to the north and had been brought south by the Vikings.

After O'Coffey's death, the scrolls and manuscripts he had brought remained in the monastery as the Druid Library. Few monks were allowed to consult with the scrolls and the Library was kept in the monastery simply to limit its evil influence. However, in 1203, St. Columcille's Seat was burned to the ground by riders from across Lough Foyle. It's said that the contents of the Druid Library was somehow removed before the attack and was broken up throughout the surrounding area.

The Iron Book was supposedly taken to the Church of Screen where it remained hidden for many centuries. What became of it thereafter is unclear, for the Old Church of Screen no longer exists and local people are unsure of where it stood when it existed.

However, it is said that before St. Columcille's Seat was sacked in 1203, the Book and other scrolls were placed in a great box (known as St. Columcille's Chest) and hidden somewhere in the countryside. The Chest was found again in 1785 in a concealed cave at Downhill many miles away by workmen building the Mussenden Temple for Frederick Hervey, 4th Earl of Bristol and Bishop of Derry. They brought the Chest to the Bishop who managed to open it and examine its contents. What he read there disturbed and alarmed him so much that until his death in 1803, he was unable to sleep in the same place for three consecutive nights and spent much of his time traveling.

Another story says that the Iron Book passed into the hands of the Culdees. The Celi Dei (Friends of God) were the only Irish order of monks and were founded by St. Maelruan of Tallaght. They were an eremitical Order and were sometimes regarded as great mystics. It was into the hands of the Culdees that the great bachalls (the sacred staffs of the early holy men) were entrusted. An austere and withdrawn Order, they wrote some of the most beautiful holy poetry and martyrologies. It was said that the Iron Book was delivered into their hands and remained there until the 16th century when the last of the Order disbanded. The last of the Culdees to possess the Book was Ruri MacGillamurra who was the Abbot of the last Culdee house in Armagh in the late 1500s. What then became of it afterward is unknown.

Could any of these places or writings have been the prototype for Lovecraft's hideous *Book of Eibon?* Is it indeed a frightful past somehow reaching into the present through its pages? Who would truly dare to say?

The Forbidden Library
Cultes des Goules

In the early months of 1703, a curious volume bearing the title *Cultes des Goules* began to circulate in Paris. Its author was unknown, but the contents of the work both shocked and outraged genteel Parisian society, for it dealt with topics such as necromancy and necrophilia, and it drew attention to grave robbing, which was often associated with the occult. It spoke of the activities of witches in graphic detail, and linked their practices to a subterranean species of degenerate beings in the Parisian catacombs. It drew attention to partial resurrections carried out by sorcerers, as well as the walking dead, who were the results of such Black Magic. The book also included spells that taught how to raise the dead for the purposes of divination and other less savory activities, as well as horrific descriptions of very ancient fertility rites relating to Shub-Niggurath (see later in the book) and Nyogtha. The Church authorities almost immediately condemned the publication and the civil powers took great exception to the idea that cannibal cults and cults of the dead were operating in France. Indeed, although the book shocked much of French society, certain individuals took great interest in it for dark and sinister purposes.

The *Cultes des Goules* was originally a private printing thought to be around 600 quarto pages. No more than 60 copies were published, some of which were destroyed. An expurgated French edition was printed in Rouen around 1737, and several hand-written Spanish and Italian versions as well as one German edition exist, but these are probably the work of individual sorcerers intent on copying some of the spells contained in its pages. There is also a partially translated English version that was carried out by a scholar named Lazarus Garvey. There are said to be just 14 copies surviving, the last surfacing in 1906 in the library of a chateau in the Massif Central region of France.

A number of Mythos writers have given differing identities for the author of the *Cultes des Goules*. The first possible figure is Antoine-Marie Augustin de Montmo-rency-les-Roches, sometimes described as "the second Comte." As a young man, he became interested in folk religions, which were practiced in regions of the Pyrenees and in the Massif Central. This led him to further explore the occult, allegedly investigating the tombs of alleged sorcerers in remote areas of Brittany and Burgundy. An aloof and aesthetic man, he was long suspected of holding anti-Catholic sympathies, which did not make him terribly popular at the court of a Catholic monarch. As the author of the first handwritten copy of the *Cultes des Goules* he proclaimed himself as a member of a clandestine society of French necromancers. He detailed the activities of a group of magicians that he referred to as "goulas" or "ghouls," who used dead bodies in their magic. It was shown to King Louis XIV by the Comte's enemies, and the monarch was appalled and disgusted by the revelations that it contained. What subsequently befell Montmorency-les-Roches is not clear, as he vanished around 1681. It is possible that he was arrested on the order of the monarch and was thrown into prison. Regardless, the date of his death is given as 1693. The handwritten copies of his book were burned under Royal Edict.

The second alleged writer might have been the Comte Francois-Honore Balfour, the so-called "third Comte." The self-proclaimed Comte d'Erlette was immediately declared *persona non grata* and was excluded from the upper echelons of French society once it was suspected that he was the creator of the dark text. Somewhat of an eccentric, a rumor that circulated in the early 18th century claimed that Balfour had three of his own copies bound in human skin.

Interestingly, writers such as August Derleth say that, while staying at the Chateau Montmorency in 1701, Balfour found a handwritten copy of the original version of *Cultes des Goules* in the library there. He allegedly rewrote the work, adding several chapters of his own, and had it secretly published with a printing of around 400 copies. Although he described the rites of the ghostly corpse-cults, Balfour denied ever having been a member. He claimed the book was written for occult and scientific reasons. In the preface of the book he stated:

LEST SOME SHOULD LABEL IT BLASPHEMY: *I HAVE CHOSEN TO EXPLAIN CERTAIN ACTIONS AND BELIEFS AND LET GOD BE THE JUDGE OF US ALL.*

Nevertheless, the Church demanded that the work be burned and Balfour was openly denounced from the pulpit. Although he was not formally prosecuted, the opprobrium of the upper French society was enough to drive him into exile. He retired to a house near Erlette where he lived an almost monastic existence. His name was abhorred in all parts of France and he was regarded as a monster of the foulest kind.

In 1724, the Comte disappeared for four days and, at the end of that period, his son found his partially devoured and dismembered body in the woods near his house. His son stipulated that his remains should be placed in a sealed lead coffin and buried in a stone crypt—a burial that was believed by many to be consistent with that of a dead witch.

Although it was not originated by Lovecraft, there has been a fierce debate as to exactly who invented both the terrible book and the mysterious Comte. August Derleth, for instance, strenuously claimed that *he* invented it and that the Comte d'Erlette was a title originally held by his own ancestors, although there is absolutely no evidence for this, nor was Derleth able to provide it from family records. Another writer, Robert Bloch, claimed that it was in fact *he* who had invented the title; others hint that Lovecraft might have suggested the idea in correspondence with either of these authors.

La Sorciere

The *Cultes des Goules* is perhaps a much darker and extended version of another book that Lovecraft would certainly have known about and probably read. Written in 1862, *La Sorciere* was a history of witchcraft written by the French historian Jules Michelet. Michelet was not a wild libertine in the style of the alleged Comte d'Erlette, but a respected man of letters who had written on a number of historical topics. His most famous and monumental work was *L'Histoire de France*; it took him more than 30 years to complete, but some have argued that it is one of the best accounts of the development of the French nation.

Of Huguenot origin, Michelet's writing carried a distinctly political tone. This is the underlying theme of his book on witchcraft which, perhaps as a Protestant, he saw as a grass-roots peasant rebellion against the power and oppression of the Catholic Church in France. Although his evidence for the assertion appears scant, Michelet suggested that this rebellion took the form of an alternative and clandestine peasant religion. Such a revolutionary religion was intertwined with belief in old gods and fairy lore, and it was largely maintained by women. In fact, the leaders of such religions were females who met in great gatherings; the Church declared that these were Witches Sabbats, so many of the women were executed at the behest of the Church. Unfortunately, Michelet allowed his sympathies, both for the laboring classes and for women, to cloud his judgement, so the book is largely inaccurate—especially when it dramatizes some of the European witch-trials that Michelet "investigated."

Could the *Cultes des Goules* have been based in part upon Michelet's *La Sorciere*? Certainly there are some similarities—the idea of a secretive cult operating just beneath the surface of conventional society, the worship of old and primal gods, the reaction of adherents of the religion against the establishment, and the linkages with fairies and the dead all seem to connect with the idea of the demon sect. But the Mythos seems to take such ideas even further, connecting them with necromancy, obscene sexual desires, and eating of the dead. It is unlikely that Lovecraft or other Mythos writers were unaware of Michelet's work—especially as it was (and still is) available in an English translation, which was first published in 1863.

Cannibalism

Throughout Lovecraft's works, such as "The Rats in the Walls," "The Lurking Fear," and "The Picture in the House," cannibalism is a theme that runs and is perhaps inspired by the *Cultes des Goules*.

The word *cannibal* derives from a 16th-century Spanish word describing the people of the Caribbean who practiced the eating of human flesh as part of their culture. However, cannibalism as a cultural phenomenon has existed since earliest times.

Prehistoric bones found in Gough's Cave in the Mendip Hills in Cheddar, Somerset, England, show the marks of what appear to be human teeth. The Bible states in II Kings that two women agreed to kill and cook their children during a siege in Samaria. After the first mother cooked her child, the second mother ate it, but refused to reciprocate by cooking hers. Writing in the fourth century, St. Jerome castigated a number of people who he had heard ate human flesh.

It was thought that during the Middle Ages, cannibalism was a much wider social phenomenon than was first thought. The 12th through 14th centuries were a period when winters were particularly severe and villages were sometimes cut off for weeks at a time by heavy snow. As starvation set in they turned to the weakest in society—the young, the very old, and the ill. In some instances, historians believe this was the norm rather than the exception. It is thought that a good number of villages in Hungary carried on in this way during the winters. So widespread was the practice that the French word for Hungarian—*hongre*—formed the basis of the English word *ogre* (a flesh-eating giant). There were also widespread reports of cannibalism during the First and Second Crusades allegedly committed by both Christian and Muslim warriors.

Although many of the later stories of cannibalism were said to originate in the Holy Land, a number of tales concerning "home-grown cannibals" circulated in Scotland around the mid-14th and early 15th centuries. Once again, some historians such as Fiona Black have suggested that such stories were designed by the English to discredit the Scots in the latter half of the 18th century following the Jacobite Rebellion.

The most celebrated tale concerned the infamous Alexander (Sawney) Beane, which appeared in a chapbook entitled *Traditional Tales Connected With the South of Scotland* published in 1843 by John Nicholson. It tells the story of Alexander Beane, who was born in Galloway at the end of the 14th century. His dates roughly correspond with the reign of King James I of Scotland (1394–1437). Confusingly, though, some accounts state that he lived during the reign of James IV (1473–1513). Sawney did not appear to work at all, and at some point left home to take up with a woman who was as lazy and ill-disposed toward work as he was. This unprepossessing pair then took up residence in a cave on the Galloway/Ayrshire coast. From there, they attacked travelers on a nearby road, killing them and dragging their bodies back to the cave where they drank their blood and ate their flesh. The cavern that they inhabited seemed to be the entrance to an underground cave system, and they spawned an equally monstrous brood that mated among themselves, producing even more cannibals. Soon there were approximately 46 individuals living in the cave system who attacked, killed, robbed, and ate passers-by.

In this way they continued for many years as Sawney's ever-expanding family slowly became the terror of the countryside. This hideous gang operated for almost 25 years and in that time, more than 1,000 men, women, and children were murdered and carried off while venturing along the Galloway roads. Sawney and his children scavenged further and further through the countryside in search of fresh meat. Once they had set upon their victims, the ghastly mob robbed them, slit their throats, drank their blood, and carried away their corpses to be pickled in brine so they could be eaten at a later time. The entrance to their cave was so well concealed that they weren't easily spotted, so the authorities were at a loss to explain all the disappearances. Local innkeepers were blamed and several were even charged with murder (although no bodies were ever found), and a couple were hanged on the flimsiest of evidence. As Sawney's murderous tribe increased to include cannibal grandchildren, the deaths along the roads multiplied.

Eventually, one of their victims managed to escape from their awful clutches. It is not clear how he achieved this, though it's thought he was taken to their cave and memorized the way back there. Some variations of the tale said that it was a married couple who managed to evade the Beanes. The survivor(s) managed to make their way to a nearby hamlet and report the matter. Curiously, no move was made against the family right away, but the matter was referred to King James I. It was the monarch who put together a force of local militia to hunt down the cannibal tribe. Just as dawn was breaking, this force stormed the cave using bloodhounds to track down their quarry and find the entrance. Sawney and his children put up a good fight and a number of local men were killed. However, the cannibals were eventually dragged from their lair. When the militia explored deeper into the cavern system, however, they found a sickening sight. Human remains hung on hooks from the walls and the rock floor ran red with blood. In one corner were great pitchers of human blood, stored like water, from which the cannibals drank.

The Beanes were taken to either Leith or Glasgow where they were all executed in a most brutal manner. Their hands and feet were cut off and they bled to death in the public street while women and children were forced to watch. Some men and women connected to the clan were burned alive and the entire brood was wiped out—except one. Sawney's eldest daughter Elizabeth had left the family and had actually married and moved to Girvan. Local tradition says that she was a vampire and was a suspect in the deaths of some of the town's citizens, draining blood from them and chewing their flesh, unable to shake off her horrid ancestry. After the death of the last Beane, her true connection to them was discovered and she was hanged. The location of the cannibal cave is a matter for debate, but this has not stopped the local council from marketing one of the coastal caverns as the actual site for tourism purposes. So successful has this been that the pathway up to the cave mouth has been greatly improved and new signage put up.

Another Scottish cannibal, a figure who bears a remarkable resemblance to Sawney, is Christie o' the Cleek, who lived at the end of the 14th century. His real name was Andrew Christie, a butcher in Perth around the early 1300s. During a severe winter around 1340, he set off with a gang of scavengers into the foothills of the

Grampian Mountains to look for meat. However, because of the severe conditions, there was little game to be had; when one of the group suffered a fairly severe injury, Christie killed the man and cooked the corpse, providing a meal for the remainder of the band. In order to survive in the wilds of the Grampians, they began ambushing travelers through the mountain passes, killing and eating both them and their horses. Christie was now the leader of the gang and he personally pulled his victims from their horses by means of a hook on the end of a rod (known as a "cleek" or crook), and this became his nickname. It is said that throughout the years, Christie and his gang killed and ate between 30 and 40 individuals. Eventually, they were defeated by a militia from Perth who attacked the gang in the Grampians. Christie, however, supposedly escaped and eventually settled in Dumfries, where he became a prosperous merchant in the town—presumably with some of his ill-gotten gains—and married into the minor aristocracy of the district.

The parallels between Sawney Beane and Andrew Christie are obvious. However, of the two, the Christie stories appear to be older—all references to Sawney start to appear from around the late 18th century, and those concerning Christie are documented from around the 15th century. Andrew of Wyntoun's *Orygynale Cronykil of Scotland*, written around 1420, mentions a Chwsten Cleek who "set up traps for women and children," so that he could eat them during hard times. Even earlier, John of Norwich in his *Marvelles of the Kingdome* (possibly written around 1350), speaks of someone called Kristie, "a fearsome robber and murderer of men" who allegedly ate a part of his victims "for sport." Raphael Holinshead in his *Chronicles of England and Ireland* (1577), mentions in an entry for 1341 "a Scottish man, an uplandish fellow named Tristicloke, spared not to steal children and kill women on whose flesh he fed." Certainly, as in some other parts of Europe, the harsh conditions of the winters in Scotland would have made cannibalism an attractive option (and perhaps even a real necessity).

In Ireland there are references regarding a haunted medieval figure to whom cannibal tendencies were attributed. This was the notorious Scaldbrother who operated in the Stoneybatter section of the city and around the Smithfield area where many of the early markets were situated. Scaldbrother dug a system of tunnels that connected various parts of his domain, down which he was able to escape after committing his crimes. He was reputedly a very small man and was able to escape with ease after committing robberies. He may have also stolen babies, which he took to his underground lair and devoured. What became of this mysterious criminal is unknown.

As the Western civilizations began to expand into other lands, travelers began to bring back stories of flesh-eating cultures in far-flung parts of the world. Religious missionaries expressed abhorrence and horror at the cannibalistic customs that they encountered in some of the places they visited. The Spanish bishop of the Roman Catholic Archdiocese of the Yucatan, Fray Diego de Landa, for example, was against the flesh-eating practices of his congregation. Other reports came from Colombia and from the Marquesas Island of French Polynesia, where a human being was known as "the long pig"—probably because of a similarity in taste between human flesh and pork. In some cultures, it was believed that by eating the flesh of another person, one could acquire his or her attributes through a process of osmosis. Therefore, warriors killed in battle were often consumed in order to acquire their strength and bravery.

This was also true with Native Americans. In 1913, *The Handbook of the Indians of Canada* claimed that a number of Indian groupings still practiced cannibalism. Among those cited are: the Algonquin, the Micmac, the Assiniboine, the Cree, the Kickapoo, the Chippewa, the Attacappa, and the Winnebago. There is also a tradition of eating flesh among the Mohawks, the Ute, and some branches of the Comanche. This devouring of flesh among the Native Americans was either carried out during times of starvation or for ritualistic purposes.

However, the most lurid tales of cannibal cultures came from further south in New Zealand. Known as "Maoris," they were traditionally feared as man-eaters by travelers; not only did they eat the living, but they also ate their own dead. Part of this fear may have arisen from the Boyd Massacre in 1809 when the Maoris of Whangaroa Harbour in the northern island killed and ate around 70 people. This was done in retaliation for the whipping of a chief's son on board the brigantine *Boyd* on the orders of her captain John Thompson. Te Ara, the young man in question, was publically flogged for disobeying an order. In retaliation, the Maoris attacked the ship and killed and devoured nearly all of the *Boyd's* crew and passengers. This constituted one of the bloodiest acts of cannibalism on record. A rescue mission was quickly mounted—Captain Alexander Berry commanded the *City of Edinburgh* and set sail for Whangaroa where they found half-eaten bodies on the shore. The *Boyd* itself had been completely burnt out. As retaliation, a group of whalers attacked the *pa* (fortified village) of another Maori chieftain (Chief Te Pahi) about 60 kilometers to the southeast, mistakenly believing that he had ordered the massacre. More than 60 of Te Pahi's warriors were killed. The incident sent shockwaves around the world and was being reprinted in American newspapers as late as 1814 with exhortations to traders not to visit the cursed shore for fear of being eaten alive by cannibals. Throughout the next four to five years, trade with New Zealand more or less dropped off.

And there is a chance that cannibalism still exists today. I recently spoke to an anthropologist colleague who had worked with one of the tribes in the New Guinea interior who were still suspected of cannibalism during the late 1980s and early 1990s. One night, the tribe brought in the body of a man from another tribe whom they had shot over a disagreement, and proceeded to cook him over a fire. When it came time to eat him, they cut the first slice and presented it to my friend as an honored guest. He was faced with a dilemma: Should he eat human flesh or should he insult his hosts by turning it down? In the end he ate it, but did so out of respect for his hosts. Similarly, another friend who is a lay-preacher showed me a book that had been written by an old cannibal chief who had converted to Christianity and was describing his former life. In it, the chief instructs the reader not to eat English, German, or Dutch men, as their flesh is heavy and stodgy. He says to eat Spanish, Italian, or Greek men, as they cook better and their flesh has more flavor.

Did these tales of flesh-eating men form Lovecraft's basis for the ghoulish Parisian cult about which he writes? Did cults from long ago inspire his writing? What were these cults, and how far back did they exist?

The Cultes des Mortes

Beginning in the 16th century, French explorers began to travel out into new lands to exploit their resources and settle there. The territories of New France began to stretch out to Africa, South America, and the Caribbean with the establishment of trading posts in Senegal, French Guiana, and St. Kitts in the West Indies. Soon trading routes were being established between far-flung islands and the French markets. The growing import from this part of the world was sugar, a commodity that was rising in popularity in Europe. The *Campagnie des Iles de l'Amerique* developed and expanded throughout the early 1600s with colonies established on Martinique, Guadeloupe, and St. Lucia. All of these colonies were sustained by slave labor on which they depended to send exports back to Europe and keep their European overlords wealthy.

One of the most important colonies was Saint-Dominigue (Santo Domingo), founded on the Western half of Hispaniola. It became the foremost sugar colony in the Caribbean, depending heavily on thousands of black slaves who worked on the plantations there. But the French planters always lived in fear of a slave rebellion and there were stories that native Indians were cannibals who would turn on their owners and kill and eat them. Indeed, there were whispers of an organized slave cult that was cannibalistic in nature, and was comprised of *hungans* or *bokors* (native witch-doctors brought from Africa) who had magical powers known as *vudou*, and might have powers to raise the dead, turning them into flesh-eating creatures that they would send against the planters. These creatures were known as *zombi,* allegedly named after a snake god whom the pagan slaves worshipped, and the cult that controlled them was known as the Cultes des Mortes (the cult of the dead).

In 1929 (eight years before Lovecraft died), the writer and journalist William Seabrook wrote a book entitled *The Magic Island,* which was a personal memoir regarding Haiti (Hispaniola). In it, he claimed he was in contact with members of the Cultes des Mortes and wrote about them in some detail. He claimed that he participated in cannibalism when he was on a trip to West Africa. He was given a meal of stew made of rice and meat, which resembled rump steak. He said that it was "mildly good," tasting like veal, but rather unlike anything that he'd ever eaten before. Later on, he realized he was eating human flesh.

Could Lovecraft have known of Seabrook's book or the Louisiana death cult and used them to form the basis of the terrible *Cultes des Goules?*

The idea of cannibals living somewhere among us, and cults that deal with the dead all form a rich and horrific tapestry that translates itself into the nightmare pages of the *Cultes des Goules.* And who is to say that the mysterious and shadowy Frenchman who penned that terrible text did not, perhaps, know far more about such horrors than we do?

THE FORBIDDEN LIBRARY
THE PNAKOTIC MANUSCRIPTS

Throughout the centuries there have been tales of mysterious texts that originated from now-extinct civilizations, which left the modern world with many secrets and knowledge to decipher. They might describe a vanished world or perhaps bestow wonderful—or deadly—wisdom, which may be best left untouched. Modern-day investigators do not understand the content of the texts, and it often frustrates the minds of those who try to read them. People from these civilizations were perhaps more astute and wiser than we are, and had access to greater knowledge about the Universe and our place in it. Such an idea postulates the theory that there were pre-human beings in this world long before the coming of man.

The notion of such knowledge is a major theme in Lovecraft's work and the Cthulhu Mythos. Fragments of arcane wisdom from often unrecognized and legendary prehistoric eras are preserved on ancient scrolls, on bits of pottery, or as carvings on ancient stones and rocks. Some are written by one particular individual, others have been penned by various scribes. Part of this ancient and usually dangerous knowledge lies in a corpus of material known as the *Pnakotic Manuscripts* first mentioned by Lovecraft in his short story *Polaris*. Later, they appear in *The Dream-Quest of Unknown Kadath*, to which subsequent Mythos writers such as Lin Carter and Brian Lumley have added the Eltdown Shards and the G'harne Fragments.

The *Pnakotic Manuscripts* originally existed in a scroll form of indeterminate age and origin. There have also been rumors that there was an English version made somewhere in the 1400s, but it only existed in manuscript form. According to writers such as Daniel Harms, a complete set of the *Pnakotic* scrolls may be in the Temple of the Elder Ones in the Dreamlands town of Ulthar on the River Skai, but this is not known for sure, because only certain dreams can access them.

The *Pnakotic Manuscripts* are of immeasurable antiquity and may not have originated on Earth to begin with. They certainly predate human kind and speak of an almost unimaginable world long before the dawn of Earth. Their actual point of origin may lie on the planet Yith, which is the fourth of five worlds circling the ancient star Ognatlach on the other side of the galaxy. At one time, it was home to The Great Race and might have been their point of origin. The *Manuscripts* represent the accumulated wisdom of the Race, which was stored in a massive archive on the planet. It should be pointed out that The Great Race did not have bodies in the corporeal sense, but were able to take over the bodies of others as they saw fit. They were entities of immense intellect and mental powers, but were unable to create their advanced technologies without the aid of physical form.

It is said that on Yith, the Race took over the bodies of an amphibian species and used them to build spherical containers in which their consciousnesses could be housed. With the addition of some technological equipment, they began to construct advanced machinery that enabled them to travel through time. Such an invention came at the right time, for the Ognatlach star-system was in an upheaval. For eons, Yith had been under attack from hordes of flying polyps, possibly originating on the second planet of the system. Although these had been subdued for a time, they continued to multiply and attacked once more in even greater numbers. Subsequently, the race abandoned Yith and fled across the Universe, eventually arriving on planet Earth.

However, it turns out that there was already a form of life here, which the Great Race immediately took over. The inhabitants were immense rugose cone-shaped beings who were of vegetable origin and who dwelt in monstrous cities. Using these bodies, the Great Race fought off groups of the flying polyps that had followed them across space, imprisoning them far beneath the surface of the Earth. Successfully defeating the invaders, they set about building fabulous cities with buildings that were thousands of feet tall. Much of their power was nuclear and they used it to construct great machines that could travel through time, flying vehicles, and other fantastic equipment. It was found that they could not interact with the past and could only travel to the future in their pure, non-corporeal sense. And they could only do so to a limited extent, meaning that scholars traveled individually rather than collectively. This also made it relatively normal for the lone scientists who traveled into the future to stay and observe the period by taking over the body of an individual within that time frame. Both groups and cults were set up in order to allow scientists from the past to assimilate into the existing civilizations unnoticed.

Roughly about 50 million years ago, the flying polyps that had been imprisoned in subterranean caverns broke out, attacked, and defeated their former enemies. In order to survive, the Race sent the minds of its best and brightest entities into the future and into space. They lived for a while on a moon of Jupiter and then on a world orbiting the dark star Taurus before returning to Earth. In the planet's far future, they occupied the hive-mind of a beetle-race. When this species becomes extinct, it is thought that the Race will inhabit an intelligent vegetable life form, growing in the dark areas of the planet Mercury. Some may even wander the darkness of space, eventually returning to Earth in order to wreak havoc on the inhabitants there and reclaim it for themselves.

After all of this, the *Pnakotic Manuscripts* only became part of human history when the people of Lomar unearthed them. In "The Mound," Lovecraft locates it somewhere near the present-day North Pole. These people were fleeing from an advancing ice-sheet, which marked the beginnings of the great Ice Age. They swept aside the hairy, cannibal Gnophkehs that dwelt in the southern lands and established their kingdoms there. They were also greatly influenced by people who emerged from the underground realm of K'n-yan, who brought with them a clay image of the toad-like god Tsathoggua, together with the scrolls of the *Manuscripts*. The great scholars of Lomar diligently studied the text and gained much knowledge from them. According to Lovecraft, Lomar was invaded around 24,000 B.C. by squat, hellish yellow creatures known as Inutos, which he identifies at the present-day Inuit (a description that perhaps reveals his underlying racism). However, in *The Dream-Quest of Unknown Kadath,* he suggested that the cannibal Gnophkehs overwhelmed Olathoe, the "many-templed" central city of the country, and killed all the great heroes there. What became of the *Manuscripts* in this event is not specified.

This was Lovecraft's basic premise on the ancient text. Other writers, however, developed and added to the text's history. For example, in a posthumous collaboration between Lin Carter and Clark Ashton Smith (after Smith's death), it is suggested that the *Manuscripts* were held by the Voormis, a fur-covered, cave-dwelling humanoid species who dwelt in primal Hyperborea. Subsequently, the *Pnakotic Manuscripts* entered formal history and were translated into a form of Greek. Among other lore, they contain the secrets of the Great Race, give an account of the nature of Chaugnar Faugn, detail the wars of the peoples of Lomar, and give the knowledge and secrets of ghouls and rituals of various gods and entities such as Rhan-Tegoth. They also provide a map to the shunned Plateau of Leng and details on the terrible cults that dwell there.

It is said that the *Manuscripts* have been closely guarded by a certain human cult know as the Pnakotic Brotherhood whose agents are everywhere in the world. There is also said to be some sort of supernatural Guardian who visits those who have read the *Manuscripts* and exacts some sort of terrible price from them.

Closely related to the *Pnakotic Manuscripts* are the Eltdown Shards, disturbing and debateable pottery fragments covered in curious markings that may also relate to the Great Race. The Shards were allegedly discovered by Doctors Abel Dalton and Nigel Woodford of Cambridge University during an archaeological dig at Eltdown in Sussex in 1882. However, other sources say that the Shards were discovered in Greenland by unnamed archaeologists in 1903. Shortly after their discovery, the two scholars pronounced the fragments untranslatable and probably unimportant. They did, however, send them to a colleague, Dr. Gordon Whitney at Beloin College in Hanover, Wisconsin. Whitney, who had seen certain occult texts relating to the *Pnakotic Manuscripts,* noted the similarity to the characters on both, but made no attempt to translate them.

One of those who had assisted with the dig was the Reverend Arthur Brooke Winters-Hall, a local clergyman and historian. He took copies of the figures on the Shards and worked to decipher them throughout the next 30 years. The results of his work, *The Eltdown Shards: A Conjectural Translation,* was published as a 48-page booklet in 1912. Winters-Hall could only afford to print 50 copies, but an anonymous benefactor funded the publication of another 300 copies in 1917. Although Reverend Winters-Hall stressed the links between the Shards and the *Pnakotic Manuscripts,* some scholars have argued that, given the relatively small amount of writing actually found on the Shards, the pamphlet is far too long to be an accurate translation. Others state that important elements of the translation have been deliberately omitted. Furthermore, much of the Winters-Hall document is mixed up with local fairy lore—particularly connecting the Great Race's time-travel abilities with the time-dilating effects of encounters with the Little Folk—so that parts of it are a mixture of human folklore and imagination. There is also some speculation that author Gordon Whitney also did some work on the Shards and *did* attempt to translate them, privately publishing his findings in a restricted monograph entitled *The Eltdown Shards: A Partial Translation.* This supposedly confirms much of Winters-Hall's work and formed the basis for some of the work of Whitney's colleague, Dr. Everett Sloan. Sloan tried to place the Shards in the context of what was known regarding certain pre-human races, but the conclusions were confused and jumbled, and therefore never published. The Shards are supposedly retained in Beloin College Museum, although not on public display. Much of the material that they contain is to be found in the *Pnakotic Manuscripts.*

There is also speculation surrounding another set of pottery shards known as the G'harne Fragments and whether or not they are connected to the *Pnakotic Manuscripts* and the Eltdown Shards. The Fragments were an addition to the Mythos by Brian Lumley in works such as *The Vaults Beneath* and *Cement Surroundings.*

The *Fragments* may have originated in Africa and were brought back to England by the explorer Sir Howard Windrop from an expedition in the early 1900s. He allegedly acquired them from a tribe in the African interior, in whose possession they had been for countless centuries, although exactly how he got them is uncertain. Cryptologists immediately noticed the similarity between some of the markings and the writing in the *Pnakotic Manuscripts.* Certain tests carried out on these pottery fragments revealed that they were probably from the Triassic Period of Earth's history—the same period as the Eltdown Shards.

The Fragments attracted the attention of the noted but eccentric archaeologist, Sir Amery Wendy-Smith. A scholar of some repute, Wendy-Smith had worked with Sir Flinders Petrie on a dig at Tell l-Hessi near Jerusalem between 1891 and 1892 and his major book *On Ancient Civilisations,* published in 1916, was regarded as something of a classic. He had also become interested in ancient African civilizations and the legendary city of G'harne, which was said to lie somewhere near the center of the ancient continent. Reading Windrop's attempt at a partial translation of the Fragments, which appeared in the *Imperial Archaeological Journal* in 1912, Wendy-Smith became convinced that these shards had come from that prehistoric city. It was

Wendy-Smith who dubbed Windrop's discovery the "G'harne Fragments" and it was he who completed the first full translation of the text in 1919. That same year, he led an expedition into Central Africa in order to determine the location of G'harne. The expedition was gone only several months when Wendy-Smith stumbled into an African village in a confused and disorientated state. Later, he would reveal that the other members of the expedition had been killed in a great earthquake in the African interior, which he alone had survived. However, his translation of the G'harne Fragments still continued to circulate in the form of a 128-page chapbook, which eventually printed 958 copies total. The Fragments describe lost prehistoric civilizations (the ancient city of G'harne is described in some detail) and ancient deities such as Bokrug and Nug. The Fragments supposedly give the history and location of a colony of serpent men who co-existed with Mankind in the early days of the planet. There are also fairly accurate star-maps included within the text, as well as reference to an ancient monstrosity named Shudde-Mell and his children who lived under the earth.

Sir Amery retired to Yorkshire in 1920 in poor health. He began a revision of the fragments and, according to Lumley, he may have been aided in this work by the renowned occultist Titus Crow. However, before he could complete the work, an earthquake destroyed his house in 1933 and many of his notes were lost in the wreckage. Wendy-Smith perished in the disaster, and his body was never found. However, his nephew Paul put several of his scattered notes together with the intention of publishing a memorial monograph, but these too were lost when his own house in Yorkshire was destroyed by a similar earthquake. Nevertheless, a copy of Wendy-Smith's original manuscripts are said to have been deposited in the British Museum and remain there to this day.

Wendy-Smith's book, though largely ignored during his lifetime, was examined again by two other scholars. The first was Professor Gordon Walmsley, a retired Cambridge Fellow who published several chapters of the Fragments in the *Imperial Archaeological Journal* in 1963. Similar to Windrop, the article was ridiculed and Walmsley's reputation was more or less ruined. The second study was completed in 1963 by Ryan Millbue entitled *The Annotated G'harne Fragments,* which linked the Fragments to the *Pnakotic Manuscripts,* but was once again discounted.

Madam Blavatsky and the Root Races

The idea of ancient, vanished races possessing arcane knowledge that has been completely lost to the world is a fascination of Mankind. The idea of prehistoric and unknown civilizations has intrigued both scientists and writers alike. For Lovecraft and succeeding Mythos writers, these early races may not have been altogether human and they may have been influenced by forces from outer space.

Lovecraft may have taken his inspiration for various inhuman prehistoric races from the work of another writer, theosophist and occultist H.P. Blavatsky. Born at

Ekaterinoslav on the Dnieper River in Southern Russia, it was clear that little Helena wasn't like other children from the beginning. She was very sensitive and seemed to possess psychic powers. In 1842, Helena's mother passed away, and Helena was taken to Saratov to be raised by her grandparents. During that time, she started to possess many talents—she was a gifted musician and painter and very sensitive to nature. However, she was wilful, resentful of any form of authority, and extremely self-centred.

At the age of 18, she married Nikifor V. Blavatsky, then Vice-Governor of the Province of Yarivan. Her grandparents opposed the marriage, as Nikifor was quite a bit older than she was. However, the marriage was in name only and was never consummated; a short time later, Helena left her husband and, using what monies she had obtained from him, began to travel around the world. When Blavatsky's money ran out, she wrote to her father who sent her more.

In 1851, Helena traveled to London where she ran into a figure who had appeared to her in visions that she had experienced. An Indian gentleman of Rajput birth, his real name is unknown, although she does refer to him as the Mahatma Moyra or sometimes just as "M." He took Helena as his pupil and began to train her in the ways of Eastern religion and occultism. He told her that she had a great future in occult spheres and in this he was correct; Madam Blavatsky became one of the most colorful and controversial figures of the mid-to-late 19th century. He also told her that her future lay somewhere in the East, perhaps in Tibet.

In 1855, after many years of travel, she entered Tibet through Kashmir and sought out some of the occult masters that M had told her about. In 1858, she made her way home to Russia where it is said that she suffered a severe psychic crisis. Regardless, she returned to Tibet in 1868. There she met an important Master who she referred to as Koot Hoomi.

By the age of 42, she had achieved great acclaim as an occultist and was well-known in occult circles. In 1873, she traveled to New York, and that is where she came into contact with Colonel Henry Steel Olcott, a veteran of the American Civil War. He introduced her to a young Irishman named William Quan Judge, who would be a great influence on Madam Blavatsky. Later, she would claim that these meetings had been engineered by Koot Hoomi in far-away Tibet. On September 7th, 1875, the three of them founded an organization that they named The Theosophical. The focus of the Society was the collection and distribution throughout the wider world of the occult laws that govern the Universe. Two years later in 1877, Madam Blavatsky completed her first major work, *Isis Unveiled*, in which she traced the history and development of magic and how it related to early Christianity. She also revealed secret mystical teachings that had been passed down from primordial times. In July 1878, Blavatsky became a naturalized U.S. citizen, an act that drew the attention of newspapers all around the world. That same year, Blavatsky and Olcott left for

Bombay, which would become the Society's headquarters. There they founded their first theosophical journal, *The Theosophist*, which is still in existence today. They also made contact with important publishers such as A.P. Sinnett—author of *The Occult World*—who may have financed some of their projects and allowed them to buy a large estate at Adyar near Madras. However, Madam Blavatsky was not in good health and there were allegations against her by two disaffected former theosophists concerning fraudulent psychic phenomena and her manipulation of various events for monetary gain. To allow things to settle, Blavatsky and Olcott lived in Germany for more than five months. Madam Blavatsky used the time to write what would become her most monumental work, *The Secret Doctrine*. Whilst writing this, she would move back to England.

The attack on her turned out to be false, but it had greatly damaged Madam Blavatsky's authority in the Theosophist Movement. She had all but lost control of *The Theosophist,* and in 1877, she began to publish another magazine entitled *Lucifer*, which was widely lambasted, even by theosophists. Throughout all of this chaos she was working on her most monumental work, *The Secret Doctrine* and, in December of 1888, she released it in two volumes together with a skeleton abstract of the secret *Book of Dzyan*, stanzas of which were originally included in both volumes.

In 1889, despite her failing health, she wrote *The Key to Theosophy*, which reinstated the founding principles of the Movement, together with *The Voice of Silence* that contained selections from Eastern Scriptures (mainly from an obscure work entitled *The Book of Golden Precepts*) and their explanations. In July 1890, Helena Blavatsky established the European Theosophical Headquarters in St. John's Wood, London. It was here that she died in May 1891 during a severe outbreak of the flu. However, she left behind a formidable body of occult and mystical teachings that are still considered to be of value today.

Part of these teachings said that the world had been populated long before the coming of Mankind by the Root Races, who went through various incarnations to blend with their constantly changing world; some of these had passed into the mythology and folklore of Humankind. This is an account of evolution, though not a scientific or religious one, but Madam Blavatsky declared it was a true one.

To date, there have been five root races and there are provisions for a sixth and seventh, which we will eventually become. The First Root Race was the Polarian Race, named that because it was somewhere in the vicinity of the North Pole. The Earth was in a less-material form at this time and the creatures that evolved then reflected this. They had little physical solidarity, possessing no skeletons, flesh, or internal organs. They had huge oval bodies that were either transparent or translucent without hair or skin. As time wore on, they grew more solid, but never attained full physicality, as we understand it now. They had no real consciousness either, but moved through their world like someone in a dream, vaguely aware of their surroundings and having no real understanding of them. The Polarians reproduced pretty much as the amoeba does today and were not even conscious that they were doing so—they were guided by what the Mahatmas call "a spiritual instinct." According to Blavatsky, the Tibetans called this race their Lunar ancestors and the continent on which they dwelt as the "Imperishable Sacred Land." When their time was past, they left no physical remains.

The Second Root Race was the Hyperboreans. They were still semi-astral, but more opaque in color. Although the species was still more or less gelatinous in form, it had begun to develop the beginnings of bone and internal organs. The species may have also developed some sort of skin and the formation of hair. Similar to the Polarians, the Hyperboreans had little knowledge of the world around them, which was also beginning to take on a more concrete form. Rather than splitting by cells, this species reproduced by budding like a plant. The creatures ejected a filament from a swelling on their bodies and this eventually grew into another of their species.

The Third Root Race, the Lemurians, was the first species on Earth with physical form. They had bones and rudimentary internal organs, and are described as a race of three-eyed giants (an eye on the top of the head being a primary eye) inhabiting the lost continent of Lemuria, which was one of the world's first land masses. Eventually, volcanic activity within the new continent caused it to sink beneath the newly formed ocean, taking much of the evidence for this Race with it. The Lemurians reproduced by budding and egg-laying. According to Madam Blavatsky, they were initially hermaphrodite and asexual, but gradually two separate species (male and female) began to develop. And they were the first Race that was self-aware. Madam Blavatsky called this event the "incarnation of the manasaputras" ("the sons of mind"). With the development of intellect, the Lemurians also became spiritually aware, and as their physical bodies developed the world around them became more material. A conflict developed between the spiritual and material aspects of Mankind.

The Fourth of the Root Races was the Atlanteans. Although greatly skilled in the occult arts, this race was physically coarser than ourselves. As the world became more refined and spiritual, the Atlanteans sank more and more into materialism and the abuse of their magical powers. They inhabited Atlantis, which they destroyed by misuse of their powers and, similar to Lemuria, it sank beneath the waves of the Atlantic Ocean. However, there were survivors that had evolved on the island-continent who managed to settle elsewhere in the still-developing world. Some of these sub-species included the Semites, the Toltecs of America, the Akkadians of the Fertile Crescent, and the Mongol peoples of the Eastern Steppe. Their descendants have continued down to the present day and are still thought to be evolving.

The Fifth Root Race is thought to be the Aryan. This species is beginning to develop its spiritual aspect once more after the brutal and materialistic Atlantean phase of evolution. The word *Aryan* in Sanskrit means "noble" and it is this goal to which Madam Blavatsky suggested the next Race was aspiring. Unfortunately, the term "Aryanism" was appropriated by Adolph Hitler and the ancient Indian swastika became the symbol of the German Nazi Party (even though it was reversed). The Aryan race is, according to the Mahatmas, striving toward racial purity. However, there seems little doubt that H.P. Blavatsky and a number of her followers held racist views. Much of their occult writings are full of the white ethnocentrisms that were prevalent in the late 19th and early 20th centuries. The sub-species of the Fifth Root Race include many of the races currently found on the surface of our planet. The coming species will be more mystical than us and will have powers of telepathy, high intelligence, and an advanced intuition.

Although there are no "giant rugose cone-shaped beings" among any of these Root Races, Madam Blavatsky's writings do present a picture of a race evolving through mystical and supernatural means. It vibes well with Lovecraft's own notions of race development from the time of the Great Race's arrival on Earth, and like his description of ancient prehistoric times, provides a quasi-scientific picture of our existence on this planet. Could it be that Madam Blavatsky's theories either influenced or were partially mirrored in Lovecraft's work? There is no way a student of the arcane and the outré could *not* have known of Madam Blavatsky and her work.

Lovecraft and Religion

Blavatsky's idea of cleansing or clearing the world of its former inhabitants in order to make way for a newer, better species can also be found in Christian mythology. There are hints in the Scriptures of previous races that may have inhabited the world. For example, the book of Genesis mention a race known as the Nephilim, many of whom were destroyed by the Flood. Although he was not overtly religious—he shunned religion as "superstition" for most of his life—Lovecraft came from a New England Baptist faith. Such churches lay a heavy emphasis on the Bible, and the Old Testament in particular. Could stories of ancient, evil Semitic monsters surviving from prehistoric times have influenced the imagination of a younger Lovecraft? Maybe in some way they found their way into his vision of the *Pnakotic Manuscripts*. Surely he would have known about such things if he had studied his religious traditions even a little bit.

The Nephilim were considered to be the spawn of supernatural beings and humans. According to Enochian lore, God sent a group of angels to watch over men (known as the Watchers) as they settled throughout the world. However, these angels found the daughters of men to be fair and mated with them. The Nephilim were the result of that union. Although we are unclear as to what they actually looked like it is thought that they may have been humanoid giants.

The notion of "the Sons of God" may have sprung from the religions of the Northern Semites (Canaanites in the Bible) living around the Palestine and Lebanon areas. El was their chief father god with more than 70 sons, many of whom became gods in their own right. They took wives from among men and lived with them in the wilderness. The Israelites later equated these with angels who had turned away from God and whose offspring became the Nephilim. However, this does not equate with some of the other descriptions of the Nephilim. Traditional legend says that they were brutal, violent beings and that their evil spread across the world.

The book of Jubilees tells how various races of giant men and monstrous creatures fell upon each other in this early period and killed an devoured each other. The Nephilim, for instance, fell upon another race of giant people, the Eljo, and murdered and ate them. The Eljo had already attacked humans and devoured them. This could not continue and God intervened.

According to traditional sources, the Flood was sent by God in order to cleanse the world of the evil giants. Noah was spared because, although not necessarily a wholly righteous man, he was needed to repopulate the earth with more wholesome beings. However, two types of giant species appear to have survived as well.

A species called the Anakim (Anunnaki) continued to populate the areas of the Middle East. Some sources say that they may have been found in parts of early America and in Africa. According to the book of Jasher, these were not unlike the Nephilim in that they were 100 meters high and lived for roughly 120 years. Their point of origin is somewhere in Mesopotamia, although they also appear in Babylonia and Semitic myth. They were the children of An, an old Sumerian god who had descended from the heavens by a great stairway known as Kur. They lived about 44 million years ago and built large cities in what would become the Fertile Crescent. In order to do this they used monstrous servitors—two slave species called the Igigi and the Sebitti. The Igigi were given the task of digging out waterways and canals to irrigate the land. They rebelled, forcing the Anakim to create a new worker-species. This they did by magically splitting a gene and splicing it with the most advanced human primate on the planet, possibly *Homo Habilis*, and in doing so may have created the Neanderthal species of human. Their cities continued to thrive into the time of Genesis and it is said that Nimrod the Hunter, the king who built the Tower of Babel, made war against the cities of the Anakim and caused great slaughter among them.

A second gigantic ancient race that the Bible mentioned in the books of Genesis, Deuteronomy, Samuel, Joshua, and Chronicles, were the Raphaim. They were a powerful and important race that survived the Deluge and continued to create problems in the newly emerging world. The Raphaim take their name from Rapha, an ancient monster or giant who existed long before the Flood. A number of his monstrous descendants survived and created problems for the emerging Israelite nation.

According to the Biblical book of Numbers, Og made war on the Israelites who subsequently invaded his Argob kingdom under the Judge Jair. Og was defeated, as was another of the Raphaim named Sihon. It is worth noting that archaeological digs carried out in the ancient land of Bashan in 1918 revealed a number of dolmens and gigantic tombs suggestive of a giant race. The area of Argob was said to contain 60 Raphaim cities, which the Israelites took in battle. As Israel made war on the gi-ant survivors of the Flood, they marched north into Northern Canaan where they encountered the Horim (a branch of the Raphaites) or Perizzites who fled before them into the forests. They were finally defeated in the ninth century B.C. by Chedor-laomer, king of Elam.

It is clear that ancient creatures—often the spawn of supernatural beings—had survived the Flood and continued to make trouble into the Israelite Iron Age. But it was not only in the past that there were changes in the development of Mankind.

Skellig Michael

So far, much of the suggested inspiration regarding the *Pnakotic Manuscripts* has come from old folktales, the Bible, and quasi-religious texts. But what if there were an actual physical representation of some of these early writings?

Off the coast of southern Ireland stands the impressive rock of Skellig Michael. The name *Skellig* derives from the ancient Irish word *skeilic* meaning "rock," and it is dedicated to St. Michael, patron saint of high places. Around the sixth century, a rocky island became the refuge for a small group of ascetic monks who built a monastery on the north-eastern side of a tiny valley. They built the distinctive bee-hive-shaped cells known as *clochans*. The monks there completely withdrew from the world and moved into remote and inaccessible places.

The monastery was simply referred to as "Sceilic" in the ancient annals and mar-tyrologies of the eighth and ninth centuries such as *The Martyrology of Tallaght* and *The Annals of Ulster.* Sometime after the 10th century, however, it appears in records as Skellig Michael, which means that around that period it must have been dedicated to St. Michael. Two references in the *Annals of the Kingdom of Ireland by the Four Masters* seem to suggest this. A stone church dedicated to St. Michael also appears to have been built there, the ruins of which are still extant and seemingly consistent with the architecture of the time.

The first reference that we have to any of the monks comes from the *Martyrology of Tallaght* written at the end of the eighth century, which commemorates the death of a Brother named Suibni in Scelig (Sweeny of Skellig). The *Martyrology* was an im-portant book at the time, so for the death of a simple monk to be recorded in its pages shows the veneration and awe with which the remote Skellig monastery was held.

Indeed, the ascetic "hermits of the Skelligs" seemed to be the heirs to a supernatural knowledge which other holy men may not have had.

There are many legends associated with the isolated settlement. Perhaps the remoteness and romance of that frontier post of the Christian faith added a kind of mystery to the life there. There was the belief that a book had been written on the island that contained detailed knowledge of demons and powerful exorcisms for driving them away. It also contained a history of the skellig and the forces that had been encountered there by the monks. Written by "Aed Sceilic, the noble priest, the celibate, and the chief of the Gaedhil in piety," the book was so potent that it had to be bound in covers of iron. This was supposed to have been a distillation of the knowledge of the "Skellig hermits"—of things unknown to the surrounding world—which has long since been lost.

In the 13th century, however, living conditions on the rock had deteriorated to such a degree that a year-round occupancy of the monastery had become impossible. From around 1200, colder weather and ferocious sea storms actually made living on the skellig extremely dangerous, so the monks were forced to abandon their lonely outpost and withdraw to the mainland at Ballinskelligs Bay near Watertown in County Kerry. By this time, the Church was also changing from a largely monastic structure to a diocesan one. Furthermore, European orders of monks with no tradition of island monasticism were establishing themselves in Ireland and the idea of eremitical communities began to fade away. The monks of Ballinskelligs still maintained the island monastery and may have held services there from time to time. It remained in their hands until 1578 when, in a response to the Desmond Rebellions, Queen Elizabeth I dissolved a number of monasteries that were under the protection of the Earls of Desmond. The island and its monastic site passed through the hands of several private, secular landlords until 1820, when it was purchased by the Corporation for Preserving and Improving the Port of Dublin and two lighthouses were erected there.

It was during the construction of these lighthouses that a startling find, which could have come right out of the pages of Lovecraft, was discovered by the men who came to Skellig Michael to erect the lighthouses. The monks had cut a system of staircases from the rock—some of which are still intact—but the men had to clamber about on the towering rock face in order to erect and adjust winches and hoists. It was after one of these falls that a local workman named Michel Ryan found himself trapped in an area of the skellig somewhere near Christ's Saddle. He had been working alone and a small fall of rock had cut him off from access to the rock steps, which would take him back down to safety. He began to look for another way down, but it proved tricky as the rocks were still loose and dangerous. Avoiding a small shower of loose stones, he clambered into what seemed to be a cleft in the rock and found himself entering a small opening. Walking along a short rock passage, he found himself in what seemed to be a medium-sized cave. The place had a very crude altar and what looked like a rough kneeling bench. But what caught Michael's eye was a small statue that had been placed on the altar. At first he had thought it was a statue of the Virgin, but as his eyes got used to the gloom of the cave, he saw that it was something else. It was something inhuman. Michael refused to describe or talk about what he had seen in the cavern in any detail, but it had shaken him greatly.

He managed to get out of the cave-chapel and eventually found his way down the rock face to where others found him. He told them what he had seen up among the crags, and with ropes and hoists they made their way back up to the secluded and sheltered place. Several others saw the terrible image still sitting on the rough altar. Some of the men were openly terrified, but a foreman crossed the cave floor and lifted the idol, dashing it to the ground. It was too barbarous, he believed, for anyone else to see. What it represented none of them know. In a crevice in a corner of the cave, they found yellowing parchments of great age, covered in a strange and unwieldy scrawl. With a flint, they set these alight, making a fire in the center of the cave and then destroyed all traces of any occupation of the place. Had they burned the celebrated *Book of Skellig Michael?* Perhaps the shattered idol, the crude altar, and the ashes of the book still lie somewhere deep within that forbidding rock even today.

The Room of Scrolls

During the late 19th and the early part of the 20th centuries the Far East was a place of exotic mystery. Tucked away in remote valleys of the high mountains of Tibet were remote communities of Buddhist monks or lamas, some of whom were privy to secrets older than time.

One of the early explorers in the Tibetan region was Alexandra David-Neel. An early follower of Madam Blavatsky's theosophist teachings, the young girl traveled to India in 1890 and later to the Kingdom of Sikkim in 1911. Her most famous journeys, however, were to the forbidden city of Lhasa in Tibet and to the Tibetan Highlands in 1937. She wrote extensively, her most famous book being *Magic and Mystery in Tibet*, which was published in 1929. One of those whom she inspired was the traveler, explorer, and writer David Amory who, like Alexandra, visited the high Himalayas in search of enlightenment in 1935.

While visiting the kingdom of Mustang, he traveled to a monastery somewhere to the north of the kingdom's capital, Lo Manthang. Because he was being guided in this area by agents of the *gyelpo* or ruler of the country he was unsure of where the monastery was, but it seemed to be on the edge of what he described as a rather squalid village. The monastery itself was dark and gloomy, so Amory only intended to spend the night there. All the same, the monks made him feel welcome and showed him certain treasures, such as an alleged Yeti skin. However, he was taken by a lama to a curious room deep within an old section of the building. The room was a kind of library with recesses set into the wall and packed with yellowing scrolls, some of them obviously very ancient. By the light of a flickering butter lamp and speaking through an interpreter, the monk explained that these scrolls contained the history of the world and of worlds that had existed before this one, stretching back to before the dawn of creation. Amory dared not touch some of them—they looked as if they hadn't been touched in hundreds of years—and anyway he might not have understood them, for the monk explained that most of them were written in the language of the gods.

The next day they set out from the monastery with its curious room and Amory never returned. If the room is still there, its location has been lost. Amory was not even sure of the name of the place. What knowledge did such a place hold and what could it tell us about our world and about our place within it? Could Lovecraft have been aware of this location? There are some who say that the account is nothing more than a fabrication, designed to give Amory some status as an explorer, but maybe there *is* an element of truth somewhere in it.

Could the suggestions concerning one or even several of these have melded together in Lovecraft's mind to form the basis of terrible literature that has filtered down to us in the form of the *Pnakotic Manuscripts*? One can't help but wonder!

It is impossible to cover *all* the texts to which Lovecraft and other Mythos writers make reference. Although there are recurrent volumes—the *Necronomicon, De Vermis Mysteriis*, and the *Book of Eibon*—there are a number of books and manuscripts that deserve a more in-depth look into the mysteries they provide.

Unaussprechlichen Kulten

Also known as *The Black Book,* this work was probably the brainchild of author Robert E. Howard, although Lovecraft used it in "The Haunter of the Dark" and "Out of the Aeons." It is a scholastic work compiled by the German occultist and explorer Friedrich Wilhelm von Junzt. The first reference to it appears in Howard's *The Children of the Night* and later in *The Black Stone.* The name *Unaussprechlichen Kulten* was suggested by August Derleth, as Lovecraft had struggled to come up with a name for a book of details on nightmarish cults.

Similar to other authors of blasphemous books in the Mythos, von Junzt remains something of a hazy figure. Born in Cologne in 1795 to Ava and Heinrich von Junzt, he enjoyed a fairly privileged lifestyle. However, his mother died while giving birth to his brother Augustus in 1804. His father, devastated by Ava's death, began to seek out mediums, spiritualists, and ghost-seers in an attempt to contact Ava in the afterlife, so Friedrich found himself in the midst of magical and spiritualistic figures. This had a profound influence on him, and provoked a deep interest in the occult.

In 1914, von Junzt entered the University of Berlin, and it was there that he met Gottfried Mulder. The pair graduated together and spent a year traveling through Asia, supposedly investigating occult groups. Following this, Mulder went off to do his own research somewhere in the East while von Junzt returned to Germany to complete his doctoral thesis entitled *The Origin and Influence of Semantic Magical Texts.* After that, he settled down as a teacher at the University of Wurttemberg where he remained for four years. However, some of his lectures on early cults outraged several Christian groups on the University campus, and there were whispers regarding his alleged homosexuality, which haunted his University career in a conservative Germany. Following the death of his father, von Junzt inherited enough money to allow him to travel once more. He journeyed extensively in Europe, America, Africa, and parts of Asia, tracking down (and trying to join) various cults and secret societies. In Paris, he

met up with a Frenchman named Alexis Ladeu, who would become his traveling companion for some time. While on his travels, he published two monographs
reflecting his obsessions at the time: *Les Vampires* (published in 1827) and *Les Lupines*
(a short treatise on werewolves published in 1828/9). In 1835, however, he and Ladeu
parted ways and von Junzt returned to his family estates in order to write his most
famous work, *Unaussprechlichen Kulten*, which was partly based on his travels.

The research for the *Unaussprechlichen Kulten* was incredibly detailed and exhaus-
tive. Von Junzt had access to the manuscripts and libraries of many obscure sects; he
allegedly saw one of the original Greek translations of the *Necronomicon*. He was also
one of the few who saw the original, unexpurgated version of the *Book of Iod* (a book
translated by the monk Joahnn Negus that deals with Iod, the Shining Hunter, and
its arrival on Earth), as well as the only extant copy of the *Ghorl Nigral* (the *Book of
Night*, mentioned in the *Book of Eibon* brought to Earth by the sorcerer Zkauba from
his homeworld of Yaddith).

The original volume of *Unaussprechlichen Kulten* was published in Dusseldorf in
1839. Some Lovecraft scholars suggest that it was printed by Gottfried Mulder, but
this seems unlikely, because Mulder was an academic and printed nothing else. The
book would have been more or less forgotten had it not been for a limited French
edition that was printed in St. Malo in 1843, three years after von Juntz's mysterious
death.

After the manuscript's original publication, von Junzt mysteriously disappeared
until he showed up in Dusseldorf a year later, claiming that he had been in Mongolia
working on another major book. In 1840, he was found dead in the same room he
had written the book, with the marks of tremendous claws on his throat with the
chambers' locks still intact. The papers on which he had been working were torn and
scattered across the room. Part of von Junzt's estate (including the torn fragments)
passed into the hands of his former friend Alexis Ladeu, who attempted to put the
final pages together. Having read what was in them, he burned the entire manuscript
and cut his own throat with a razor.

Following von Junzt's allegedly strange death, many of those who owned copies
destroyed them in panic, lest some similar horror befell them. It is said that only six
copies survived. The original German version boasts a set of particularly fine, if utterly
horrific, engravings by the German artist Gunther Hasse.

A disreputable London bookseller named M.A.G. Bridewell, however, obtained a
copy of the French edition from a London bookshop and produced a pirated English
edition of it in 1845. This was meant to "shock and titillate" the English populace,
but it is a shoddy and very much incomplete work. Under the title *Nameless Cults,*
the so-called "Bridewell edition" is a slim, octavo volume, leather-bound with almost
indecipherable text. It is filled with mistranslations, misprints, and typographical errors.
Parts of the text have been omitted and sections have been misplaced within the book.

The most famous and much more reliable English translation appeared in 1909, again under title *Nameless Cults,* published by Robert E. Howard's fictional publisher, Golden Goblin Press of New York. The edition included color plates by the artist Diego Valasquez. The Golden Goblin volume was much more accurate than the "Bridewell edition," but the translation was incomplete. More than a quarter of the original text had been expurgated, perhaps because of its questionable material.

A copy of the original German *Unaussprechlichen Kulten* may be found in the Restricted Literature Section of the Sanborne Institute for Pacific Antiquities in Santiago, California, and in the Huntington Library in San Marino, California. It may also be found in Lovecraft's fictional Library of Miskatonic University. Also, a copy was supposedly held in the Great Library of Calderstane Castle, Loch Arrow, near the village of Pittmirkie, Western Scotland, but this seems to have vanished when the Castle burned down in 1925.

Running more than 1,000 pages long, the German work relates to the familiar societies that had something of a sinister reputation: The Assassins, the Thuggee, the Sons of Ying, the Leopard Societies of Africa, and the Jaguar Men of South America. There are, however, descriptions of other, more obscure cults together with their rituals and their literature.

Although set out in an ordered and formalized style, the descriptions of these cults breaks down to a disjointed series of ramblings and bears no comparison to the earlier section of the book on the better known cults and societies. The latter third of the book is taken up with fantastic series of gibberish concerning bizarre artifacts and creatures such as the Lamp of Alhazred and alticorns (unicorn horns). There is also a claim that the author visited Hell. Much of the final section was not included in the Golden Goblin edition and was used by his critics to show that von Junzt was mentally unstable. To add to the confusion, it has also been suggested that von Junzt may not have died, but faked his own death and produced several other monographs under an assumed name. To this day, his life and work still remain something of an enigma. Nevertheless, his book became, and still remains, a classic of dark and academic study.

Did Lovecraft base von Juntz on someone who actually lived? Did he actually exist, only with a different name? There are a couple historical figures off whom Lovecraft may have based his fictional character.

William Seabrook

One of the prime contenders for the inspiration of von Junzt was the American writer and adventurer William Seabrook, who has already been alluded to (see *Cultes des Goules*). Seabrook was born in Westminster, Maryland, in February 1884. In 1913, he moved to France and, in 1915 he joined the French Army. After his tour, he returned to America and joined the staff of the *New York Times,* but found it difficult to fit in and resigned to become a freelance writer.

In 1918, Seabrook journeyed to French-speaking West Africa to study tribal customs. He had become fascinated by cannibalism and wished to see for himself. He traveled to the lands of a tribe called the Guere; whether or not the tribe existed as Seabrook described is open to question, but he supposedly lived among them for approximately eight months and ate human flesh. Returning to America, he wrote the experiences as a section of the book *Jungle Ways*, which was published in 1930.

In 1924, he traveled to Arabia where he claimed to have visited the Devil-worshipping Kurdish Yazidi. His account of the experience, *Adventures in Arabia: Amongst the Bedouins, Druses, Whirling Dervishes and Yezidi Devil Worshippers*, was published in 1927 to wide interest and acclaim. The monies that he received from the book allowed him to travel to Haiti, and he recorded his adventures there in another book called *The Magic Island* (published in 1929). Included in these writings was an alleged encounter with a powerful secret society in Haiti, the Cultes des Mortes. This was a society of bokors and hougans (local magicians) who wielded great powers, both political and supernatural in their respective areas, and who even had the power to raise cadavers from the dead. They came together to work great magic and to see zombies as slaves to local plantation owners. Seabrook claimed to have met with them and learned many of their secrets, some of which he included in his book.

His interests, particularly in the occult, were beginning to wear on him both physically and mentally. In 1933, he was admitted to a mental facility in Westchester County, New York, to receive treatment for acute alcoholism. There, he continued to write, recounting various aspects of his life and stating that he hadn't really witnessed anything that couldn't be explained by scientific or natural means. He discharged himself and wrote up the experience in another book *Asylum* (published in 1935) in which he detailed events in the institution as though they were part of a scientific experiment or a journey to some exotic locale.

On September 20th, 1945, Seabrook committed suicide in Rhinebeck, New York. He was certainly an extremely controversial character and could well be the model for the enigmatic figure of von Juntz. But was he the only one?

Percy Fawcett

Perhaps another contender might be Colonel Percy Harrison Fawcett. Born in Torquay, England, in 1867, he was interested in the occult and a follower of Madam Blavatsky. He led his first expedition into South America in 1906 at the behest of the Royal Geographic Society (which he had joined in 1901), which wanted to map the border region between Brazil and Bolivia. Fawcett's expedition lasted a year, during which he noted strange animals including monstrous anacondas and massive spiders. He returned to the South American jungles several times, tracing the source of the Rio Verde in Brazil and, in 1910, made his way into the near impenetrable Heath River country (on the borders of Peru and Bolivia), returning with many stories which many thought improbable.

Fawcett began to formulate wild theories about the occult and the origins of Mankind, allegedly based on his South American discoveries. Canadian explorer John Hemming referred to Fawcett's writings for the National Geographical Society as "eugenic gibberish," and there is some suggestion that he had become influenced by the teachings of Madam Blavatsky. Nevertheless, the National Geographical Society continued to employ him as a surveyor and an explorer.

In 1925, he acquired money from a consortium of wealthy businessmen who went under the umbrella title of "The Glove" to lead an expedition deep into the Brazilian Mato Grosso region. He was convinced that a great city, which he named "Z," lay somewhere in the jungle depths. This city had been the home of a wise, literate, and compassionate race that had been mysteriously wiped out. The city was the subject of a mysterious document known as Manuscript 512 housed at the National Museum of Rio de Janeiro. It is an account given by the Portuguese *bandeirante* (explorer/slave trader) Joao da Silva Guimaraes, who came upon the ruins of a massive city during an expedition in 1753. Although descriptions of the actual journey are fairly detailed, the location of the metropolis is extremely vague. The city may have been Kuhikugu, a massive agricultural complex consisting of 20 settlements at the headwaters of the Xingu River, which existed perhaps about 1,500 years ago.

Backed by The Glove, Fawcett put together a team and the expedition set out into the interior of the Mato Grosso where Fawcett expected the lost city to be. His last letter came from a location known as Dead Horse Camp on May 25th, 1925, in which he expressed doubts about the hardships he was facing. He also said that he was pressing further on into uncharted territory. That turned out to be his last communication with the outside world. In 1927, a nameplate bearing Fawcett's name and a compass was found among the Baciary Indians of the Mato Grosso. However, these may have been gifts from one of Fawcett's earlier expeditions. The Kalapalo Indians of the region said that Fawcett and the others had most probably been killed by some "very fierce Indians" living near the Upper Xingu, although these Indians have never been identified.

In 2004, the filmmaker Misha Williams claimed that Percy had never intended to return to civilization. Inspired by the writings of Madam Blavatsky he intended to set up some sort of theosophist commune deep in the jungle under the rule of his son Jack. However, this story was largely discounted. It is generally assumed that Fawcett and his party were killed either by wild animals or local Indians—probably the latter. Two Indian tribes, the Kalapalo and the Alioque, fell under suspicion. Each tribe blamed the other, but the Brazilian political activist Orlando Villas-Boas claimed that he had heard from several of the Kalapalo that they had murdered the entire group. Villas-Boas and the Danish explorer Arne Falke-Ronne said that Fawcett and his company had lost the gifts they were carrying in a river flood and had turned up in a Kalapalo village without the requisite presents, which was a serious breach of etiquette.

Subsequently, Jack and Raleigh Rimmel's bodies had been dumped into the river, but Fawcett being an old man had been treated with respect and buried in a secret grave in the forest.

Strangely enough, scientist may have found evidence of his lost city of Z not by exploration, but by satellite technology. Looking down on a section of jungle along the Brazilian-Bolivian border (where Fawcett had assumed it might be), they located what appears to be a complex of buildings and a network of roads covering an area of approximately 7,700 square miles, which may have been a home for almost 50,000 people. Also, the anthropologist Michael Heckenberger has uncovered stories of a large and wealthy civilization that may have flourished in the region at one time.

So did Lovecraft model von Junzt on William Seabrook or Percy Fawcett? Whoever he was, he was certainly an enigmatic character, and *Unaussprechlichen Kulten* remains one the Mythos's more terrible and formidable volumes.

The King in Yellow

In terms of the Mythos, *The King in Yellow* is something of a peculiarity. The work is a collection of short stories that are connected by a blasphemous two-act play of the same name, the reading or performance of which will drive readers (and audiences) insane. The style of the writing is late-Victorian Gothic, and the stories are classified as supernatural and horror, as well as science-fiction and fantasy. Lovecraft read Chambers's work and was so impressed by it that he incorporated elements of it into his own work. Thus, far from being a minor fantasy novel, *The King in Yellow* became an important volume of the awful tomes that made up the Lovecraftian corpus of shunned books.

No one knows exactly who wrote *The King in Yellow*. It was supposedly written sometime in the late 19th century by a relatively unknown playwright named Castaigne, however, author Daniel Harms has suggested that the first two scenes may have been written by the English Elizabethan tragedian Christopher Marlowe, who is one of England's greatest playwrights. Marlowe was certainly a colorful character and was the author of plays such as *Doctor Faustus* and *The Jew of Malta*. He was described as a heretic, a tobacco-user, a spy, a counterfeiter, a magician, a homosexual, and a necromancer.

Harms suggests that Marlowe's folio draft of the first section of *The King in Yellow* found its way into the hands of William Shakespeare who attempted to complete it. This section of the work was destroyed in the Great Fire of London in 1666, 50 years after Shakespeare's death. However, the Marlowe section survived and an unknown gentleman included it with a privately printed collection of poems by his wife.

Author Keith Herber has stated that the original play was in French (*Le Roi en Jaune*). However, Daniel Harms suggests that it was initially printed in English between 1890 and 1895, although it was originally performed in Paris in 1895. The French Government immediately banned it at the behest of the Church. Since then, there have been clandestine publications and performances in places such as Zagreb, Prague, Budapest, London, Edinburgh, Berlin, Warsaw, Belgrade, Sarajevo, and Dublin. Performances have also taken place in both Chicago and New York.

Despite its relative obscurity, the work has been influential in the field of strange literature. Fragments of it appear to turn up in the works of the playwright Charles Vaughan, in the writings of the occultist Kenneth Grant (author of the *Chronicles of Kralnia*), and beat writer Charles Bukowski.

There are allegedly two rather different versions of *The King in Yellow.* The first version begins in the city of Yhtill under the star Aldebaran. The main characters of the play are the Queen, Thale, Cassilda, Uoht, Aldones, and Camilla, all of whom are claimants to the throne of Yhtill. However, Cassilda is chosen as the new Queen by her father over Aldones and with the compliance of Uoht. In revenge, Aldones convinces Uoht to forge a set of documents bearing the Queen's seal and then instructes Camilla to arrest him for doing so. The whole episode is watched by Thane, the king's third child, who expresses his grave doubts about the succession.

Meanwhile, a strange and ghostly city inexplicably appears on the other side of Lake Hali. The city's Royal Court hears of a mysterious stranger who appeared in Yhtill. A curious symbol known as the Yellow Sign also appears with the stranger's passing. The Royal Family takes the stranger prisoner, but learns nothing of value.

In the second act, the Court throws a masked ball and the stranger reappears again. When the time comes to unmask, he reveals that he wears no mask and that this is true face. Camilla goes mad at this disclosure and tortures the stranger to death. At the same time, she orders the death of all prisoners in the Court cells, including her own son Uoht.

The ghostly city on the other side of Lake Hali suddenly vanishes just as suddenly as it appeared, and madness begins to sweep the land. There are rumors of an invading army and suddenly the King in Yellow appears in Yhtill to tell them that their time is over. He has come to rule, and in order to do so, he kills Aldones and Thale.

In the second version of the play, the first scene is the city of Hastur, which has been at war with its neighbor Alar for countless years. The Queen of Hastur is Cassilda who, although weary and ill, will not relinquish the crown in favor of her three children—Thale, Uoht, and Camilla—though they demand that she now choose her successor. As Cassilda grows ever weaker and her children pressure her to continue the dynasty by naming one of them, news reaches the ailing queen that a stranger wearing a pallid mask and carrying the Yellow Sign on his garments has inexplicably appeared in the city. On the advice of the High Priest, Cassilda summons the figure to the Palace. The stranger, who is named Yhtill, offers the Queen a way to break free from the domination of the mysterious King in Yellow who lives on the other side of Lake Hali. The King, who rules Carcosa across the Lake, exercises his power through the Yellow Sign, which all must wear as a symbol of his domination. Only by wearing a pallid mask like him, the stranger tells the queen, can the domination of the King in Yellow be broken.

Believing everything that the stranger has said, the queen holds a masquerade ball at which all the guests must wear a Pallid Mask in the same style as he. When the time comes to unmask, Yhtill reveals that he actually wears no mask and that he has come from Alar to destroy Hastur's people. Cassilda goes mad, but her city is rescued by the intervention of the King in Yellow from the other side of the Lake. He arrives in Hastur and casts Yhtill to the other side of the Lake. Before he departs, the king promises Cassilda that he will allow the victor of the war with Alar to rule the world, but there is one condition: All the people of Hastur and their descendants must wear the pallid masks forever. The king now departs, bringing the play to an end.

In the play, the King in Yellow appears as a gigantic human creature dressed in tattered yellow robes and wearing a pallid mask, which conceals truly awful features. The King might have been human in the past, but he has been subtly altered, possibly through the power of the Old Ones. His speech is also strange and hideous. Some commentators have suggested that the King might actually be Nyarlatothep, one of the Mythos creatures.

Sometime after the play first appeared, a set of stone tablets was found in a cave in China. The text on them seemed to hint at an actual being on which The King in Yellow might have been based. What these tablets actually meant is not known, but they became known as the Xanthic Folio, or the Yellow Codices, and were treated as a companion to *The King in Yellow*.

The actual book that Lovecraft probably read was a Gothic fantasy written in a relatively cumbersome prose, as was fashionable for such work. Only the first four chapters directly relate to the play, but some of the other tales contained scattered references to it. However, the later stories in the book do not specifically follow the macabre themes of the first four, as it has to be remembered that Chambers was primarily a writer of romantic fiction.

Chambers drew his influences for the play from a number of other writers. Perhaps the most obvious is that the setting for the masqued ball at which the stranger appears contains a number of elements in Edgar Allen Poe's *Masque of the Red Death*. Here, as in Chambers's play, the decadent aristocracy seclude themselves from a terrible disaster that is sweeping the country, besporting themselves in festivity. Toward the end of the story an unknown guest appears in a blood-soaked shroud and wearing a red mask, which the other guests try to dislodge. When they do so, there is no face beneath it, and they realize that this is the embodiment of the Red Death. This knowledge kills them all. The element of the stranger at the masqued ball and the portent of doom as embodied by the stranger in *The King in Yellow* are remarkably similar.

Lovecraft seems to have read *The King in Yellow* around 1927 and, greatly taken with it, started incorporating some of the names and locations into his own work. The Lake of Hali and the Yellow Sign, for example, appear in *The Whisperer in the Darkness* (1931). Gradually, the dreadful play became one of the seminal texts in the Mythos lexicon. However, in Lovecraft's fiction some of the terms remain very vague, for instance, there is no real indication as to what either Hastur or the King in Yellow might be. It was August Derleth who developed Hastur into one of the great Old Ones, although in Chambers's writing it is definitely a place. However, Lovecraft compounds even more confusion in his cycle of poems, *Fungi from Yuggoth*, when he refers to a dreaded ancient god whose face is covered by a "yellow veil" sitting alone at the end of time.

The King in Yellow can therefore signify a number of different things and most recently it has been updated for a Cthulhu Mythos role-playing game by Kevin Ross. Throughout Mythos fiction this figure keeps resurfacing and menacing those who have the misfortune to encounter it.

The Book of the Wolf

We have already noted a number of books whose contents are so powerful that the reader's head must be encased in a circlet of iron for protection. This was a feature of several Gaelic witchcraft manuals that appear in both Irish and Scottish folklore. Some were said to be so potent that a mere perusal of the contents could blast the eyes of the reader.

The most famous of these terrible and dangerous texts was *The Book of the Wolf*. The wolf in question was Alexander Stewart, Earl of Buchan, third son of Robert II of Scotland, and brother to King Robert III, widely known as the Wolf of Badenoch. Stories concerning Alasdair Mor mac an Righ (to give him his proper Gaelic name) portray only his extreme cruelty and rapacity. He was certainly a stern and rather ferocious man who interpreted the law of the land as he saw fit, but he maintained some sort of discipline in the Highlands. His feud with Alexander Burr, the Bishop of Moray, was legendary and culminated in the burning and destruction of Elgin Cathedral by the Wolf's ketterins (personal soldiers), resulting in him being declared outlaw by the outraged Bishop.

It was in the years leading up to the burning of Elgin in 1390 that rumors started circulating about him. These rumors were written down in a great book that was bound with iron hasps. The content of this and the secrets it contained were so terrible that they would blast the eyesight of any reader, save that of the Wolf himself. It was also said that unearthly powers came down to the stone circle at Kingussie (now long demolished) where the Wolf had held court and that he had consorted with them. *The Book of the Wolf* supposedly contained the magics of a prehistoric race that had existed in Scotland long before the time of the Picts, as well as spells and incantations for raising ancient and slumbering spirits from the earth.

For a long time the weak and ineffectual King Robert III did little against his brother, but after the attack on Elgin and the plundering of the Abbey at Forres, even *he* had to act. He limited the Wolf's power in the north and confiscated some of his lands. Nevertheless, he still maintained a formidable presence until his death in 1405. What became of the Book afterward is unknown, although it was allegedly passed down among the kings of Scotland and was certainly in the library of the enigmatic James III, who was deeply interested in magic.

The People of the Monolith

Early in 1926, a slim volume of poetry bound in bright red buckram was issued by the Erebus Press of Monmouth, Illinois. This comprised the work of a relatively unknown poet named Justin Geoffrey and was entitled *The People of the Monolith*. Although he had produced some works before—his fragmentary verse *Out of the Old Land* had been published in *Etchings,* a small, limited-edition magazine in New York—very little was known about Geoffrey, and early sales of the book were slow. However, after news of the poet's mental collapse reached the literary world, the book sold out.

The book was privately printed and funded in part by John Tyler, a businessman in New York. Erebus Press produced 1,200 copies, only a few of which survive, most of them in private collections.

The Geoffreys were an old Planter family that had come to New York around 1690 and become relatively prosperous merchants. Justin enjoyed a fairly privileged youth, which enabled him to spend days wandering through the Catskill Mountains of upper New York State. When he was 10 years old he was on one of his walks when something mysterious occurred, which turned his intellectual direction toward poetry. Details concerning this experience are scant, but there are those who say that story is just fantasy, that no such experience ever occurred, and that Geoffrey was simply a strange and moody child with a wistful interest in poetry.

Whatever the source of his inspiration, he quickly extended the scope of his reading tastes to include Rimbaud, Huysmans, and Beaudelaire. In 1917, he drifted to New York City where he wrote a number of poems, many of which were strange and outré, but without attracting much acclaim beyond a tiny circle of friends and acquaintances. In 1920, Justin set out for Europe and spent the next two and a half years wandering. In 1922, he visited a small village in Hungary, which had a rather dubious reputation. There, in the shadow of a strange-standing stone close to the village, he experienced a very strange dream that would serve as the basis of his most famous work, *The People of the Monolith*. The name of the village is usually given as Stregoicavar ("witch town"), but it was also known by an older name of Xuthltan.

He returned to America late in 1922 or early in 1923 and made contact with an old friend named Edward Derby. Those who met him around this time described him as being changed and distant and, though he wrote to some close friends on his return, his letters made very little sense. He met with Derby and together the two of them did a series of late-night poetry readings in Arkham's Desolate Highway Café, which was a hang-out for the city's bohemian faction and "artsy" groups. At one of these readings he gave a poetic outline of *The People of the Monolith* and appeared on-edge, as though he expected something to emerge from the darkness of the night and attack him. This only added, of course, to his air of bohemian mystery. After the last reading he suddenly disappeared, and for almost two years nothing further was heard from him, although late in 1923, a small folio volume appeared in Arkham entitled *Secrets of the Hanged Man*, followed by a book of about half a dozen poems called *Voices from the Stones* in 1924. Both works were dismissed by both literary and occult groups, though it is not clear if they were actually written by Geoffrey at all. Indeed, the style of his poetry has remained something of an enigma through the years with a number of critics saying that it appears to be the work of several people rather than by an individual. If these were the work of Justin Geoffrey, nothing was heard from him thereafter. It is thought, however, that he did send several letters to his friend John Ernest Tyler asking for money.

In early 1925, Geoffrey was found again in Chicago. He was an alcoholic and addicted to morphine. However, he brought with him the transcript of his major poem and several other pieces that he had been working on. For several months, he lived in New York as the guest of his friend John Tyler while he completed his work. However, one evening he wandered off and was found two days later in an alleyway. Back with Tyler he began to experience fearful nightmares and episodes during which he could become exceptionally violent. He would also wander off with increasing frequency and had to be brought back, usually under the influence of alcohol or drugs. However, in 1926 he returned to Chicago where, several weeks later, Tyler found him living in a house on the bad side of the city and had him committed to the Illinois State Asylum for his own safety. For a while he appeared more settled and even resumed some of his writing, but at the end of the year he was found dead in his room. No satisfactory explanation has ever been given for his sudden demise and there is a suspicion that he may have taken his own life. (According to some reports he seemed especially anxious and fearful of something toward the end of his life.)

He left behind a small amount of work besides *The People of the Monolith*; two other poetry collections were published after Geoffrey's death—*Scarlet Runes and*

Other Poems (1928) and *Out of the Old Land* (1929)—together with a small book of fantastic fiction *Towers in the Sky* (1929). *Out of the Old Land* contains variants of several of the supplementary poems found in *The People of the Monolith* (including the title poem) and reworkings of fragments of verse (possibly from *Voices from the Stones*). There is also said to be a small folio of some drawings that he made while in the Illinois Asylum, which were printed in limited edition by an unknown publisher in San Francisco in 1960. It includes a particularly eerie scene dominated by the central figure of the piece—*The Veiled Hermit*—which some have claimed is reminiscent of the land around Stregoicavar. Most of Geoffrey's work has now become collector's items, although one copy is supposedly held in the Restricted Viewing Section of the New York Metropolitan Library.

Justin Geoffrey and his terrible work *People of the Monolith* appear in a story by Robert E. Howard entitled *The Black Stone*, which was published in *Weird Tales* (November 1931). Although the work is Howard's there is no mistaking Lovecraft's influence, and the two might have corresponded at length on the idea.

The story centers around a mysterious black monolith that lies outside a Hungarian village that had been founded in some former time by an unknown race. Octagonal in shape, some 16 feet in height and about a foot and half thick, it may have been the focus for some sort of religious ritual. In fact, the inhabitants of the village are not the original ones—these were all wiped out in a Turkish invasion around 1526. The armies of Suliman the Magnificent all but obliterated the original village and gradually Hungarians repopulated it. The initial inhabitants of Xuthltan were a curious race, in the common folklore of the area they were not even wholly human and although virtually extinct, they may not have been completely eradicated from the area.

In Howard's story, the protagonist visits Stregoicavar and sees the famous Black Stone there. He notices that there are the marks of tools on its surface as though someone has been trying to destroy it. On Midsummer Night, the narrator falls asleep and wakes to find a chanting, dancing throng celebrating close to the stone. Unable to move, he sees a young girl being sacrificed to the stone and on the top of the monolith a squat, toad-like thing appears, whereupon the narrator wakes up. He decides to excavate the ruins of the old castle and finds the crushed casket and a written account of how the Turks found "a monstrous wallowing toad-thing" in a nearby cavern and slew it with sacred steel. The narrator then realizes that what he saw was not a dream, but a vision of some reality. He throws the casket and a golden idol of a toad into the Danube, but what he has learned almost maddens his mind.

This is the basic story that Howard recounted, which has formed the basis for a series of tales by other writers such as W.H. Pugmire and for references by Lovecraft. The Black Stone has seemingly grown in malevolence with each tale—even looking at it for long periods can cause insanity according to some. It, together with the poetry of Justin Geoffrey, has become one of the peripheral themes of Mythos fiction and still features in Cthulhu fiction from time to time.

The Celaeno Fragments

The Celaeno Fragments represent a more science-fiction aspect of Mythos fiction with their emphasis on distant worlds and time-traveling, undying academics. Although termed as "fragments," they are in fact a set of handwritten notes representing a transcript that was placed in the fictional Miskatonic University Library in 1915. The person who deposited them is believed to have been Dr. Laban Shrewsbury, who disappeared shortly after depositing them. The name associated with them is an intriguing one. *Celaeno* is a Greek name, meaning "dark one," and it refers to a number of mythological characters. One of these characters is a Harpie (a terrible monster with a head of an old woman and the body of a vulture, which Aeneas encountered in the Strophades Islands). He also refers to one of the Pleiades (the seven daughters of the giant Atlas). The *Fragments* consist of 50 pages of notes and give very little data. They bear some resemblance to the *Pnakotic Manuscripts* and the *Eltdown Shards* and, it is suggested by Lovecraftian scholars such as Robert Price, that it may come from the same source. They were first written about by August Derleth, although Lovecraft may have been involved in their creation.

Shrewsbury, a respected American anthropologist was born in Baraboo, Wisconsin, in 1864. However, he spent much of his adult life in the fictional town of Arkham where he occasionally taught at Miskatonic University, lecturing in comparative anthropology. In 1914, he was granted an emeritus Professorship by the University and settled into a writing career. He stayed well away from well-trodden anthropological paths, preferring to concentrate on the more bizarre aspects of his field—strange cults in Ponape (Pohnpei) and rumored religious practices and queer mythologies in Java and New Guinea. His book, *An Investigation into the Myth-Patterns of Latter-Day Primitives with Especial Reference to the R'lyeh Text* (1914), created much debate among anthropologists and scientists. It drew heavily on the so-called *R'lyeh Text*, or the *Black Tablets of R'lyeh*, a set of questionable stone tablets found in China. They make little sense and deal with a being name Cthulhu.

Shortly after publication in 1915, Shrewsbury disappeared after announcing that he was going out for a short walk. He was presumed dead, and upon investigation of his house, a selection of notes concerning anthropological aspects of the latter 19th century was found. They were eventually published under the title *Cthulhu Among the Victorians*.

Twenty years after his mysterious disappearance, Laban Shrewsbury suddenly reappeared with little explanation as to where he'd been. He told several of his colleagues a strange story, which none of them entirely believed.

He had not been on Earth at all during the missing time, but on a great library-world circling a star in the Pleiades. The place was known as Celaeno and it housed information on the early cults of the Universe, especially those relating to the worship of Cthulhu. Within its confines Shrewsbury had spent his time researching Cthulhu cults on various worlds in our own galaxy before returning to Earth.

After explaining this, he disappeared again and returned 11 years later. He had merely returned to Celaeno to investigate a few references. He seemed not to have aged and people began to wonder about him—was there perhaps some strange truth in what he was saying? This time, Shrewsbury settled down in Arkham and began work on his next book, *Cthulhu in the Necronomicon*. Once again, the use of such a questionable book as the *Necronomicon* created controversy in the academic circles of Miskatonic University. The book, however, was never published. In 1938, a mysterious fire completely destroyed Laban Shrewsbury's house and, although no body was ever found, it was assumed that he had died in the blaze. However, reports and alleged sightings of him have been recorded since.

The "Fragments" themselves are little more than 50 sheets of handwritten notes written in Shrewsbury's cramped style. They describe, in what appears to be an attempt at academic language, a plethora of beings and "gods" not known to conventional mythologies—Yog-Sothoth, Azathoth, and many ethereal beings. There are also creatures that Shrewsbury equates with elementals: Nyarlathotep (earth), Cthulhu (water), Cthugha (fire), and Ithaqua (air). There are also disjointed references to "space vampires" and "dholes," and although some of these are to be found in other works (for example *De Vermis Mysteriis* and *Cultes des Goules)*, these may simply be the ramblings of Shrewsbury's slowly disintegrating mind and raise serious questions regarding his sanity.

For the University, the *Celaeno Fragments* became something of an embarrassment. Far from furthering its reputation as a center of academic excellence, Shrewsbury made it something of a laughing stock. Curiously, a set of books that were part of the estate of a man named Amos Tuttle were also deposited with the University Library in 1936, and some of these bore sections that were slightly similar in nature to the *Celaeno Fragments*. Following his death in 1936, a person claiming to be his nephew Paul appeared and served as executor of his estate. Shortly after, Paul disappeared without a tracem, taking most of Tuttle's vast library with him. Certain books were, however, formally bequeathed to the University Library and are currently housed with the University's Abner Whatley Collection.

It is an impossible task to explore all the literature associated with the Cthulhu Mythos, particularly since writers are adding new books to the corpus of work on a daily basis and are extending the lore on already-existing volumes. These are only some of the mouldering volumes that grace the decaying shelves of the Forbidden Library. There are many others—*The Revelations of Glaaki*, *The Ponape Scripture*, *Monsters and Theyr Kynde*, and *The Seven Cryptical Books of Hsan*, some of which individual readers may explore at their leisure and risk. And, of course, who knows what other terrible literature lies rotting in the corner of some cobwebbed chamber, on the worm-eaten shelves of some forgotten library, or tucked away in some shabby bookshop, waiting to spring fresh horrors upon the unsuspecting world? The literature of the Cthulhu Mythos continues to expand; who knows what might be lurking out there?

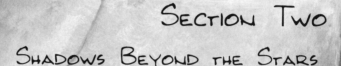

Section Two

Shadows Beyond the Stars

In Mythos fiction, the monsters and malignant entities are often a blend of creatures from the fringes of folklore, of ancient gods, and of things that have come to Earth from beyond the stars. Perhaps because of varying interests and perspectives of writers, the nature of the beings seems to shift, expand, and change. This process has accelerated as time went on, and more writers became involved in Mythos fiction. Certainly in the early days of the Mythos, there seemed to be more cohesion, probably due to the voluminous correspondence that centered around Lovecraft. As time went on, however, that cohesion has started to break down and new strands of Mythos lore have developed. Therefore, the Mythos takes on a kind of organic life of its own, evolving and expanding, but this makes the process of developing a central understanding all the more difficult. The development of role-playing games has only added to the confusion and contradictions. Perhaps not even Lovecraft understood what he was creating, and his ideas regarding the creatures that he created changed throughout the years both in their nature and origin. As his perspective shifted between horror and science-fiction, so did the emphasis of his writing and the creatures within it.

There are, of course, those who have sought to give some sort of cohesion to the concept, such as Robert M. Price, Daniel Harms, and Keith Herber. They are steeped in Mythos lore and have acted as advisors on its fiction and games. For the uninitiated, however, or for those approaching the Mythos for the first time, the process can be a rather daunting one. From where do the ideas for such beings come? From the ancient mythologies of which Lovecraft was especially fond? From tales of witchcraft? From the science-fictional viewpoints of Clark Ashton

Smith and August Derleth? From a combination of all of these? Perhaps before examining the creatures/beings and their development it is worth briefly examining the
backgrounds against which they are set.

The Great Old Ones

Arguably, many of Lovecraft's early entities belonged to a category of being
known as the Great Old Ones. They are ultrapowerful alien beings with a knowledge
of advanced alien technology and magic (in Lovecraft's universe, the two tend to be
indistinguishable). They came to Earth millions of years ago from various points in
the Universe, and have been instrumental in shaping the course of human history.
They have almost god-like powers, but are still bound by certain physical and natural
laws. It is also thought that Earth may not be the only world that they inhabit, and
they may also be dominant over other species throughout the galaxy. Since it occurred
in some distant prehistoric time, there is no record of the Great Old Ones arriving
on Earth. Their intentions do not seem terribly sympathetic toward Mankind, which
evolved later. Tradition seems to state that the first to arrive was Cthulhu (the mighti-
est of the Old Ones), who immediately ordered the building of a massive city called
R'lyeh on a large continent in the current-day Pacific Ocean. This city now lies under
the ocean and Cthulhu is still believed to be there, waiting or dreaming.

After millions of years some sort of change took place. According to Harms,
there are two theories as to what occurred. The first hypothesis suggests that the Great
Old Ones were once servants of another superior race known as the Elder Gods, and
they committed some sort of crime against their former masters. They rebelled and
appropriated some of the Elder Gods' technology (or magic) as their own. Or they
may simply have attacked the homeworld of the Elder Gods. Whatever their crime,
the Elder Gods cast them out and marooned them on various remote outposts across
the galaxy, including the planet Earth. They also imprisoned them in other dimensions. The Elder Gods then returned to their own world, a planet orbiting the star
Glyu-Uho, leaving the Great Old Ones to fend for themselves. Faced with all sorts
of supernatural restrictions imposed by the technology of their former masters, the
Great Old Ones are continually trying to break free and wreak a terrible revenge on
the Elder Gods.

The second suggestion is that the Great Old Ones have imposed these restrictions upon themselves for some unknown reason. This might remove any notion
that they are imprisoned here as former servitor of the Elder Gods. Daniel Harms
has suggested that they may have entered a cyclic period of inactivity (similar to a
natural hibernation in animals), but that they will arise at some future date in order to
conquer the world. This, he states, explains the couplet taken from Abdul Alhazred:

THAT IS NOT DEAD WHICH CAN ETERNAL LIE,
AND WITH STRANGE AEONS EVEN DEATH MAY DIE.

Even though their physical bodies are in a state of suspension, their minds remain active; their thoughts and telepathic communications go out and can be experienced by humans on the planet around them. Through time, as Harms points out, these thoughts and stories have become distorted and transformed into legends and mythologies concerning slumbering giants and great heroes, but in a number of cases, humans have been able to pick up the pure thoughts of the ancient beings. This has allowed the Great Old Ones to form groups of worshippers and servants who imagine that, when their masters return and reconquer the world, they will receive numerous benefits and powers in return for their loyalty. However, the general consensus seems to be that the Great Old Ones barely consider them and that the Earth will be left desolate and uninhabitable by human kind.

The number of Great Old Ones is unknown, and it seems to be expanding as more and more additions are made to the Mythos by various writers. There are, however, some important ones to note. Mention has already been made of Cthulhu, a massive octopoidal being that rules over the sunken city of the dead known as R'lyeh. Similar to all its brethren Cthulhu still slumbers, but might wake at any time to wreak havoc. Hastur, another powerful and important entity waits, not on Earth, but in outer space on the shores of the Lake of Hali, which supposedly lies somewhere near the star Aldebaran. A toad-like entity known as Tsathoggua slumbers far beneath the Earth in a lightless underground world known as N'kai, while Ithaqua, a water and air entity, is confined to the northern reaches of our world and to other frozen worlds in the immediate vicinity of our sun. It is this being that has given rise to the legends of the Wendigo in places such as Northern Canada. These Great Old Ones appear to be especially active in the world, but according to Lovecraft and others, many others still lie in a state of suspended animation until they can come again.

The Outer Gods

As the Mythos grew and other writers began to add their own ideas and perspectives (particularly influential writers such as August Derleth, Clark Ashton Smith, and Robert Bloch) more beings were added to the pantheon and various subdivisions were created. Of course, not all writers agree with such divisions or use them in their work. Later writers, such as Brian Lumley and Joseph Campbell, began to look for ways in which their own creations could be accommodated within the overall Mythos structure and created groupings of the beings that were deserving of special worship and attention.

One of these groups was the Outer Gods who were sometimes distinguished from the Great Old Ones, though a number of Lovecraftian scholars still do not recognize the concept and simply class them among the Great Ones. These might be described as "functionary beings" and seem to have been those who had the greatest contact with Mankind. Their names included Azathoth, Yog-Sothoth, Nyarlathotep, and Shub-Niggurath, although some of these were known by other titles in ancient folklore and mythology. This confusion is compounded by references to Elder Things in Lovecraft's tale *At the Mountains of Madness*, which may refer to the Outer Gods or to the Elder Gods.

The Elder Gods

Similar to the Great Old Ones, the Elder Gods seemed to have immense powers, which were limited by the natural order of the Universe. However, they were immeasurably older than the Great Old Ones and, according to some sources, were said to dwell on a world in the vicinity of the star Betelgeuse. This is, however, disputed by other writers who claim that they come from another dimension known as Elysia or a place known as the Hourless House, which lies somewhere in the realm of dreams.

Wherever they come from, the Elder Gods are the implacable enemies of the Great Old Ones. Indeed, some have claimed that the Great Old Ones were a servitor species created by the Elder Gods who eventually rebelled against them. Scholars have argued that the Great Old Ones raided the vast archive-library on Celaeno and removed certain texts, thus gaining knowledge to stand against their former masters. The Elder Gods, however, were powerful enough to imprison the rebels on a number of worlds (including Earth) where they maintain a constant watch in case the Great Old Ones break free and menace them again.

No one knows the origins of the Elder Gods. However, it is thought that they were born when the Primal Entity, Ubbo-Sathla, split asunder, creating the Universe and everything that dwells within it. They are, in effect, primal energies that have existed since the dawn of time, some of which may have taken on physical (though not necessarily human) form.

In the myth, the names of certain of the Elder Gods include Nodes, Khalid, Yad-Thaddag, Zehirete, Adaedu, Urthuvn, Othkkartho, and Xuthyos-Sibh'Bz. Extremely little is known regarding any of these.

Of course, there is sometimes confusion among Myths writers concerning the distinction between the Great Old Ones and the Elder Gods, and some names seem to have been transposed between the two. However, it is generally believed that Nodens, Lord of the Great Abyss, will lie in wait for his ancient enemies to arise and at that time he will defeat them, thus establishing the rule of the Elder Gods in the Universe once more. Some have supposed the Elder Gods to be the forces of light and the Great Old Ones as the dark powers, which seek to rule all existence. Lovecraftian scholars have stated that the distinction isn't quite so simple.

Lovecraft authorities such as Kenneth Grant, Daniel Harms, and Keith Herber have suggested some origins and features of the Elder Gods that serve as a more subtle distinction from the Great Old Ones. They suggest that the Elder Gods may be an earlier incarnation of the Great Old Ones themselves. To add further confusion they refer to them as "the Great Ones" who emerged from the Great Old Ones' dreams. Finding the Great Old Ones in their tombs, the Elder Gods became terrified and sealed these tombs with the Elder Sign, withdrawing back into the Dreamworld (where they now rule) under the leadership of Nodens. Nodens is said to be awake for aeons, but when It eventually sleeps, the Elder Sign will be broken and the Great Old Ones will re-emerge to wreak havoc on the Universe and the Elder Gods will be powerless to stop them.

Another suggestion is that the Elder Gods were the original creators of the Universe and into its fabric they wove much pain and suffering, which is experienced on countless worlds, including Earth. The Great Old Ones therefore plan to destroy the Cosmos and remake it in a much better form. Again, the Elder Gods may actually be known as the Antarctic Elder Things who have been imprisoned on Earth by the Great Old Ones for unspecified reasons.

Lastly, it is suggested that although the Elder Gods do exist, they are little different from the Great Old Ones and their ultimate intentions (to clear the Earth of human beings) is basically the same. Although they oppose the Great Old Ones, it is not out of any altruistic motive to protect Mankind or make the Universe a better place—it is simply a power struggle.

The portrait that emerges of the Elder Gods is therefore both confusing and contradictory. They become entwined with the Great Old Ones, as well as with other beings, which have allegedly come to Earth. However, even today, their exact nature and purpose here remain largely shrouded in mystery.

The Elder Things

These beings are also referred to as the Primordial Old Ones and refer to another type of intergalactic being that came to Earth sometime in the dim and distant past. They contain elements of both the animal and vegetable kingdoms and arrived here by flying through the "interplanetary aether," possibly from the worlds of Uranus or Neptune (or one of their moons). Physically, they resemble an immense cone or cylinder, sprouting a large starfish-shaped head with five distinct points. One tapering end has a huge eye that rests there. The creature has a number of appendages with another eye at the end of each one and a set of cilia, which enables the being to sense its surroundings without the aid of light. It also has five feeding tubes, each topped with a mouth and five retractable wings that gather around its middle like a skirt. The Elder Things prefer to live underwater if they can, but they can also live on land or in the air.

They came here in the Earth's infancy, showering the upper atmosphere of the young planet with their seeds (which is their main method of regeneration and how they conquered many other worlds) and proceeded to build a massive city at the South Pole. Daniel Harms marks them as the creators of Ubbo-Sathla, which he claims is the source of all Earthly life; a race known as the shuggoths (a servitor species); and of initiating the genetic experiments from which humans sprang.

As they spread across the globe, they created huge buildings of spectacular construction—many displaying the five points of their own anatomy. Their writing was based on their anatomical configuration, a system of dots and circles along five radii, and their five-pointed coinage was made of green soapstone. Their religion simply consisted of worshipping the DNA helix, which they viewed as the source of all life, although it's believed that they also feared an unknown entity lurking on the moon of Neptune or on the moon Charon, orbiting Pluto.

In order to conquer the Earth, they fought against a number of other space-born races, including the Great Old Ones and the Great Race of Yith. Their shuggoth servitors also rebelled against them and, although the insurrection was put down, the Elder Things were so decimated by the conflict that they were forced to abandon many of their great cities that were left to decay. However, as the Ice Age began to creep across the world, the Elder Things took measures to save themselves. They withdrew from the Earth's surface and traveled to a great lake of fire, which they had discovered deep underground near the South Pole. There they constructed another mighty city and continue to live there largely undetected until the present time. However, several scientific expeditions to the Pole site encounters with them noting a loss of sanity to some of their members.

Recent scientific experimentation with telepathy and telekinesis have shown that some subjects display significant abilities in these areas. This has led to the suggestion that the Elder Things have specifically "programmed" certain types of individuals to have particular ability in these fields and may be part of a master plan to control the world. What the purpose of this might be is only speculative, but it may have something to do with a conflict against the Great Old Ones.

The Great Race of Yith

In order to confuse and confound matters even further, reference has been made by Lovecraft, Derleth, Walter DeBill, and others to the Great Race of Yith. Unlike the Great Old Ones and the Elder Gods, the Great Race of Yith do not have a true physical form, but can inhabit whatever bodies they desire.

Although usually referred to as the Great Race of Yith, the species did not originate there. Yith is a planet circling the star Ogntlach, supposedly in the Constellation of the Great Fish. There is a great dispute among Lovecraftian scholars as to where exactly this world might lie—some say that it orbits on the other side of the galaxy, others in intergalactic space or in another galaxy, and some have even put it just beyond the orbit of Pluto. Despite being some way from its sun, Yith's seas are geothermally heated and were at one time home to a semi-intelligent amphibious race that the Great Race took over. They used this species to build metal receptacles for their minds. They built vast laboratories on the planet and began to develop a wormhole technology there to enable them to spread out across the Universe. Using this technology they eventually reached Earth.

Our planet became inhabited by huge cone-like creatures, the minds of which the Great Race immediately took over. At the time of their arrival here, Yith had been invaded by a species known as the Flying Polyps, which had come from the second world of the Yithian system. Details of this species are extremely hazy, but it is thought that they possess the power to make themselves invisible, leaving only five-toed tracks to mark their presence. They also control the elements in a way that is not fully understood, but which may be related to their special relationship with the Zarrians (an amphibious race from a world near the galaxy's core). The Flying Polyps also used the wormhole technology to pursue the Great Race to Earth and began to prey on the conical beings. The Great Race defeated them and confined them to a series of underground caverns far beneath the Earth. Although there have been periodic attempts to escape this prison the Great Race have managed to keep the Polyps there.

Following the defeat of the Flying Polyps, the Great Race began building great cities of immensely high buildings all across the face of the planet. Many of these buildings were used for research, for the Great Race had an insatiable curiosity about the worlds they had conquered. Their advanced minds began to make the possibility of mental time-travel a reality. Eventually, they were able to cast their minds back into the past, but were physically unable to interact with anything they found there. The future proved a slightly difficult outcome. By projecting their minds far into the future, scholars of the Great Race found that they could sometimes take over the minds of the individuals who dwelt there. This opened up a possibility of intense scientific observation for the naturally curious species. The Great Race began a grouping known as the Motion, which was aimed at helping travelers to a particular time assimilate into that period. The Tower of Babel, for instance, was a project in building some sort of guiding beacon using enslaved minds to construct it. This project singularly and spectacularly failed, resulting in mental confusion across the world.

In the past, however, the Flying Polyps managed to escape their prison and defeated their captors. In desperation, the Great Race sent the minds of its brightest scientists and thinkers through time and space in an attempt to preserve their species. Some of them dwelt on a moon of Jupiter and from there to a dark star in the constellation of Taurus where they inhabited a species very similar to our own. From there, they have traveled to Earth again many millennia in the future where they take up the hive-mind of the race that now dwells here. Fleeing a global catastrophe, they will then take over the minds of a vegetable species dwelling on the planet Mercury. From there they will return to our own world becoming known as Dark Ghosts, incapable of taking any physical form of their own.

The theme of the Great Race of Yith has been taken up by several writers other than Lovecraft, Walter DeBill, Denis Detwiller, and David Conyers to name a few. They each added and expanded on the original theme. And who is to say that they are incorrect in stating that ancient aliens, somehow disguised as members of our own species, are moving and working among us—covertly observing us for their own obscure purposes.

Of course, this is all fiction created by Lovecraft and others to astound and terrify, but might there be a *germ* of truth in any of this? Could *something* or even *some things* have come from beyond the stars and settled on our world, covertly and subtly shaping our history and even our current perceptions? It is an idea that has intrigued many and formed the basis of much writing.

Strangers From the Stars

According to some, the idea of visitations from the stars in the distant past is nothing new. Since the very earliest times, men and women have looked at the points of light twinkling in the night sky and wondered if other beings—whether supernatural or human—might dwell up there among the aethers.

In early mythologies (religious or otherwise) there are myriad stories of celestial beings descending to earth from the skies. Indeed, *Sulam Yaakov* (Jacob's Ladder), mentioned in the book of Genesis and other religious texts, speaks of angels moving up and down a column of light that ascended into Heaven. Some have translated this to mean some sort of transportation device from a spaceship or interplanetary vehicle and the "angels" as celestial travelers. The 12th-century chronicler John of Naunton records a strange cloud appearing over a village in what is now Gloucestershire and sending down long beams of light. He says many men saw angels among the light and assumed that it was the Second Coming. Of course, this could be just a peculiar cloud formation coupled with a "trick of the light" or optical illusion, but the notion of beings from outside the normal spheres of existence loomed in the popular mind. But as Lovecraft suggests, have beings from the depths of space actually visited us in the past?

The idea of vaguely humanoid (or indeed non-humanoid) beings descending from the heavens on a ladder is not confined to Jewish, Islamic, and Christian traditions. According to Bon (the religion that flourished in Tibet before Buddhism), the first king of the country, Nyatri Tsenpo descended from the heavens on a golden rope onto the top of Yalashangbo, a dome-shaped mountain in northwest Tibet. When he arrived he was venerated as both god and king and ordered that a great palace be built for him—this would become the Yumbulagang Monastery above the Yarlung Valley, which is supposed to be one of the oldest (if not *the* oldest) building in Tibet. He would also found the so-called Yarlung Dynasty. The monarch had certain physical peculiarities that differentiated him from other humans. For example, his hands and feet were webbed and his eyelids closed from the bottom rather than the top. According to legend, his skin was a slightly different color, almost green, and he had features that resembled gills on both sides of his neck. It is also said that he did not sleep. All these things combined made Tibetans believe that he was a god and worthy of being their king. Nyatri Tsenpo was also immortal and, when he decided that he had reigned for long enough, he returned to the mountain where he had first appeared and climbed up into the Heavens once more on the same golden rope that had brought him to Earth. And it appears that he was not the only one of his kind, for the 28th king of the Yarlung Dynasty, Lha Thothori Nayantsen (the prefix *Lha* denotes that he was a sky god), who ruled in the late 600s, is also descended by a golden rope and bore a number of characteristics, similar to the first monarch. Is it possible that both these beings were from the same species and that they both came from somewhere in space? It is certainly an intriguing mystery, but the idea of celestial visitors goes back in time even further.

Writer Robert K. Temple has written numerous books and several articles for *Time-Life*, mainly on Chinese culture and history. However, his most controversial book, *The Sirius Mystery* (1976), looks at an African people in northwestern Mali called the Dogon. It is Temple's belief that this tribe was visited by ancient astronauts around 5,000 years ago and an account of this visitation has been preserved. He quotes various pieces of evidence from Dogon mythology and tradition, including some astronomical data, which they could not have acquired otherwise. The most puzzling piece of evidence is that the tribe knew about a star, Sirius B, which is an invisible companion to the star Sirius A. Basing some of his work on that of the ethnographers Marcel Griaule and Germaine Dieterlen, Temple draws similarities between Dogon mythology and that of ancient Egypt and Sumer. He concludes that they probably all come from contact with extraterrestrial beings, which explains the Dogon's knowledge of the heavens. The notion has been criticized by many scholars who point out flaws in the work. They state that the Dogon could have obtained such knowledge through contact with Europeans and others. They state that the Dogon tribe may have been hoodwinking the investigator with false traditions and stories. Nevertheless, many of Temple's followers continue to maintain that very early extraterrestrial contact remains the only feasible explanation.

The connection between the supernatural and extraterrestrial visitations (such linkage is evident in many of Lovecraft's tales) was a common one in ancient times. Early men interpreted such visitations as the intervention of gods or lesser cosmic beings. The sacred Hindu writings tell of the gods and their avatars traveling in miraculous flying cars or flying houses, known as Vimanas. One such text is the Ramayana, a sacred Sanskrit epic attributed to the Hindu sage Valmiki. It formed an important part of Hindu teaching, particularly in places such as Nepal and Sikkim. It portrays the ideal world with ideal individuals living within it and was written about the fifth or fourth centuries B.C. Book 6 Canto CXXIII (*The Magic Car*) states:

Is not the wond'rous chariot mine,
Named Pushpak wrought by hands divine
This chariot, kept with utmost care,
Will waft thee through the fields of air,
And thou shalt light, unwearied down,
In fair Ayodhya's royal town.

Some adherents of ancient celestial visitation, such as Erich von Däniken, have suggested (in his popular book *Chariots of the Gods*) that these were some forms of advanced flying vehicles used by spacemen from beyond our world. He mentions a quotation from another sacred Nepalese work, the *Mahabharata*, which states that Bhima flew in his Vimana (translated as "chariot") along a ray of light, which was as bright as the sun and made a noise like thunder. This once again is cited by von Däniken as something like a force or travel beam, which may have guided the flying vehicles.

Of course, it is not only in ancient Hindu scriptures that we find supposed reference to early visitors from the stars. Both Jewish and Christian traditions refer to supernatural celestial beings that have come to Earth and interacted with Mankind. As noted previously, the book of Genesis makes several references to the "sons of God," who mated with the daughters of Men, producing the Nephilim. The apocryphal *Book of Enoch* expands on the story, stating the "sons of God" were the Watchers: angels whom God sent to guard Mankind. Enoch describes them as a force of roughly 200 angels who disobeyed God's wishes and descended to Earth to meet with human females. They taught the humans many "secrets" including astronomy, metalworking, cosmetics, and sorcery. Fragments of *The Second Book of Noah* mention the Watchers and state that they had been cast out of Heaven and were looking for somewhere to settle. Men granted them a place in return for learning from them, including expertise in growing crops. (It is said that the Watchers first taught men how to grow vines and introduced them to wine.) This has led some to think that the "Watchers" were actually renegades from the stars who had been cast out of their homeworld and were looking for somewhere to settle. They established themselves on Earth and began to help Mankind flourish and develop along certain lines. This idea of interstellar fugitives might have appealed to Lovecraft, as he often portrays his "visitors" as fleeing from something else. It has been argued by UFOlogists such as Chuck Missler and Mark Eastman that the Watchers may have been here to observe the rise of humanity and they somehow got involved in it. The cross-breeding of the genetic species resulted in the rise of a race of monsters—the Nephilim—which finally had to be destroyed by manipulating planetary weather systems and producing the Great

Flood. The ancient Biblical texts seem to endorse at least part of this theory by making a distinction between the line of Seth (who was the son God gave Adam and Eve to replace Abel) and the line of Cain, which appears to evolve into something rather separate. Missler has argued that the "orthodox angel" is of the general line of Seth, who was not spared the Flood.

According to Von Däniken, another section of humanity may have been destroyed by something resembling atomic weapons. This occurs in Genesis 19 with the destruction of Sodom and Gomorrah. Two "angels" visit the holy man Lot and his family and tell them they are to be spared. Von Däniken argued that these are not supernatural beings, but interplanetary travelers who spare Lot and his offspring (his wife is destroyed because she turns back) for some unknown purpose.

The book of Genesis and other early Apocryphal texts apart, the first chapter of the book of Ezekiel also creates something of a mystery. Here, the prophet experiences a "vision" in which he sees an immense and fearsome cloud that emits light. "The center of the fire," he says, "looked like glowing metal, and in the fire was what looked like four living creatures." These creatures were described as being humanoid with wings that sped back and forth "like flashes of lightning." They seemed to be within some sort of vehicle that Ezekiel describes as being "a wheel intersecting a wheel." Various shining metallic-looking objects moved around them and the winged beings moved with these objects. "When the living creatures moved, the wheels beside them moved; and when the living creatures rose from the ground, the wheels also rose."

The prophet interprets this as a vision granted to him by God, but von Däniken and others place a different meaning on it. What Ezekiel has seen, they suggest, is some form of spaceship taking off, and this proves that celestial beings were active on Earth. The theory was backed up by Josef F. Blumrich in his book *The Spaceships of Ezekiel* (1974). An engineer and designer at NASA, Blumrich became interested in the descriptions of Ezekiel's "vehicle," which the winged humanoids appeared to operate, and wondered if it could be some sort of advanced design for an interstellar craft. If so, could he design something similar? The book he produced provides details, schematics, and designs for a workable spaceship built along the lines of the Ezekiel story. The book was, of course, rubbished by church groups and others who claimed that Blumrich had manipulated some of the Biblical quotations in order to suit his own purposes. Even so, the text and designs remain intriguing ones and well worthy of study.

Still looking at both Jewish and Biblical evidence other scholars have suggested that some of the events in the ancient texts of both Judaism and Christianity might boil down to alien intervention. For example, writers such as Robert Steinman have suggested that Joshua's destruction of the walls of Jericho might be due to the influence of an extraterrestrial sonic weapon that aided the Israelites. It is also suggested that the Ark of the Covenant may have contained something that was of alien origin (whether technological or otherwise), which was venerated by the ancient Israelites. These, of course, are simply speculations.

Besides the main Judeo-Christian tradition, other cultures also carry legends regarding beings who have come from "somewhere else" to settle on Earth and teach those around them. Similar to the Tibetan story of Nyatri Tsenpo, the ancient Sumerians believed that a being named Oannes descended from the Heavens and brought philosophy and various crafts to Earth. Oannes is described by the Babylonian chronicler Borossus as having the outward appearance of a fish but underneath that of a man. It was thought that he could not live for long outside a watery environment, so he dwelled in the Persian Gulf, rising out of the waters from time to time to interact with those who came to see him and teaching them the basis of writing, the arts, and certain sciences, such as agriculture and metalwork. What eventually became of him is unknown. Historians have connected him with a form of the Babylonian god Ea, or with Adapta, the first king of Eridu. The story was dismissed simply as myth, but more recently cosmologists such as the late Carl Sagan and Josif Shklovsky have suggested that the stories be taken seriously and investigated for evidence of early alien contact.

Arising out of what some have described as a pseudo-scientific approach, a wave of literature appeared linking ancient civilizations with alien encounters. One of the foremost exponents of the idea is Zecharia Sitchin, an Azerbaijani-born writer who sought to explain the development of human culture through the intervention of alien beings. He produced a series of eight books together with a number of companion books known as *The Earth Chronicles* stating that aliens were mostly responsible for the rise of the Sumerian civilization in Mesopotamia around the 4th millennium B.C. His first book, *The 12th Planet*, published in 1976, which was immensely popular and is still in print, postulated that aliens had come to Earth from a planet named Niburu primarily to mine raw materials such as gold, which did not exist on their world. Niburu was supposedly an undiscovered planet on the outer reaches of our Solar System and its inhabitants were known as the Anunnaki (the name was originally given to a group of Sumerian gods who were supposed to have descended to Earth). He used this theory to explain certain megalithic sites across the world, which he claimed had been raised by the aliens. As his books became more and more popular, Sitchin's claims became ever wilder. He drew on the Oannes story, claiming that this was the result of an early experiment in genetics by the Anunnaki, who went on to create a proto-human being (the creation of Adam). His theories have all been debunked. Modern astronomy has completely ruled out any possibility of a planet anywhere near the position that Sitchin described, and has described his "solar history" as "fanciful rubbish." Serious Babylonian scholars have dismissed his account of early Sumerian history and religion as being entirely fictitious, and state that he made up an entire Sumerian mythology in order to sell his books.

Further evidence for the activity of ancient aliens derives from certain unexplained megaliths that still exist today. Lovecraft and many other Mythos writers enthusiastically embraced this concept and speak of "cyclopean" megalithic ruins deep in the jungles or among the Arctic snows. Ancient monuments and megaliths, however, provide an intriguing and often mysterious look into the past. For example, the great stone heads on Easter Island speak of a vanished race of impossibly long-eared men; the technology required to raise the Egyptian pyramids at Giza; the intricate architecture of the "lost" Inca city of Machu-Picchu in Peru; or the construction and linear alignment of Stonehenge in England. All of these have both amazed and baffled scientists and engineers right down to the present day. Even the walls of certain Mycenaean cities during the so-called "Greek Dark Age" defy engineering explanation and this has been used by certain writers to suggest the use of alien technology and techniques. Other UFOlogists have mentioned strange glyphs in out-of-the-way places such as the Wondjina rock paintings in Australia or the celebrated Nazca Lines etched into the geography of the Nazca Desert in Southern Peru. These were not really discovered until the 1930s when aeroplanes panning over saw gigantic figures carved into the earth below, comprising stylised geometric forms, depictions of animals and birds, and at least one human figure. It has been argued that such work was far in advance of the local Nazca people of the area and that these have been done by aliens using powerful technology. It has even been suggested that these were used as the landing coordinates for spacecraft in some ancient time. This places the Nazca Lines on par with some of the other ancient megaliths mentioned previously. But of course there is little evidence for any of this. Ancient man may have been more resourceful and much more skilled than we imagine, and these are simply the results of early thinking and invention by civilizations that have come and gone. Lovecraft and others state that many of the "Cyclopean cities" perished with Atlantis, Hyperborea, and Mu, and now lie beneath the waters of the ocean or sheathed in snow and ice at the Poles. And because such visitations/invasions occurred millions of years ago, all trace of them and what they achieved may have vanished and we have no way of knowing about them. But did the concept of some of Lovecraft's beings simply have their origins in the idea of visitors from the stars or was there, perhaps, another source for such entities?

Mystery Religions

In many of the Mythos stories, much of the menace can come from some form of clandestine or specialized cult, which worships some ancient god. The worship of such deity has probably existed from time immemorial and has percolated in various forms to the present day. Layer upon layer of mystery and ritual surround many of these groups, and their nature and function has often become more and more complex. Furthermore, writers add their own perspectives to the Mythos. But did such cults (or anything like them) exist anywhere in ancient history?

Possibly the nearest grouping that resembles Lovecraft's "degenerate cults" is that of the Greco-Roman "mystery religions" in the first through fourth. The description "mystery" derives from the Latin *mysterium* and from the Greek *mysterion* meaning "secret or hidden." Unlike some of the more common religions—say, for example, early Christianity—admittance to such congregations was not by simple declaration or "profession," but through *initiation*, which could involve complicated procedures and rituals. An individual who gained such admittance was usually described as a *mystes* or mystic (from the word *myein* meaning to close or shut—particularly with regard to the mouth and eyes—and signifying secrecy) and was usually bound by an oath of secrecy.

It should not be thought, however, that the Mystery Religions were an alternative to the more formalized types of religion. Certainly some of the worship involved local gods and, as such was opposed to the mainstream religions, but in the main the Mystery Religions acted as a *supplement* to mainstream beliefs and often offered new interpretations and perceptions regarding them and concerning the world in general. Indeed, certain elements in mainstream worship may even have been assimilated from the Mystery Religions. However, many of these religions did lie outside the mainstream and, because of their intense secrecy about initiation and practice, both were viewed with distrust and suspicion by the more formal faiths. In fact, the Religions of the Late Antiquity (around the 4th century) were heavily persecuted by the now-Christianised Roman Empire. This did not destroy them, but only served to drive them further underground, making them even more clandestine in their ways and worship.

The most famous of all the Religions was probably the Eleusinian Mysteries, which involved worship of the goddess Demeter and her daughter Persephone in the Greek city of Eleusis. Initiation ceremonies were held every year in the city, amid great secrecy. The Mysteries were said to be extremely old, even pre-dating the Greek Dark Age (roughly 1,200–800 B.C.). They were probably the last vestiges of an old agricultural cult (Demeter was the Greek goddess of agriculture and fertility) and may have been used to explain the difference between summer and winter. (Persephone was carried off into the underworld causing the earth to freeze and no vegetation to grow—Zeus revoked this and allowed her to remain on earth for six months of the year, when vegetation would return.) Little is known about these Mysteries since they were not written down, and no Scriptures concerning them survive. However, it is known that in Eleusis, the religion held a huge sacred box that resembled the Ark of the Covenant. Some scholars have argued that this was a massive chest (*kyste*) very much in the style of the Ark, while others have suggested it was a smaller lidded-box (*kalathos*), which was held by the priests. Only the initiates knew what either of these two receptacles contained, and any knowledge of the contents has been lost to history.

The Eleusinian Mysteries were thought to be far older than the city states of Greece. In fact, they supposedly went back to Bronze Age Greece (1900–1100 B.C.).

Some scholars have even identified them with early religions in the Minoan civilisation, which had been influenced by some of the beliefs of the early Near East. Their purpose was to "elevate man above the human sphere into the Divine and to assure his redemption by making him a god and so conferring immortality upon him." This, it has to be stated, was also the purpose of many of the Mystery Religions, for example, the cults of both Isis and Osiris in Egypt. In other words, the real purpose of the ancient Mystery Religion was to give the initiate a greater knowledge and understanding of his or her god and how to be more like that celestial being.

The Mystery Religions usually fell into three categories: those influenced by the formal Hellenistic religions; an imperial cult (who may have worshipped either an individual ruler or a dynasty of rulers as gods); or an ethnic or civil religion particular to a specific area. All of them flourished in the Mediterranean sphere of influence and many were open to all.

Eventually, the Catholic Church condemned those congregations. Christians alleged all sorts of terrible things against the religions—that they ate children and practiced homosexuality and that they practiced bestiality at their gatherings. In his *Apology*, the second century Churchman, Justin Martyr, described them as "demonic imitations of the true faith" and that "devils in imitation of what was said by Moses, asserted that Persephone was the daughter of Jupiter and instigated the people to set up an image of her under the name of *Kore.*"

The Mystery Religions were only the most well known of the pagan continuances into the developing ancient world, but they were not the only forms of worship lying outside the mainstream religions of the time. In other parts of Europe and the Near and Middle East, the cults of local deities persisted. Some modified themselves as new religions and began to spread into their homelands, but basically retained much of their traditions. They worshipped a variety of gods and goddesses in a variety of ways—some involving sacrifice, others not. The objects of their worship adopted a wide variety of guises, from idols to standing stone to sacred animals, all seemingly deserving of their followers veneration. Particularly during the period of the Late Antiquity, as Christian persecution became more pronounced, these congregations met in out-of-the-way places dotted across Europe, ranging from secret temples hidden away in the hills to open air worship and wells, stones and rivers, all away from prying eyes. With his wide reading on esoteric Oriental and classical subjects, Lovecraft may have known of the Mystery Religions, and their secretive nature and ritual may have appealed to him. Small wonder then, he created such religions for himself, equating them with old gods and survivals from near-forgotten times. The beings that he created now form a kind of pantheon, which lies at the very center of the Mythos. But exactly who or what *are* these beings and from where did the idea for them come? Where did Lovecraft and other Mythos writers derive their ideas? Perhaps we should take a slightly closer look at some of them and try to find out.

SHADOWS BEYOND THE STARS

CTHULHU

"PH'NGLUI MGLW'NAFH CTHULHU R'LYEH WGAH'NAGL FHTAGN."
("IN HIS HOUSE AT R'LYEH, DEAD CTHULHU WAITS DREAMING.")

One of the most famous phrases in Lovecraftian fiction, the former quote marks the Being that has given the entire Mythos its name. The phrase is written in a strange, possibly pre-human language, and appears in Lovecraft's *Call of Cthulhu*, which was written in 1926 but not published in *Weird Tales* until 1928. It has been repeated in many other Mythos tales and by many other writers. It contains many of the themes of Mythos fiction: the occult invocation, the ancient deity (one of the Great Old Ones), and the sunken or lost city/land. It also gives a sense of monstrous foreboding, which is one of the features of the Mythos.

As with a number of Lovecraft's creatures, the physical description of the entity is sometimes slightly vague. It appeared to be human in form, but had bat-wings and claws with a huge octopoidal head. Other accounts simply describe it as a mass of gigantic and writhing tentacles with a number of fanged beaks and many massive burning eyes, some of which seem to be in at least three sections. Robert M. Price has claimed that the Kraken was the main inspiration for the entity. A poem called *The Kraken* was written by Alfred Lord Tennyson around 1830, which spoke of a huge and slumbering leviathan lying on the ocean floor and waiting to be summoned. In order to devastate Mankind, suggests Price, this might have been the being behind Cthulhu. The Kraken was, of course, not a god—although in early Scandinavian mythology there were only two of them in the world—and perhaps in Lovecraft's initial conception neither was Cthulhu, but It later began to assume almost god-like qualities.

Although it is known that the Being is one of the Great Old Ones, the exact nature of Its origins is both fragmentary and unclear. It is thought, however, that It came into being on the planet Voorhl, somewhere deep in the 23rd nebula. At some point in Its existence, It traveled to the green double star Xoth, where on a frozen world It mated with another being named Idh-yaa. Together, they produced several of the Great Old Ones, such as Ghatanothoa, Ytogtha, and Zoth-Ommog. From Xoth, Cthulhu migrated to Saturn with Its children, and from there they all descended to Earth.

Similar to many of the other Great Old Ones they set about establishing a colony here and settled on an unnamed continent on which they built a massive black stone city named R'lyeh. They were not the first extraterrestrial creatures to arrive here, however, for the Elder Things had been on Earth for countless millennia before them. A war erupted between the two species in which Cthulhu and Its offspring destroyed the cities of the Elder Things. They were aided by another species known as the Star Spawn, which may have descended from Cthulhu. The Star Spawn is now Cthulhu's servitors and lie dreaming in R'lyeh with It. The conflict between Cthulhu and the Elder Things continued for a number of centuries before a truce was finally declared and each species agreed not to interfere in the affairs of the other.

In the dim and distant past some sort of catastrophe occurred on Earth. Whether it was a massive earthquake caused by a certain alignment of stars, effects of a great war with the Elder Gods, or a result of a secret weapon created by the Elder Things, the continent on which R'lyeh stood suddenly broke apart and sank. By this time, however, Cthulhu and Its minions had entered a period of hibernation, and were unaffected by the cataclysm. Today, R'lyeh is said to lie somewhere beneath the south-western Pacific Ocean, although some place it near Ponape or near the coast of Massachusetts. While it lay beneath the ocean, uncounted aeons passed and Mankind evolved. The deepness of the gulf in which R'lyeh lies has blocked off most of the telepathic signals from the Great Old Ones who remain there, and so much of the communication with the hibernating entities occurs only in dreams. From time to time, however, undersea earthquakes will throw portions of the monstrous city to the surface, although it does not seem to remain there for long before disappearing beneath the waves once again. However, it is said that "when the stars are right" it will rise once more in its full majestic glory as the world as we know it comes to an end, and Cthulhu will reawaken.

In some of these upheavals, however, Its tomb has re-emerged above the waters, Cthulhu has stirred, and Its influence in the world has become slightly more pronounced. This causes some excitement in variations of Its cult, which exists across the world. Through dream communication Cthulhu (although It theoretically lies dormant) had managed to recruit a series of followers who have come together in various countries to worship their Master and to hear Its words and further Its aims. It has even been suggested that some of these followers may exist in the highest echelons of world government and are simply waiting for a sign to bring about the Final Apocalypse.

Much research in the field of Cthulhu cults was done by Professor George Gammell Angell, a senior scholar in Semitic Languages at Brown University. Professor Angell was an expert in ancient inscriptions and was frequently consulted by Universities and museums from all around the world.

However, he passed away at the age of 92, so his great-nephew Francis Wayland Thurston brought the notion of Cthulhu to a wider world. Among the artifacts is a curious box stuffed with papers—disjointed notes, ramblings, and jottings—and also a peculiar bas-relief clay figurine, which is supposedly a representation of Cthulhu. At the time of his death, Angell was supposedly investigating the worship of the being and was coming up with some strange and terrifying results. Thurston's own investigation into the box also uncovered a number of references to instances of the being's cults in America and in other parts of the world. The origin of the Cthulhu cult is said to be somewhere in the Arabian Desert, possibly Irem, City of the Pillars, once visited by Abdul Alhazred. Here, there was a Black Temple built by the djinn.

However, cults existed far beyond Arabia. In some of the southern islands the Polynesians told the story of the squid-god Kana-loa who was confined to an underwater prison by the great god Miki-Miki. It's said that when enough followers gather on a certain island and call upon Kana-loa, he will rise again and the seas will overwhelm the land. And something strange lies off the coast of County Kerry, Ireland, along Ballyheague Strand near the church at Ardfert. It is said that this strange something that still waits out there in the sunken town of Kilstaveen, an evil place that slid into the ocean. Although several descriptions are given for the Thing that dwells under the sea it is thought to be vaguely octopoidal in form, similar to Cthulhu. From time to time several of its servitors come ashore robed and shrouded, and anyone who sees their faces beneath their veils is driven instantly mad. It is said that the ocean deity is still worshipped by those who escaped the destruction of Kilstaveen.

Similarly, in the remote Cemetery Bayou in Assumption Parish in Louisiana, the top of what appears to be a mausoleum rises above the bayou waters. This is supposedly the burying ground of the now-lost Church of St. John the Benevolent, which was flooded as various waterways were cut through the Parish. *Something* that was found out in the swamps is interred there and lies within the walls of the drowned mausoleum, though what it is remains unclear. All these ancient fables may have contributed in some way to the idea of Cthulhu in sunken R'lyeh.

Cthulhu occupies an important part in the Mythos and is mentioned more frequently than any other being. This may be because his rising is thought to foreshadow the general coming of the Great Old Ones.

As with many other Mythos entities, the exact nature of Cthulhu is a confused one and has been changed and altered by a multitude of writers. Some say that Cthulhu does not exist as an entity at all, but rather as a manifestation of other beings. For example, Daniel Harms stated that Cthulhu may be nothing more than an emanation of Yog-Sothoth. Others argue that It is an avatar of Nyarlathotep. This idea is allegedly taken from the *Sussex Manuscripts,* which are a set of fragmented tablets that bear a striking resemblance to the *G'harne Fragments.* Others still try to connect the entity to the Aztec god Huitzilpochtli, although the two entities do not resemble each other in any way. With regard to the worship of Cthulhu there are certain texts that may guide the votary both in the appearance of the creature and the proper nature of its worship.

The R'lyeh Text and the Ponape Scriptures

In the world of forbidden books, the *R'lyeh Text* is extremely old. The Text was originally written on tablets of black stone, which came from the sunken city and were widely known as "The Black Tablets of R'lyeh." They are said to be Hyperborean in origin, but many have suggested that they are far older than that. The text is written in characters that resemble Chinese, but are of an older pre-human tongue. Curiously, a fragment of it was supposedly translated into Chinese using slightly similar characters.

The Chinese translation is, of course, not the only attempt at interpreting these texts. In the course of its existence the *R'lyeh Text* has traveled through Babylon and Greece where translations were made. There is also supposedly a Latin translation that dates from around A.D. 150. A Greek translation also exists in and is thought to be in a private collection. A German translation was transcribed in the 18th century and entitled *Liyuhh*. It was privately printed at the end of the century and again at the beginning of the 19th century, but it is unclear as to how many copies were actually printed and what became of them.

Lastly, an English version was translated by John Wilmot, 2nd Earl of Rochester (1647–1680). Wilmot was a notorious libertine and in his time was something of a poet, who was allegedly associated with witchcraft and sorcery. Because his book was privately published, nothing further is known about it and no copies appear to be in circulation.

Much of what we know regarding the *Text* (and indeed regarding Cthulhu Itself) comes from the work of Harold Hadley Copeland and Professor Laban Shrewsbury. Copeland was a leading anthropologist who had graduated from Miskatonic University in 1881. After graduating, he traveled to a number of areas in the Pacific, subsequently publishing a series on Polynesian culture. His first scholarly work, *Prehistory in the Pacific: A Preliminary Investigation with References to the Myth-Patterns of South East Asia,* was published in 1902, and was incredibly well received.

The success of the work inspired Copeland to delve into the more obscure myths of the Pacific region. His next book, *Polynesian Mythology with a Note on the Cthulhu Legend-Cycle,* published in 1906, showed the first stirrings of what was to become a dangerous obsession with Copeland—a probing into the notion of an ancient species. In the work, he made references to the obscure *R'lyeh Text*, which raised certain questions regarding his sources and his sanity. Although still considered to be a major contribution to the field of anthropology, the new book was not greeted so warmly in academic circles as the first. However, Copeland threw himself into his work and now turned his attention to the translation of a text known as the *Ponape Scriptures*, which came into his possession. A translation appeared in 1907 mainly to academic disdain.

Copeland published two other questionable works after that—*The Ponape Figurine* (1910) and *The Prehistoric Pacific in Light of the Ponape Scripture* (1911). Both of these abandoned much-recognized academic research and were almost hysterical in their tone. The first dealt with a mysterious statuette that Copeland had come across; he connected it with a hideous veneration, which he claimed was carried on in the lost continent of Mu. He made reference to queer ruins, which he stated were on several remote Pacific islands. Other anthropologists agreed that, although the ruins were intriguing, they seemed to be entirely consistent with early Pacific cultures. Copeland also quoted extensively from the *Ponape Scriptures*, which had been brought from the South Seas by Captain Abner Ezekiel Hoag. *The Prehistoric Pacific* was widely derided in academic circles, and subsequently Copeland was forced to step down from the Presidency of the Pacific Area Archaeological Association.

In the end, Copeland decided to set off with his companion and academic colleague James Ellington for Central Asia in 1913. His destination was a series of mountains beyond the Plateau of Tsang where Copeland declared that survivors from Mu were still living. The expedition was an unmitigated disaster. Ellington died within the first few weeks, most of the group's bearers deserted and took many of the supplies with them, and Copeland himself disappeared. He turned up again three months later in Mongolia with his mind more or less gone. He raved about the things that he'd seen in those nightmarish mountains but, more importantly, he carried 10 stone tablets with him, which were carved in an unknown language. These, he claimed, were the words of a Muvian High Priest named Zanthu who had shown him many dreadful things. He returned to America where he lived pretty much in seclusion near Providence. Three years later, he moved to California and released yet another book, *Zanthu Tablets: A Conjectural Translation*. This was a large and rambling account that mentioned Cthulhu and detailed "abhorrent rites" in worship of that being. Much of what he wrote was similar to the *R'lyeh Text* and proved its authenticity. The book was largely dismissed by the academic world and readers alike. Shortly after, Copeland was admitted and confined to a San Francisco sanatorium where he later slit his throat with an open razor. For some months before he committed suicide, Copeland had been conducting a steady correspondence with Dr. Henry Blaine, who was the keeper of manuscripts and Curator at the Sanborne Institute for Pacific Antiquities in Santiago, California. Following his death, Blaine received a large package of Copeland's papers with the dead man's instructions that they should be published. It was while he was sorting these out and checking them for publication in 1928 that Blaine suffered a mental breakdown and had to be confined. When he died in a Santiago mental hospital the documents passed to his assistant Arthur Wilcox Hodgkins

Hodgkins studied Copeland's material, and then made a hurried and unexpected trip to Arkham. On his returned, he went back to the Institute where on March 26th, 1929, he allegedly murdered a night watchman, attempted to torch the gallery, and attempted to steal an artifact called "the Ponape Figurine." He was captured and committed to the same mental institution where his predecessor was detained pending a full investigation. He hanged himself before such an investigation could be carried out.

However, not all academics were dismissive of Harold Copeland's work. Laban Shrewsbury, on the other hand, was involved in anthropological studies in the South Seas and Asia relating to Cthulhu (as well as the *Celaeno Fragments*).

What did the *Text* say? The translations, even including those by Copeland and the references by Shrewsbury, are extremely uncertain and are not to be trusted. However, they seem to deal with both the nature and history of Cthulhu and the construction of the city of R'lyeh. There are also details of some rituals and worship, which were carried out in praise of Cthulhu. However, it is not clear as to which of these sections were added at a later date or which were added by the translators. It's speculated, for instance, that in his "translation," Copeland possibly added certain themes that he had heard in Asia and the South Seas.

It's also thought that while relying on the *R'lyeh Text* both these academics used part of another work in their studies, which was just as mysterious and abhorred. This was the *Ponape Scripture,* a text of uncertain age and origin brought back from a trading trip to the Carolines by Captain Abner Ezekiel Hoag in 1734. They were allegedly written on parchment made of dried palm leaves in what appeared to be human blood (or the blood of some human-like creature), and were bound using the wood and fibers of what seemed to be a long-extinct cycad. Hoag was unable to read what was written but claims that he had a manservant named Yogash on one of the islands who helped him to translate.

The *Scripture* was allegedly written by Imash-Mo, a priest of the god Ghatanothoa in the sunken land of Mu. The text dealt with the veneration of Cthulhu, but also of another ocean-being named Dagon. The book saw an extremely limited printing in the late 1730s, and was immediately opposed by many religious groups because of its references to Dagon, which was considered to be a "false god" in the Bible.

There was a second printing shortly after Hoag's death, which began to circulate in the occult circles of the time. Later, his granddaughter Beverly Hoag Adams published some of his written work in a volume entitled the *Ponape Scriptures*, which was abridged and riddled with errors. A handwritten edition, possibly translated by Hoag with help from Yogash, can still be found in the Kester Library in Salem, Massachusetts. Hoag reputedly bequeathed it to the library upon his death. Despite its dubious content, Miskatonic University published a version of a translation of the *Scripture* in 1907.

The document appears to be the work of a Cthulhu follower who was drawing others into the cult. It details the history of the lost continent of Mu and the deeds of several wizards there, including Zanthu. Several copies of the *Scripture* are known to exist and one may have been taken to the run-down coastal hamlet of Innsmouth where it influenced the establishment of the Esoteric Order of Dagon.

As for the idea of Dagon, the concept is a confusing one. Although a god of that name was worshipped by the Assyro-Babylonians, it was a god of grain and fertility rather than a sea-god. It later became a Semitic deity of the ancient Canaanites and the Amorites, and as such is referred to as the enemy of Yahweh, the centralizing God of the Old Testament.

The name first appears around 2,500 B.C. in records from the Tel Heriri region of Syria (the Mari Texts) and in the names of an Amorite trinity (the others being Ilu and Adad). It is possible, too, that some of these gods were the localized deities of certain cities and were known as *dingirs* in Babylonian cuneiform, denoting a lesser god or a supernatural figure, and Dagon may well have been one of these. He was certainly worshipped there in a massive temple complex known as E-Mul ("The House of the Star") and a sector of that ancient city was named after him.

Sometime during the 1st millennium B.C. the cults of Dagon seem to have grown in power and status. This may have been because of important patronage, some form of alleged supernatural occurrence associated with the entity, or a simple consolidation of sects and cults. By 1,400 B.C. he was one of the most significant gods in Syria with a massive and imposing temple at the ancient Syrian port of Ugarit. Although primarily still a god of grain and fertility, it's thought that his influence may have extended to the bounty of the sea, and hence the establishment of his temple at a major port.

The idea that Dagon may have been some sort of sea-being may have come from a misinterpretation of his name sometime in the 11th century. The Hebrew Biblical commentator Rabbi Schlomo Yitzhaki suggested that the name of the being may correspond to the ancient Hebrew word for "fish" and equated Dagon with the Babylonian fish-deity Oannes. This was the name given to a mythical fish-like being who had taught Mankind wisdom and was said to dwell in what is now the Persian Gulf. A number of other rabbis followed his example, interpreting an obscure passage in the first book of Samuel that Dagon had the body of a man but the tail of a fish.

The image took hold of the medieval Christian imagination. If Dagon was the enemy of God as the Old Testament suggested, then he must be a monster and a dangerous fiend who would destroy believing Christians if he could. And once again the motif of the fish-god took over, making Dagon a kind of sea-monster. And there were sea-monster aplenty in the early Biblical world with whom Dagon could be identified.

One of these was Tiamat, the "Mother of Dragons," a female Babylonian monster that resembled a massive serpent. Although no clear description of her exists, her name is referenced in the *Enuma Elish*, which seems to suggest that she is half-human and half serpent. She also apparently gave birth to many dragons and sea-going monsters. Some of these characteristics may have been transferred to the medieval idea of Dagon, which has filtered down to the present day.

Medieval Biblical scholars also sometimes equated Dagon with another Hebrew monster, Leviathan (whom Christians viewed as the alternate ego of the Devil). Early Sumerian writers were terrified of a seven-headed serpent. It was supposed to be an aspect or emanation of the god Lotan who slept in a palace under the sea and was closely associated with the ocean. In the book of Isaiah he is referred to as "the crooked serpent" who dwells in the sea, while the book of Job suggest that the Leviathan is more of an animal than a supernatural being.

Jewish texts such as those written by Rabbi Schlomo Yitzhaki describe Leviathan as a massive monster, living near the Sources of the Deep in the far oceans who will rise up against Yahweh and attempt to destroy Mankind together with the land-based monster Behemoth. Both will be ultimately destroyed by Yahweh and their carcasses will be picked over by humans.

In Christian writings, St. Thomas Aquinas firmly connected Leviathan with Satan, making the creature one of the Princes of Hell. The being was the very personification of envy and would lead God's people into sin. When sinners died, they were caught up and devoured by the Leviathan. Indeed, Leviathan may have been the prototype for Hellmouth, a monstrous tentacled demon that sometimes appeared on Protestant woodcuts during the Reformation with a gaping mouth into which the damned disappeared. In both Catholic and Protestant eyes, Leviathan was an enemy of God and one of the Four Crown Princes of Hell. In some Protestant teachings, however, particularly when studies were taken from the Old Testament, the ideas of Leviathan and Dagon became somewhat confused. The creatures became the last great symbols of paganism and were also identified with the god Zeus.

Although there have been many monsters in the ancient world, some of them have been linked with *aliens* and evil—similar to Cthulhu. Could such beings be commanded by their worshippers? Certainly beings such as Tiamat and Dagon might be summoned, and it was said that reputedly the most evil man in Icelandic history— Gottskálk grimmi Nikulásson (Gottskalk the Grim) had a book of runes that could summon the Kraken and bend it to the sorcerer's commands. It is said that he sent the creature against several sea-captains who had crossed him in some way, causing their deaths. It was thought, therefore, that priests and sorcerers could control these great ocean-going entities from time to time and use them in evil ways.

The short story *Dagon* was written by Lovecraft in 1917 and was one of the first recorded tales that he wrote as an adult. It was not published until 1919, however, in an issue of W. Paul Cook's *The Vagrant*. Cook had encouraged Lovecraft to write some amateur fiction for the magazine and he replied with two stories—*Dagon* and *The Tomb*. Lovecraft ascribed the tale to a dream he had experienced, although later critics said that he may have been more directly influenced by a story written by the American satirist Irvin Shrewsbury Cobb, entitled *Fishhead*, about a piscine human. They also speculated that he "borrowed" certain elements of the tale from Edgar Rice Burrows novel, *At the Earth's Core*, which appeared in 1914. He would use the motif of Dagon again, however, in his *The Shadow over Innsmouth* (1936) as detailed above.

Although bearing the name of an Assyrian-Babylonian fertility and harvest god, the worship of Cthulhu forms a significant part in the rituals of the Esoteric Order of Dagon. Reference to this cult appears in Lovecraft's novella *The Shadow over Innsmouth* written in 1931 (but not published until 1936), the themes of which have become one of the staples of Mythos fiction. The cult flourished in the early to mid-1920s in Innsmouth, Massachusetts. It is thought that the Order was founded by Captain Obed Marsh, a trader from the area who conducted much of his business in Polynesia and the South Seas. On returning from one of his trading ventures Captain Marsh arrived at Innsmouth "greatly changed" and bearing quantities of gold. He had been dealing with an island tribe who had amassed a great wealth through dealing with a race of fish beings—he received payment in return for human sacrifice.

Marsh continued to trade with the natives throughout the years, gradually becoming one of the most prosperous and influential man in Innsmouth. In 1838, he journeyed to the island once more to find that his business partners had been wiped out in an attack from another island and there was no more gold. The village went into decline and the people there turned on each other. They tried to develop their fishing industry but a number of families began to gradually drift away.

Soon after, Marsh began to follow a new religion that he claimed would be "the salvation of Innsmouth." The beliefs were partly based around the religion of the South Sea islanders and partly on Christian teachings. A significant element in it, however, was the relationship with the creatures with whom the Polynesians had dealt. Marsh claimed that these creatures also lurked off the coast of Massachusetts at a place known as Devil's Reef. He founded the Esoteric Order of Dagon in the village, stating that if the inhabitants worshipped the fish-god (Cthulhu) of these inhuman beings they would enjoy prosperity once more and their fishing nets would be full. Soon the Order grew and all churches in the locality had been forced to close down. Marsh's followers became almost a political force in Innsmouth, becoming both a church and a strong-arm fraternal organization as the Order spread its tentacles into almost every branch of local society. Innsmouth was swept by a virulent plague in 1846, which decimated much of the village's population and made Marsh the most prominent figure there, a position he held until his death in 1878. The Order, however, continued, blending Polynesian legends Middle-Eastern fertility beliefs and Holy Scripture.

Indeed, it became such a potent force in the area that it attracted the attention of the authorities. Notice of the Order's activities landed on the desk of the director of the FBI, J. Edgar Hoover. It is said that Hoover kept an extensive file on the activities of the Order and it was he who personally authorized FBI involvement when the Federal authorities raided Innsmouth in 1928. There were a number of arrests and a number of items seized, but no one was ever charged. The Order in Innsmouth, however, more or less disintegrated, although fragments of it may exist elsewhere along the New England coast and in other coastal regions.

One of the "items" supposedly seized by the authorities was a book called the *Codex Dagonensis*. Similar to other books of its kind—the *Codex Maleficium* and the *Codex Spitalsk*—this volume first appeared in Northern Germany around the year A.D. 400. Among the material found within it are certain complex rituals for the invocation of Cthulhu and a great deal of information on the Elder Sign. The original volume was brought to Innsmouth by Obed Marsh who used it in the rituals of the Esoteric Order. Some Mythos writers suggest that the book is consulted from time to time, under some special arrangement, by surviving members of the Order, which is no longer seen as a threat to National Security. But who were these ichthyic beings with whom the South Sea islanders and Obed Marsh had dealt?

The Deep Ones

From the descriptions that exist, the Deep Ones are fish-like humanoid beings that dwell in cities far beneath the surface of most oceans. It's reported that their faces *appear* human, but with bulging frog-like eyes and pronounced gills on either side of the head. They often have scales and webbed hands and feet. A description of them compares them to "human frogs." This sound tends to be more of a discordant croaking than any form of recognized language.

The Deep Ones (as they are known) are believed to be immortal and can only be killed by an act of violence. They believe that this immortality is conferred upon them either by Cthulhu, Mother Hydra, or Dagon. Indeed, Father Dagon and Mother Hydra may be the oldest of their species and are venerated as such. Even illness or starvation will not cause a Deep One to die, although it may diminish it in both size and power.

According to some speculation the Deep Ones may have arrived on Earth with Cthulhu and Its minions to act as servitors to them. Their natural home is an aquatic world circling a dim star in a dark galaxy far away. Although they were extremely primitive upon their arrival they developed and evolved through time and are now at the height of their powers. Others who have had contact with them, however, believe that they evolved on this planet and are, in fact, another species of Mankind.

Whatever their origin, they have built complex and fantastic cities out of stone and mother-of-pearl beneath the waves of nearly all the major oceans of the world.

These metropolises include Y'ha-nthlei, which lies off the coast of Massachusetts; Ahu-Y'hola, which is close to the coast of Cornwall in England; and G'll-hoo on the very edge of the Witch's Hole in the North Sea. There is some form of connection (perhaps telepathic) between these cities, and it is thought that in some instances the Deep Ones act as a sort of "hive mind" the way that some insects do. However, although there is a kind of communal consciousness among the Deep Ones, each one seems rather individualistic.

Some of the creatures remain apart from the main cities and colonies giving rise to tales of "mermaids," "kelpies," and the Adaro aquatic race of the South Seas. Sometimes, as in the area around Innsmouth, isolated members of the Deep Ones will mate or marry with human land-dwellers and the children that result from these unions will appear human in many respects, although each one of them will sport what is sometimes referred to as "the Innsmouth look." This is a kind of developing metamorphosis in which the subject physically decays over a period of time with gradually peeling and scaled skin and bulging eyes. They may also experience a slight webbing of the fingers and toes and a faint wattling of the skin around the neck where gills should be. The condition is also accompanied by a shambling, shuffling gait and a general slumping of the body. In some cases, there is also a slight change in the shape of the individual's skull. The final outcome of this condition may be a transformation into a full member of the Deep Ones and a return to the ocean and its underwater cities.

The Deep One's religion is centered around the concepts of Dagon and the Hydra, but the most central point of all their worship is Cthulhu, which they serve blindly. The mighty cities that lie beneath the waves are said to contain temples to the being and Its telepathic messages are regularly received in such places. From time to time, the people of the sea will trade with Humankind (particularly in the region of the South Seas) and it is thought that this is how the Ponape Figurine came among Mankind. Deep Ones will also form land-based cults that will worship Cthulhu, and many of these are said to be dotted all over the world.

Ocean Monsters

Could *something* really lie beneath the ocean waves waiting to re-emerge when conditions are right? Clearly, Cthulhu belongs to a deep-seated fear that has troubled Mankind since the earliest of times. Stories of terrible ocean creatures have existed almost as long as men have sailed the seas and appear in nearly all sea-faring cultures. The fifth-century writer Avienus details the voyages of the Carthaginian explorer Himilco the Navigator, who traveled along the Iberian Peninsula (Spain) and far beyond the Pillars of Hercules (Gibraltar). Himilco encountered sluggish sea monsters that sometimes threatened his ships, while Pytheas of Massalia, a Greek explorer and cartographer in the fourth century B.C. encountered ferocious creatures with long and sharp teeth (perhaps walruses) during an expedition to the seas off Northern Europe around 325 B.C. Perhaps more significantly, the 17th-century Dutch explorer Adriaen Block encountered a massive, tentacled squid-like creature while exploring off the Massachusetts coast in the early 1600s.

One of the most famous of the early water monsters (and one which is mentioned in the Mythos) was the Hydra. The chthonic being, which resembled a large serpent with multiple heads, dwelt in the area of Lerna, Greece. This was a swampy area containing a number of springs, and the remnants of a former lake in an eastern coastal region of Peloponnesus in southern Greece. One of the springs in the area was said to be sacred to the sea-god Poseidon, who had placed the Hydra there to guard it. It was supposedly the offspring of Typhon, a monstrous figure with poisonous snakes and serpents growing from certain parts of his body, and Echidna, "the Mother of All Monsters," who was a half-woman, half-snake. The beast was also reputedly sacred to the goddess Hera. The mythology surrounding the creature stated that if a head was cut off then two more would grow in its place. A number of Greek warriors had tried to slay the monster, but all had perished, not only killed by the snake, but by the noxious and poisonous fumes that wafted up from the stagnant swamp all around its lair. The hero who slew the Hydra was the warrior Hercules, who did so in order to complete his Second Labour. He fired flaming arrows into a cave at the Spring of Amymone where the creature dwelt, drawing the monster out. Then he proceeded to cut of the heads off the Hydra while his nephew Iolaus cauterised the stumps with a flaming torch. Although Hera (seeing that Hercules was winning against her creature) sent a giant crab to attack them, Hercules defeated that as well (Hera turned this into the constellation in the Heavens that we know as Cancer). However, the idea of the Hydra as a water-monster remained legendary for many years afterward and the creature is still a classical Greek monster even today. The writhing coils of the great serpent might be suggestive of the coils of the Cthulhu and may have at least partially inspired the idea of the underwater being somewhere in the back of Lovecraft's mind. It could have spawned the phrase "Mother Hydra" among members of the Esoteric Order of Dagon.

The Kraken, on the other hand, was a fearsome, gigantic, octopus-like creature that dwelt along the coasts of Norway and Iceland, but was sometimes seen further south. The name may come from the Old Norwegian *Krake* meaning "a withered tree." The Orvar-Odds Saga refers to two great monsters—Hafgufa and Lyngbakr—which were so immense that they could feed on whales. A Saga from around 1250 gave an account of the two beasts, which it named *krake*, but it also suggested that they might be one animal that had been viewed at different times. If these actually *were* two beasts, the text suggested, then they must be the only two in existence and may be a unique species.

Erik Pontopiddan, the Danish Bishop of Bergen in Norway, also described the Kraken in his book *A Natural History of Norway* in 1752. Legend says that Pontopiddan had seen something that appeared to be a Kraken off the coast of East Jutland when sailing as a boy and had been intrigued and fascinated by the creature ever since. He claimed that the creature was not really aggressive, but that the real danger to sailors and fishermen came from the whirlpool that it left in its wake. Nor were these creatures legendary monsters, but some undetermined species of marine life. He would set the scene for a number of other naturalists who speculated on what the nature of the kraken might be. From certain descriptions it was assumed that these were giant squid or some sort of gigantic mollusc, which lived an incredible depth, but came up to the surface from time to time. The French scientist Pierre Denys de Montfort speculated that there were in fact two types of kraken: a kraken octopus that had been seen by Norwegian sailors and mariners off the coast of America, and a colossal octopus, which was sometimes found in the southern seas.

Poets were also mesmerised by the thought of something lurking in the depths far beneath the ocean. The poet Alfred Lord Tennyson composed a sonnet to the mighty beast:

> FAR, FAR BENEATH IN THE ABYSMAL SEA,
> HIS ANCIENT DREAMLESS, UNINVADED SLEEP
> THE KRAKEN SLEEPETH....

Could *this* have been the inspiration for the dreaded Cthulhu, "dreaming in R'lyeh," beneath the Pacific waves?

Merfolk

But what of the Deep Ones themselves? Do the servants of Cthulhu have any place in mythology and folklore? The answer may partly lie in a belief in mermaids.

The word *mermaid* is a combination of both French and English—*mer* being French for "sea," and *maid* being the English word for a young and beautiful girl. The common perception of such beings is as the upper torso of a woman and the lower portion as a great fish. Although this perception is largely a medieval one, there are instances in ancient lore, many concerning supernatural beings.

The earliest recorded tale concerning a mermaid comes from ancient Assyria and dates from around 1,000 B.C. It concerns Atagartis, "the great goddess of northern Syria." Her name is taken to mean "without fish" and usually refers to an ancient Assyrian queen who forbade the eating of fish throughout her kingdom. Another legend concerning her says that she gave birth to an illegitimate child of which she was ashamed, and threw herself into a lake to drown. She did not die, but was transformed by the gods into a fish with a human head.

The sister of Alexander the Great, Thessalonike, is also a mermaid. She would sit on rocks in the Aegean Sea and call to passing ships, always asking the one question: "Is King Alexander alive?" The correct response was "He lives and reigns and conquers the world," whereupon she would wish the vessel well and allow it to pass on its way. Any other response elicited an angry response in the form of a storm, which wrecked havoc on the vessel. Perhaps this latter story was based on the legend of the Sirens, the three daughters of the river god Achelous who inhabited three small rocky islands on the southern side of the Isle of Capri. Although partially bird-like, they lured sailors onto the rocks though sweet singing and the illusion that they were beautiful.

A number of explorers also claim to have seen mermaids. Christopher Columbus, for example, supposedly saw three off the shores off of the coast of Haiti, while Sir Henry Hudson's crew reported seeing one near Nova Zembla in 1610. During the 18th century, a ship supposedly captured a mermaid off the coast of Borneo in 1745, the famous "mermaid of Amboina." She was held for four days, made noises like a mouse, and refused to eat anything. What became of this particular mermaid is unknown, but it is assumed that she died. Although no trace was ever found of her, the ship's captain asserted that he could not prove his story because the flesh of a mermaid rotted more quickly than that of a human being. This was used as an explanation as to why mermaid's bodies were never found at sea or on beaches.

In ancient China, mermaids were believed to swim in the warm waters off the southern coasts. If captured, they were forced to cry, because their tears would turn to pearls as soon as they touched the ground, providing great wealth for the captor. Chinese mermaids also had a peculiar, though not unattractive, smell when they emerged from the water and, if sad or alarmed, this smell could turn putrid and cause illness among humans. Thus, their tears provided wealth on one hand, but also sickness and death on the other. The Tainos of the Caribbean believe that the mermaid is a manifestation of the goddess Jagua and that gifts must be left for her. She is also known in Voodoo and Santeria religions (particularly in coastal areas of South America) as *La Serene* ("the mermaid"), as the manifestation of the Higher Pantheon, and is considered an extremely powerful *orisha* (emanation of a god or power).

Some cultures believed that an entire society lived beneath the waves in cities and in settlements, which often mirrored those on the land. *The One Thousand and One Nights* contain a number of stories that deal with undersea civilizations, which are not all that different from their land-based counterparts. Indeed, the people who lived there are not anatomically different from those who dwell on the land. In fact, the only difference between them and land-dwellers is their ability to breathe water instead of air. In the tale of *Abdullah the Fisherman and Abdullah the Merman,* the underwater society is portrayed as a communal one, and is much more socially compassionate than that which lies on the land.

But perhaps it was the Celtic idea of a mermaid, prevalent in Ireland, Scotland, and some parts of England, which influenced Lovecraft most. Here, the mermaids (and mermen) did not have fish's tails and they walked on two legs like land-dwellers. In order to swim through the cold sea currents they would wrap themselves in fur cloaks and were often mistaken for seals or other sea-going creatures. Whoever discovered a mermaids cloak and was able to retain it had power over the mermaid.

The merfolk in Celtic Christian countries were believed to be fallen angels. When Lucifer led a rebellion against God, some angels supported neither one side nor the other, and they were brought before God. They were not evil enough to be cast into Hell with Lucifer or good enough to be allowed back into Heaven. So they were condemned to Earth, becoming the forerunner of fairies and the powers of the world. Mermaids had been cast into the sea and were condemned to remain there until the Say of Judgement. Consequently, they were opposed to humankind who enjoyed God's forgiveness for their sins and were always seeking to do humans harm—usually by luring them away into the sea and drowning them. It was inadvisable to fall asleep on the beach or near to water unless it was near the sound of church bells, which could be rung in order the drive the creatures off.

The close resemblance between Celtic merfolk and humans also formed the basis of legends. There were differences between the two species, of course, but they were minimal. Mermaids were supposed to be inordinately fond of fish, have extremely flat feet, and in some cases be unable to enter a place of Christian worship—all these differences were negligible. And given the right circumstances, mermaids could actually live on land for long periods with relative ease. In his *Fairy and Folk Tales of the Irish Peasantry* (1888), the writer W.B. Yeats notes:

NEAR BANTRY (CO. CORK), IN THE LAST CENTURY, THERE IS SAID TO HAVE BEEN A WOMAN COVERED ALL OVER WITH SCALES LIKE A FISH.... (MERMAIDS) HAVE IN THEIR OWN SHAPE, A RED CAP CALLED A COHULLEN DRUITH, USUALLY COVERED IN FEATHERS. IF THIS IS STOLEN THEY CANNOT AGAIN GO DOWN UNDER THE WAVES.

Yeats explains that the woman was the offspring of a mermaid and a human man. Such unions were not uncommon in some Irish, Scottish, and English coastal areas. There were even tales of marriages between humans and people from the ocean.

There are also stories of mermaids who lured men away into the deep, magically living with them under the waves. Cornish mermaids were particularly adept at this. The most famous of such tales is that of the Mermaid of Zennor on the very southernmost tip of England. She was one of the very few mermaids who could enter a Christian church and actually sing in the choir. There, captured the heart of a young man, Matthew Trewella. They started going out together and one evening she led him down to Pendour Cove and into the sea. He was never seen again, although the mermaid was. A ship's captain saw a mermaid sitting on some rocks who told him that she lived under the sea in a large town with her husband Matthew Trewella. In memory of the lost boy (and as a warning to others), the figure of a mermaid is carved on a pew-end in Zennor church, bearing a mirror in one hand and a comb in the other, the symbols of vanity and heartlessness. The Cornish folklorist William Botterell makes reference to a certain healer named Matthew Lutey of Curey, who captured a stranded mermaid from the sea and took her comb. Later, in some accounts, he married her and she bequeathed upon him great powers of healing and prophesy, which made him one of the greatest "pellars" (wise men) in all of Cornwall. Botterell, however, gives no date for this event. An old song from England warns that once married, a man can never divorce a mermaid, as there is "no separation beneath the sea" and must remain with her for life.

In Wales, mermaids do not live in the sea but in lakes and deep ponds—perhaps they are related to early Celtic and Germanic water sprites. However, they are hostile toward humans and will frequently emerge from the water to seize those passing by, drag them down, and drown them. Some tempt individuals into their watery domain with gold coins and large jewels, which they hold out invitingly.

Inspector Legrasse

One of those who fought against the Cthulhu cults was John Raymond Legrasse, a New Orleans police inspector. In 1907, he led a raid against a particularly mysterious and loathsome cult, which appeared in a squatter camp in the bayou region of Louisiana. The cult was supposed to be a voodoo congregation, but Legrasse suspected that it was much more than that. In 1908, the Inspector spoke at a meeting of the American Anthropological Society and asked them to identify a small idol made of a greenish-black stone, which had been captured during the raid. This, he revealed, was what the cult had been worshipping. No one could identify the thing with any certainty.

Legrasse, however, began to interrogate some of the 47 prisoners that had been captured during the raid. One of them, "Old Castro," was particularly talkative. He told Legrasse that they worshipped the Great Old Ones and their priest, the great Cthulhu, who currently lay dreaming in the sunken city of R'lyeh. This was the first time that Legrasse had ever heard the name "Cthulhu," but he was convinced that behind the old man's rambling fantasies were *some* truths. "Old Castro" identified the center of the Cthulhu cult as being Irem, City of the Pillars, in the Middle East, but told him little more. However, Legrasse was now approached by one of the academics who had attended the meeting, William Channing Webb, who told him of rumored degenerate worship on the Greenland coast by a strange tribe of Esquemeaux (Eskimos), which piqued the Inspector's interest.

Although Lovecraft left the narrative of Inspector Legrasse at this point, other Mythos writers such as Lin Carter, Joseph Payne Brennan, and C.J. Henderson would revive the character and give him fresh adventures dealing with the followers of Cthulhu. In subsequent tales, Legrasse returned to the bayou region and investigated further by attending a séance with Carter's famous occult detective Anton Zarnak. What he learned troubled him deeply and he resigned from the police force. He became something of a recluse, spending all of his time studying Mythos lore. After returning to society in order to fight off an invasion of New Orleans by the Deep Ones, he set out for Nepal where he believed a significant Cthulhu cult existed. He returned, shaken and disturbed, withdrawing from society once more. The arcane knowledge that obtained seems to have broken Legrasse, as he is often used as a warning to those who would probe too deeply into the affairs of the creature.

Could these underwater beings have somehow served as a template for Lovecraft's Deep Ones, the servants of great Cthulhu? And could their queer offspring have inhabited such dilapidated and nearly abandoned coastal settlements such as Innsmouth? Maybe under the continually rolling ocean *something* or *some things* really are waiting!

Shadows Beyond the Stars

Nyarlathotep

Few Mythos entities are worshipped in so many guises or appear in so many forms as Nyarlathotep, the Mighty Messenger. And although many of Lovecraft's other beings are either exiled to the stars, or lie slumbering in the deeps or in inaccessible places in the world, the Crawling Chaos is perhaps one of the most active and one of the most important of them all. It is also the one that interacts most frequently with human beings.

Nyarlathotep dwells in a cavern at the very center of the world where It waits with two mindless flautists, which accompany It wherever It goes. It acts as an intermediary between the Great Old Ones and Humankind, carrying messages between them and their worshippers, and performing services for them and their adherents.

The Crawling Chaos first appeared in Lovecraft's work in a prose-poem entitled *Nyarlathotep* written in 1920, albeit in a much different guise compared to later tales. Initially, the entity appears as a tall, gaunt, and swarthy man, perhaps reflecting Lovecraft's early interest in Egypt and the Middle East. In this form Nyarlathotep travels the world, revealing magical powers and strange supernatural instruments to many people. In his verse, Lovecraft suggests that Nyarlathotep is the instigator of the world's collapse and general destruction, as It takes over the minds of Its followers and causes them to lose interest in the planet.

However, It re-emerges as a central character in *The Dream-Quest of Unknown Kadath* written in 1926 and 1927. Once again, the being resembles a human pharaoh-like individual when It confronts the story's protagonist, Randolph Carter (who is a thinly-disguised representation of Lovecraft and appears in a number of other tales). By the early 1930s, Nyarlathorep has changed, though It still maintains a quasi-human form. Now, It appears as the Black Man, a creature that haunted the European with-cults. It now takes on the guise of a dark-skinned being that is closely associated with the Devil. This would mirror the historical accounts of alleged 16th-century witches and the fevered imaginings of the witch-hunters who accused them. It first appears in this form to the witch Keziah Mason and later to Walter Gilman in Lovecraft's story "The Dreams in the Witch House" (published in Weird Tales in 1933).

It has to be noted that Nyarlathotep is described as a humanoid figure in many stories. In the story "The Rats in the Walls," written in 1923 (but not published in *Weird Tales* until March 1924), It is mentioned as a faceless god that dwells in a dark cavern at the Earth's core. The non-human element of the entity reveals itself again in *The Haunter of the Dark,* written in 1936. Here, Nyarlathotep is the object of veneration of the Starry Wisdom cult in Providence and is described as a nocturnal, bat-winged, tentacled entity, dwelling in the steeple of a dark and ruined church. The idea had moved from that of an ancient and evil Pharaoh to an almost amorphous and malignant horror.

It is difficult to know where Lovecraft's inspiration for the being comes from, but Lovecraft suggested that it might have manifested from a terrible dream that he'd experienced early in life. Writing to Reinhardt Kleiner in 1921, he spoke of a vivid nightmare that he dreamed at age 10:

> *I WAS IN GREAT PAIN—FOREHEAD POUNDING AND EARS RINGING—BUT I ONLY HAD ONE AUTOMATIC IMPULSE—TO WRITE AND PRESERVE THE ATMOSPHERE OF UNPARALLELED FRIGHT; AND BEFORE I KNEW IT, I HAD PULLED ON THE LIGHT AND WAS SCRIBBLING DESPERATELY.*

The source of his terror was Nyarlathotep, which he claimed had come to him in the dream. He also experienced a "curious tugging" of the nerves and muscles around his eyes, which he also attributed to the work of the entity, even though the obvious suggestion was that his eyesight was failing and that he needed glasses. However, the "tugging" allegedly went away after the horrid dream and he attributed that to the machinations of Nyarlathotep. The dream, he claimed, formed the basis of the prose-poem "Nyarlathotep."

Of all the bizarre and formidable entities that he created, Lovecraft arguably seemed most obsessed with Nyarlathotep. Although the being appears as a character in four of his stories and two of his sonnets he makes various references to It in several other of his works such as "The Whisperer in Darkness" (written in 1930) and "The Shadow out of Time" (first published in *Astounding Stories* in 1936). In some of his correspondences he refers to the entity as "the Crawling Chaos," which may mark another discernable shift in his perception of It. And yet in his story using the same title, written in 1920 (revised in conjunction with Elizabeth Berekley and Lewis Theobald Jr.) he makes no reference at all to Nyarlathotep.

But an intriguing question also arises as to whether Nyarlathotep may have had Its origins in an actual person because, in the dream, Lovecraft received a letter from his good friend Samuel Loveman who advised:

> *DON'T FAIL TO SEE NYARLATHOTEP IF HE COMES TO PROVIDENCE. HE IS HORRIBLE—HORRIBLE BEYOND ANYTHING THAT YOU CAN IMAGINE—BUT WONDERFUL. HE HAUNTS ONE FOR HOURS AFTERWARD. I AM STILL SHUDDERING AT WHAT HE SHOWED.*

Writing on the subject of the dream, Lovecraft stated:

*I HAD NEVER HEARD THE NAME NYARLATHOTEP BEFORE, BUT SEEMED TO UNDER-
STAND THE ALLUSION. NYARLATHOTEP WAS A KIND OF ITINERANT SHOWMAN OR
LECTURER WHO HELD FORTH IN PUBLIC HALLS AND AROUSED WIDESPREAD FEAR
AND DISCUSSION WITH HIS EXHIBITIONS. THESE EXHIBITIONS CONSISTED OF TWO
PARTS—FIRST, A HORRIBLE AND PROBABLY PROPHETIC, CINEMA REEL AND LATER
SOME EXTRAORDINARY EXPERIMENTS WITH SCIENTIFIC AND ELECTRICAL APPARATUS.
AS I RECEIVED THE LETTER I SEEMED TO RECALL THAT NYARLATHOTEP WAS ALREADY
IN PROVIDENCE.... I SEEMED TO REMEMBER THAT PERSONS HAD WHISPERED TO ME
IN AWE OF HIS HORRORS, AND WARNED ME NOT TO GO NEAR HIM.*

Even before Lovecraft's time, traveling showmen were visiting the towns of
America, demonstrating electrical and scientific "miracles" to local people. Many of
these were no more than hucksters and quacks who claimed to reveal the "mysteries
of the East" to a wondering public. Some couched their demonstrations in mystical
or quasi-scientific terms, often suggesting that they were representative of an antique
(or even "lost") knowledge. In order to do this, some even adopted strange-sounding
names and even assumed fanciful titles, such as "Dr. Chian-yi" or "Professor Abin-
azer." Some claimed they could reveal "the secrets of the Pharaohs handed down
from Mystic Egypt" or "the Wonders of the Future through the medium of electrical
magic." (It must be remembered that in the 1920s there were many parts of rural
America that did not have electricity, so it was still a great wonder.) Therefore, these
demonstrations verged on the supernatural in many places, and the traveling showmen often played that element up. Although there may not have been an actual showman named Nyarlathotep, could the idea of such a supernatural figure have played on
Lovecraft's mind and conveyed itself into the overall shape of the demonic messenger?

Lovecraft seems to have initially envisaged Nyarlathotep as some sort of Egyptian
man (with arcane and mystical powers). In "Nyarlathotep" he states:

*AND IT WAS THEN THAT NYARLATHOTEP CAME OUT OF EGYPT. WHO HE WAS NONE
COULD TELL, BUT HE WAS OF THE OLD NATIVE BLOOD AND LOOKED LIKE A PHA-
RAOH. THE FELLAHIN KNELT WHEN THEY SAW HIM, YET COULD NOT SAY WHY. HE
SAID HE HAD RISEN UP OUT OF THE BLACKNESS OF TWENTY-SEVEN CENTURIES, AND
THAT HE HEARD MESSAGES FROM PLACES NOT ON THIS PLANET. INTO THE LANDS
OF CIVILISATION CAME NYLARATHOTEP, SWARTHY, SLENDER AND SINISTER, ALWAYS
BUYING STRANGE INSTRUMENTS OF GLASS AND METAL AND COMBINING THEM INTO
INSTRUMENTS YET STRANGER. HE SPOKE MUCH OF THE SCIENCES—OF ELECTRICITY
AND PSYCHOLOGY—AND GAVE EXHIBITIONS OF POWER WHICH SENT HIS SPECTATORS
AWAY SPEECHLESS, YET WHICH SWELLED HIS FAME TO EXCEEDING MAGNITUDE.*

In this extract Lovecraft seems to portray Nyarlathotep as a traveling showman or as a pseudo-scientific Carney entertainer, mixing feats of electrical and psychological prowess with lecturers and talks. The entity appears human, though seemingly mysterious and mystical, but a man nonetheless. Commentators such as Will Murray have suggested that he might have been influenced by some of the "traveling inventors" of the day—quasi-showmen who gave lectures and demonstrations in the hope of interesting wealthy patrons in their inventions or to raise money to fund them. Many used electricity in their demonstrations; one of the most famous was Giovanni Aldini (thought to be the basis for Dr. Frankenstein in Mary Shelley's novel) at the start of the 1800s. Murray has argued that Lovecraft may have chosen Nickola Tesla as his model. Tesla was both a mechanical inventor and electrical engineer who made huge contributions to the development of the commercial application of electricity and electromagnetism. However, in order to raise funds, he did give a series of well-attended lectures and demonstrations in the early 20th century, which involved electricity. A number of religious groups campaigned against him. Could he have been seen by Lovecraft and become the human template for the dark entity?

Three years later in 1923, in the story "The Rats in the Walls," Nyarlathotep has taken on something of a much different aspect. Here Lovecraft notes:

It was the eldritch scurrying of those fiend-born rats, always questing for new horrors and determined to lead me on, even unto those grinning caverns of Earth's centre where Nyarlathotep, the mad, faceless god, howls blindly to the piping of two amorphous, idiot flute players.

Nyarlathotep is no longer a fantastic showman, traveling from town to town, giving weird and terrifying lectures and demonstrations, rather It is something that dwells and shrieks at the Earth's core and can extend Its attentions and powers into the world above. It is no longer, it seems, the wandering entertainer who can change his form and style to suit his audience, rather It is some sort of terrible deity, trapped in the lightless caverns at the center of the world. And yet perhaps the idea of the traveler who can terrify those who see him with his illusions may not have completely gone away.

Whether the entity is a specific member of the Great Old Ones or not is unclear, although It seems to enjoy some form of special relationship with them. Nevertheless, It also seems to have a distinct personality different from the majority of them and may not even share the same form of thinking as them. Indeed, in some cases It appears to be openly contemptuous of them. They may view themselves as the "masters," but how It regards *them* is open to question. The entity Cthugha (a Great Old One that takes the form of a great air conflagration), displays a distinct and constant enmity toward It. Others display a variety of attitudes ranging from a cool friendliness to open dislike. And it is thought that while most of the Great Old Ones look upon Nyarlathotep simply as a servitor and messenger, the entity Itself assumes that It is a god in Its own right.

Nyarlathotep may also bring about the end of our world. It is thought that in the Final Days the Outer Gods will simply clear away humanity from the planet. It is believed they will wait on a signal from their messenger, which will appear in the skies, dressed in red and with the wild beasts licking Its hands (or tentacles). The Crawling Chaos will then travel the world—it is not completely clear if this is an emanation of Nyarlathotep or something else—giving demonstrations of both science and magic in all the major cities. The Outer Gods will then take this as a sign that they are to clear humankind from the face of the planet and will act accordingly. According to some predictions, the entire Universe will be turned into an infinite graveyard. Indeed, the process is already underway as Nyarathotep has already revealed to Its followers the secret of nuclear energy and this knowledge has passed into the mainstream of Humanity.

It is said that the entity's true form is that of a vast expanse of viscous and corrosive yellowish slime, but that this can take any form that It chooses. This power has been granted to It by either the Outer Gods or the Great Old Ones in some former time. In such an infinite variety of guises, It can carry out whatever functions they desire. From time to time, however, It will take the form of a yellowish gas, which boasts a devious and malignant mind, and some scholars have argued that *this* is Its true form.

In a number of these guises Nyarlathotep has been worshipped throughout the ages. It was worshipped as *El-Ker-Laat* in the ancient land of Mu (and possibly in Atlantis as well) through what form it took is unknown. It is speculated that it was in the form of a gigantic eye placed on top of a gold-sheathed standing stone. Some representations were supposed to depict a shadowy humanoid form seated on a throne of bones, but it is not clear if this indeed was Nyarlathotep. Its most celebrated form of worship was in the Hyperborean land of Stygia where It was known as "Nyarlat"; and from there Its veneration traveled to Egypt. According to some funerary tablets and magical papyri, the Crawling Chaos was one of the most important deities worshipped on the Lower Nile though, again, what form the god took is open to question. Its adherents were some of the most powerful sorcerers and witches, and Its dark and malicious powers were often concentrated in secret temples and isolated shrines across the landscape. Through time, however, the Egyptian people became fearful of the dark god and began to remove all references to It from their written records, assigning some of Its attributes to other gods such as Thoth and Set. At certain periods in Egyptian history there have been further attempts to repress any reference to Nyarlathotep and these have been successful. However, through the years there were some resurgences in worship. The most celebrated of these was during the reign of Nephren-Ka, the so-called Black Pharaoh, a mythical ruler of Egypt and one of the last of the Egyptian Third Dynasty. However, a document known as The Secret Papyri of Turin makes reference to Nephren-Ka as a magician of some repute. It is said that Nephren-Ka made a deal with Nyarlathotep in the vanished city of Irem, though the details of this agreement are not known. When he returned from the wilderness, he revived the cult of Nyarlathotep (in fact some even say that he *was* Nyarlathotep), which spread throughout the Lower Nile. He became one of the most powerful rulers in the region and, during his reign, the cults of Bast, Anubis, and Sebek flourished in Egypt. Through Nyarlathotep, Nephren-Ka received an artifact known as the Shining Trapezohedron, or Crystal of Chaos. This enabled the possessor to gaze across space and time, but can also be used to summon Nyarlathotep in Its form as the Haunter of the Dark from the subterranean cavern where It dwells, although such a summoning is fraught with danger.

However, despite his formidable powers, the Dark Pharaoh ruled largely as a dictator and his people became discontented with his reign. They prevailed on Sneferu to overthrow him and, after receiving help from the goddess Isis, Sneferu did so, causing the Black Pharaoh to flee. He made his way toward the coast, intending to escape to "a Western island," but was cut off by Sneferu's forces somewhere near the site of modern-day Cairo. There he and many of his followers entered an underground vault, and although Sneferu's forces attempted to capture them, they simply vanished allegedly into the earth. Not knowing what happened Sneferu declared the Black Pharaoh dead and had his name and details of his reign stricken from all records and monuments.

Meanwhile, in a subterranean world, Nephren-Ka sacrificed 100 of his followers to Nyarlathotep and, in return for this, the entity bestowed the gift of prophesy upon him (although some asset that the Black Pharaoh already had acquired the gift through the Shining Trapezohedron). Now alone in the underground vault Nephren-Ka spent the last days of his life drawing the future of the world until the coming of the Great Old Ones/Outer Gods on the walls of his tomb.

Allegedly, the Black Pharaoh did not die, and his essence lived on and reappeared in the form of Queen Nitocis during the Sixth Dynasty. The priests of Nyarlathotep flourished again and human sacrifices were allegedly common during this reign.

During the 18th Dynasty, between 1550 and 1292 B.C. the worship of Nyarlathotep came to the fore yet again. The Pharaoh Amenhotep IV (or Akenaten) allegedly discovered the remains of Nephren-Ka sealed in an underground vault and attempted to revive the sorcerer by magical means. In any case, the wizard supposedly influenced the pharaoh, making him turn the religion of the land toward the disguised avatars of the creature Itself. However, the time was not right and the stars were not in the right positions, so the entity left and returned to Its tomb, leaving Amenhotep and his reign to fall.

After these events the formal text regarding the Dark Pharaoh ceases, although there is some traditional oral evidence. It's thought that the followers of Nephren-Ka fled Egypt and disappeared into remote regions of the Sudan where they set up new temples and shrines. It has even been suggested that some of these followers even fled to parts of France and Britain, taking their worship and their dark literature with them. There are also some who state that these followers traveled down to the Arabian Gulf to what is now Yemen, where certain of them were later encountered by Abdul Alhazred.

The tomb of the Black Pharaoh also remains something of a mystery. Although many authorities state that he probably lies in an underground vault at some unknown location, there are others who say that he is interred within one of the Pyramids. Two possible locations from the period are good candidates. One is the Pyramid at Maidum on the Dashur Plain about 40 miles south of the mouth of the Nile, which is known as the Persistent Pyramid or the Collapsed Pyramid. Although its building is attributed to either Hani or Sneferu, according to Mythos scholar Daniel Harms, it may have been initially constructed for Nephren-Ka. This was originally a seven-tiered structure, but at some point it seems to have collapsed. Archaeologists believe that the stress levels within the structure were incorrectly calculated and contributed to the pyramid's collapse. The monument stands alone on the edge of a desert, well away from any other such structure, and is a rather spectacular site. It is suggested that somewhere beneath it lies the vault of Nephren-Ka.

Another contender for such a gravesite is the Bent (or Black) Pyramid at Dahshur lying south of the Mustaba Faraoun near Saqqara. Similar to the Collapsed Pyramid this also dates from the time of Sneferu and, according to historians, was one of the pyramids that he commissioned. It may have originally been conceived as a true pyramid, but its dimensions may have been changed halfway through the construction. It was perhaps designed by Imhotep, who acted as chief architect, vizier, and advisor to the pharaoh and may have also been the designer of the Step Pyramid at Saqqara. It is said that under one of these pyramids Nephren-Ka lies sleeping, waiting to be wakened at the end of time. Although he is described as being of the Third Dynasty, confusion surrounds Nephren-Ka. In his story *Fane of the Black Pharaoh* (1937), Robert Bloch refers to "biblical times," which places him at a much later date, possibly the 19th or 20th Dynasties.

Around 1786 to 1575 B.C., Egypt was invaded and occupied by a group of people known as the Hyksos or the Aamu. Archaeologists suggest that these were an "Asiatic people" and their name has incorrectly been translated from the works of the Jewish historian Josephus as being Hyksos (a Greek word) or "shepherd kings." The Egyptians referred to them as "hikau khausut," which meant "rulers of foreign countries." Mystery still surrounds them and some historians have queried if there was an invasion at all. There may have been armed incursions—the Hyksos were described as having new and advanced weaponry, a composite bow, new forms of swords, and arrowheads—but it's now thought that this was simply a migration of peoples who took some of the lands in which they settled by force. The extent of the Hyksos kingdom lay on the eastern part of the Nile and did not extend through Egypt entirely. The Hyksos seem to have been a confederation of Semitic peoples, and many of them appear to have had Canaanite names.

By the early 1700s B.C. Egypt was starting to politically fragment, with independent states rising up and assuming some form of autonomy. The Semite and Syro-Palestinian peoples may have taken advantage of this political upheaval and migrated into the country, establishing their own kingdoms. With them they brought strange and unfamiliar gods that made the Egyptian people rather uncomfortable. Some have argued that Nyarlathotep may have been among the gods that they worshipped, and this may have constituted a slight revival of the entity's fortunes in ancient Egypt. Whether or not this is true, a number of Lovecraftian scholars have continued to assert the notion, and the reign of the Hyksos still presents as a fascinating and mysterious part of Egyptian history. Nyarlthotep is associated with destructive machinery and weaponry so the technology for some of the advanced weaponry of the Hyksos may have sprung from that infernal source.

In *De Vermis Mysteriis*, Ludvig Prinn refers to Nyarlthotep as "the all-seeing eye" and states that It knows all about science and technology. Sometimes It appears to chosen individuals and grants them a charm or perhaps a piece of scientific technology, which may lead inevitably to conflict and violence. For the individual concerned the knowledge will only lead to madness and death, but it is sustenance and energy to the Dark One to see humankind destroying itself.

Nyarlathotep has appeared in various guises, sometimes instigating warfare in various parts of the world. As Ahtu, It appeared in the Congo where It obtained a substantial following. Here, It takes the physical form of a large mass of dark and viscous material with a host of golden tentacles sprouting from it. Ahtu's followers often tend to be deformed or have some mental problems, but are urged on to feats of fantastic prowess and strength by the whispers of their god. In the 1950s, it is thought that Nyarlathotep was behind much of the violence against the Belgian administration of the Congo. Several of the Europeans who dwelt in the Congo may have been part of the cult of Ahtu, but only if they were deformed in some way.

The entity also manifests itself in the form of Aku-Shin-Kage in Japan and takes the physical image of a man in ancient Samurai armour with many small mouths instead of a face. The entity may be responsible for a great deal of the warfare in Japanese history, particularly between 1568 and 1603, known as the Era of the Warring Kingdoms. The being is sometimes counted as *Tengu*, a Japanese demon, although exactly where it fits into the country's demonology is not terribly clear. And in Kenya, It takes no form at all, but is rather known as The Black Wind. In this form, it destroys crops, spreads disease, and creates mayhem and violence between tribes. In Kenya it is also known as the God of the Bloody Tongue and may have been behind the Mau-Mau uprisings in the 1950s.

Nyarlathotep also appears in China as part of the Cult of the Bloated Woman. Here is assumes the guise of a huge and obese woman with at least five slobbering mouths in her belly and a mass of dark tentacles around her. It carries a Black Fan, which magically disguises Its true nature from Its victims (portraying her as young and beautiful) until It has ensnared them. Books concerning this awful deity once circulated widely in China—among them *The Book of the Black Fan*, *The Goddess of the Black Fan*, and *Tales of the Priest Kawan*

In Haiti, the entity is referred to as the Floating Horror. In this part of the world, Nyarlathotep can really only physically reveal Itself through a follower or a sacrifice, which has been specially chosen and prepared as a host body. When the host body has been killed the entity will briefly manifest Itself in a localized form. This is akin to a reddish jellyfish-like, floating organism with a single huge eye and a faint bluish tinge. This form or emanation is closely associated with some peripheral voodoo cults on the island. In Turkey, however, the Dark Messenger is revered as a human figure whose skin would appear to have been flayed and who hangs in the air, Its mouth open as if perpetually screaming. Its commands are allegedly experienced as a series of echoes.

The entity is also recognized in Australia as the Black Faceless One or as the Haunter of the Dark. It is worshipped by certain cults of aborigines dwelling in the slums of a number of the country's most prominent cities. Their areas are designated by a curious spiral sign drawn on the walls of shanty buildings. It is said that one of these cults actually possesses the Shining Trapezohedron through which the Haunter can enter our world. Nevertheless, it is said that Nyarlathotep regularly appears in the slums of places such as Sydney or Darwin with a frightening regularity and is known as the Father of Bats, Fly-the-Light, the Sand Bat, and Face-Eater.

Another guise of the Dark Messenger is to be found in Malaysia. Here It is known as the Shugoran and is represented by a dark humanoid figure blowing a horn. This is worshipped by the Tcho-Tcho people in remote corners of Burma and Indonesia. The Tcho-Tchos are another species of human—possibly older than ourselves—who some Lovecraftian scholars argue may have emerged from the Dreamlands, but now live in Northern India or Tibet. They have some way of commanding It and can call It forth at will, usually to take revenge on those who have offended them in some way.

In Eastern Europe and in the Carpathian Mountains, the Dark Messenger is worshipped in the form of a great black bull and is mentioned in Magyar folklore. It is believed that this animal will appear in monstrous form at the End of Days and will trample the countries of the world under Its feet, signaling the coming of the Great Old Ones.

In some parts of New England, Nyarlathotep takes on yet another form: This is the White Man. Records of this incarnation only appear to certain groups of early religious cults in the region such as Mother Ann Lee's Shakers or Shadrach Ireland's Brethren of the New Light where It is counted as an emanation from God. In this form, Nyarlathotep appears as the White Man, a humanoid figure, swathed in what looks like a white winding sheet that covers Its entire body. Accounts of this figure appear in a number of New England witchcraft and heresy trials. In some other parts of the region, however, It appears as the Tatterdemalion, a great ragged scarecrow-like figure that appears in rural areas and speaks to Its followers in an insidious whisper. In earlier times, Nyarlathotep appeared to Its followers in England and seems to have traveled with some of them to the New World. In this form the entity appears in some witchcraft trial accounts both in America and in England.

But it is not only in our own world that Nyarlathotep can take these many guises. In the Dreamworlds, according to Lovecraft and others, It can appear in a variety of in-carnations. For example, It materializes as the Queen in Red, a dangerous woman com-pletely dressed in red, wearing a red mask, and sometimes displaying demonic features. Her fingernails are impossibly long and her teeth seem almost vampiric in length and sharpness. She is often counted as a female counterpoint to the King in Yellow, although the exact nature of the relationship between these two entities is unclear.

Linked to this is perhaps another guise of Nyarlathotep often referred to as the Thing in the Yellow Mask. This is an entity entirely draped in yellow rags or fila-ments, which allegedly sits in a stone chamber at the very center of the ruined city of 'Ygiroth on Mount Lerion above the River Skai in the Dreamlands. Others say that it is a veiled High Priest that sits behind a screen in an isolated monastery on the Plateau of Leng. It communicates with those who approach It through a series of hideously fluting pipes that It holds in Its paws. Some Mythos writers have stated that this is an emanation of the avatar of the entity Hastur, but most believe it to be that of Nyarlathotep.

Within the Dreamlands, Nyarlathotep can also take the form of a writhing mist, which is a sickly, pallid color moving of its own volition across the ground in the direction in which the Dark Messenger intends to go. If touched by this mist an indi-vidual will go mad and possibly die within a short time.

And beyond our own world, Nyarlathotep is worshipped as Lrogg on the planet L'gy'hx (thought to be Uranus or a moon thereof). The natives here are metallic and have joined with some of the renegade insect beings from Shaggai in order to wor-ship the Dark Messenger in the form of a two-headed bat, which dwells in the deep caverns of that world. The rites involved in such worship are particularly complicated and involve the preparation of one living sacrifice each planetary year.

One of the most potent and terrifying images adopted by Nyarlathotep is that of the Black Man. According to both Lovecraft and Robert Bloch, this guise manifested itself primarily in medieval and early modern England, but had been brought there from the Holy Land by the returning Crusaders and may be of Egyptian origin. The Black Man is the very embodiment of Nyarlathotep, and is described as hairless with dead black skin and sometimes cloven feet.

Since the dawn of antiquity the color black has been associated with negative as-pects of the Universe and often with evil. The Christian Council of Toledo meeting in

447 did not hesitate to describe the Devil as a monstrous figure, but made his color uniformly black. In Christian eyes, black was the color of sin and of wrong-doing. It was the antithesis of light and purity. It was the color of the sky at night, which Man feared. Consequently, evil manifestations—or those deigned to do Humankind harm—often adopted this color in order to perform their malignancy. Creatures that wrapped themselves in dark cloaks or wore dark clothing were usually regarded as dangerous.

Thus, the Black Man became a malignant, Satanic figure in many cultures, but especially in Western European Christian ones. Within the Christian mind it was the symbol of demonic activity and the way through which the Enemy of Mankind conveyed his wishes and instructions to his followers. The Black Man was the very center of witchcraft and dark ritual—the very archetype of evil. This concept was enhanced as Europeans made contact with the dark-skinned peoples of Africa. Stories came back to the West of ghastly ceremonies conducted by African tribes, which involved human sacrifice to strange gods, cannibalism, and mutilation.

The Black Man soon became the center of witch-gatherings and the figure around which the Sabbat rotated. He was also the great Tempter who sought to lead God-fearing people away from the path of Righteousness and into sin and damnation. In Scotland, for instance, the Black Man frequently appeared in various places, offering all sorts of inducements to abandon the ways of the Lord. The being might appear either at a gathering of witches to individuals along lonely roads, or in isolated places in order to instruct his followers or to tempt the vulnerable.

For example, during the 1590 witch trials in North Berwick (the first major witchcraft trial in Scotland) more than 70 people from East Lothian were accused of witchcraft and "Black Airts." The Evil One appeared in front of St. Andrews Auld Kirk to a gathering of witches, who were plotting harm against King James VI of Scotland. One of them was Agnes Sampson, a local healer and midwife known widely as "the Wise Wife of Keith," who described him as a great dark-skinned man, naked, and with a huge member, who appeared in the nave of the church and struck both awe and terror into them all.

At another trial in 1660 in Forres, Morayshire, Bessie Forbes—a healer and fortune-teller)—was accused, along with her daughter, of meeting with the Devil in an old abandoned Catholic cemetery near their home. After being tortured using a "witch's bridle" (or branks bridle) she confessed that she had met with a grandly dressed, black-skinned man walking among the grave markers who had lured both her and her daughter away from the true Christian path and instructed them in the "ill arts."

Near Elgin several years later, an old man named Neil McGregor was brought before a Court of the Kirk Session and accused of heresy. He claimed that on a lonely path, he had met with a black-skinned man who engaged him in conversation, and led him into "dissolute ways." The man instructed him to raise his cap while passing a large standing stone on a nearby common and to wish it "good day."

So strong was the notion of the evil Black Man in the Scottish psyche that it appears in one of the most famous Scottish witchcraft short stories, Robert Louis Stevenson's *Thrawn Janet*. In the tale that is told in the Scottish vernacular, the minister of Balweary, the Reverend Soulis occasionally saw a Black Man (the Devil) who came to his parish and, as is eventually revealed, had possessed his housekeeper Janet McClour. When he questioned Janet regarding the Black Man, he was met with the response:

A BLACK MAN! QUO' SHE SAVE US A'! YE'RE NO WISE MINISTER! THERE'S NAE BLACK MAN IN BA'WEARY.

Nevertheless, the Black Man *had* possessed her and tuned her into his servant. In the story, Stevenson was simply articulating that the Devil (or some evil fiend) went furtively about the countryside in the guise of a Black Man, possessing individuals and gathering followers around him. The idea of an evil creature with black skin lurking somewhere close by was always a fear in the back of the Celtic mind.

In France, the idea of a Black Man prowling the lonely forest tracts filled many Christian people with abject fear. In early 1570, the misanthropic Giles Garnier lived with his wife in a ramshackle cabin deep in the wooded countryside of Armanges, near the town of Dole. It's thought that he'd come to the area from Lyons, but kept to himself and stayed away from local people.

At the beginning of 1573, Giles Garnier was brought to trial before the Parlement at Dole and was accused of being a werewolf where he told a fantastic tale: He had been out walking in the Woods of St. Bonnot when he had encountered a tall black man, grandly dressed and wrapped in a black cloak. But it was his eyes that had initially attracted Garnier, for they were large and burning. He had engaged Garnier in conversation and the lonely hermit had met him several times in the woodlands. This man taught him various forms of sorcery including how to transform himself into a wolf, and it was in this form that he roamed the countryside attacking both livestock and children. Under magistrate Henri Camus, Garnier was put on trial, but could say nothing more about the man. On January 18th, 1573, he was found guilty of witchcraft and of being a werewolf and was executed. Afterward, several people passing through the Woods of St. Bonnot claimed that they had seen a very tall man wrapped in a black cloak passing among the trees. Although many had thought that the old hermit had been wandering in his mind, some now began to doubt this.

Garnier's confession had echoes of another case from Poligny almost 50 years earlier. The region, in the Jura region of France, was the location of a major werewolf trial around 1520. Here, three men were accused of becoming werewolves through sorcery. One of these, Pierre Bourgot (known locally as Big Peter), claimed he was visited by a Black Man while working in the woods near his home. The stranger was one of three horsemen and Bourgot had never seen him before, but nevertheless he felt able to tell him his troubles. Later, the horsemen visited him at his home and the stranger taught Bourgot certain things that would enable him to become a werewolf.

He gave Pierre a vessel of magic ointment which, when smeared on his naked body, conveyed him to a Grand Sabbat, a coven of local witches at which the Black Man presided. There, he was instructed to recruit others to follow the creature, which he did, and brought in the two other men. Faced with a catalogue of horrors, local magistrates had really no other option but to find the men guilty, sentence them to death, and have their bodies burned. However, the idea of a dark man traveling through the country turning weak-willed people into werewolves remained a common theme in French folklore right up until the time of Giles Garnier and beyond.

In Germany, there were whispers of a supernatural black figure that often threatened Mankind. In the Brocken Peak, which is part of the Harz Mountain chain in the north of the country, the dark figure of a gigantic man appeared in the skies above the mountain top when the conditions were right. The Spectre of the Brocken (also known as Mountain spectre, or Glockenspectre) has a supernatural significance, and can appear in any mountain area. It is strongly associated with witchcraft, giving the Brocken and Herz Mountains a rather sinister reputation. It is said that the figure was an immense Black Man who oversaw gatherings of witches who congregated in the remote mountain area. The earliest note of it was written by the German theologian and naturalist Johann Silberschlag in 1780, but stories about it had been circulating for many years previously. Even though Silberschlag identified it as a perfectly natural occurrence, the belief still persisted that it was a physical manifestation of the Devil or of some other evil entity.

Near the small town of Mittelberg, Germany, a local woodcutter met the Black Man while walking in the woods. Like some sort of showman, the traveler showed the woodcutter many marvels, which he brought out from a pack that he carried. Here, there are overtones of Lovecraft's initial vision of Nyarlathotep as a traveling showman or packman. The woodcutter described him as a tall man, very dark and swarthy. He instructed the other in the ways of witchcraft and urged him to turn against his neighbors and to accept a heretical Protestant faith. The Black Man appeared several times more to the woodcutter in his house and told him many secret things concerning his neighbors, which he was able to use against them. However, he was charged with possessing preternatural knowledge through witchcraft and devil-worship and was subsequently executed.

So what, in fact, *is* Nyarlathotep? Is It the human traveling scientist and showman that Lovecraft probably envisaged him to be? Is It an ancient pharaoh whose name has been struck from official Egyptian records? Was It the Black Man who appeared to Giles Garnier and who features in Robert Louis Stevenson's *Thrawn Janet*? Or is It the myriad manifestations that appear all across the world and is worshipped by secret cults? Is It in fact *all* of these? Whatever It may be, Nyarlathotep unarguably remains one of Lovecraft's most complex and enigmatic creations.

SHADOWS BEYOND THE STARS
YOG-SOTHOTH

One of the most important Outer Gods in the mythos, the entity known as Yog-Sothoth, has been described in a number of ways. It is the Lurker at the Threshold, the Key and the Gate, the All-in-One, and the Opener of the Way. The being was first mentioned by Lovecraft in his novella *The Case of Charles Dexter Ward,* written in 1927, but has since become an important entity in the Mythos and has been referred to perhaps more than many other of the entities.

The Outer Gods maintain a special distinction from most of the Mythos entities, although this is not recognized by all Lovecraftian scholars. Some argue that they are simply a branch of the Great Old Ones with whom they have an uncertain relationship. Perhaps they arrived on Earth at a slightly different time to the main body of the Great Old Ones; perhaps they come from a rather different species. The connection between the two groups is unknown. Some scholars have even suggested that the Great Old Ones are actually larval Outer Gods, but this view is not widely held. It may also be that the Outer Gods may be some sort of embodiment of the primal forces that have shaped the Universe and, as some have suggested, are working toward its eventual decline and destruction.

The Outer Gods seem to gravitate toward certain entities, one of them being the Daemon-Sultan. However, other scholars challenge this and centered the pantheon on the entity Abhoth, a being connected with filth and disease, which dwells beneath the Grey Barrier Peaks in the Dreamlands. It takes the form of a long string of mucus-like grey slime, which forms into a pool when It rests and continually spawns offspring, most of which It devours as soon as they are born. Other Mythos writers take issue with this and state that the Outer Gods are centered on an entity named Daoloth, also known as The Render of the Veils. This being resembled a cluster of multi-colored rods between which eyes seem to come and go and peer out at the space surrounding it. It dwells in a pocket of time-space and is continually moving in order to avoid stagnation. It was worshipped in ancient Atlantis and has the power to confer on its worshippers the ability to see both the past and the future, as well as other dimensions. It also has the power to make a summoner behold the true nature of the Universe, though such knowledge usually drives the individual mad. Daolath is also a blood-drinking entity and can only be summoned with an offering of the caller's own blood.

Just where Yog-Sothoth fits into this hideous pantheon is unclear, but it is speculated that It is one of the central entities of such a grouping. In physical form, it appears in a number of guises. Its most common appearance seems to be as interlinked collection of iridescent spheres, but It can also appear as a mist or in liquid form. In August Derleth's 1945 short novel *The Lurker at the Threshold* (which contained two fragments written by Lovecraft) It takes the form of a black, amorphous shape. Anyone who is touched by Yog-Sothoth is always almost destroyed in the most horrific manner.

According to Friedrich Von Junzt's *Unaussprechlichen Kulten*, Yog-Sothoth is the spawn of a Nameless Mist. This is a creation of the daemon-sultan Azathoth which, according to Von Junzt, spawned Yog-Sothoth during the Hour of the Spiral Wind, which came from the world of Nith. Other sources say that it was Azathoth Itself that created Yog-Sothoth, and as such It is a co-ruler of the Cosmos with the demon-sultan. Still, others say that the entity is in fact one of the Great Old Ones that has been changed in some special way.

If the entity is indeed one of the Great Old Ones then it differs from them in various aspects. The most important of these is that Yog-Sothoth can exist everywhere in time and space at once. However, there is a curious paradox here in that the Lurker at the Threshold would appear to be shut outside our own dimension and can only enter it when It is summoned. Lovecraft expert Daniel Harms has suggested that Yog-Sothoth may have been imprisoned in another dimension by the Elder Gods where time and space converge; because of the gravitational effect of such a point, it may not leave except on rare occasions and by the force of another will. It may also be possible that Yog-Sothoth inhabits another dimension that is closed to us, but can transcend the dimensional barrier if called upon to do so. Once It is called into our world, however, It can ignore any physical, conventional, or traditional boundaries and this makes It an extremely dangerous entity indeed.

Yog-Sothoth can only be summoned at certain times of the year and only by following certain prescribed rituals. The traditional time for summoning the entity is on August 1st (Lammas) or Halloween (October 31st). The actual summoning requires the building of a tower of stones or creating a circle of standing stones into which the entity is called. It also requires a human sacrifice and the spilling of blood, although this does not necessarily have to take place within the tower/circle. A proper spoken summoning ritual is then called for, although those who use this should be aware that the slightest error or mispronunciation will result in the summoner's immediate destruction.

The being can also manifest Itself in a number of forms through avatars of emanations. One of these is Aforgomon, an emanation of the entity created by Clark Ashton Smith. Aforgomon is a curious figure that flickers in and out of time, which It can manipulate as It sees fit. Nothing is known about the physical appearance of this emanation, as It only reveals Itself to those who have angered It, however, It is thought to usually take the form of a blinding white. The emanation is implacably opposed to another entity known as Xehanoth. This entity was summoned from the Timeless Void by the Atlantean priest Calaspa in order to destroy Yog-Sothoth. In being opposed to Aforgomon It is also opposed to Yog-Sothoth Itself.

Yet another of Yog-Sothoth's manifestations is an avatar known as Umr At-Twil or in Its Arabic form, Tawil al-Umr. The entity appears cloaked and cowled like a monk in grey fabric. It holds a sphere of iridescent metal, which is thought to be the very essence of Yog-Sothoth. Beneath the cloak, Umr At-Twil might appear as a huge bipedal canine with a human torso. Some have compared It to the Egyptian god Anubis.

In this incarnation, Yog-Sothoth is the leader of a group of entities known as the Ancient Ones. These are beings that have passed through a distortion in space and time known as the Ultimate Gate, which lies between the known Universe and the place where Yog-Sothoth now dwells. Those who pass through the Gate meet with the entity and become one with It. Other writers have suggested that the Gate leads into a portion of the Dreamworlds, but those who cross its Threshold can never return to their own Universe. Umr at-Twil is the Guardian of this Gate, and those who would wish to cross will have to face It. Just beyond the Gate, the Ancient Ones lie sleeping on pedestals, some carrying scepters in their hands. They will only awake if someone wishes to pass through the Ultimate Gate and join their number. Some have specu-lated that the Ancient Ones are simply the Great Old Ones and that in its guise as Umr At-Twil, Yog-Sothoth is their jailer. The *Book of Thoth* warns against any dealings with this incarnation of Yog-Sothoth which, it says, are fraught with peril and can only result in the destruction of the individual concerned.

Some scholars, such as Harms and Price, have speculated that Umr At-Twil is really a mental barrier, which a person must overcome if he or she is to obtain a true understanding of the Universe in which we live. The Ultimate Gate, it is argued, is really the final obstruction to attaining this knowledge. This is certainly in keeping with some ancient forms of Middle-Eastern Gnosticism, which held that Adepts had to pass through several "Degrees" before attaining the True Gnosis concerning both the world and the Cosmos. The Ultimate Gate is the final test that Yog-Sothoth sets those who would be with It. The occultist Kenneth Grant has linked Umr At-Twil with an entity that he identifies as Choronzon, Guardian of the Great Abyss, and that this refers to a psychological abyss, which the Adept must cross in order to gain the True Knowledge. Others have linked UFO activity with Umr-At-Twil, claiming that what we classify as Unidentified Flying Objects are really manifestations of the creature's psyche.

Bugg-Shoggog *may* be an emanation of Yog-Sothoth, although It may be an en-tity in Its own right. In Lovecraft's tale "The Dunwich Horror" (written in 1928, and published in 1929) it is the mysterious name that is uttered by a dying Wilbur Whately. A number of scholars have interpreted it as part of an invocation to Yog-Sothoth, but this is not certain. It may also be a generic name for the offspring of the entity, or the name of Wilbur's monstrous brother, or Wilbur's own name in the mysterious city of Yian-Ho. An unknown monster is said to dwell in the very center of the city—something that has been spawned on the terrible Plateau of Leng. Von Junzt claimed he visited Yian-Ho, but was very vague about what he found there, and a strange four-handed clock owned by Titus Crow supposedly came from that city.

Other commentators such as Ronald Marsh have hinted, however, that Bugg-Shuggog may be an entity in Its own right, although subservient to Yog-Sothoth. It is described as the Grim Sentinel of Ild-Ryn, whose seal appears in the *Book of Eibon* and will destroy anyone unworthy who attempts the rituals of Yog-Sothoth. Apparently a representation of the Seal is housed somewhere in the Vatican and that the agents of several popes have used it against those whom they determine as "heretics."

Another version of the mysterious Bugg-Shoggog is said to be *Bugg-Shash*, although Bugg-Shash may be one of the Great Old Ones. It takes the form of an inky blackness with myriad compound eyes and slobbering mouths, which make loud chittering sounds. The entity was known and worshipped in ancient Atlantis where sorcerers had called it from another dimension. In some accounts, however, the being that they attempted to summon was in fact Yog-Sothoth but, as their invocation was incomplete, the entity sent Its emanation or avatar instead. When summoned, the entity must be told immediately where It might find a victim or It will take the summoner instead. It can be restrained to some extent in the Pentacle of Power, which is described in the *Necronomicon*, but the powers of the pentacle may only have a limited effect upon It. Once called, It cannot be easily dismissed and will only return to Its own dimension once It has feasted and the appropriate rituals have been completed. It also has power over the recently-buried dead, so dealing with It and Its followers may be an extremely tricky business.

Although it is thought to be an emanation (or servant) of Yog-Sothoth, there are some who claim that Bugg-Shash is no more than an interdimensional parasite that preys on creatures in alternate realities.

Whether Bugg-Shoggog or Bugg-Shash are simply emanations of Yog-Sothoth or whether they are Its servants is still a matter for debate. What is known is that they are inextricably tied to the creature in some way and that all of these entities should be avoided where possible.

Theories Concerning Yog-Sothoth

Aside from the notions about emanations and avatars of the entity, there are several theories about Yog-Sothoth and Its history.

The first is that the entity is opposed to the mysterious being known as Nodens, Lord of the Great Abyss. The nature and cause of this enmity is unknown, but it is thought to run extremely deep. According to an interpretation of a reference in the *Necronomicon,* this hostility will continue until the end of time when both entities will destroy each other.

Another theory links Yog-Sothoth with Biblical lore. It is said that when It first appeared on Earth, the entity was imprisoned using the Elder or Yellow Sign beneath a Black Mountain. It lay asleep until It was disturbed and awakened by Moses who freed the entity for his own purposes. In fact, there is a theory that Yahweh is a manifestation of Yog-Sothoth. Because of the complexity of early Biblical teaching and study, this theory may well be discounted.

Still, there is another suggestion that Yog-Sothoth is not a single entity at all, but is made up of a trio of separate entities who appear to contribute to a cohesive whole. Each of these entities can function separately, but if they are summoned together using a certain ritual they can cross into our dimension as Yog-Sothoth. In this respect, Yog-Sothoth appears almost as a rather perverse version of the Christian Trinity. If certain rituals are carried out then the entity can remain in our dimension indefinitely. However, none of these theories have gained much acceptance.

Liber Damnatus Damnationum

Although there are references to Yog-Sothoth in a number of ancient works (the most notable being the *Necronomicon*) perhaps the most sinister is the *Liber Damnatus Damnationum*, also known as the *Liber Damnatus*, or the *Book of Damnation*. This is also mentioned in Lovecraft's *The Case of Charles Dexter Ward* and is reputedly a volume of dubious antiquity. It was supposedly written in Latin during the Middle Ages by a monk named Janus Aquaticus, about whom little is known. The book did not get published until 1647 in London. There were two handwritten copies in existence, one of which is now held by an organization known as the Brotherhood of the Green Flame, who worship Tulzcha, another of the Great Old Ones, which appears as a pillar of fire and Juk-Shabb on the planet Yakub. Interestingly, it is thought that perhaps Juk-Shabb may be a manifestation of Yog-Sothoth. Another copy was said to have been in the library of Joseph Curwen, one of Providence's most influential citizens. It is not certain whether this was a handwritten or printed copy, but it was most probably the latter.

The book contains a lot of information about what it calls "The Time of Great Dying," when the Great Old Ones clear away Mankind from the world and will permanently establish themselves on Earth. In this period, Yog-Sothoth will dominate an otherwise-barren planet. However, those who have aided the Great Old Ones will be admitted to their ranks and Yog-Sothoth will transform them. The volume contains a formula that allows a sorcerer to call down the entity and to become immortal through merging with one of his or her descendants on a future Earth. The formula contained in the book, however, can only be used at certain times of the year, specifically at the equinoxes when the Veil between the dimensions is particularly thin and the being can cross over into our world. Great care must be taken in using this formula, as it might also draw wandering dimensional shamblers across the interdimensional barrier. Such creatures are humanoid, but with wrinkled hides and massive, tearing claws. They either wander the dimensional barrier or else dwell alongside Yog-Sothoth in Its dimension. Some say they are further manifestations of the entity, or are connected to it in some unknown way. They can occasionally appear in our dimension without being summoned, but this is very rare. When the shamblers encounter humans they usually seize them and disappear with them into another dimension or into the space between the dimensions and they are never seen again. According to the *Liber Dam-natus,* the shamblers may be the servants of Yog-Sothoth.

Something similar appears in a section of the so-called *Book of the Black Star* or *Book of Darkness*, which was translated several times and in to several languages including a partial transcription into English. The tome reveals what the world will be like at the end of time and when it is under the rule of a combination of the Great Old Ones and the Outer Gods, particularly Yog Sothoth. It may have been from the pages of this book that Wilbur Whately knew what he would look like and what he would be called (Bugg-Shoggog) in "The Dunwich Horror."

The Worshippers of Yog-Sothoth

Humans are, of course, not the only species to acknowledge and worship Yog-Sothoth. Chief among the entity's followers are a race known as the Mi-go. These are beings with a vast stellar empire all through the Galaxy and possibly beyond. Their nearest outpost to Earth is Pluto, which they call Yuggoth. They are crustaceans with wings and egg-shaped heads, which constantly change color. These heads appear to be their main means of communication.

They came to Earth during the Jurassic period for mining purposes, and they have bases in the Appalachians, the Andes, and the Himalayas, where they are kept secret by an unknown scientific means. They also recruit the local populace from time to time in order to keep their activities hidden. Even so, word of their presence sometimes filters out and becomes part of rural folklore and legend. The Mi-go eat a variety of fungus, which they transport from various worlds since it cannot grow on Earth. They consume this by passing a metal cylinder containing the fungus through their bodies.

From time to time, the Mi-go will conduct experiments on humans in order to find out if their potential as servitors can be developed. Through the years, however, these experiments have declined as the species recognizes that humans have a very different mentality than they do. Much of their current scientific research now revolves around ob-servation, though on occasion they will kidnap a human to study him or her more closely.

Many of the Mi-go bases lie underground and, along with their laboratories, there are a number of hidden temples dedicated to the worship of Yog-Sothoth. Indeed, when Earth has been secretly attacked in the past, the Mi-go have always fought on the side of the Outer Gods because of this attachment. In fact, the Mi-go have always aided the forces of Cthulhu and Its spawn because of a perceived connection between this entity and Yog-Sothoth. They revere the entity as "the Beyond One," perhaps because It dwells in another dimension into which they cannot go. However, it's though that some of those whom they have kidnapped are sometimes offered up to the entity as a sacrifice.

Besides the Mi-go a number of other entities worship Yog-Sothoth. One of these are a series of vaporous minds that dwell in the Infinite Darkness beyond space, and which continually mull over certain of the affairs of our own Universe. Very little is known about these minds except that they are very intelligent and very ancient. They somehow both observe and consider our own Universe, although what their motives are is unknown. The being is also worshipped by various pallid plant creatures that dwell in the fungus jungles lying far beneath the surface of Mercury. These creature who are half-plant, half-fungus experience Yog-Sothoth as an echo, which travels across the Solar System.

On our own world, a number of individuals and cultures have worshipped the entity under various names and guises. For instance, it was worshipped by certain cults in the woods of Averoigne, although such devotion does not appear to have been widespread, and may have died out over time. Among the ancient Aztecs there is evidence of such worship although, once again, it is difficult to determine its extent. Certain sorcerers and shamans have venerated the entity in the hope of gaining some measure of control over space and time. Their motives for contacting the entity vary from the wish to hold a specific individual in a time warp to stepping outside of space and time themselves. But possibly after a period of time Yog-Sothoth will take some of these souls and destroy them or consume them.

Anubis

The phrase "Opener of the Way" may give some clue as to what Lovecraft may have been thinking as he invented the entity Yog-Sothoth, as the nickname is often specific to one of the ancient Egyptian gods. The deity in question is Anubis. He was responsible for judging the souls of the dead and for guiding them to another level of reality beyond this mortal world.

Anubis was initially known in Egypt as Inpu or Anapa. Indeed, many believed that it was his duty to guide those of lordly rank safely to the Afterlife, and he was also said to oversee the burial rites of the ancient kings. He was also the Keeper of the Gate into the Otherworld and none could pass over into the next world, except with the permission of Anubis. In order to allow souls to cross, Anubis had to weight the heart of each individual against *ma'at* which was the ancient Egyptian concept of Truth. It was his decision as to who should pass on into the next level of existence or should languish in the Underworld. The "way" into another existence could not be accessed unless Anubis opened it, hence his nickname.

In some Greek texts he is referred to as "the Barker" and also as a barbarian god. However, during what became known as the Ptolemaic period (roughly 332 B.C. to 32 B.C.), Anubis became worshipped as a Greek god under the name Hermanubis. Similar to his Egyptian counterpart, Hermanubis was "an Opener of the Way," guiding souls into another realm of reality.

The idea of Yog-Sothoth certainly seems to be a complicated one, perhaps drawing on a number of influences to which numerous Mythos writers have added. Could *something* like Yog-Sothoth lurk out there? Is this the Thing that waits behind Lovecraft's perception?

Shadows Beyond the Stars

Father Yig

Although he is an integral being in a number of Mythos stories, the original idea of Yig (sometimes known as "Father Yig" to his disciples), the serpent-man may not have been completely created by Lovecraft. "The Curse of Yig" appeared in the November 1929 edition of *Weird Tales* under the name Zealia Bishop (a writer of romantic fiction and one of Lovecraft's correspondents) and was later published in 1953 by August Derleth's Arkham House Press. There is no doubt that Lovecraft aided her in the writing, but scholars have argued about the extent of his input. It has been suggested that Bishop supplied Lovecraft with a rough story, which he may have rewritten. David Harms and Donald Tyson have stated that Bishop did all the background research and supplied Lovecraft with her notes so he could ghost write the story for her. It was the first of three tales that he would work on with Bishop— the other two being *The Mound* (1930) and *Medusa's Coil* (published in *Weird Tales* in January 1939, nearly two years after Lovecraft's death).

The figure of Yig is a bit confusing. According to Lovecraft and other Mythos writers, he is one of the Great Old Ones who came to Earth from the stars in the distant past, though it is unknown as to how Zealia Bishop envisaged the entity. It's thought that her story may have been originally intended as a love story centered on old Indian myth. Set in Oklahoma around the 1880s, "The Curse of Yig," centered around a young married couple who learn about an ancient Indian snake-god named Yig, which can turn ordinary humans into its less-than-human servants. The effects of the legend aren't helped by the fact that the husband has a snake phobia and that his wife accidentally disturbs a nest of rattlesnakes on their property. They suspect that Yig may be lurking nearby and may be trying to influence them. They attempt a number of rituals in order to keep Yig away, but in the end the woman kills her husband believing he is the creature. She is subsequently confined to a hospital for the insane where she dies, but not before giving birth to a half-human, half-snake being.

This is a straightforward horror story, and perhaps that's what Zealia Bishop intended it to be. Lovecraft, however, appears to have given it a depth of cosmic eeriness, which shaped the entity named in the title. Yig, therefore, took on many of the attributes of the Mythos and became one of its central entities.

In Mythos terms, Yig arrived on Earth countless millennia ago from a world called Zandanua where Its brother Rokon still dwells. Yig was something of a scientist and Its experiments with genetic material resulted in all the reptiles and insects that exist in the world today. According to some, humanity itself is a by-product of the creature's experimentation.

Other Mythos authors argue that this is completely wrong and Yig did not fall from the stars at all. They argue that Yig is the offspring of a great dragon or serpent named Mappo no Ryujin, who allegedly slept on an island in the center of a lake far beneath the fabled continent of Mu. Leaving its awful parent, Yig traveled to the underground caverns of K'n-Yan, a county of red or blue-lit caverns, which lie somewhere far below Oklahoma. They contain the ruins of abandoned cities that were built by the serpent-men of Valusia, who fled there after the destruction of their lands on the surface world. When they abandoned the worship of Yig for that of the toad-god Tsathoggua, the serpent-god brought his wrath upon them and the few who remained loyal simply fled to even deeper caves. According to some texts, Yig now dwells in the Pit of Ngoth in the caverns of Yoth, which are part of the underground land of K'n-Yan.

However, the worship of the serpent-man appears to have spread to the surface of the planet, possibly into the south-western states of America and Mexico, where the entity was venerated as Quetzalcoatl or Kulkulcan. Some of this worship may even form the basis of a few fringe voodoo cults. Many of Yig's followers share the same consciousness as their god and are able to perceive things in special ways; this has become the basis for shamanism in some places.

Certain Indian tribes of the Great Plains still worship Yig secretly through their shamans. Some of these are actually the children of Yig, who have taken on human form. Sometimes the human disguise decreases as they approach adulthood and they become more reptilian in appearance and generally shun contact outside their own community circle. These are usually shamans with specialized gifts such as the gift of prophesy.

As an entity, Yig has an ambiguous nature—sometimes malevolent toward humanity and sometimes rather benevolent. Its mood can change in an instant, however, and therefore it is not to be trusted. It is also wise to placate the being with offerings, particularly in the fall of the year. This can constitute drum beating, gifts of corn and wine, and by carrying out various rituals. If a human should harm a serpent it incurs Yig's wrath. Such wrath manifests itself in the madness of the individual, who has wronged the entity, but it can also take the form of mutated and deformed offspring or of "visitations" by those snakes Yig commands, which It deems as Its "children." Those who especially displease the entity are transformed into snakes or snake-like beings.

In art, Yig is often portrayed as a being that has the lower body characteristics of a serpent and the upper torso of a man, as a huge winged serpent (sometimes spitting fire), or simply as a great dragon. He usually sits on a heap of human skulls with smaller serpents coiling about close by. According to some accounts, when in human form, Yig's head appears slightly larger than that of an ordinary human, he has no real nose (although he may have some small breathing slits), and his eyes are extremely narrow and slanted like that of a snake. Some even say his mouth is exceedingly fanged. From time to time, Yig will send out his avatars—emanations of Itself—into the world, but like their master, these creatures must hibernate, especially in the warmth.

In the *Necronomicon*, Alhazred states that Yig and Nyarlathotep are bitter rivals though the reason for this enmity is unclear. This means that the followers of one may be the opponents of the other. There are also supposed connections to lesser entities such as Nug and Yeb, two minor beings whose significance seems to remain a mystery. They may be the children of Yig, although authorities claim that they are the children of Shub-Niggurath and Yog-Sothoth. Yig is also credited as being the father of Han (or Dark Han), a minor entity of divination, which appears in the pages of *De Vermis Mysteriis*. Han often appears in human form as a dark, cloaked man with huge, burning eyes, continually shrouded in a kind of mist. His dwelling place is the shunned Plateau of Leng, but he is somehow connected to Yig in the caverns of K'n-Yan. Because of their suggested similarities, Yig has sometimes been linked with Byatis, but it is unclear whether these two entities are the same or not.

The main text that deals with Yig is known as *The Ssthaat Scriptures.* Reference to it appears in James Ambuehl's *The Snake Farm* (1998) and Allen Mackey's *The Caller from Oklahoma* (1993–94). It is said that the 17th-century Native American monks wrote the text, though its specific origin is largely unknown. Details of the text are also very sketchy, but it seems to be an account of Yig's battles against creatures that would invade Its Oklahoma land, which It has vowed to protect. It also contains certain rituals for invoking the snake-god and one that may even stop time itself.

Even more interesting is a work known as *The Vatican Codex.* Although this document bears no actual title, it is held in a Restricted Section of the Vatican Library and is not available for any form of study except by special dispensation. It is supposedly Mayan in origin, brought back from the New World by Spanish priests.

It depicts the Mayan creation myth in a somewhat similar fashion to the *Popol Vuh,* the document translated by Father Ximinez in the town of Santo Tomas Chulia in Western Guatemala in 1701. In the text, reference is made to a being known as either Ghatanothoa or Yig, who came to Earth from the star Arcturus. Seeing a goddess bathing at dawn, the being leaps upon her and attempts to rape her. She manages to escape and flee, however, and Yig's semen falls into the sea, giving birth to all the creatures and animals on the Earth. In retaliation for Yig's outrage, the Old Ones imprisoned him far beneath the surface of the Earth on an island in the middle of a great lake of fire. But they also took some of his seed and used it to create Humanity. However, Yig continues to plot against them and to destroy humankind.

A number of writers also take issue with this explanation stating that Yig did not come from Arcturus at all, but rather was a god of the serpent people who dwelt on our planet in some primordial time.

History of the Serpent

The serpent is, of course, one of the most ancient images of evil in existence. In Hebrew tradition it is the serpent that tempts Eve in the Garden of Eden. However, the worship of snakes and serpents is recorded in a number of old cultures representing the fear and awe with which the creature was viewed.

Serpents (or nagas) were highly regarded in Hindu society. Indeed, the word *naga* in Sanskrit means "deity." The word can also refer to the King Cobra, which is regarded as a "royal" snake and a lord among serpents. Although snakes feature heavily in various forms throughout Hindu mythology, perhaps the nearest version to that of Yig is the goddess Manasa (or Vishahara) destroyer of poisons, who is worshipped in north-eastern India. She is a fertility goddess, and is also the sister of Vasuki, king of the serpents. She is also said to be a daughter of the powerful Hindu god Shiva. She is supposedly capricious and self-pitying and needs to be placated regularly. In art, she is depicted as a woman, covered in coiling snakes, seated upon a lotus or standing upon a huge snake, and sheltered by the hoods of seven cobras. She sometimes carries a child on her lap in the fashion of the Christian Madonna—the child is generally assumed to be her son Astika, who protected the serpent-race from some of the ancient Hindu kings. In some depictions, she is shown as one-eyed, as one of her eyes was burned out by her step-mother. She appears in the *Mahabharata* and also the Scriptural *Puranas*, emphasising her importance as a deity.

In the Near East, the ancient Sumerian peoples believed that snakes were immortal, because they could shed their skins and seem forever young. It was also believed that snakes could confer this attribute on their followers and worshippers. Prior to the establishment of the Israelite kingdoms and the dominance of Yahweh, snake worship flourished widely through parts of the Middle East, particularly among the Canaanites. Powerful snake cults supposedly thrived in two of the larger Canaanite cities—Megiddo and Gezer. The cults may have influenced the religions of the region, as elements of them appear in Hittite worship as well.

In Greece, snakes were equated with wisdom, thus a Cretan goddess (who was reputedly worshipped at the court of King Minos), is shown carrying two serpents in her hands as twin symbols of power and knowledge. Snakes appeared time and time again in Greek legend as monsters. For example, the massive serpent Typhon, the father of storms and volcanic activity, is often portrayed as a massive snake. He was an enemy of the Olympian gods and usually depicted as a massive reptile with more than 100 heads.

The Gorgons were three fearsome female snake-headed monsters that supposedly dwelt on an island near present-day Corfu. Their hair was made up of continually coiling snakes, which dripped venom while their snake-like gaze had the power to turn men into stone. They also wore belts of twining snakes around their middle. Two of them were immortal, but the third sister, Medusa, was not, and was killed by the legendary Perseus. From the blood of the dead, Gorgon sprang the famous winged horse Pegasus. It is also said that when Perseus flew over the Libyan Desert on Pegasus, carrying the Gorgon's head, the blood dropped to the ground and gave birth to the Amphisbaena—from the Greek meaning "both ways"—a miraculous snake with a head at each en of its body.

The most famous of all the serpent-gods, however, was the female monster Python, the earth-serpent at Delphi. Python was the former enemy of the god Apollo, who slew her and took over her sanctuary as his own. The area became one of the most celebrated oracles in the entire world. Indeed, so famous was the priestess at Delphi that many seers in many other lands became known as "Pythonesses." In fact, when the Israelite king Saul went to consult the Witch of Endor, she was described to him as a "woman with a Python."

One of the most celebrated scenes involving people being destroyed by serpents is that of Laocoon and his sons being crushed to death by large serpents that arose out of the sea. Laocoon was a priest of Poseidon who warned the Trojans against accepting the Trojan Horse as a gift from the departing Greeks. Poseidon, who had supported the Greek cause, became so enraged that he sent great serpents to destroy Laocoon and two of his sons.

There is also some evidence that serpent-worship was widespread in parts of Europe before and during the time of the Roman Empire. Rumors of ancient temples dedicated to snake-worship on the Iberian Peninsula are recorded in several accounts of that area, and it is mentioned in Roman texts that the Slavs may have kept serpents in some of their temples as a manifestation of their early gods.

The Vikings too, believed in serpent worship; their most famous great serpent was the Midgard Serpent, who slept at the foot of Yggdrasil, and whose coils were entwined around its roots. This was one of the children of Loki, the Norse god of mischief and the giantess Angrbooa.

In Africa, the center of serpent worship was Dahomey (now Benin) on the western coast. It is probably from this area that the idea of the great serpent Damballah found its way into voodoo worship in both Haiti and America. One of the oldest forms of the voodoo belief is known as Rada Voodoo which takes its name from Arada, a village in Dahomey. The worship centered on the great snake known as *Le Grand Zombi* (in certain forms of voodoo religion the *zombi* is not a walking dead, man, but a huge serpent), which was the embodiment of the god Damballah-Wedo. The *veve* (emblem) of the god includes two intertwined serpents, and he is revered as a massive snake. This form of voodoo is prominent in certain parts of the southern states of America, particularly in New Orleans.

The main form of serpent worshipped in Dahomey is the *dang-gbi,* a type of python that is native to the region. In the ancient kingdom of Whydah (also known as Huedah or Hueda), snakes were especially revered. There is still a sanctuary there through which between 50 and 60 pythons glide at any time. It is expressly forbidden under local law to kill any snake and, up until around 1857, there were processions of snakes from which the uninitiated were excluded—this was reputedly *Le Gand Zombi* and his many wives. It is also said that a snake was carried around on a cushion and was shown to worshippers at such gatherings.

Much has been made of snake worship in Egypt, particularly in relation to the god Set. However, this notion is more from the imagination of Robert E. Howard. In one of his Conan the Barbarian stories—*The Phoenix and the Sword*, which appeared in *Weird Tales* in December 1932—he described Father Set, a seven-headed serpent-god in Stygia, which was worshipped by the priest and magician Thoth-Amon. Howard was so struck by the image that he incorporated it into his King Kull stories, stating that Set had been worshipped by the serpent men of Valusia. In ancient Egyptian religion, Set or Sutekh was the god of the desert, of storm, and of foreigners. The main Egyptian snake god was Apep, an evil deity whose worship flourished during the time of the New Kingdom between the 16th and 11th centuries B.C., and who was the implacable enemy of the sun-god Ra. Its name simply meant darkness and wrong-doing, and it was seen as a massive snake or a dragon that lived in the desert. Later on, such a creature became strongly associated with the Devil.

Among the Celts, serpents were worshipped, although they were not found in every part of the Celtic world. However, in some parts of England and Wales, rocks that are known as "snake stones" have been found, and this may be an indication of snake or serpent worship. But curiously, it is in Ireland (where no snakes exist) that such worship seems to have been widespread. In Glenshesk, deep in the Glens of Antrim in Northern Ireland, on the site of what appears to have been an ancient pagan enclosure, a stone stands bearing the symbol of a rearing snake. Snakes also feature heavily in early Irish Christian art, which perhaps shows the importance of pagan snake cults around the arrival of Christianity. Some scholars have suggested that these representations may have been initially phallic in nature, but James Bonwick, in his *Irish Druids and Old Irish Religions* suggests that Christianity may have supplanted many of the snake cults that existed in various parts of the country.

A singular sculptured cross at Killamery, Kilkenny, shows two snakes twisted around the upright in a rather menacing fashion. No legend is attached to this cross, but it is thought to represent the triumph of the Church over the forces of pagan darkness. There is a similar but less explicable carving on a baptismal font in Cashel, Co. Tipperary, with a number of serpents adorning headstones and sarcophagi in the same place. Serpents seem to be strongly associated with the site and this prompts the notion that the area may have been the location of an important serpent cult. Indeed, the Crozier of Cashel, which was found during the last century, has two serpents intertwined around the lower part of its staff. The handle is also carved with the figure of a man standing on a serpent, the head of which is rearing to bite him.

Other carved stones include a magnificent serpent carved in a Celtic cross at the monastery of Clonmanoise in County Offaly. At Lough MacNean in southwest Fermanagh, St. Patrick's dog supposedly destroyed a great serpent that rose up out of the water and threatened the saint. An ancient carving of the dog with a serpent in its mouth was said to have once existed near the village of Belcoo (*Beal Cu*—the mouth of the hound). Similarly, at Banagher, near the village of Dungiven in North County Derry, a local holy man, St. Murrough O'Heaney, supposedly defeated the last great serpent in Ireland at a place that is still known as Altapaist (the Height of the Serpent). The shrine tomb of St. Murrough still stands in the cemetery of Old Banagher Church, with the church now in ruins. Stories of paiste (Old Irish for serpents) exist all over Ireland, many of them appearing to be defeated by holy men and early Christian saints. The most famous story in Ireland, of course, concerns St. Patrick, who drove the entire snake population out of the country. This mass exodus is supposed to have taken place at the formerly pagan site of Cruachan Aigle and is supposed to be the reason why there are no snakes in Ireland.

Father Yig and the Serpent People

Mankind are, perhaps, not the first intelligent lifeforms to inhabit our planet. According to Mythos writers, a species of highly intelligent bipedal reptiles appeared during the Permian period about 299 million years ago. With their vast intelligence they became skilled magicians, harnessing the primal powers of the Universe for their own ends. Their power centered on the fabled Cobra Crown, which was a tall conical piece of wrought gold, wound in the shape of a coiled serpent and encrusted with diamonds. The Crown was also the focus of great supernatural power. It allowed the wearer to read the thoughts and control the actions of those near to him on her. The power of the Crown varied according to the sorcerer who wore it—if the mage was weak then only one mind could be controlled, but if the wizard was powerful, thousands might be manipulated. This artifact was worn by the wizard kings of Valusia—an area of the great prehistoric continent of Thuria, a fictional period of history created by Robert E. Howard, which was the stronghold of the serpent people. In Valusia, the serpent-men built mighty stone cities comprising both laboratories and temples—most of their worship revolved around Yig, Byatis, Han, and Tsathoggua. The coming of the Triassic Age brought new climatic conditions that were unfavourable to the serpent-people and the race went into decline as many of them fled underground.

As the reptilian people disappeared, the Cobra Crown was carried off to an Atlantic island where it was placed in a shrine to be worshipped. However, it was stolen by pirates and carried East. It later fell into the hands of the powerful Hyborian wizard Thoth-Amon, but before he could use it to dominate the world around him, it was wrested away from him and drained of its power. Since then, it has vanished and its whereabouts are unknown. However, the loss of the Crown was not the only problem that beset the serpent race.

Human evolution was difficult for the serpent people and ultimately led to the downfall of their empire. The new and emerging race swept the old species aside and, although some of the reptiles provided certain knowledge in order to help the humans develop, they were largely consigned to history. To escape the decimation of their culture, many of the serpent-folk disappeared into the hills of Wales or deep into the caverns of Yoth. Many put themselves into a kind of hibernation, although others disguised themselves as humans using their magical abilities. Apart from a few abortive attempts to reinstate themselves in what was once Valusia, they have never posed a serious threat to humanity. However, their worship of Yig continues to this day.

Today, the serpent people are small in number, but they may still be among us. There are suggestions that there may be another rising of the species—an attempt to take back lands that were formerly theirs and to recreate Valusia. Those who may dwell among us certainly have magical skills and, perhaps more importantly, knowledge of poisons, which they can use against us.

Lambdon Worm

Medieval folklore is full of stories of saints and Christian knights defeating massive serpents or "dragons." In Eastern Europe, the holy knight Iorgi defeated a "dragon "somewhere in Romania, while in Transylvania one of the Bathory ancestors supposedly slayed a great serpent that lived in a cavern in the Carpathian Mountains. The greatest English folktale, however, is that of the Lambdon Worm, which comes from a slightly later period. Could the old English legend of the Lambdon Worm that appears in many ballad sheets and books of folktales all over the world (including America) have somehow set the idea for the notion of Yig in the mind of Lovecraft and several other Mythos writers? Is the deadly worm the forerunner of the ancient Father of Serpents?

During the time of the Crusades in the 11th, 12th, and 13th centuries the Lambdon family held estates in County Durham, England. At the time, a certain John Lambdon skipped church to go fishing in the River Wear. On the shore of the river he found a large serpent or *wyrm* (the ancient Saxon word *wyrm* is often used to denote a snake or serpent). He thought it was an eel and decided to take it home to make mischief. On his way, Lambdon met an old man on the road who issued two dire warnings—first about missing church in order to go fishing, and the second concerning the creature that he carried in his bag. Badly frightened by the queer old man, John tossed the worm down a nearby well and promptly forgot about it. Several years later, he regretted his earlier misdemeanors and went to fight in the Crusades.

While he was away, the worm grew very large and became poisonous, even poisoning the water of the well around it. Livestock started to go missing and villagers suspected that the worm had grown so large that it had escaped from the well. Eventually, the Worm fully emerged and wrapped itself around a nearby hill. It began to devour everything around it, including small children, and eventually John Lambdon's aged father had to placate the beast by feeding it the milk of nine good cows from a wooden trough each day. Soon the estates became destitute as the Worm began to consume more and more food. It moved itself from the hill and settled in the River Wear where it wrapped itself around a large rock.

After seven years, John Lambdon returned from the Crusades to find his father's estates in ruin. He resolved to kill the worm but in order to do so, he went to consult a witch who lived near Durham. The old woman revealed that he was responsible for the worm, so it must be him that kills it. However, she also warned him that, if he defeated it, he must also kill the first living thing that he meets on his way home, or his family will be cursed for nine generations and will not die in their beds.

John went and prepared the armor according to the witch's instructions and he arranged with his father that if he killed the worm he would sound his hunting horn three times, whereupon his father would release his favorite hound. He then went down to the Wear to fight the worm. The creature attacked, trying to wrap itself around him, but was cut to pieces on the spearheads—the bits of it being washed away before they could reform and heal themselves. With the worm now destroyed, John sounded his hunting horn. On hearing it, his father was so overjoyed that he forgot about releasing the hound and ran to congratulate him. He was the first living thing that John Lambdon met. John could not bring himself to kill his father, and so the curse was activated.

As a result, John's son, Sir Robert, drowned while crossing a river at Newrig. Two of his descendants, both called William (father and son) were both killed in the English Civil War, while another, Sir Henry, died in his carriage just outside Lambdon Village in 1761. Their deaths contributed heavily to the legend of the foul worm.

Strange serpent worship from around the world, accounts of mysterious scaled humanoids, and whispers of a mysterious serpent race dating back into prehistory may all have contributed to the overall legend of Yig. Or did Lovecraft know something that we don't? Perhaps Yig or something like it *does* exist somewhere out there....

Shadows Beyond the Stars

Ithaqua

Of all the Great Old Ones who came to Earth from beyond the stars, few are as dangerous as Ithaqua, The Wind-Walker. Thankfully, It is confined to areas of the far north where encounters are limited, although that does not diminish Its ferocity or malignancy.

General descriptions of Ithaqua are vague, and it is difficult to determine Its physical form. Sometimes it appears as a gigantic, quasi-anthropomorphic being with huge burning red eyes and webbed feet; in other accounts, it appears as a massive cloud or snow formation with the same burning eyes. The physical form of It is called a Wendigo, a creature of Canadian and North American myth and folklore. It can travel on the winds and can achieve tremendous speeds and cover a great deal of ground in minutes. It has been known to tear humans apart limb from limb with its ferocity, so this not an entity to be trifled with.

With some of the Great Old Ones, it's possible to pinpoint where they've come from, but not Ithaqua. However, it is speculated that the entity may have come from a dark, freezing planet orbiting a nameless star on the very fringes of the Universe. From there, it traveled to a similar cold world named Borea where it rested on a plateau before traveling to Earth. There is some dispute as to where Borea might lie; John Sterman suggests that it might lie far out in outer space (perhaps in the galaxy of Andromeda) and that it is an ice-world, while Daniel Harms and Brian Lumley suggest that it may lie in a parallel dimension in which Ithaqua was initially imprisoned. They also state that Ithaqua also has a cult on Borea known as the Children of the Winds, which boasts thousands of members. Ithaqua was trapped on the moon Numinos, but was freed by his adherents and fled to Earth. However, It returns to Borea on occasion to receive the worship of Its followers. Through the years It has brought many beings and creatures from our own world to this distant planet in an attempt to colonize some of its remote areas.

On our own world, Ithaqua sought out a habitat that vaguely resembled the environment from which it had come: the North Pole. The entity now dwells in a building named the Temple of the Winds, which may only appear to humans at the Winter Solstice. However, when the stars are right, Ithaqua can travel south to more temperate climates, although It can't stay there for long. It isn't known if the being can manifest itself in the Antarctic, as there is little knowledge of It in that region, however, such a journey around the world may be possible. Certainly It is not confined to our world, but appears to have the ability to "fly" through space and visits the planet Borea from time to time. When It returns from the Outside, the Wind-Walker will reinvigorate Its cult all through the North and urge them to act violently against some more settled communities. Its return is always accompanied by frenzy among some of the Northern Indian tribes.

Shortly after Its return from the coldness of the interstellar depths, Ithaqua will sometimes venture south to warmer climes by walking on the winds. No matter where the winds blow in the world, Ithaqua can be there, as they provide a ready path for wherever It wishes to go. There are some who say that It actually has command over them and other atmospheric elements as well.

Ithaqua's history is difficult to ascertain, and it's possible that It has been worshipped under a number of other names in various parts of the world. For instance, It was supposedly worshipped in Atlantis under the name Avaloth. Avaloth is one of the entities mentioned in the *Eltdown Shards* and is referred to as a voracious and rapacious god. At one stage in Earth's history, it tried to encase the entire world in a great sheet of ice, although Its purpose for doing this is unknown.

Daniel Harms suggests that Ithaqua may have been worshipped in some of the Nordic counties by the Vikings as Thor, but given the amount of information that exists on the Norse deity this would on the face of it seem extremely dubious. He is also of the opinion that the entity was worshipped in the guise of Quetzalcoatl by the Mesoamerican cultures and as Enlil by the ancient Sumerians, Hittites, and Canaanites. However, much of Its worship is now confined to the northern reaches of Canada and America, though the majority of Its cults died out in the late 19th century. Some secret centers of worship still remain in places like Stillwater, Manitoba. Here, the inhabitants of the town vanished overnight without a trace, although it's claimed that certain individuals have heard voices crying for help in the area of the former town. In Cold Harbor, Alaska, there is thought to be a thriving cult operating within the town. Cults such as these are reputed to engage in human sacrifice and child abductions. Although a number of official investigations have been carried out into the existence of such a cult, nothing concrete has been found.

There are also non-human worshippers of Ithaqua among these snowy wastes. Deep in the misty forests of Greenland, survivals of extremely ancient times still lurk. These are species of the Gnophkeh, described as horned, furred creatures that walk on two, four, and sometimes six legs. Some anthropologists say they are a form of proto-human, which has managed to survive to the present day; other scholars state that they are a form of servitor race, which the Great Old Ones created soon after they arrived on Earth. They probably existed in the kingdoms of the world before the Great Ice Age. Legend states that they were a slave race of the serpent men of Valusia, but managed to break free and establish their own kingdom, which was then attacked by the Voormis, who drove them into the area of the polar wastes, which they still inhabit. They are highly intelligent and great hunters, and through inherent magical powers they can call up storms in order to conceal their presence. They are believed to be worshippers of Ithaqua and have constructed invisible temples to the entity among the northern snows.

The early Gnophkeh were not the only ancient beings to worship the Wind-Walker. Legends from Hyperborea speak of a pre-human race known as the Ptetholites, who called down demons and avatars of the Great Old Ones (particularly Ithaqua) on their enemies. Their history is written upon the Broken Columns of Geph, a series of shattered monuments located within the coastal jungles of Liberia. These pillars may date from the time of Hyperborea, although some date them as much older and state that they are mentioned in the writings of Teh Atht, a wizard from the primal land of Theem'hdra. The writings on them resemble that which is found on the Eltdown Shards, and may come from a similar source. It was at these pillars that the elders of the Ptetholites carved the history of their species, as well as warnings against those who would call on the magic of the Great Old Ones. Their enemies allegedly tried to strike out these inscriptions and even to destroy the columns themselves, but the monuments still lie deep in the jungle today.

According to the Columns, the Ptetholites made the mistake of calling down demons against the formidable wizard Edril Ghambiz of Esipah, who was able to turn the magic back upon them tenfold. The doom that came upon them simply wiped out the Ptetholites, and the Columns of Geph remain as their only marker. However, the writings on them contain a hymn of praise to Ithaqua, among many of the other invocations.

Aside from those who worship It, it is also thought that the Wind-Walker is responsible for a number of strange disappearances within the northern regions, especially Canada. There are stories about people who have disappeared in the snowy wastes for several months, only to reappear again not far from where they disappeared, usually encased in a thin film of snow. In most cases, their minds will be gone and they will babble wildly of Ithaqua and of the strange things that this creature has permitted them to see. Some of them carry strange items, which have clearly originated in other parts of the world from where they were found. Curiously, the victims of the Wind-Walker survive the coldest temperatures while they are gone, however, after their return, the individuals do not live all that long.

Some students of Lovecraft suggest that there is some link between Ithaqua and another of the Great Old Ones named Hastur—perhaps Ithaqua is Hastur's servant? Indeed, there seems to be some sort of enmity between Ithaqua and some of the other Great Old Ones who would appear to shun the Wind-Walker. It is also known that Ithaqua is one of the few Great Old Ones who will readily attempt to mate with the human females that It carries away. In doing so, it hopes to create beings that can transcend the limitations that have been imposed upon It by the Elder Gods. And the results of such matings are scattered across the northern wastes and also remote mountain areas. None of them have been even slightly successful, but have often produced deformed and monstrous creatures.

The Yeti

It's here that Mythos fiction may mix with folklore and legend. High in the Himalaya Mountains between Nepal and Tibet, a strange hominid being is said to dwell and this, argue Lovecraftian scholars, may be a servant of Ithaqua or some manifestation of the entity. Known as the Abominable Snowman, Yeti, Meh-Teh, or Shukpa, the creature has become one of the most intriguing mysteries of our modern world. Scientists have argued that it is another form of human life, coexisting with us, but some also say that it might be some sort of supernatural being. The idea of the creature living high amid the mountain snows has become one of the enduring facets of Western popular culture in the 20th century. Although generally regarded as something of a myth, there are many naturalists who still believe that the idea of an unknown hominid creature still has some merit. So, is there something there, and is it somehow connected to Ithaqua?

The name *Yeti* could be a compound of Tibetan words that may mean "bear of a rocky place," or "bear *in* a rocky place." There are other local names for it such as *Mirka* meaning "wild man" or *Jo Bran* meaning "man-eater." Of particular interest of Lovecraft readers is an alternate Tibetan name for the creature: Mi-go. In the Mythos the Mi-Go are a race of winged beings that came to Earth from Yuggoth (Pluto). The name "Abominable Snowman" was coined by the American press in 1921 following a British Royal Geographical Reconnaissance Expedition to Evert led by Lieutenant-Colonel Charles Howard-Bury. As they crossed a ridge in the deep snow, the expedition came on a set of tracks that Howard-Bury suggested were those of an extremely large wolf, but which bore a distinct resemblance to those made by a bare humanoid foot. The native Sherpas who were with him immediately identified them as the tracks of the metoh-kangmi *met-oh* translates as "man bear" and *kang-mi* as "snowman." Upon their return to Darjeeling, the expedition was interviewed by the journalist Henry Newman for the *New Statesman*. Newman mistranslated the word "metoh" as meaning dirty, filthy, or abominable and thus the name "Abominable Snowman" was born.

Prior to the 20th century information regarding the creature had been scant. There were, according to some travelers in the region, references in ancient Nepalese Buddhist tales concerning a glacier god who lived among the snow. This was the mir-god or "wild man," who was regarded as a physically fierce supernatural being. Blood from the being and portions of its skin and fur were used in various mystical ceremonies in the remote mountain villages and monasteries. The being is more likely to be connected with the ancient Bon religion, which was a Tibetan form of worship before the advent of Buddhism. The entity took a form that was somewhere between an ape and a bear, and it would carry large armfuls of stones, which it would hurl down on travelers passing in the valleys below. Sometimes it screamed like a woman and sometimes it made a queer whistling sound, which hurt the ears of those who heard it.

In 1832, an account was published of the explorer and ethnographer Brian Haughton Hodgson's travels in Nepal. In it, Hodgson makes passing reference to an incident in which his guides reported seeing a tall man-like figure among the snows, and fled from it in terror, believing it was an ancient god. Hodgson believed it was an orangutan or some unclassified sort of ape. Another explorer, Thomas Church, reported the same in 1845, but believed it was a Himalayan bear. The first tracks of the creature were found by the British explorer Laurence Waddell in 1899. Similar to

Church, Waddell believed that the tracks he discovered were made by some form of bear and more or less dismissed them. He claimed he heard many stories of an ape-like mountain "god," but never uncovered a shred of proof that such a thing existed.

Nevertheless, in 1921 there was the first real recorded sighting since Church's half-obscured vision nearly a century earlier. The Greek geologist and photographer N.A. Tombazi, working for the Royal Geographic Society on the boarders of Nepal, distinctly saw a figure crossing the Zemu Glacier in Sikkim. It was pointed out to him that this was the god of the snows, but Tombazi was more inclined to believe that it was a hermit monk. The creature stopped to devour some rhododendrons growing on the slopes below, but Tombazi still remained unconvinced. However, he did acre that the prints were far too big to be those of an ordinary man and that they seemed to be the tracks of a huge biped.

Forty years later, the myth appeared to take on some real substance. During an expedition to Mount Everest in 1951, the photographer Eric Shipton shot what appeared to be large human-like footprints crossing otherwise unbroken snow. These created a lot of controversy within the scientific world. On closer inspection, a number of scientists stated that these were no more than the prints of some ordinary animal—a bear or large cat—which had been distorted by the melting snow. Others stated that it was proof positive that the Yeti existed. The Zemu Glacier popped into the debate in 1948 when Flight-Lieutenant Peter Byrne revealed that he too had found tracks quite close to the mountain when on holiday in Sikkim. And in 1953, Sir Edmund Hillary and Sherpa Tenzing Norgay also claimed to have seen large tracks while on their way to conquer Mount Everest. Hillary would later discount the Yeti theory and suggest that he'd been mistaken.

With excitement about the Yeti at its peak, there were several expeditions to remote monasteries where sacred paintings of the "god" were photographed as "proof" of its existence. The most famous of these drawings was at the mountain monastery at Tengboche in northern Nepal, which was taken in 1954 by John Angelo Jackson. Jackson's photographs were printed in the British *Daily Mail* and caused a great stir. For good measure, Jackson had also photographed some footprints in the snow, which he claimed were Yeti tracks, and the expedition was given a number of hairs from what was claimed to be a Yeti scalp at the Pangboche monastery. The hairs were dark brown in color, but showed slightly red in a strong sunlight. On return, Jackson and his team submitted the hairs for analysis. This was carried out by Professor Fredric Wood Jones, one of the experts in human and comparative anatomy of his day. He compared the hairs with other specimens taken from bears and foxes of the area and also from several known species of ape. He concluded that the "scalp" hairs were actually taken from the nape of the neck of an unidentified primate, but was unable to identify what sort of animal it was. The hairs corresponded to nothing that he knew. However, he was certain that they were not those of a bear or an ape.

A roughly similar set of circumstances occurred in 1957 when a German expedition, together with the photographer Herman Baum, visited the Rongbuck Monastery in a remote area of Sikkim. Here the members were shown what looked to be faeces from the Yeti that had been frozen and were venerated as "the droppings of the glacier gods." Baum brought a tiny sample of the excrement back to Germany to be tested. Apart from stating that the creature was vegetarian in nature, the German tests remained inconclusive. However, Baum's findings were enough to inspire the wealthy Texan oilman and cryptozoologist Tom Slick to mount several expeditions into the area. In 1959, one of Slick's expeditions also returned with alleged Yeti feces, which were analysed in the United States. Again, the tests were inconclusive, however, one interesting discovery was made: All animals (including humans) have parasites in their bodies, which are largely unique to them. A parasite was found in the droppings that was completely unknown and could not be identified.

Slick was now convinced that he had found evidence of some other sort of human or even some major unknown creature, and resolved to provide even more proof. He was a friend of many influential people, including a number of Hollywood actors. In 1959, he reputedly persuaded his good friend—the movie star James Stewart—to undertake a "smuggling" mission for him. In 1957, one of Slick's expeditions visited the monastery at Pangboche to photograph the images of the glacier god there. While they were there, they were shown one of the monastery's most secret treasures—the skeletal hand of a Yeti, which they photographed and made public. Interest was naturally piqued and, in 1959, Slick mounted another expedition to the monastery ostensibly to inspect the hand once again. In their luggage, they carried a replica of the hand made out of human bones, which they substituted for the real treasure when the monks allowed it to be removed for inspection. They took the real hand with them to Nepal and had it shipped to India. Stewart was in India at the time and Slick asked him to hide the Pangboche Hand in his luggage when he flew to London. It was taken to the London University for study by expedition leader Peter Byrne. The examination was carried out by one of the leading primatologists of the time, William Osman Hill, who concluded that it was indeed the remains of a hominid. He suggested that this might be some sub-species of man or near-man, although in 1960, he revised his findings stating that the hand was *possibly* closer to that of a Neanderthal.

In 1991, the story took a further twist. The celebrated American television show *Unsolved Mysteries* claimed that they obtained bone fragments from the Pangboche Hand and subjected them to further analysis. They were found not to be human, but not of an ape, either. Shortly after the program aired, the entire hand was stolen from the Pangboche Monastery (it has been suggested that before his death, Slick had ordered the stolen bones to be returned to the monks) together with the bone fragments used by the television company, and so far they have not been found. Prior to his death in 2000, George Agogino supposedly transferred some important files to cryptozoologist Lauren Coleman, but allegedly these have also disappeared. The Hand of the Yeti still remains a mystery today and has led some to speculate that there is some sort of cover-up involved—maybe even by some sort of cult. Very Lovecraftian!

Mythos adherents have suggested that the Yeti is perhaps a specially created life-form that is designed to serve Ithaqua in the remote mountains. They further claim that the creature is protected by a human cult that worships the entity and destroys any evidence relating to its servitors. On the face of it, and with the mysterious disappearance of artifacts like the Pangboche Hand, there may be something in such a belief. But are the Yeti truly artificial servitors created by Ithaqua, and are they the only such servants?

Bigfoot

Similar to the Yeti, Bigfoot is considered to be a monstrous creation of Ithaqua serving the entity on the North American continent. Also known as the Sasquatch, it is said to inhabit forests in the Northwest Pacific area where the Wind-Walker is known to venture from time to time, although it has been seen in other regions as well. The word *Sasquatch* is thought to derive from the Native American word Sesquac, which is the Salish word meaning "wild man of the forests." Similar to the Yeti, it has been largely dismissed as folklore by much of the scientific community, but legends about it still persist all over America and further afield.

Perhaps unlike the Yeti, which arguably appears to display more bear-like qualities, Bigfoot seems to exhibit more of the characteristics of a large ape with large eyes and a pronounced ridge instead of a brow. From personal accounts it would seem to be slightly larger than the Himalayan Yeti with footprints that measure 24 inches long and 8 inches wide. Unlike most great apes, however, Bigfoot often boasts six or seven toes on each foot and sometimes the tracks of claws are also visible. Some sightings also state that Bigfoot may have a crest, similar to that of some species of male gorilla, and that its shoulders are round in a distinctly simian way.

A number of tribes in the Pacific Northwest have folktales about hairy giants living in the mountains or forests, but in this they are little different from many other Native American peoples. Each of these giants seemed to have a name that was specific to the area. Local people in Washington State spoke of skoocooms, a tribe of man-eating cannibals that lived somewhere near Mt. St. Helens. On the Washington coast, the creatures are known among the Coastal Salish as ts'emekwes, and are primarily fish-eaters, existing on a diet of clams. Further upstate they are known as stilyah, and are mainly vegetarian in nature. However, all of these can be extremely aggressive when crossed or when humans venture too close. Of particular interest to Lovecraftian scholars (and a concept that might link the creature to Ithaqua) are a series of articles written for various Canadian newspapers by the folklorist J.W. Burns in the 1920s. Burns linked the name *Sasquatch* with the Halkomelem language group of Western Canada and said that the origin of the being had come from legends in the north and west of the country. He argued that the idea of the "wild man of the woods" had come from Northern Canada, and had made its way south to the tribes of the Northwest Pacific coast. This idea ties in with the Mythos assertion that Ithaqua was/is confined to the Northern Canadian area, and that this is where many of Its servitors are said to be based. However, many of the tales were generally disregarded as superstition.

The photograph of the Yeti footprint by Eric Shipton generated considerable interest in the hominid, so a number of "monster hunters" in the United States were on the lookout for similar tracks within their own country and they were not disappointed. Unusual tracks were discovered in Del Norte County, California, in 1958 by a workman named Gerald Crew. While working machinery in an area known as Bluff Creek, Crew found a number of tracks apparently made by multiple animals of the same species, which he claimed resembled some of those that Shipton had photographed. His claim was greeted with a great deal of scepticism—some thought that Crew had read about Shipton's images and decided to copy them. In order to prove his story, Crew had his friend Bob Titmus make a plaster cast of one of the footprints, which he then displayed to the local press. The story was printed in the *Humboldt Times* in Eureka with a photo of the cast. In his interview he referred to the creature as "Big Foot," which the newspaper itself shorted into a single word "Bigfoot." The *Humboldt* article was picked up by several more papers including the Associated Press News Agency. The story gained momentum with a number of reported sightings not only in California, but in other states such as Wyoming. The story also made the career of Ray Wallace, who was working as a local logger at the time. Wallace's career as a "monster chaser" really took off and he appeared as an "expert" on a number of television programs and helped on a number of magazine articles, earning himself the nickname "Bigfoot" Wallace. Upon his death in November 2002, Wallace's son Michael claimed Wallace had been in possession of some large wooden feet with which he made the tracks. He was playing a joke on Gerald Crew, but later realized the potential in his prank. Michael's story was confirmed by the widow of the editor of the *Humboldt Standard*, who stated that her husband had been in on the hoax with Wallace.

However, back in 1958 Bigfoot fever was gripping the nation, and Tom Slick sent several investigative teams to the Bluff Creek area to find evidence of the strange ape man. They allegedly found nothing, not even fresh tracks. Sightings in other parts of America, however, began to multiply. Early reports were reportedly unearthed, though some may have been deliberately faked. The most famous account was Albert Ostman who had been allegedly captured and held captive by Sasquatch in British Columbia in 1924. While searching along the Powell River for gold, Ostman was allegedly kidnapped while sleeping in his camp and carried for more than 3 miles by a female Sasquatch. He was taken to a plateau where he was deposited in a cave with a family of Sasquatch—three adults and one child. He was held prisoner among them for six days. They were reasonably good to him, giving him a "sweet-tasting grass" to eat. He eventually made his escape by feeding the Sasquatch some snuff, which made them groggy. For many years the tale was counted as accurate, but in 2007 a number of ethnographers and folklorists cast doubts on it. Many of them drew parallels from old Indian stories that Ostman would undoubtedly have heard. And although the incident is alleged to have happened in 1924, Ostman did not make it public and release details of it until 1957 at the height of Bigfoot interest. It is thought that he was probably simply trying to cash in on Bigfoot mania. Also in 1924, a miner named Fred Beck claimed that he and his colleagues were attached by an ape man in upstate Washington near Mt. St. Helens. The site would later be referred to as Ape Canyon. Several Sasquatch attacked the miners' cabin and pelted them with rocks. The miners fired on them and might have killed one, but its companions dragged it away. Beck recounted the incident several times but in a book written in 1967, he became very mystical. He said the ape men were from another dimension and were actually supernatural beings. They had attempted to communicate with him through dreams. They were gods in their own right and do not appear to be close to Lovecraft's visions. The story was exposed as a fraud when a local man recounted that as a teenager, he and a number of other youths had been responsible for the attack on the cabin and throwing rocks at the miners.

So is there something out there in the American wilderness? And could it have somehow been created by Lovecraft beings as Ithaqua? The idea of a physical manifestation of Ithaqua or his alleged servitors may not lie with either the Yeti or the Bigfoot, so it is necessary to perhaps look elsewhere for a connection—perhaps to some other folkloric monster.

The Wendigo

Lovecraft and many other Mythos writers have specifically linked Ithaqua with the mythological Algonquian spirit-creature, the Wendigo. Once again, given the variety of tales and imagined connections, the picture is a rather confused one. Basically three theories exist regarding this legendary creature. First, the Wendigo is simply another name for Ithaqua. A second theory is that the Wendigo are actually a star-race and Ithaqua is part of that species. These beings have created the Shantaks, which prowl the edges of the Dreamworld and are sometimes hunted by Nodens.

A third strand of thinking suggests that the Wendigo might be a servitor race, created specifically by Ithaqua for Its own unfathomable purposes. It is thought that these creatures worship Ithaqua and provide It with the supernatural sustenance that it needs to survive on our world. In some variations, the Wendigo are transformed humans that Ithaqua has altered through Its magical powers.

There seems little doubt that Lovecraft took the idea of the Wendigo from Algernon Blackwood's story *The Wendigo*, which was published in a 1927 collection entitled *Ancient Sorceries and Other Tales*. It was published again in the 1932 abridged version entitled *The Willows and Other Queer Tales*. In the story, a group of hunters encounter something that they can't explain. The story gives a sense of open and barren landscapes in which a shadowy and growing menace lurks; this may have appealed to Lovecraft and fit with the ideas of desolate and threatening places, which feature in his works. It is an ancient evil lurking just below the surface of the countryside—the very essence of Lovecraft's fiction.

In standard folklore, however, the Wendigo is a common myth among a number of tribes in the Algonquian language group and is known under various names, such as Windiga, Witikow, and Wihtikow. In these myths it is often a cannibalistic spirit that can sometimes take on physical shape and "possess" those whom it encounters. Descriptions of it often differ from tribe to tribe, but it is always considered to be malignant and is strongly associated with bitter cold, famine, starvation, and sickness. Its abode is somewhere in the Far North, but exactly where is unclear. Sometimes it is portrayed as an emaciated human with a pale white skin pulled over a gaunt and almost-vampiric face; sometimes it is a human skull balanced on a shaggy body. Some describe its lips as being bloody and its teeth impossibly long; in almost all cases it gives off the odor of death and decay.

Among the Objibwe, the Naskapi, the Eastern Cree, and the Swampy Cree, as well as some other tribes, Wendigo are giants who dwell in the forests. They did not start out as giants, but because they are cannibals, they consume human flesh, which adds to their stature as they devour their victims. In this way, they are never satisfied and are always hungry and are always seeking prey. In other Algonquian-speaking tribes, they are usually the same size as humans, but have a voracious appetite. Although they consume a good number of victims, however, they always appear gaunt and emaciated. Wendigo, therefore, were the spirits of gluttony and greed, and it was said that anyone who engaged in the eating of human flesh would surely become possessed by the spirit of the creature. Those who were possessed by the Wendigo spirit would become excessively violent by eating human flesh. In some instances, the spirit of a suicide would return in the form of a Wendigo in order to torment and threaten the tribe.

The Assiniboine or "Stone Sioux" of the Northern Great Plains also performed a certain ceremony mocking the Wendigo as part of their Sun Dance rituals. This ritual was known as a *wiindigookaazhimowin* among the Ojibwe, who also performed it from time to time. A figure wearing a horrendous mask represented the Wendigo and danced backward while beating on a drum until he had danced out of the village or group. Some of these rituals were performed in secret places to avoid annoying other gods. According to William Warren in his book *History of the Ojibway People*, this ceremony was last performed within the United States at the Leech Lake Indian Reservation in Northern Minnesota, although he does not give a date for the event.

In Algonquian lore, the most powerful shaman to stand against the ravages of the Wendigo was Jack Fiddler in what is presently North-Western Ontario.

Jack was born between Sandy Lake and North Spirit Lake in Upper Ontario around 1839. He was given the Anishinaabe name Zhauwuno-geezhigo-gaubow (a man from the southern skies), although his father named him Mesawetheno (Swampy Cree meaning "stylish man"). After his birth, his father disappeared, leaving Jack to grow up in a time of hardship for the Oji-Cree. They had initially lived by fur trapping, however, many of the other clans in the area increased their own trapping and soon the native animal life of the area declined. Jack moved to Big Trout Rapids and later to York Factory in north-eastern Manitoba. In 1860, the Hudson's Bay Company reopened its post at Island Lake and the Suckers returned to settle there, making Jack their chieftain.

Because of his mysterious father, Jack was counted as a great shaman among the surrounding tribes. He also had a formidable reputation for defeating Wendigos; Fiddler claimed he killed 14 Wendigos, which had been sent against his people by enemy shamans. In some cases, Jack Fiddler was brought in by families whose loved ones had been somehow "taken over" by Wendigos. In most cases, the victim simply craved human flesh or was very sick (and might turn Wendigo), and Fiddler was forced to kill the individual concerned. Fiddler's own brother, Peter Flett, had turned Wendigo while on an expedition, and had to be killed. On several occasions Cree ministers were approached and asked to intervene, but Jack would not pay any attention to the Christian message.

In 1906, local authorities were approached by Norman Rae, who was an in-law of Jack Fiddler. Rae told them of Jack's allegedly "magic powers" against Wendigos, saying that he drew his powers from a spirit deep in the forest.

At the start of 1907, two officers from the North West Mounted Police arrived at the Sucker settlement and question Jack before arresting him. All across Canada, newspapers picked up on the arrest. They were intrigued by the stories of spirits and demons that Jack and his people worshipped. Jack's brothers were charged with the murder of his brother Joseph's daughter-in-law, which Jack admitted, saying that she had been a Wendigo. They were taken to a white holding center at Norway House while Churches called for their execution and the authorities called for at least a serious conviction.

At the end of September, Jack was taken for a walk as part of his exercise regimen. He managed to slip his guards and escape into the surrounding forest. He was found a little later hanging from the branch of a tree where he had committed suicide. Joseph's trial went ahead with witnesses from the Sucker people agreeing that their clan had no knowledge of Canadian law, and that they had considered the killing of the girl as a way of preventing her body from being possessed by an evil spirit. One witness, Angus Rae, said that he had seen Jack and Joseph deliberately kill the girl, as they were the only ones in the clan who had the spiritual strength to do so.

It was now easy for the Canadian authorities to subdue Jack Fiddler's people. The Severn River and Deer Creek communities were now told they had to accept both the formal legislature and the Christian Church without question and, in 1910, Robert Fiddler (Jack's son) signed an agreement with the authorities, which became known as Treaty 5. Most of the Sucker clan moved to Sandy Creek and became part of Treaty 9, the formal treaty between the British Crown and the tribes of northwest Ontario. All talk of the Wendigo died away in the development of the Christian religion, although it's said that some beliefs continue today. However, for most people—even for many of the Cree—the idea of the Wendigo has become nothing more than a piece of folk history.

Does Ithaqua exist somewhere in the frozen Northlands as Lovecraft and other Mythos writers? Are eerie creatures such as the Yeti and the Bigfoot Its specially created servants? Can It truly walk on the wind wherever It wishes as the tales suggest? As the faintest of breezes blows past your windows, perhaps it is better to stay indoors!

Shadows Beyond the Stars

Nodens

In the Mythos, Nodens is named as one of the Elder Gods, a group of beings who *may* have preceded the Great Old Ones, and may be either their leader or one of their most important members. Nodens may be important to Humankind as well, because he is often described as Lord of the Great Abyss. As usual, there is much dispute among Mythos writers as to exactly what this term means. Some, including Lovecraft, take it to mean a cavernous region far beneath the Dreamlands city of Sarkomand. There are towns and cities there over which Nodens rules and whose inhabitants have never seen either the sun or the moon. However, the writer and mystic Kenneth Grant thinks that the term refers to a region of hypothetical space that separates humans from the True Universe. This "celestial buffer zone" prevents humans from gaining the true knowledge about the Universe around them and keeps them sane. There are even those who say that Nodens acts like a kind of jailer, keeping the Great Old Ones who have been imprisoned on Earth. However, there will come a time when Nodens will sleep and the Great Old Ones will be free to roam the Earth once more as they did in former eras.

There is also some confusion about what Nodens might look like. In most depictions he is shown as an old man with a long beard and oaken staff, riding on a seashell chariot that is drawn by fantastic sea creatures. This identifies It clearly with the ocean, so it is assumed that in the early incarnation of the being, Lovecraft envisioned the being as a kind of sea-god similar to Poseidon. As a human figure, Nodens seems extremely old (Lovecraft describes him as "hoary"), but other writers have described It as a great tentacled writhing mass. However, it seems to be the human form of the entity that is more readily accepted in Lovecraft's "The Strange High House in the Mist":

> *THEN HOARY NODENS REACHED FORTH A WIZENED HAND AND HELPED OLNEY AND HIS HOST INTO THE VAST SHELL.*

Nodens first appeared in Lovecraft's short story "The Strange High House in the Mist," which was written in 1926, but was not published by *Weird Tales* until October 1931. It was originally rejected by *Weird Tales* when it was submitted in an initial draft in July 1927. Lovecraft then submitted a revised version to W. Paul Cook, a friend and correspondent, but who was also a printer and publisher. Cook had just set up The Recluse Press and had published one issue of a Gothic fiction magazine, *The Recluse*. He had promised to print a book of Lovecraft's work, as well as preview one of his stories in *The Recluse*. Lovecraft eagerly submitted "The Strange High House in the Mist" for the second issue. However, Cook did not have the money to maintain the magazine and it soon became apparent that no second issue would materialise. Lovecraft then did a number of revisions of the story and submitted it once more to *Weird Tales* who accepted it this time, paying him $55 for it. At last, Nodens saw print.

The idea for the entity, however, may have come from Lovecraft's reading of one of his favorite authors, Arthur Machen. Machen was a Welsh writer and mystic whose stories had a profound influence on the development of British supernatural, horror, and fantasy genres. His novella, *The Great God Pan* (written between 1890 and 1894) is considered to be a classic. He is also noted for his use of Celtic, Roman, and medieval folklore, of which he was an ardent student. Machen also had a deep interest in the occult and it is claimed that he was a member of the Order of the Golden Dawn.

Machen's philosophy centered around the idea that behind our everyday existence lay ancient and primeval forces that were continually working against us, and that we would become aware of their machinations. The idea was applauded by many mystics and occultists including Aleister Crowley, who described Machen as "a true visionary."

Lovecraft discovered Machen around 1923, and the Welshman's work had a profound effect on him. In fact, it might be argued that his underlying thinking about ancient forces paralleled that of Machen, and that he tried to replicate the idea of things lurking beneath the Welsh hills in New England. He also took some of Machen's references and expanded upon them; Nodens is an obvious example. In his book, *The Great God Pan*, Machen refers to an inscription on the side of a column that he visited:

To the great god Nodens (the god of the Great Deep or Abyss) Flavius Senilis has erected this pillar on account of the marriage which he saw beneath the shade.

The phrase "The Great Deep or Abyss" *could* be taken to mean the ocean and some have thought that Nodens (in his original form) may have been a sea god. Lovecraft may have initially felt the same and surrounded the entity with a kind of marine imagery, such as great shells and semi-aquatic beasts. Lovecraft began to see Machen's pagan imagery in short stories such as *The White People* with its hints at dholes, voolas, and witchcraft all lurking beneath a pastoral setting, and he began to amend his ideas regarding Nodens. Lovecraft's enthusiasm for Machen's work was evident—in his essay *Supernatural Horror in Literature*, he describes him as "one of the four great modern Masters" of supernatural fiction—the others being Algernon Blackwood, Lord Dunsany, and M.R. James—so it is only natural that Machen influenced some of his characterization.

According to the Mythos, Nodens came to Earth millions of years ago from somewhere in outer space and was worshipped by a race of beings about whom we know nothing. However, it is known that they possessed some rudimentary form of time-travel, which Nodens may have brought with It from Its homeworld. When the Great Old Ones arrived, Nodens and Its followers fled into the distant future where Nodens would rule again. It has been suggested that Nodens took this step because of an enmity with Yog-Sothoth, but no one is exactly sure if this is indeed the case.

Other accounts in the Mythos state that Nodens was worshipped in Atlantis under the name of Chozzar, God of Magic, although little is known about this deity. There are also references to the entity in works on English Druids, where It is referred to as "the serpent of the waters," making it either a snake or water god (or both). There is also a Roman temple dedicated to a god named Nodens in the small Gloucestershire town of Lydney. A pre-Roman site also existed in the area, but this could only be found by those who were dying—on which the Celtic god could bestow healing—and exact a price for doing so. The inscription (unearthed in the 1920s) may have been included in a revised and expanded version of Machen's *The Great God Pan*, which might have inspired Lovecraft.

Gradually, Nodens's nature began to change as Its place in the Mythos developed. No longer was It served by fantastic marine creatures like some ancient sea-god, but by nightgaunts. This fits in with Lovecraft's Dreamlands stories and placed Nodens in an alternate Universe. Nightgaunts are humanoid entities who inhabit the desolate places of the Dreamworlds. They have a rubbery, whale-like skin along with large and membranous wings, are black in color, sport horns on either side of their head, and have no faces, simply an empty blackness where one should be. They also have barbed tails with which they "tickle" their victims when they pounce upon them from the skies. Sometimes they carry tridents, but usually they have no tools or weapons of any kind. According to Daniel Harms they are linked in some way to ghouls, although the exact nature of the connection is unknown. They blindly serve Nodens and will attack any who dares to disobey the entity or mock Its rituals. Nightgaunts can also be summoned by individuals using a certain type of stone marked with the Elder Sign.

Usually Nodens is beneficent toward Humankind although, as a deity, It can be extremely capricious. The being will usually not intervene directly on behalf of a human, but will offer help in the form of advice or suggested incantations. For example, he offers such advice to Randolph Carter in his battle with the entity Nyarlathotep when things look dangerous for him in Lovecraft's *The Dream-Quest of Unknown Kadath*: "…and archaic Nodens was bellowing his guidance from unhinted deeps."

Nodens also appears as a hunter walking through the Dreamlands in search of prey. The creatures that he hunts are usually evil and malicious toward humans. These are Shantaks—great winged, flying lizard-like birds with the heads of horses that live either in the Cold Waste in the North of the Dreamlands or in the mountains near the Plateau of Leng. They also exist in our own dimension, and built massive stone structures on other planets. In our world they supposedly built the ruined city of Zimbabwe in Africa. They are also the servants of several of the Great Old Ones including Nyarlathotep. However, they fear Nodens and the nightgaunts who hunt them down relentlessly. Nodens also turns his attention to other servants of the Great Old Ones wherever they are to be found.

Nodens is something of a complex entity, shifting slightly in nature and description. But does he have parallels in history and legend—something that writers like Machen drew upon?

Nodens at Lydney

Mention has already been made of a temple dedicated to Nodens at Lydney in Gloucestershire, England. However, this was not the only place where temples and shrines to the god were found—others existed in Gaul (France) and on the Iberian Peninsula (Spain and Portugal). Many archaeologists believe that in these places, he was largely a Roman god and he was viewed as an alternate entity to Neptune (god of the sea) or Mars (god of war). The name *Nodens*, however, has been suggested by J.R.R. Tolkein to originate from the Germanic *Nodents* meaning "to take or to have use of." This links him to a Germanic hunting deity with Celtic connotations (Tolkein refers to him as "Nodens the Catcher").

Nodens was certainly associated with the sea, but also with nature and healing. In fact, the complex at Lydney was generally thought to have been a healing site with the temple, including an incubatio, a chamber where sick pilgrims could be laid. It is thought that the temple had been built on an even earlier site that overlooked the River Severn and may have been a defended shrine.

The site was excavated in the 1920s by the eminent archaeologist Sir Mortimer Wheeler who established that the temple-complex was probably founded slightly after A.D. 364, and continued well into the fifth century. Some of the excavations were of great interest and may have inspired Machen in his descriptions of Nodens. Several of these were stone tablets, one of which reads:

FOR THE GOD NODENS. SILVANUS HAS LOST A RING AND HAS DONATED ONE HALF (OF ITS WORTH) TO NODENS. AMONG THOSE NAMED SENICIANUS PERMIT NO GOOD HEALTH UNTIL IT IS RETURNED (TO THE TEMPLE OF NODENS).

This appears to be a simple votive request to find lost property. It was perhaps believed that Nodens could locate property that was either lost, mislaid, or stolen if the proper offerings were made. Another inscription on a bronze plate is dedicated to the god Mars:

TO THE GOD MARS NODENS. FLAVIUS BLANDINUS, THE DRILL INSTRUCTOR WILL-INGLY AND DESERVEDLY FULFILS HIS VOW.

What exactly the vow entailed is unknown, but the inscription portrays Nodens as perhaps something akin to a war god. A similar plate that is incised with the image of a baying hound states:

PECTILLUS DEDICATES THIS VOTIVE OFFERING WHICH HE HAD PROMISED TO THE GOD NUDENS MARS.

It is not clear if the votive offering was the inscribed plate or the hound that was depicted on it. If the latter was the case, then perhaps Nodens sometimes demanded an animal sacrifice from his followers. However, the image might be some sort of Celtic survival since dogs were equated with healing all across the Celtic world. Further inscriptions seem concerned with healing and equate Nodens with the Roman god Mercury, who was the deity associated with healing. It is possible that in a revision of Machen's *The Great God Pan* references to these tablets were included—the inscriptions seem so close to the work thus providing a base for some of Lovecraft's fiction.

The floor of one of the rooms, however, adds further confusion to the identity of the god since a mosaic there seems to link Nodens with the sea-god Neptune. It depicts a figure rising from the waves surrounded by fishermen, sea monsters, and tritons. The floor dates from around the founding of the temple in the fourth century and was dedicated to the worship of Nodens by one Titus Flavius Senilis, who may have been a wealthy local merchant or some sort of local politician. Whoever he was, he seems to have made the temple a site of some importance in the area. In the same room are nine carved dogs some resembling Irish Wolfhounds, one of which has a human face, a bronze arm, and a plaque of an unknown woman. The dogs are suggestive of some shrines in Gaul, but they may also have been Irish or Welsh, suggesting the temple's connections with certain other parts of the ancient world. It has been suggested that they represent hunting (and the image of Nodens as a hunting god), but they may also suggest healing. In the same room were the impedimenta of healing, such as an oculist's stamp (which was used by Roman physicians to distinguish between cakes and vessels of eye ointment). Could it be that this unnamed sea-deity was also associated with healing? The location of the site may also have some significance. The temple was positioned on a rise overlooking the Severn Estuary, and this close association with water may suggest that some sort of marine deity may have been worshipped there. The clear view of the Severn Bore may have had some relevance to the worship carried on at the temple.

There is evidence too of some sort of temple priest who would have officiated there. One of the objects recovered from the dig in the 1920s was a bronze artifact that might have been the head-dress of such an individual. The artifice is elaborately carved with a sea-deity surrounded by *puti* (small cherub-like figures suggesting innocence) and tritons. This may have been part of a priestly garb or perhaps some sort of ornament worn by some prominent and important person in the cult of Nodens. It may have been worn by Flavius Senilis himself.

Nodens, then, seems to have been a shifting deity within the Romanized world, taking on the aspects (and being substituted for) a number of other, more familiar gods. Nodens as a Roman god would be difficult to pin down, but is there perhaps an even older deity upon whom the Roman perceptions might have been based?

Nuada of the Silver Arm

Some researchers and scholars have suggested that the British god Nodens may have his roots in the Celtic demi-god Nuada Airgetlam (Nuada of the Silver Arm).

According to the ancient Irish *Annals of the Four Masters,* Nuada was a king of the Tuatha de Danann (the people of the goddess Danu) who are also mentioned in the *Book of Invasions* (a collection of stories written by monks around the 11th century). According to these venerable texts, the Tuatha were a wave of prehistoric invaders who took over Ireland in some distant time before formally recorded history. They were the fifth in several waves of invaders who arrived, each defeating previous peoples who had settled in the country before. The Tuatha, however, were rather different from all previous invaders. They had learned magical and occult skills, and are thought to have been the ancestors of the fairy folk who were said to (and perhaps still do) inhabit the country up until recent times. According to some sources, they arrived from the East not in ships, but in a golden mist or in a dark cloud, a symbol of their magical powers.

When the Tuatha arrived, Ireland was occupied by the Fir Bolg, who had been the previous invaders. Where the Tuatha might have come from is unknown, and some have suggested that they were not an actual people at all, but rather a representation of old pagan gods that were once worshipped.

According to legend, Nuada had been king of the Tuatha de Danann for seven years before they arrived in Ireland. His people, he claimed, were originally descended from another wave of invaders who had occupied Ireland—the Nemedians—who had founded four cities in the North of the country—Falias, Gorias, Murias, and Finias. Through trading with other nations, sorcery, and connections to the spirit world they had accumulated great knowledge of sorcery and dark arts, but were driven out by the arrival of the Fir Bolg. Now, after learning even more dark lore in far countries they had returned to reclaim their birthright. They arrived in either a cloud or in long ships, which they beached in the West of Ireland (in Connemara) and then set light to them so that none would think of retreating. Initially, they wanted their settlement to be peaceful, so Nuada tried to negotiate half of the country as their own. The kings of the Fir Bolg, however, refused and threatened to drive them from the country, thus precipitating a war.

The major battle of the initial conflict was the First Battle of Magh Tuireadh (the Plain of Pillar) at which the Fir Bolg were defeated and driven back. The site of this battle is unknown—some accounts say that it took place near the village of Cong on the borders of Mayo and Galway; others say that it lay somewhere in County Sligo. Wherever it was, it marked a heavy defeat for the Fir Bolg, as the kings were scattered following the battle. However, as they regrouped they issued a challenge directly to King Nuada: face one of their champions in one-on-one battle. Nuada accepted the challenge and the Fir Bolg put up their champion, a near-giant known as Sreng. The fight was long and hard, and in the end Nuada won, but in doing so, he lost an arm. Since he was now "blemished" he could no longer continue as king. Therefore, Nuada was replaced by Bres, a half-Fomorian and something of a tyrant. The smiths of the Tuatha de Danann made Nuada an artificial arm forged from silver. When being fitted, the God of Healing, Dian Cecht, muttered a spell: "ault fri halt di freith fri feth" (joint to joint and sinew to sinew), which caused flesh to grow over the silver arm. This meant that Nuada could be reinstated as king. The deposed Bres, however, was not at all pleased and sought help from his kinsmen, the Formorians. They began a war against the Tuatha de Danann, which culminated in the Second Battle of Magh Tuireadh. During this conflict Nuada was killed by the lethal rays from an eye of one of the Femorian giants—Balor of the Evil Eye. His sword was removed and taken to a secret place, becoming one of the Four Great Treasures of the Tuatha de Dannan. The others were the Spear of Lug, the Stone of Destine (which would cry out the name of the next king), and the Cauldron of the Dagda (which could feed any company that sipped from it, no matter how many). Nuada's sword became the Irish equivalent of King Arthur's Excalibur.

Although Nodens does not appear to be one of the major entities of the Mythos (It appears only peripherally in some of the tales), It is nevertheless an intriguing entity whose identity and function seems to continually shift. It can help those who travel through the Dreamworlds, and in our own world It serves to keep the Old Ones in check within their tombs—It can therefore be seen as an ally to a struggling Humanity against cosmic forces. And It is also a hunter, attacking those who would seek to threaten us. Whether the god is an alternative to the Roman gods of Neptune, Mars, or Mercury, or whether it comes from an earlier Celtic era, the shadowy form of Nodens waits in the Great Abyss maintaining a constant and watchful eye over our own fragile and increasingly vulnerable world.

SHADOWS BEYOND THE STARS

TSATHOGGUA

Perhaps none of the ancient entities is more baleful or repulsive than Tsathoggua (the Sleeper of N'Kai), the toad-god who squats in the caverns beneath the earth and whose High Rites are held at May-Eve and Halloween. In the Mythos, Its first appearance in print is a reference in Lovecraft's story *The Whisperer in Darkness*, which was written in 1930 and published in *Weird Tales* in August 1931. The main description of the entity comes in a Clark Ashton Smith story *The Tale of Satampra Zieros*, which was written in 1929 and published in *Weird Tales* in November 1931. In the physical description of Tsathoggua, Lovecraft and Smith vary greatly, and it's thought that perhaps Lovecraft envisaged the entity as a bat-god or even as a sloth-god, whereas Smith thought it was a great toad-like thing. In "The Mound" (one of Lovecraft's revisions for Zealia Bishop) he refers to the "very terrible black toad idol found in the red-litten world and called Tsathoggua in the Yothic manuscripts. It had been a potent and widely worshipped god…." Also, according to *The Dream-Quest of Unknown Kadath*, an idol of Tsathoggua stands near the entrance of the Vaults of Zin in the Dreamworlds, where it may be worshipped by the frightful Gugs (a race of mute, black-furred, horrifying giants). Smith developed the idea of the toad-god, and the mythology that surrounds it is often complex and contradictory.

Tsathoggua is believed to be one of the Old Ones that takes the form of a great fur-covered toad with sleepy eyes, a drooling jaw, and a lop-sided sloth-like grin (containing elements of how Lovecraft had actually initially envisioned It). The creature is said to be the offspring of two entities Ghisguth (who is a destroyer of worlds in a distant galaxy) and Zstylzhemghi (an insectoid being who has also spawned a number of flies and pests, and may reside on Uranus). His grandfather, however, is Cxxaxukluth, who is the formless and perhaps sexless spawn of Azathoth. As It approached old age Cxxaxukluth became cannibalistic in nature and began to consume Its own children, which It had produced by meiosis. Fearful that Its grandfather would consume the infant Tsathoggua, the parents hid It away in some deep caves on the planet Yuggoth, where Cxxaxukluth could not reach. Later, they opened a doorway to the planet Saturn and deposited Tsathoggua there. Other writers state that it was an unknown race from a dark galaxy who opened the doorway and sent the entity through. This race ultimately inhabited a dark planet just outside our Solar System and transferred Tsathoggua to Earth for some unspecified purpose. According to the Mythos as outlined by Keith Herber, the entity was established in the ruined city of Yuth within the stone desert of the primal land of K'li-Phon-Nyah, where It was worshipped by the nameless entities that still dwelt there. Despite such worship, It soon left Yuth and moved to the underground realm of N'Kai. Some say that It dwells within a cavern beneath the ancient land of Averoigne, but Daniel Harms suggests that this is unlikely. According to Harms, the toad-god seems to have been worshipped in Hyperborea, but such worship ceased after the Great Ice overwhelmed the land. According to Clark Ashton Smith's *The Parchments of Pnom* (mentioned in a letter to Robert Barlow in 1934), Tsathoggua mated with an unknown entity named Shathat to produce Ossadagowah (another toad-like entity that now dwells on a planet of the star Algol and can only be summoned by 13 wizards acting in unison). It also mated with another reptile being with whom it created Kazadool-Ra, which It then consumed, displaying some of the cannibalistic tendencies of Its grandfather.

Although it is disputed by some other Lovecraftian scholars, Harms states that the serpent-men from the caverns of Yoth were the first to worship the toad-god. From here, the worship may have spread to the underground city of K'n-Yan—a blue-lit cavern far below Oklahoma in which the survivors regrouped following the destruction of Lemuria. Here, the entity was worshipped by Voormis and later by humans. A Voormis is a humanoid, cave-dwelling race who first appear in Lin Carter's reworking of Clark Ashton Smith's story *The Scroll of Morloc* first published in 1976 in *The Year's Best Fantasy Stories*, and later in *Lost Worlds* in 1980). It was they who carried the worship of the toad-god back to Hyperborea and from there to Atlantis. After the sinking of the island continent, this worship was carried even further by the survivors. One group made their way to what is now France and settled in the region of Averoigne. Prominent among this party was the Atlantean priest Klarkesh-Ton (this was used by Lovecraft as a nickname for Clark Ashton Smith; Smith liked it so much that he incorporated it into his own stories and ultimately into the Mythos) who led the people into dark ways, which blighted the country ever after. Klarkesh-Ton established an oracle in the dark groves of Averoigne, which was the Voice of Tsathoggua. The French Cult of Tsathoggua became a powerful one and may still exist in some form today.

A second dispersal from doomed Atlantis made it to the coast of America. There they settled among the natives who were forming their Mesoamerican culture. The cult continued right down to the 1800s when the Narragansett and Wampanoag of the Eastern American seaboard still worshipped the god in secret. They would later give up this veneration and the cult would die out. However, Tsathoggua's cult may secretly flourish in underground temples in various parts of Europe and America, drawing its power from sacrifices, orgies, and hideous rituals. Some scholars claim that much of the instability and uncertainty in the present world stems directly from the activities of the cults, and many leading figures in the world of finance and politics are members of them. Others claim, however, that the toad-god has received so little worship throughout the recent centuries that much of Its essence has dispersed, and those who attend Its rituals are only gratifying their own animalistic lusts and desires. However, there are others who claim that Tsathoggua will still be worshipped in Zothique, which according to Smith, will be the final continent on Earth at the very end of the world. There, the entity will be known and revered as Zathogwa the Outcast, although Smith has not revealed exactly how he knows this.

History of the Toad

It's probably no coincidence that Smith decided to portray Tsathoggua as a "squamous toad-like entity." Arguably throughout history no creature has been as closely associated with darkness, madness, and evil as the toad. Sometimes referred to in English lore as the borax or stelon, there are few animals (aside from the cat) that have been more closely linked with witchcraft. Similar to the serpent, the toad was often considered to be the enemy of Mankind—its body often provided a habitat for evil spirits, its venom was highly toxic, and even its gaze could cause madness. Its skin and innards could be used in the foulest of spells by those who intended harm.

Perhaps the earliest known reference to a toad's evil power comes from the Middle East. In ancient Persia, around B.C. 700–600, the followers of Zoroaster lobbied that all toads should be killed, as they represented a baleful influence against society. Acting quickly, the authorities ordered toads to be stoned and crushed no matter where they were found, although toad's blood should not touch exposed skin, as it was highly poisonous. Although suspicious of the toad, other cultures sometimes took a more lenient view. In ancient China, for example, the toad was the symbol of the moon and was therefore the repository of ancient knowledge. The toad represented the principle of "cool shadiness"—which as the sun rose new wonders might be revealed. The toad was both ancient and wise, and therefore had to be treated with respect. And yet, in the minds of the ancient Chinese, there was an element of mystery to it, too.

However, European Christians began to view the toad with suspicion and associate it with evil. It became the symbol of the Devil, who had three toads upon his coat-of-arms. It was believed to be inherently poisonous, and the spittle of a toad could be used by poisoners in the preparation of the most lethal substances. Since poisoning and witchcraft were often considered to be related in the medieval mind, toads quickly became associated with witches. They were classed as "familiars"— the Devil's servants who were bound to carry out his or her commands on behalf of the Satanic master. In other cases, the toad was considered to be the very embodiment of the Devil who dwelt with a witch and acted as his or her protector. Therefore, one had to be extremely careful when destroying a toad in case some sort of supernatural evil might occur, either through the witch's spells or from the Devil directly.

Witch-hunters in local communities were also familiar with the lore of the toad. In many cases, their examinations of suspected witches often focused on a supplementary nipple, which the witch often used to feed the toad on his or her blood, as a mother would suckle a child. The finding of such evidence was considered an important factor in the identification of a sorcerer. In the Basque region of France, it was also considered that a witch would have the mark of a three-toed toad's foot somewhere on his or her body as a mark of a pact with the Devil. In the Pyrenees mountain area and in some parts of Germany the image of a toad was to be found reflected in the left eye of the witch. This was considered to be an infallible indication of the presence of the Evil One.

In Devon and other parts of England, the crushed body of a toad was used by witches in their most potent spells. The sap of cow parsley or sow thistle was mixed with the spittle of a toad, which would create an ointment that would render the witch invisible to the human eye. Similarly, mixed with vervain and the gall from a farrowed sow, a mixture could be created that would enable the witch to fly.

Some taught that toads could spit venom at their enemies; others that they could vomit fire. Such fire was also said to have a poisonous element to it, so even the fumes of it were harmful. A toad was also said to be able to inflict a severe and poisonous bite. If an individual was bitten by a toad then the only remedy, according to folklore, was to pour scalding hot water over the alleged bite, making the cure actually worse than the supposed problem. Each toad also embodied a certain magical stone, which would detect the presence of poisons in food or anywhere else. If poisons were present, the toadstone would become warm to the touch and might even change color (it was supposed to be a uniform emerald green). When set into a magical ring it would become paler, almost pure white, and poisons were then assumed to be present.

In addition to the toadstone, each toad was supposed to have a precious jewel concealed within their skull. Romany (gypsy) folklore said that when a toad was killed this wonderful gem vanished within the space of a minute, so if the creature was skinned quickly enough, the jewel could be extracted and the stone could grant the finder great knowledge. It was also said that the knowledge had been passed down since the time when great toad gods were worshipped among the Romany (could these be forerunners of Tsathoggua?). However, the knowledge gained from toads would bring neither happiness nor contentment, and those who gained it would never rest easy again, because they knew all the secrets of the world.

Although associated with poisoning and death, the toad also seems to have been associated with fertility. For instance, in some parts of Scotland it was believed that women wishing to conceive should sleep on their backs with a toad on their belly. After several sessions of this, they were assured of becoming pregnant. In the Brocken Mountains of Germany, women were supposed to hold a small statuette of a toad between their legs in order to make themselves pregnant. Furthermore, a man who carried the dried tongue of a toad in a silken pouch next to his skin was sure to charm any woman he wished.

Pieces of a toad were also said to be infallible charms against disease—the legbone of a toad carried in a muslin bag was a protection against King's Evil (swelling of the lymph nodes in the neck), as well as conditions of the throat or chest. Sometimes the entire body of the toad was placed in the bag after being decapitated in front of the patient. The bag would have to be carried until the remains decayed, whereupon the protection was complete. In Devonshire, the skin of a toad carried in a bag of fine linen would give both a cure and protection to the onset of rheumatism, and toad skins were often used in a variety of harms and cures all across England.

Witches also used toads in order to control the weather and to summon up storms. By either using a toadstone or by slaying a toad, a sorcerer had great power to control the elements and bend them to his or her will. In the 1662 witch trial of Isobel Gowdie in Aulderdearn, Scotland, the accused admitted that she and her coven frequently used the bones of toads and newts to call up storms to do harm to their neighbors' crops. The idea that toads could influence the weather was not uncommon, and there are also accounts from several German and Austrian witchcraft trials from a slightly later period stating exactly the same thing.

The ancient Society of Toadmen in Cambridgeshire, England, also had great powers derived from toads. For instance, it was said that no horse could resist the whisper of a Toadman and would carry out his every instruction. The Society is suggestive of other such groupings—for example, The Horseman's Word, a secret workingmen's society in the Angus and Mearns area of Scotland, which was said to possess ancient words of power that gave them mastery over "the beasts of the field." There was also the Brothers of the Plough in Northumberland, who possessed words that gave them command over any plough horse. It is also suggestive of the "horse whisperers," who were at one time common in many parts of England.

The ritual for becoming a Toadman was an elaborate and complex one, and it was said to have continued in some parts of Cambridgeshire up until the late 1930s and early 1940s. It involved catching and killing a toad and then skinning it in a certain manner. The bones were then buried and ants were allowed to pick them clean. They were then carried by the prospective Toadman next to his skin until they were completely dry. At the first full moon, he took the bones to a place with running water and cast them in. They would then separate and one would float upstream, making a screaming sound as it did so. The prospective Toadman would then recapture this bone and keep it safe in a graveyard, stable, or barn for at least three nights. Then he would face his final test as he was brought in by several others to meet with the Devil, who would try to persuade him to give the magic bone back. If he refused—as he invariably did—he became a Toadman and learned the various words of power that the Toadmen knew. The Society of Toadmen was extremely powerful among the labouring classes in rural Cambridgeshire and there are even rumors that it still may exist today. Could Lovecraft have been aware of one of these and based Tsathoggua's cult of worshippers on something like it? Far-fetched as it may sound, such a theory may not be beyond the realms of possibility.

The Book of K'yog and the Codex Dagonensus

Two blasphemous tomes detail the history and rituals of Tsathoggua. The first is the *Book of K'yog*, which refers to a work that is far older than even the *Book of Eibon*. It has been lost for many millennia and is only referred to in old texts such as the *Book of Karnak*, a tome of occult knowledge supposedly found in the ruins of the Egyptian city of Karnak where it was used by priests and oracles. *The Book of K'yog* allegedly tells how Tsathoggua was brought to Earth and some of Its earliest histories here. However, it gives little information regarding the rituals surrounding the toad-god and how It may be summoned.

Much more informative is the so-called *Codex Dagonensus*. This work bears a striking resemblance to two other Codices that are also kept in the Vatican—the *Codex Maleficium* and the *Codex Spitalski*. In fact, the *Codex Dagonensus* may be a copy of *Spitalski* (which is probably the oldest of all three Codices), but with certain additions relating to Tsathoggua. Although very little is known about its origins, the *Codex Spitalski* could have been written somewhere near present-day Uppsala in Sweden around A.D. 400 and was copied in various other editions around 200 years later.

The additions to the *Codex Dagonensus* include material such as the *Nyhargo Dirge*, a set of Tsathogguan rituals designed for the worship and summoning of the entity, as well as variations of the Elder Sign for possible protection against It. There are also many added pages of protective sigils and for the construction of talismans.

Frog Hybrids

What about the *physical* attributes of Tsathoggua? Could the actual form of the toad-creature be based on something that exists or has existed? Although stories of a curious hybrid between human and frog, dwelling in swampy areas and along drainage ditches near Loveland, Ohio, had been circulating in the area for many years, it did not get full attention until around 1955.

The "frog" was supposedly a small humanoid with a face that resembled a frog or lizard, and appeared to be covered in green scales. It stood roughly 4 feet tall and walked upright. Its hands and feet were possibly webbed. The frog species was first witnessed in May 1955 by a businessman on his way home late in the evening. Stopping by a bridge over a drainage ditch he suddenly spotted three small creatures squatting under it, unaware of his presence above them. He described them as being 3 feet tall and nearly naked (they each wore something resembling a loincloth), and as completely hairless with wrinkles across their chests, which looked like scales. Their faces were "frog-like" with bulging eyes and thin, lipless mouths. One of them was holding up an electrical device in what looked like a webbed hand. They suddenly became aware that they were being watched and disappeared under the span of the bridge; when the businessman went to look further, they were gone. There was, however, a strong odor of almonds and alfalfa where they had been.

For 20 years there was no sight of any such creature. Then in March 1972 a 4-foot tall creature was seen once again close to an irrigation ditch, which ran along beside a railway branch line. It was spotted by a guard on a wagon that was being moved. Once again, the creature was holding up something that looked vaguely metallic and seemed to be monitoring the engine that was pulling the train. Alarmed that this might be some sort of criminal activity, the guard called the police, but before they arrived, the being had become aware that it was being observed and jumped over a restraining barrier. Two weeks later, police officer Mark Mathews saw it squatting by the side of the road, apparently taking great interest in some passing traffic nearby. He drew his gun and moved in on it, but the creature spotted him and leapt away. Mathews shot at it, but missed. He described it as being about 4 feet tall and about 50 to 75 pounds, covered in a leathery, grey skin that was scaled, with a possible tail and with a face like a frog or lizard. Shortly afterward, a local farmer reported what he suggested was the same creature riding a small bicycle along a nearby farm road. The creature moved too fast for him and was soon gone.

Similar to the Loveland Frog, there were many stories regarding an amphibious, batrachian humanoid around Thetis Lake near Victoria, British Columbia. Some would say that the legends there had persisted for centuries. The Lake is the first Canadian conservation area, established in 1958, and taking in not only the Lake itself, but the surrounding forests and protected parkland.

In August 1972, a local newspaper, *The Victoria Daily Times,* reported that a couple of teenagers who had been walking up by Thetis Lake had been attacked by something that had emerged from the water. It was described as roughly resembling the monster in the film *Creature from the Black Lagoon* and was certainly humanoid in shape. It was alleged that one of the teenagers had been slashed on the hand by the creature, which had long, taloned fingers, webbed toes and hands, and a line of barbs along its skull and arms. Its upper torso appeared to be scaled like a fish. There were certainly deep cuts on the hand, which the Canadian Royal Mounted Police who investigated described as "being triangular in nature." The police decided to investigate and nicknamed it "the Gill-man" after the monster in the film. The boys never wavered in their story and seemed very sincere about what they had seen.

Four days after the initial report, two anglers spotted the monster on another stretch of the Lake. One of the men said that the creature had simply emerged out of the water, looked around, and then disappeared beneath the surface. He was described as roughly the same height as a human, but with a monstrous toad-like face, scaled, and with a razor sharp crest running along the crown of its head. Its hands—at least what they could see—appeared to be webbed. They gave its color as blue to silvery-grey. However, they didn't hang about in case the creature returned, so if it reappeared they could give no further account of it. Canadian police searched the area, but found nothing—not even tracks where the creature might have come ashore.

At the end of August/beginning of September, another paper, *The Province*, received a call from a local man who had lost a Tegu lizard. They can grow up to 4 feet in length and are carnivorous. Some people can keep them as pets, although they do not settle well in domestic environments. Police thought that what the witnesses had seen might be this animal that had somehow found its way to Thetis Lake. They claimed that many elements of the descriptions given matched that of the Tegu species, although they had been "slightly altered" to fit with the 1954 film. Nevertheless, sightings of *something*—perhaps the "Gill-man"—continue to be reported from time to time in the Thetis Lake area.

Fens

The Fens are an extremely marshy area of eastern England, parts of which were virtually inaccessible and shut off from the rest of the country until fairly recently. They are very low-lying compared with the chalk uplands, which surround them and are often still liable to flooding. Although much of the fenland has now been reclaimed, this marshy area was dotted with small islands on which abbeys and hermitages were established, as monks sought isolation for contemplation and study. Indeed, they became known as "the Holy Land of the English," because of the numbers of holy houses that existed there. Even today there are great cathedrals dotted all through this area.

The inhabitants of these dark, ancient, and waterlogged lands have always considered themselves a race apart, and the inaccessibility of the Fenland countryside ensured that this was so. There are tales from the pagan past of an even older pagan race dwelled there long before even the Romans came to Britain. Descriptions and legends of them are sparse, but they were said to be not human—having webbed feet in order to fit in with their watery environment, and being able to live underwater. They were said to be "very hideous to look upon" having faces resembling those of toads or frogs, and were believed to be extremely warlike and intensely pagan. In an account of the life of the 8th-century holy man, St. Guthlac of Crowland, there is a description of a holy house being attacked by a group of these Fenmen and of a number of monks being slaughtered. They were "extremely barbarous and given over to the worship of strange gods," which they worshipped deep in the Fenland swamps. The holy Guthlac supposedly drove them back into the deep marshlands and destroyed certain heathen idols, but stories about their activities continued into the 12th and 13th centuries.

And it's not only in England that such stories are found. In the Dunamoos Marshes of Bavaria, Germany, there are tales of peculiar creatures and peoples. Until 1790, much of these marshes, similar to the Fens, were completely inaccessible, and it was not until around 1800 that any drainage system of the boglands was commenced. During this time, there were tales of curious beings that were disturbed by the work.

For example, a group of strange humanoids were seen at a distance, observing the work as makeshift pumps were being installed in a certain area. Assuming that these were locals, a workman approached them, and when he did so, the beings moved away with curious hopping movements. They were not seen again, but stories concerning a strange village deep in the swamps where blasphemous worship was carried on circulated among some of the workmen.

Such stories may have been encouraged by the strict Protestants who moved into the area around 1802—some of them Mennonite Anabaptists. The area became largely non-Catholic, and those of other faiths who settled there were often viewed with intense suspicion. Also, some of the work on the drainage systems was carried out by convict labor—a number of whom actually escaped into the swamplands. Stories said that these fleeing convicts had mated with strange swamp people to form hideous hybrids. There undoubtedly *were* rather strange and reclusive communities living in these boglands at various times, and this may have contributed to the area's rather sinister reputation.

Queer tales of toad-like entities still continue to circulate, just as they have done for countless years. Could Lovecraft have known about them and used them as the template for Tsathoggua? And exactly *what* sort of entity waits out there in the marshes to serve as such a model?

Shadows Beyond the Stars

Azathoth

Somewhere beyond space and time, beyond the very boundaries of Lovecraft's reality, sits the blind idiot god Azathoth, sometimes referred to as "the daemon-sultan," the "Primal Chaos," or "Nuclear Chaos." More recent writers developed and described this Outer God in its natural form: a shapeless and amorphous mass of unchecked and highly dangerous energies, although it could take other forms when it desired, as well as when it was summoned into our world. The lack of cohesive form did not diminish its immense power or malignancy for, according to lore, Azathoth somehow gave birth to the Universe and will ultimately bring about its end. In the interim, it bubbles, mumbles, and blasphemes to itself, all but oblivious of the Universe that it has spawned. Perhaps drawing on the Eastern imagery of which he was fond, Lovecraft further portrayed the entity in "The Haunter of the Dark" as being surrounded by a court of mindless, flopping, and amorphous dancers, lulled by the music of pipes played by nameless hands. This idea has overtones of a Turkish seraglio—an enclosed space where an Eastern potentate relaxed while his concubines danced and performed, therefore hinting at Lovecraft's interest in the culture and lore of the "mystic East." Azathoth, however, takes little interest in the activity around it, only dimly aware of what is going on while it stays lost in its own black madness. It is thought to be blind, though whether this is a physical blindness is opened to question. And the term "idiot god" is also inaccurate, as it has a deep and arcane knowledge of all things within the realm of Man and of other realms beyond. This is how Lovecraft envisioned the daemon entity, but could such a creature exist, and where did the idea come from? Perhaps there is more to Azathoth than meets the eye!

Similar to many entities in his Mythos, Lovecraft's description of Azathoth remains extremely vague. Perhaps this was because Lovecraft wasn't exactly sure what he was describing, and he may have changed his mind as his approach to the Mythos changed. Maybe more than any other entity, Azathoth marks the change from a supernatural cosmology to a more science-fiction-orientated one. In other words, the entity changes from a mysterious god-like Eastern caliph figure, ruler of some far away realm, to a mass of seething nuclear energy at the center of cosmic chaos.

Using Middle Eastern tradition and legend, some writers such as August Derleth and Colin Mayers have placed Azathoth in what would appear to be a quasi-Biblical tradition. Both ancient Sumerian and Semitic legends have spoken of a war in Heaven in which certain angels—for example Lucifer—were cast down. Taking their lead from Babylonian, Hebrew, and Biblical texts it was suggested that Azathoth was not always blind nor an idiot. Some Lovecraftian writers (particularly those involved with role-playing games) have suggested that there was once a great war between the Elder Gods based in the star Betelgeuse and the Outer Gods who were "instructed" by Azathoth. Thos who had allied themselves with his "instruction" were ultimately defeated along with Azathoth. The defeat unhinged his mind and he was cast out into some sort of outer darkness where his shape somehow changed to a mass of seething energy that continually bubbles in maddened fury.

Although the deity's actual origins remain hazy, such an explanation places it within an extremely ancient Middle-Eastern tradition of warring gods, and connects it to Judaism, Islam, and Christianity. In fact, within the Christian mind, it firmly connects Azathoth to the Devil and gives the Being an added emphasis of evil and malignancy in Western minds. The idea of a cosmic war centered around certain stars, however, maintains the element of science fiction within the concept.

The name *Azathoth* first appears in Lovecraft's notes in 1919 when he simply records it as "a barbarous name." No context is given for it, though Lovecraft may have connected it with the Eastern gods, djinn, and rulers that he had read about in books such as *One Thousand and One Nights*. Later, and in another note written that same year, he develops the name and hints at a story idea concerning "a terrible pilgrimage to seek the nighted throne of the daemon-sultan Azathoth." The idea has overtones of a quest-story, the motif of which appears in many legends from the chivalric tale to Eastern fable. Although it gives Azathoth some form of status as a sultan, it offers no description of him, nor does it even say if he even *sits* on the throne. Nevertheless, the context is clearly a supernatural one. As a student of arcane lore and books, Lovecraft may have been aware of such books at the *Dictionaire Infernal* by Simon Collin de Plancy, or the *Ars Theurgia Goetia*, the second book of the 17th-century grimoire *The Lemegeton*, both of which gave a detailed hierarchy of hell with the ranks of demonic forces. Azathoth is malignant in design, its very throne is evil and abhorrent. Perhaps Azathoth is envisaged then as a supernatural being of great power and occult magic, that is to say a creature to be avoided by any rational person.

However, after he wrote "The Dunwich Horror" in 1928, Lovecraft's position on occult horrors begins to change slightly. In a letter to Willis Conover, the jazz producer, broadcaster, and editor of *Science Fantasy Correspondent*, he states the following with regard to supernatural and occult books:

YOU WILL UNDOUBTEDLY FIND ALL THIS STUFF VERY DISAPPOINTING. IT IS FLAT, CHILDISH, POMPOUS AND UNCONVINCING—MERELY A RECORD OF HUMAN CHILDISHNESS AND GULLIBILITY IN PAST AGES. ANY GOOD FICTION WRITER CAN THINK UP "RECORDS OF PRIMAL HORROR" WHICH SURPASS IN IMAGINATIVE FORCE ANY OCCULT PRODUCTION.

Lovecraft commentators such as Daniel Harms and John Wisdom Gonce have suggested that it was a turning point for him, and that afterward he looked toward science fiction. This meant that he no longer envisioned his Old Ones as either gods or demons in the supernatural sense, but as extremely powerful aliens or as the products of a mad science. These beings had come to Earth somewhere in its dim and prehistoric past (thus maintaining the theme of arcane and lost knowledge, which he seemed to hold dear), and had established themselves in secret places beyond mortal knowing. There had been hints in some of his earlier works that this process was taking place, but this, it is argued, marked a substantial shift in emphasis as far as the perception of Lovecraft's beings were concerned. He did not change their names, but some of their characteristics appear to have been altered to fit this new perception.

In the novella *The Dream-Quest of Unknown Kadath* he gives a rather scientific description of the daemon-sultan:

OUTSIDE THE ORDERED UNIVERSE THAT AMORPHOUS BLIGHT OF NETHERMOST CONFUSION WHICH BLASPHEMES AND BUBBLES AT THE CENTRE OF ALL INFINITY—THE BOUNDLESS DAEMON-SULTAN AZATHOTH WHOSE NAME NO LIPS DARE SPEAK ALOUD AND WHO GNAWS HUNGRILY IN INCONCEIVABLE UNLIGHTED CHAMBERS BEYOND TIME AND SPACE AMIDST THE MADDENING, MUFFLED BEATING OF VILE DRUMS AND THE THIN MONOTONOUS WHILE OF ACCURSED FLUTES.

Within such a description, some elements of the Eastern seraglio remain, but its location seems to have changed, as does the nature of Azathoth itself. No longer is this a vague and shadowy demonic figure, rather it "blasphemes and bubbles," which suggest that it is not remotely human. This has allowed Lovecraftian writers such as Brian Lumley, and science-fiction writers like Henry Kutner, to develop the idea further and describe the daemon-sultan in terms of a fizzing, chaotic field of nuclear energy that lies somewhere beyond the normal reaches of time and space.

Azathoth had therefore changed in both location and nature, but it still remained a potent force within Lovecraft's cosmology, and would continue to darkly inspire many researchers and writers who would delve into his fiction.

Origins of the Name

Was Azathoth's name simply an invention of Lovecraft, or was there a deity that was worshipped under the name *Azathoth* somewhere in the past?

It is possible, of course, that Lovecraft simply blended the names of differing deities from different periods in time, and from different civilizations, into one single name. Syntactically, the name Azathoth would appear to have two separate components that may be the result of such a blending. The name could be composed by connecting the name of the Babylonian demon *Asag* with that of the Egyptian god *Thoth*.

Asag is a fairly central demon to Sumerian cosmology, and is immortalized in the Sumerian mythological prose-poem *Lugale*. Asag is so hideous that its very gaze can petrify an entire forest or make the lakes and rivers boil, killing all the fish within them. Its breath, like the scorching wind, could devastate a fertile land, turning it into an empty desert. Indeed, Asag's title was often "Lord of the Waste," but he was also known as "the demon that caused sickness" and was closely associated with malaria. Asag had also mated with the mountains, and from that union emerged a legion of rock-demon creatures, which were subject to his every command and would turn upon humans if called upon to do so. He was defeated in a prehistoric time by Ninurta, Lord of the Plough and Protector of Lagash.

The name *Thoth* from Egyptian mythology is much better known. Thoth was a god of judgement and wisdom, and was one of the most important deities in the Egyptian pantheon; he was known as either Tehuti or "the tongue of Ra." He was also often seen as an arbiter figure between the warring Egyptian gods. More importantly, however, Thoth was also seen in certain Coptic Christian circles as "the mind of God" and the basis for the Platonic Logos; as such, he is believed to maintain the balance of the Universe. The connection between the Lovecraftian Thoth-element and this deity is strengthened slightly by the sacred *Book of Thoth*. This was a hidden book of magic spells, lore, and incantations, the existence of which was widely taken as undisputed fact during the Middle Ages. It was written by various mages at some point during the Ptolemaic period of Egyptian history under the direct influence of the god himself. The volume, which was a series of scrolls, was supposedly a distillation of ancient Egyptian magic, most of it dating back into prehistoric times with a list of ancient names of various forces and how to summon them. It also contained two extremely important spells—one of which would enable humans to understand the language of birds and animals, and one that would aid them to perceive the gods. The book was supposedly hidden in a series of boxes, which lay somewhere at the bottom of the Nile near the small town of Qift. These boxes were guarded by fierce serpents that could not be overcome, no matter how hard one tried—it was not good (said the legend) for humans to know how to perceive (and perhaps even control) the gods.

The idea of the hidden book may have served as a template for Lovecraft's own *Book of Thoth*, although its creation is largely attributed to Thoth-Amon, a wizard of Prehistoric Stygia. It was thought to be destroyed at the Library of Alexandria, but was somehow spared and taken back to Egypt where it was held by the High Priests of Thoth. The Roman Emperor Caligula brought it from Egypt in order to experiment with it, but it was destroyed before his death in A.D. 41. According to Lovecraft, Abdul Alhazred may have perused a copy of it and elements of it may have formed the basis for the *Necronomicon*.

It may have served as a template for the actual *Book of Azathoth*, mentioned by writers such as Robert M. Price, which appears in two distinct volumes. One of these is carried by the terrible messenger Nyarlathotep, which, as in the ancient Egyptian tome, contains an incantation that can allow men to perceive the likeness of the Outer Gods. All those who swear allegiance to these Gods must sign the book in their own blood. Such an act has overtones of medieval witchcraft; witches were supposed to sign names in their own blood as a proof of their allegiance to the Devil. The second book is a rambling pseudo-account of Azathoth's relation to the creation of the Universe, written in an unknown hand and found in a spiral-bound notebook in Midium's Hotel in New York. It appears in a story by David Hensler entitled *The Higher Mythos*. The volume, of course, connects the entity with the quasi-historical *Book of Thoth*. The Egyptian god of wisdom, therefore, could play a central role in the creation of the name Azathoth, and it *may* spring from the combination of a hideous Sumerian demon and an Egyptian god of wisdom. However, as Robert M. Price has pointed out, while the name may indeed be a fusion of existing names, the source may be different to Sumerian or Egyptian lore. He has suggested that its origins may be Semitic and Biblical, and Lovecraft simply combined the Old Testament name Anathoth (the town from which the prophet Jeremiah came) with that of Azazel, one of the Watcher angels who sinned by lusting after the daughters of Men. Azazel is also referred to briefly by Lovecraft in, "The Dunwich Horror," so there is little doubt that he was familiar with the fallen angel.

Lovecraft may have been familiar with the concept of "azoth," and this, too, may have served as an inspiration in the creation of the name. Azoth was one of the legendary substances that were sought after by the medieval alchemists—it was both a universal medicine that could cure any sickness, as well as a mystical solvent that could dissolve anything to which it was applied. According to lore, Azoth had been found by early Arab alchemists. Azoth's ability to burn through any material from cloth to stone fascinated some of the rulers in the West who recognized its potential as a weapon, and a number of alchemist were employed to find it. Might this not have somehow suggested to some writers the corrosive energies of Azathoth as it seethed and bubbled at the center of the Universe? However, it has been suggested by some scientific historians that Azoth was simply another name for mercury. Taking the concept slightly further, some have even suggested that the name referred to a form of "spiritual mercury," which was some kind of healer for the soul. In fact, the word was used as the title of a book written by the occultist and mystic Arthur Edward Waite, whom Lovecraft used as a model for the wizard Ephraim Waite in his story "The Thing on the Doorstep."

Although the name may originate in Sumerian or Semitic lore, there may also be a connection between Azathoth in its nuclear state and the Egyptian sun-disc Aten. Aten was initially the emanation of the sun-god Ra, and was inferior to him. However, during the reign of Amenhotep IV, worship of the solar corona with various names became widespread. In turning the worship of the corona into a country-wide religion, the pharaoh raised the importance of what had once been a relatively minor cult to new levels. Because the deity was the actual embodiment of the sun's rays, Aten was composed of a fiery energy that could take human form when it chose, and because it could take on the attributes of both Horus and Ra, it also took on various names, one of which may have been connected with the god Thoth. So it's possible that Azathoth may have been connected to the corona of an ancient sun, and this might have given him his name. Was Lovecraft perhaps aware of this? If so, it not only have named the daemon-sultan, but might have given it it's later scientific characteristics.

Vathek

As far as the *character* of Azathoth is concerned, many researchers point to another source of inspiration. In 1782, a Gothic novel appeared entitled *An Arabian Tale* or *The History of the Caliph Vathek*. It was written by William Thomas Beckford, who was certainly a colorful and controversial character.

Similar to Lovecraft, Beckford was fascinated by many things Oriental and part of his work, including *Vathek*, reflects this. Beckford started working on the next novel at the age of 21, and it is something of a sprawling affair concerning an Oriental ruler and his unsuccessful quest to gain supernatural knowledge. Set in 1782, it reflected the late 18th and 19th centuries' fascination with the East and Middle East (as an art collector, Beckford owned a large collection of Middle Eastern artifacts, some of which are now in the National Gallery in London). Supposedly he based his central character on the Abbasid ruler Al-Wathiq ibn Mutasim. The Abbasids reigned over much of what had been the Persian Empire, establishing their capital at Baghdad. At the height of their power during the ninth century, they were unrivalled throughout the ancient world in their wealth and opulence. This era may be what Beckford had been thinking of when he penned his Gothic novel.

The tale is long and complex and tells of hideous-looking strangers who appear at the caliph's court, of swords with indecipherable inscriptions cut into their blades, of ritual child sacrifice, and of djinn, efreets, and Islamic dwarves who torment and threaten humans. This was all set again the splendor and luxury of Vathek's court. In the end, Vathek is guided down to Iblis (Hell) where he is trapped and immediately regrets the mistakes and sins throughout his life.

Although originally written in French it was quickly translated into English by the Reverend Samuel Henley and was published in that language in 1786. However, Beckford's name was omitted from the publication. It was simply entitled *An Arabian Tale from an Unpublished Manuscript*, and purported to have been translated from an ancient Arabic scroll, which gave it a distinct air of authenticity. Indeed, it must have seemed that the events described therein were real. It is probably this translation that was available to Lovecraft.

There is also mention of several characters within the text that may have their origins in actual historical figures. The most notable of these is Belkis, who appears several times within the novel; he may have been based on Belquis, which is the name of the celebrated Queen of Sheba. She appears in several other books, most notably the Hebrew Old Testament, the Bible, and the Qur'an, and was said to be a woman of great learning and intelligence. In sacred texts she consulted the great Semite king, Solomon. Beckford's authorship, although already known, was not formally acknowledged until the early 20th century, and the work was not published with its inclusion until mid-century.

It is not surprising to see how such a work of bizarre Orientalism would have appealed to Lovecraft and fired up his imagination. The idea of the dark and nebulous potentate haunted Lovecraft; in June 1922 he began a major work based around the entity. It was described as "a weird Eastern tale in the 18th century manner" and would probably be reflective of Vathek, along with a number of other French writers, such as Voltaire, who wrote some of their work in the same vein. This was clearly the pre-nuclear version of the daemon sultan, which had been influenced by folklore rather than science-fiction, and was probably designed to be a magnum opus. Lovecraft had hinted as much in a letter to Frank Belknap Long around the same time.

The novel floundered, however, and was abandoned. What was written of it—roughly 500 words—was published in the journal *Leaves* in 1938, a year after Lovecraft's death. However, according to Lovecraft scholar Davis E. Schultz, some of the ideas from it were used in *The Dream-Quest of Unknown Kadath*, written as part of his *Dream Cycle* stories. Apart from the title, Azathoth does not appear in the text, and there is little to show what creature Lovecraft had envisioned the daemon-sultan to be.

Mana-Yood-Sushai

At least part of the image of Azathoth may have come from yet another source. Robert M. Price has suggested that, like a number of his creations, Lovecraft found inspiration for the daemon-sultan in the works of one of his favorite fantasy authors, Lord Dunsany. In his work *The Gods of Pagana*, Dunsany describes a withdrawn creator-god named Mana-Yood-Sushai, who created the Universe and then retreated from it. He supposedly sleeps eternally, lulled by the music of a lesser god named Skarl, who must drum for all eternity, because if Man-Yood-Sushai should wake he would destroy the Universe and all that he has created.

This idea may be suggestive of the Sumerian god Patesi bel-Zaub (Lord of the Deeps), who slept seated on an azure throne in the shade of a tree on an island in the middle of Lake Abzu. Patesi bel-Zaub had once before raised the seas in his anger, flooding large parts of the world. Although he was not lulled by continuous music, the heat of the island where he sat down to rest caused him to doze, and a cup of wine by the side of his throne ensured that he continued to do so. In early Middle Eastern mythology, the same is said of Yao Sabboath the Destroyer, who sits on an emerald throne in the shadow of a great rock, dreaming away Eternity. If the entity should awake, it will bring about the Great Day of Judgement.

All these figures hold echoes of Lovecraft's Azathoth and all are apparently routed in the folklore, mythology, and religion of the early Middle East. Whether Lovecraft created the mysterious caliph from his own researches or directly from Dunsany is another matter, but the similarities seem too great to be ignored. Though, it would appear that Lovecraft's Azathoth might be more malignantly *aware* than anything that Dunsany had created.

Achamoth and the Gnostics

Lovecraft's interest in Gnosticism has prompted scholars such as Daniel Harms to suggest that this is an area in which the origins of Azathoth may lie.

In Gnostic belief, it was not a Supreme Being who had created the Universe (such a Being was far too spiritual, remote, and unknowable). Rather, what we perceive as reality was created through a series of Demiurges, archons, or artisan figures who were lesser emanations of the Supreme Being. These entities molded the *pleroma* ("fullness") or matter of the Cosmos into the form that we recognize. This was also the basis of thinking of some of the early forms of Greek philosophical thinking, particularly those deriving from Plato.

Influenced by Greek thought, Gnosticism became ever more complex. The early Christian Gnostics, for instance, attributed to the Demiurges and archons human-like attributes. Wisdom, for example, was accorded the name Sophia, but there were also higher and lower levels of wisdom, and therefore higher and lower Sophias. In the complicated Gnosticism of the thinker Valentinius, one of the major Gnostic movements that spread across the Roman Empire produced Achamoth, an emanation or "daughter" of a lower Sophia. She was the mother of a Demiurge that had created the Universe we know. But while she gave birth to Creation she, like Azathoth, could bring about its destruction if she chose. Although the teachings of Valentinius were prevalent within early Christian beliefs, by the end of the 2nd century they were counted as heretical. Nevertheless, they were still transmitted in secret and became part of the "forbidden knowledge" of the early philosophies. Possibly the secrecy of such an ancient and complex way of thinking appealed to Lovecraft and may have played some part in the creation and development of Azathoth.

Cults and Worship

In the latter half of the 1920s, the transition from a folkloric to a scientific image for the daemon-sultan was all but complete. Azathoth was no longer the mystical, distant, and demonic figure of Arabian legend, but was now a swirling and unstable mass of nuclear energies that seethed and bubbled in some curiously angled corner of the Cosmos. In Lovecraft's "The Whisperer in Darkness" (written in 1930), the narrator states that he is filled with loathing when told of the "monstrous nuclear chaos beyond angled space which the *Necronomicon* had mercifully cloaked under the name Azathoth." This is no longer the mystical, distant demon-like entity of former imagination, rather, it has a science-fiction edge to it. The entity had also become part of a new, more-scientifically based vision of the Universe that Lovecraft was creating. Although certain old elements remained (Lovecraft's distinction between folklore and science could be extremely blurred at times), the Universe was undergoing a powerful change. The Outer Gods were no longer the mystical entities they once were—instead, they were ancient and powerful aliens from worlds beyond the most distant stars who had come to Earth in some dimly remembered time.

According to Lovecraft, although Azathoth was still worshipped by inbred communities and crazed hermits in the remote New England hill country or by strange gatherings in distant corners of the world, much of the information has come from prehistoric times. Earliest reference to such worship seems to have been adhered to among the Gnophkehs, a race of primitive humanoids, who were alleged to have lived in primal Hyperborea in a time before the Great Ice Age. These creatures were cannibalistic in nature, covered in coarsely matted hair, with long proboscis-like noses, and huge, protruding ears. Although they chiefly worshipped the octopoidal deity Rhan-Tegoth, it has been suggested by some writers such as Lin Carter and Clark Ashton-Smith that sections of them may also have worshipped Azathoth. Rhan-Tegoth, it seems, went into hibernation and completely forgot about them, whereupon the seething mass of Azathoth became their main deity. According to Carter, they were eventually overwhelmed by another humanoid race, the Voormis, who according to Smith worshipped the god Tsathogga. The Voormis are also mentioned by Lovecraft as the "Voormi peoples" who appear in the *Pnakotic Manuscripts* or *Fragments*. Although the Voormis were human in form, they were covered by a thick reddish fur, had three toes on each foot, dwelt in caves, and communicated by dog-like howls. According to the Fragments, they drove the Gnophkehs into very remote areas and all but wiped out their worship of Azathoth. Lovecraft seems to have established a pseudo-historical basis for the notion of Azathoth linked into some form of prehistory, which somehow underpinned our own world. Others, however, would develop the idea of primal beings even further.

The main devotees of the idiot god were supposedly the insect-race from Shaggai (also known as Shan), who also came to earth in the time before the Ice Age. This concept is the creation of the Lovecraftian writer Ramsey Campbell (although the idea came from the notes of Lovecraft), who describes their original homeworld as a rocky, inhospitable place with little light, orbiting two emerald suns. It is partly covered by a vast sea of black protoplasm, and huge and shadowy jungles of carnivorous mold. On this bizarre world, a space-faring, pigeon-sized insect people have evolved, who worship the daemon-sultan in large green pyramids. Another object of their worship— the avatar Xada-Hgla, which manifests itself as a clam-like entity from which long pseudopods protrude and great green eyes peer out from inside the shell—may actually be another manifestation of Azathoth. In fact, according to Campbell this may have been the original form that the daemon-sultan initially possessed before the gods took away its reason and reduced it to a mass of fizzling nuclear energy. Many images of this deity appear within these conical temples, which can sometimes teleport across space and time. The science-fiction element of the Mythos-story (and of the god itself)—time traveling across space from far away planets—was clearly already taking shape.

When the world of Shaggai was destroyed in a collision with a strange, celestial, red-glowing object more than 800 years ago, the Shan were not obliterated. They were able to teleport to several nearby worlds in their Azathoth temples—worlds from which they were able to spread out into the wider Universe, taking their unspeakable rituals of worship with them. According to Campbell, some of these appeared in the Severn Valley in England and have become trapped here, as our atmosphere contains an element that sometimes prevents their temples from teleporting. The transference of Azathoth from folkloric myth to science-fiction entity was now more or less complete.

Finally, the author Thomas Ligotti in his story *The Sect of the Idiot* mentions a group of small, wizened non-human beings who prostrate themselves before "the primal chaos which is Lord of All…the blind, idiot god Azathoth." In many of his tales, Ligotti describes the insidious infiltration of the Old Gods into the modern technological world, perhaps a metaphor for their adaptation, particularly in the case of Azathoth.

The Rites of Azathoth

Little is known regarding the specific rites that mark the worship of Azathoth. Ramsey Campbell, however, states that those followed by the insects of Shaggai are "utterly abominable and abhorrent." Lovecraft hints at the worshippers of Azathoth, which are "mercifully cloaked" by certain obscure passages in the feared *Necronomicon*. These are probably summoning rituals that draw the entity down from its throne—this is the only time that Azathoth may leave its "curiously angled" corner of space and time. The invocation is also said to open a special portal in the fabric of time and space, which allows the deity to enter our world. Even then, according to the *Necronomicon* and *De Vermis Mysteriis*, such a summoning requires large amounts of fissionable material in order to make Azathoth appear. Therefore, it seems that the invocation and rites of the daemon-sultan combines elements of science and technology (nuclear-fusion) with arcane and blasphemous magic reflecting the ambivalence in Lovecraft's changing perceptions. Combined with certain rituals, says *De Vermis Mysteriis,* the very use or mention of Azathoth's name gives the individual great power over lesser beings from outside the normal spheres of existence.

The *Book of Eibon* mentions something called "The Grey Rite of Azathoth," though no description is given as to its performance or context. It may be a summoning ritual or some sort of celebratory rite, and remains something of a mystery. Among the surviving text it seems there is this a ritual for calling down Azathoth and for binding the daemon-sultan to do one's bidding.

Later Visions of the Daemon-Sultan

Although the entity had changed in form, Lovecraft was not yet done with Azathoth. The Being appeared once again in his story "The Dreams in the Witch House." In this tale, the spectral witch, Keziah Mason, instructs the protagonist Walter Gilman that he must meet with a Black Man and go with him to the center of the Ultimate Chaos to stand before the throne of Azathoth. There, he must sign allegiance to the daemon-sultan in his own blood and take a secret name. Gilman recognizes the name Azathoth from something that he has read in the *Necronomicon* and he knows that it actually stands for some sort of ancient horror. Gilman later wakes from a dream in which he was conscious of the thin sound of pipes being played somewhere in the darkness—suggestive of the court of Azathoth.

"The Dreams in the Witch House" seems to suggest that Lovecraft was still slightly confused as to what form the daemon-sultan should actually take. The idea of being taken by a Black Man and the idea of a pact signed in blood are all features of medieval and witchcraft trials, whereas Azathoth is suggested as the nuclear field of a cosmic chaos. The two elements of Lovecraft's fiction therefore come together in a rather confused manner.

In "The Thing on the Doorstep" (written in 1933), Lovecraft makes reference to a "hellish" collection of poems written by Edward Pickman Derby (a character thought to have been based on Lovecraft) entitled *Azathoth and Other Horrors*. Apart from the title there is really no description as to what sort of horror the daemon-sultan suggests.

The last of Lovecraft's direct references to Azathoth appears in 1935 in *The Haunter of the Dark*. In this he speaks of Azathoth, the Lord of All Things with his court of amorphous, flopping dancers, lulled by the thin sound of a hideous flute. There is little here to describe the god, either in folkloric or science-fiction terms, and yet there is still an air of monstrous menace about the reference.

This was Lovecraft's own, rather vague vision on which others chose to expand. Some of them have chosen to change the daemon-sultan's image even further. In *Insects from Shaggai*, Ramsey Campbell, for example, mentions a huge idol, said to be that of Azathoth, found in a forest near Goatswood (Campbell's mythical town set in the English Severn Valley) by his protagonist Ronald Shea. The idol is of a bivalvular shell out of which extend a number of polypus appendages. The shell is supported by many barrel-like legs and within the shell Shea sees a bestial, mouthless face with deep eyes, covered in glistening black bristles. Later, as the tale reaches its climax, he also receives a glimpsed of a later vision of Azathoth—what the god might have metamorphosed into:

I SAW SOMETHING OOZE INTO THE CORRIDOR—A PALE, GREY SHAPE, EXPANDING AND CRINKLING WHICH GLISTENED AND SHOOK GELATINOUSLY AS STILL MOVING PARTICLES DROPPED FREE; BUT IT WAS ONLY A GLIMPSE AND AFTER THAT IT IS ONLY IN NIGHTMARES THAT I IMAGINE THE COMPLETE SHAPE OF AZATHOTH.

So what are we to make of Azathoth? Possibly Lovecraft had initially envisioned him as something out of Middle-Eastern folklore, a kind of mysterious djinn-ruler who maintained a magical court in some far away and inaccessible place. Later, however, he changed that perspective and turned him into some form of science-fiction entity— a being that is simply a changing mass of nuclear energy—dwelling in some chaotic corner of the cosmos. Even in the stories of later authors, this confusion surrounding Azathoth seems to continue, as it becomes a mighty being that made war on the alien rulers of Betelgeuse, or the shell-like god of an insect-race living on an unimaginably far-away planet. At the end of it all, Azathoth still remains something of an enigma. Perhaps there are future tales to be written that will reveal the entity's true nature and origins.

Shadows Beyond the Stars

Shub-Niggurath

Arguably, none of the Outer Gods have been the subject of as much text or the focus of as many cults as Shub-Niggurath, the dark embodiment of fertility. It has been featured throughout Mythos fiction ranging from Robert M. Price to Ramsey Campbell to Stephen King. Yet, in his own work, Lovecraft gives very little indication as to what this powerful entity might look like and what its origins are, so it has been left up to these later authors to hint at its appearance and powers.

Origins of the Name

The idea of Shub-Niggurath may originate in ancient Oriental folklore and mysticism, of which Lovecraft was particularly fond. His first mention of the entity is in the Revisionist Tales (a revised collaborative story begun by someone else and amended by Lovecraft) entitled "The Last Test," published in 1928 and jointly credited to Adolphe de Castro. Here, the name is used only as an exclamation of praise—"Ia! Shub-Niggurath!" with no real explanation as to its meaning.

The associations with Yemen and the al-Dahana give the impression that Lovecraft had initially intended Shub-Nigguarth to be some kind of Middle-Eastern entity. In his essay on *Lovecraft and Occultism* (2003), John Wisdom Gonce states the following:

> LOVECRAFT'S FASCINATION WITH *THE ARABIAN NIGHTS* (WHICH HAD BEGUN WHEN HE WAS FIVE YEARS OLD), DEFINITELY CARRIED INTO HIS ADULT LIFE, LEADING HIM TO DO FURTHER RESEARCH INTO ISLAMIC HISTORY AND FOLKLORE, AS INDICATED BY THE BOOKS IN HIS LIBRARY: THE CALIF HAROUN ALRASID AND SARACEN CIVILISATION BY EDWARD HENRY PALMER AND TALES OF GENII BY SIR WILLIAM CHARLES MORRELL (PSEUDONYM). KNOWING LOVECRAFT'S PASSION FOR RESEARCH, IT'S QUITE POSSIBLE THAT HE WENT ON TO READ SIR RICHARD BURTON'S UNABRIDGED AND UNEXPURGATED VERSION OF THE NIGHTS WHEN HE REACHED ADULTHOOD. WHAT WOULD LOVECRAFT HAVE LEARNED FROM SUCH STUDIES? HE WOULD HAVE LEARNED ABOUT A FASCINATING MENAGERIE OF ISLAMIC GENIES AND MONSTERS: A SUB-SPECIES OF DJINN KNOWN AS THE GHOUL (GHUL) THAT DWELLS IN CEMETERIES AND DESERTED PLACES AND EATS HUMAN FLESH.

Somewhere among Lovecraft's research into Islamic lore was there some creature that inspired the name Shub-Niggurath? Indeed, the name could even have some Sumerian connotations, as the prefix *Shub* occurs in some early texts from the Fertile Crescent as an addition to that of a god, demon, or minor deity. The prefix may denote that the entity is worthy of praise. It is worth noting that in Charles Abbot's *Oriental Folklore* (1901), the name *Nug* or *Nag*, which appears in Lovecraft's text is given as that as that of a djinn-type creature, which lived in the desert. This idea has been developed by the writer Clark Ashton-Smith, who in *Descent into the Abyss* describes Nug, reputedly the off-spring of Shub-Niggurath (see *Lovecraft: Selected Letters III and IV*), as "the grandfather of ghouls." This gives credence to the idea that the original creation of the deity lay somewhere in the Middle East and was connected in some way to pre-Islamic mythology. Lovecraft, however, changed that slightly.

In keeping with the Middle-Eastern theme of the entity's origins, Lovecraft enthusiast and writer Robert M. Price has suggested that the name may come from another work—a piece of prose by Lord Dunsany.

Edward Plunkett, the 18th Baron of Dunsany created a mystic realm that he called the Lands of Dream, which many people believe acted as a template for Lovecraft's Dream Worlds. Similar to Lovecraft, Dunsany was in many ways an Orientalist, and often used many exotic Eastern-sounding locations for his stories and prose. One work published in 1910 is entitled "Idle Days on the Yann" and concerns a journey along the river among thickly forested banks. In the course of the description, Dunsany notes:

AND I FELT THAT I WOULD PRAY. YET, I LIKED NOT TO PRAY TO A JEALOUS GOD THERE WHERE THE FRAIL, AFFECTIONATE GODS WHOM THE HEATHENS LOVE WERE BEING HUMBLY INVOKED, SO I BETHOUGHT ME INSTEAD OF SHEOL-NUGGANOTH WHOM THE MEN OF THE JUNGLE HAVE LONG SINCE DESERTED, WHO IS NOW UNWORSHIPPED AND ALONE, AND TO HIM I PRAYED.

Sheol-Nugganoth is one of Dunsany's own inventions, but Lovecraftian scholars such as Price believe Lovecraft may have borrowed it and turned it into Shub-Niggurath. The exact meaning of the word Sheol is almost certainly Hebrew, referring to a place that may be the earliest description of the Afterlife. The most common translation of the word is "a pit or abyss" into which the dead were cast and, according to Hebrew tradition, were "removed from the sight of God." In the Hebrew Tanach, the word occurs more than 60 times and is usually referred to in the context of a place of mourning and regret. In the Biblical books of both Ecclesiastes and Job, Sheol is the destination of both righteous and unrighteous flesh. In later Jewish lore, it appears to have been a place of unmitigated tedium in which the spirits of the departed continually drifted about, muttering to themselves in endless dark, trying to recall and reflect upon their previous lives. However, the word *Sheol* was later replaced by the Greek word *Hades* as Judaism spread through the Hellenistic world.

Others, particularly Biblical scholars, have suggested a rather different etymology for the name. They suggest that it is connected to the ancient Hebrew word *su sal* meaning "to burrow," denoting some sort of underground connotation, whereas the important theological scholar William Albright believed that the word might originally have been "shaal," meaning a place of questioning or interrogation somewhere far below the ground. Might it also have referred to some deity who stood in judgement over the souls entering its subterranean realm?

If Price and others are correct in saying that Lovecraft *did* use Dunsany's Sheol-Nugganoth as an original template for Shub-Niggurath, then perhaps the emphasis may lie in the *Sheol* prefix. This would also give the entity a Hebrew/Middle-Eastern origin, although perhaps the idea of some sort of medieval fertility god or goddess might be a much better bet.

Lovecraft gave slightly more detail concerning the entity in some of his other collaborative tales, but even then the information and description appears extremely sketchy. In "The Mound," a story that he ghost-wrote for Zealia Bishop between the 1929 and 1930, he stated that a major shrine to the deity was located in the subterranean realm of K'y-yan that extended throughout a vast underground cavern beneath Oklahoma. Bishop had employed Lovecraft to flesh out a rather conventional ghost story concerning a mysterious Indian mound that existed near the town of Binger, Oklahoma, at which the ghost of a headless Indian (possibly a woman) was said to appear. The story was both too short and too ordinary for Lovecraft, who extended the concept into a novella in order to make the mound a gateway to the underground realm. In the novella Lovecraft describes the entity as:

SHUB-NIGGURATH, THE ALL-MOTHER AND WIFE OF THE NOT TO BE NAMED ONE. THIS DEITY WAS A KIND OF SOPHISTICATED ASTARTE AND HER WORSHIP STRUCK THE PIOUS CATHOLIC AS EXTREMELY OBNOXIOUS.

The reference to Astarte is a particularly telling one, and links the origins of Shub-Niggurath to the ancient mythologies of the Fertile Crescent and Far East. Astarte was the consort of the Semitic god Baal, and was regarded as a fertility goddess. Her true origins, however, may lie further East in the cult of Cybele and her consort Attis. Cybele may be an even older Phrygian (Asia Minor) goddess of growth and fecundity. In his book *Mother of the Gods*, Mark Henderson Munn has suggested that she was also known in Greek Lydia (a region of Anatolia on the present-day Turkish borders) by the name Mountain Mother or All-Mother. Her cult became intertwined with a number of Roman fertility cults and later became Latinised in the Roman world as Magna Mater—a term beloved of Lovecraft in parts of his fiction.

Munn also draws attention to the notion that the name may also refer to a cult of Kubaba, the only queen to appear in the Sumerian lists of kings. Although a follower of the Sumerian god Marduk during her lifetime, Kubaba became a goddess after death and in the list of kings, she is recorded as the sole member of the 3rd Dynasty of Kish. She was further seen as the protector-deity of the ancient city of Carchemish on the upper Euphrates, which marked the widest spread of her cult throughout Mesopotamia. During this extension of her influence, she may have picked up the attributes and characteristics of certain localized fertility goddesses, which became incorporated within her worship. Significantly for Lovecraftian purposes, she is described as "the Great Mother of a Thousand," and her cult may have been intertwined with the worship of Astarte and Cybele.

But perhaps it is the Phrygian goddess Cybele that formed the basis for Shub-Niggurath in Lovecraft's mind, particularly with relation to her "Not to be Named" consort. Although she is described as "the Mother of a Thousand" Kubaba has no consort, and although Astarte is attached to Baal in Semitic myth, the relationship is a rather tenuous one. Up until the sixth century B.C., Cybele appears alone and as a single deity, but from the fifth century B.C. onward, she is joined by the god Attis. Ceremonies surrounding the two gods are recorded as wild and frenzied (Lovecraft hints that the rituals of Shub-Niggurath were also wild and "abominable") and included ritual castration. Attis, it was said, had castrated himself after being driven mad by Cybele. In Phrygian Anatolia, the name of Attis was specifically forbidden, because he was not truly a man and therefore he was "the One Who is Not Named," similar to the consort of Shub-Niggurath. Later, however, the writer August Derleth would identify this mysterious entity as another Mythos entity named Hastur, but there is still some speculation about who it actually is. Robert M. Price for example, as quote by Daniel Harms in his *Cthulhu Mythos Encyclopedia*, claims that he is none other than Yog-Sothoth, or the serpent god, Yig.

In keeping with Shub-Niggurath's Eastern origins and worship, Lovecraft introduces a more "English" element to the worship of the deity. In his story *Rats in the Walls* he states that: "…the great mother worshipped by the hereditary cult at Exham Priory…had to be none other than Shub-Niggurath." The deity was moving a little ways from the dusty plains and secluded temples of the Middle East to secret places in the leafy forests of England and the New World.

Descriptions of Shub-Niggurath

Despite the possible Middle Eastern connections, very little is known about the deity. Lovecraft doesn't give any real description of the being, although he does refer to it as "an evil cloud-like entity" in a letter to Willis Conover (a jazz producer and broadcaster on *Voice of America* who corresponded with Lovecraft toward the end of Lovecraft's life). Therefore, it might be possible to suggest that although Lovecraft's vision of Shub-Niggurath lay in the mystery religions of the East, he had no firm idea as to what it was or what it looked like. Indeed, its gender has sometimes been called into question, as it is sometimes referred to as "the Black Ram of the Forest with a Thousand Ewes." Generally, however, Shub-Niggurath is taken to be female.

Lovecraft's description of the entity as "evil" and "cloud-like" is once again suggestive of Eastern folklore. This creature is a type of extremely ferocious djinn that appears in the form of a smoky cloud with a glistening center, which is extremely tricky and bad-tempered. If he had read Morrell's *Tales of the Genii*, Lovecraft may have known about such an entity and may have transposed it onto the personage of Shub-Niggurath.

Given the paucity of actual description, it has been left to writers other than Lovecraft—August Derleth, Robert Bloch, Ramsey Campbell, and others—to develop the Outer God as a distinct entity and to offer some form of description. In their works, it appears as a great and noxious cloud from which cloven feet and flailing tentacles and tendrils constantly protrude and are reabsorbed. Sometimes it appears in the city of Harag-Kolath (which appears in the works of writer Richard L. Tierney) as a dark and shapeless mass with myriad eyes. Despite being an important deity in the Mythos pantheon the appearance, and to some extent the nature of Shub-Niggurath, still remains a tantalising mystery.

Residence of the Deity

Like many other aspects of its being, the domain of Shub-Niggurath is unclear. According to some writers such as Richard Tierney, Shub-Niggurath arrived on Earth from space in a distant, prehistoric time and aided in the construction of the underground city of Harag-Koth, where it now awaits the arrival of its consort (possibly Hastur). For Lin Carter, the being may have originated on the planet Yaddith, an unimaginably distant world that orbits no less than five stars. It has become infested by carnivorous worm-like creatures known as dholes (whom some believe are the servitors of Shub-Niggurath), which have left it barren and desolate. The destruction of this distant world may be one of the reasons why the entity traveled across the infinite void of space to Earth, though why it chose this particular planet is unclear.

It is also possible that Shub-Niggurath may exist in another dimension entirely. It may sit as a member of the court of Azathoth in a place where the conventional rules that govern time and space break down. According to texts such as the *Necronomicon*, wherever this entity is located, it is possible for any adherent to summon it using a properly constructed altar and with the correct rituals and invocations. Interestingly, this can most effectively be done in woodland places, thus moving the deity from its initial desert Middle-Eastern setting into a recognizable English/New England one.

Cults and Worship

According to the Cthulhu writer Daniel Harms, the cults of Shub-Niggurath may be the most widespread of any Mythos entity. The deity has been worshipped many times in many places, and there is a strong suggestion that it was one of those Outer Gods who were venerated long before the dawn of recorded history. Indeed, some have argued that even before they came to Earth several of the gods had sent messages to the planet in order to form cults that awaited their arrival. During the 1940s, for instance, a relatively obscure writer named Fred L. Pelton published a volume entitled *Cultus Malificarum* (which later formed part of *A Guide to the Cthulhu Cult*). The *Cultus* contains translations of what Pelton refers to as the *Sussex Manuscript*, which was initially written in a pre-human tongue and was allegedly translated in 1598 by a Baron Frederick I of Sussex from Olaus Wormius's Latin text. This reveals how Shub-Niggurath and several of the other Outer Gods made contact with early inhabitants of Earth in order to establish cults that would venerate them and give them power. It also discloses how a major ritual has to be performed every thousand years, which would continue the cycle of these beings on the planet. The work, which was published in three volumes, each detailing a separate aspect of pre-human history with regard to the Old Gods, is probably the most extensive study of such worship. However, much of the text relates to the more generalized worship of such deities and not to strictly specific aspects of it, such as Shub-Niggurath.

Although many of these original cults and their forms of worship have been more or less lost to history that does not mean the legend didn't continue. Shub-Niggurath is known to have been worshipped by the Tcho-Tcho peoples, the Hyperboreans, the people of Sarnath, the inhabitants of Mu, the Egyptians, the Cretans, the Greeks, and the Druids. It has been venerated in many guises, a number of which we have explored, but there were later medieval and early modern cults that also flourished and changed the nature of the entity once again.

The Goat Connection

In his story *The Whisperer in Darkness,* written in 1930, Lovecraft penned the following exchange in relation to a hideous pre-human ceremony:

> EVER THEIR PRAISES AND THEIR ABUNDANCE TO THE BLACK GOAT OF THE WOODS! IA! SHUB-NIGGURATH! THE BLACK GOAT OF THE WOOD WITH A THOUSAND YOUNG!

In this, Lovecraft seems to add yet another aspect to the entity. There is a connection here that links Shub-Niggurath to the forests and woodlands, which were supposedly centers for European fertility and witch-cults that flourished during medieval times. His description of the "black goat" is significant, because the animal would become strongly associated with European sorcery in both the medieval and early-modern minds. There is, nevertheless, still a connection to the Middle East and to prehistoric religions there.

From earliest times, the goat was an animal strongly associated with communal cleansing from both evil and sin. As early as the 24th century B.C., the animal was used to carry away evil spirits during a purification ritual preceding the wedding of a king. A she-goat (there is no indication that it had to be black) was hung with a silver bracelet or chain and was driven out into a place called Alini (the surrounding wilderness), taking away all the former evils and indiscretions of the monarch and his people with it. The marriage could not continue until this had been done or a great evil would descend on the land. If the goat happened to be pregnant at the time, then she would give birth to thousands of devils in the waste. Therefore, the goat was seen as the receptacle of sin and evil, and was now associated with devils.

Such a ritual may also have been the basis for the later Hebrew cleansing of the Holy Tabernacle in Jerusalem. On the Day of Atonement, the sins of the Children of Israel were confessed (after the appropriate sacrifices) by the laying on of hands on the head of a goat. The animal was then subsequently driven out of the city to Azazel, thus taking away the sins of the people and cleansing the Tabernacle. Once again, the goat symbolically took on the embodiment of darkness and evil. Although it was the original scapegoat, the animal, so steeped in communal evil, also acquired great and dark powers, and would later have an occult significance. At some point the personification of the animal with all its dark mystery became confused with the Greek word *Goetia* meaning "sorcery," which appears in such works as the early modern *Ars Goetia* (a work derived from Johann Weyers's 1563 work *De Preaestigiis Daemonum*, and this may have been an element in the iconic representation of the Goat of Mendes.

Mendes was the Greek name for the Egyptian city of Djedet on the eastern Nile Delta. The city was also known in Ancient Egypt as Per-Banebdjedet—the Domain of the Ram Lord of Djedet. The chief deity of the city was Benebedjedet, a ram god that embodied both the elements of good and evil. According to the Greek historian Herodotus in *Histories,* the god was represented with the head and fleece of a goat, although in later years, this was also a representation of Zeus.

The sacrifice of rams or goats was forbidden within the city of Mendes, except on one day of the year when a ram was killed and its head was placed upon a statue of Zeus that stood in a temple inside the city walls. The statue was then worshipped, both as the embodiment of Zeus and the ram-god. This image was later denounced by the emergent Greek Christian Church, and eventually served as the template for Eliphas Levi's celebrated 19th century depiction of the Goat of Mendes in his *Dogme et Rituel de Haute Magie* (published in 1854) showing a winged human torso with a goat-head and a pair of breasts, with a torch placed between its horns. Levi stated that this was a representation of Baphomet, the Sabbatic Goat, which was worshipped by the Knights Templar and brought into Western European witchcraft traditions by them.

The most celebrated image of the Satanic Goat of Mendes, however, comes from the work of the French occultist Alphonse Louis Constant, who styled himself as Eliphas Levi. His dark image was supposedly taken from a very old set of Tarot cards in which the goat symbolized Mercury. He claimed the images on the cards were taken from the original *Book of Thoth*. These scrolls were a treatise on pre-human magic, or so Levi claimed, and contained knowledge that had existed before the foundation of the world. The image of the Goat of Mendes, therefore, had an occult significance, which was deeper than any mere medieval witchcraft interpretation. This was not to say, of course, that it hadn't influenced some of the early witchcraft trials—especially those of the Knights Templar in France.

It was the Templars who really brought the idea of Baphomet as a sinister entity into the public mind. Although rumors and legends circulated that they brought certain artifacts back from the Holy Land and they were involved in some form of unholy Saracen worship, nothing could be proved. Finally, King Philip IV of France eventually moved against them in 1306/7. Aided by a French pope and the Church authorities, he accused them of blasphemy, witchcraft, and heresy. The fact that many of the Templar rites were conducted in the strictest secrecy did nothing to further their cause against such attack. It was alleged, for example, that they had brought a goat-like idol from the East and clandestinely worshipped it. This of course was Baphomet, also known as the Goat of Mendes.

But the legend of the Templars continued through the centuries. The secrecy and mystery that appeared to surround their Order only added to interpretations regarding them and elevated them to an almost supernatural status. Attempts were made during the 17th and 18th centuries to link the Templars with the early Gnostics. The notion that the Gnostics were the heirs to ancient and possibly forbidden truths certainly appealed to the 17th-century mind and became entangled with the Templar legend persisting until the early 19th century. The idea suggested that Baphomet, which the Templars venerated, somehow embodied that secret knowledge of former times and the symbolism contained might be used as a medium by which to impart it. Baphomet, therefore, became something of a slightly confused figure, symbolizing esoteric knowledge, evil, and witchcraft all at once.

In 1818, these mystical and possibly Satanic connections were even further strengthened by the publication of an essay by the Viennese Orientalist, Joseph Freiherr von Hammer-Purgstall. Entitled *Discovery of the Mystery of Baphomet by which the Knights Templar, like the Gnostics and Ophites, are convicted of Apostasy, Idolatry and of Moral Impurity by their own Monuments*, the work served to create a sort of pseudo-history around the notion of a goat god, which symbolized some arcane and blasphemous knowledge. It relied heavily on alleged medieval accounts and upon rather spurious archaeological evidence, not to mention instances of alleged Baphomets, which had been clearly faked by earlier "scholars." The essay was a mish-mash of half-truths, speculations, and outright lies, and it was written with a hidden agenda. It was specifically designed to discredit the emerging sect of Freemasonry, which was creating much intellectual interest around this period. Because of the secrecy surrounding its meetings, Freemasonry was viewed with some suspicion, and it was alleged by some that the organization was actually a front for ancient magics and mysteries. Rumors circulated that images of Baphomet were held and worshipped within certain lodges, just as the Templars did. Although there is no evidence to suggest that this was true, certain Templar churches such as Saint-Merri in Paris have carvings of squat goat-footed men with bats wings and breasts.

It was some of these drawings that may have given Eliphas Levi the idea for his illustration. Although Levi declared that the image had its roots in Templar traditions, it doesn't correspond to the descriptions given of Baphomet. However, Levi's interest strengthened the occult significance of the image and linked it with dark magic and sorcery. Throughout the years the Black Goat has become the very symbol of all that is sinister, dangerous, and supernatural.

Although there is no real evidence to suggest that either Lovecraft or his father were Freemasons, there are those who claim that lodges across America held copies of the *Necronomicon* within their precincts and this had a direct influence on Lovecraft and his work. Also, the writer Colin Wilson claims that Winfield Scott Lovecraft was an Egyptian Freemason and owned a copy of the book (this has always been strenuously denied by all of the various Rhode Island lodges) and his grandfather Whipple Van Buren Phillips was extremely active within the Masonic Orders and was a founding member of Ionic Lodge Number 28 in Greene, Rhode Island, in 1870. Nevertheless, the rumors concerning the secret rites of the Freemasons and their supposed worship of Baphomet may have influenced him in the creation of Shub-Niggurath.

Since Lovecraft's death, the being has surfaced time and time again in Mythos tales by other writers. Celebrated Lovecraftian authors such as Stephen King (*Crouch End*), Ramsey Campbell (*The Moon Lens*), and Gary Myers (*What Rough Beast?*) together with a host of lesser-known and fan writers have all paid homage to and further developed the idea of this Outer God.

SHADOWS BEYOND THE STARS
OTHER ENTITIES

Major entities among the Great Old Ones may lurk all around us—in the seas, lakes, hills, and woods, subtly working their ancient magic or sciences upon us all. However, there are some others who may be languidly watching us as well.

Hastur the Unspeakable One

Unlike most of the Great Old Ones of which It is a part, Hastur the Unspeakable One (He Who is Not to be Named) is not to be found on Earth. It either dwells or is imprisoned in a dark star near Aldebaran in the constellation Taurus. That dwelling is in a habitation on the very edge of the Lake of Hali on the fringes of the constellation Taurus, although other sources place this dwelling among the Hyades, which can also be found in Taurus.

As with many other Mythos entities, a certain confusion reigns as to the exact location of the entity's habitation. Some say that Hali can be found on Earth; the location is given as the Gobi Desert in Mongolia, which was supposedly a lake beneath whose waters Hastur lived. The lake drained, leaving only the desert behind, which was supposedly part of the primal land of Carcosa (although some state that Carcosa is a planet that orbits around a black star in Taurus). Hastur is considered to be the patron of decadence, sluggishness, ennui, nihilism, and languidness, and is closely associated with the King in Yellow.

In regard to its physical form, descriptions range from an invisible Presence, which can only be sensed in a physical way, to a great clot of expanding shadow, to a 20-foot reptilian biped covered with tentacles. It also exists as the Emerald Lama, a humanoid figure that has an alien "feel" to it, wrapped in an emerald robe and no face. This is the only humanoid shape that Hastur adopts. There are some, of course, who assert that the entity *has* no physical form.

The entity has acquired the sobriquet "He Who is Not to be Named," and this could refer to Its separation from some of the other Great Old Ones or because of the abominable rites associated with It.

Hastur was worshipped in ancient civilizations such as Attluma (which sank beneath the waves before Atlantis), Atlantis, and Hyperborea, where great temples to It were raised. Its cult was both feared and hated even back in ancient times. Its purpose was to attempt to bring Hastur to Earth in order to gain supernatural knowledge (previously it had only appeared in emanated forms such as the Emerald Lama). This could only be attempted when Aldebaran was in the sky, when it was in a Celestial Conjunction with the planet Mercury, and in the middle of nine stone monoliths arranged in a V-shape resembling Taurus. The entity could then be drawn down using the Yellow Sign.

Hastur is worshipped in the secret places of America and Asia by the Mi-go, but It is also served by a species of interstellar beings known as the byakhee. These beings seem to adapt elements of birds, bats, and rotting corpses. According to some traditions they were the inhabitants of an interstellar city that was drawn into Carcosa and were driven completely mad by the experience. They travel between worlds by flying through space, visiting and nesting on worlds such as Yuggoth and Carcosa, using either a growth or device attached to their necks, which is called a hune. The growth also secretes a liquid called space-mead, which anyone wishing to travel with them must drink. The byakhee then activates the hune and is able to travel through space at incredible speeds. Similar to Hastur, the byakhee can be summoned, but only when Aldebaran can be seen in the night sky.

The entity Shub-Nigguarth and Hastur are closely linked, having mated at some point to produce foul offspring called the Thousand Young. Hastur is also opposed to Cthulhu, although, like many other such conflicts, the cause of their enmity is not known. At some point in the distant past, the two of them have tried to destroy each other, but neither succeeded.

Hastur is not actually a creation of Lovecraft, although he was impressed with It and does refer to It several times in his works. Although the entity first appears (in a slightly different guise) in Ambrose Bierce's *Haita the Shepherd* (curiously Hastur is also the patron saint of shepherds), as far as the Mythos is concerned, the source of the name is Robert W. Chambers in *The King in Yellow*. Lovecraft had read Chambers's work and was so impressed by both it and the name itself that he began to make references to it in his own fiction, most notably *The Whisperer in Darkness*. He also makes reference to Hastur when discussing Chambers's work in *Supernatural Horror in Literature*.

The *Sapientia Magorum* (the *Wisdom of the Mages*) is a volume of incredible antiquity and mentions Hastur many times. While both Greek and Latin versions of it are known to exist, the original version appears to be Persian; it was allegedly written by the Persian mage Ostanes.

The *Sapientia Magorum* is attributed directly to Ostanes and copies were found in certain parts of the world, although during the days of the Roman Empire, copies were quite rare. There was one Greek copy at Ephesus, a Syrian edition somewhere in North Africa, and a Latin translation somewhere in Italy. No trace of any of these exists today. It is further suggested that the Greek copy was held in the Temple of Artemis at Ephesus and this was the reason that the arsonist Herostratus (driven mad by arcane knowledge) set fire to the building in 356 B.C. The text was destroyed in the ensuing conflagration.

The volume allegedly gives some detailed information on Hastur and on certain protective rituals that are to be practiced when summoning the entity. In the text, Hastur is allegedly referred to as Kaiwan, which seems to be a Middle Eastern name for the being. There are also a number of incantations and rituals to aid the reader to achieve immortality. It is possible that some of this text—including that relating to Hastur—may have been copied from the equally mysterious the *Book of Eibon*.

Another equally mysterious text to mention Hastur that provides a formula for summoning the entity is a set of clay tablets generally known as the *Yellow Codex* (or sometimes *Xanthic Folio*). The tablets were discovered in the 1920s in China's Xinjiang Province. Archaeologists unearthed the ruins of a city (known locally as Niya) and found that it contained a library in which these tablets had been deposited. However, some occultists believe the information that they contain had somehow already been in circulation in Europe since the 18th century. It is also suggested that the *Codex* may simply be an extension of the *Pnakotic Manuscripts* and are said to be in the same style.

The text deals primarily with the King in Yellow and his link to Hastur, as well as a number of summoning spells. It also contains details of a treaty between the cities of Hastur and Carcosa, although this part of the tablets remains pretty much untranslated. What has become of the actual tablets is unknown, although it is thought that they are in a restricted area of the Vatican Library in Rome.

The name and the idea of Hastur could have also come from Ambrose Bierce's *Haita the Shepherd*. The story appeared in the anthology *Can Such Things Be?* (1893) and elements of it were regarded as one of Bierce's allegorical and satirical stories, questioning the authority of religion and social values as "Bitter Bierce" was wont to do. In the tale, Hiata is a rather naive shepherd boy who blindly and unquestioningly prays at the shrine of Hastur. When great rains come and floods arise Haita begins to question the existence of the god and attempts to blackmail the deity into proving that he actually watches over the people who worship him. The god punishes him for his doubt. In the same anthology was another tale that perhaps inspired Lovecraft called *The Inhabitant of Carcosa.* It is thought that Bierce derived the name from the city of Carcasonne in Southern France, but both Chambers and Lovecraft appear to have been so taken with the name that they incorporated it into their own fiction. For Chambers (and perhaps for Lovecraft as well) Carcosa was a shadowy, cursed place, and was perhaps not on this world at all. It was described as being on the shores of Lake Hali though the location is vague. It might be on Earth, it might be among the stars.

The ideas of Hastur, Carcosa, and Hali are all interconnected throughout the Mythos, and they all remain enigmas that are still awaiting some form of solution. Perhaps their true identity and relevance lies in some future story.

Glaaki

The Mythos writer Ramsey Campbell created the entity Glaaki, which appears in his story *The Inhabitant of the Lake* (1964), and a number of other writers and role-playing games have used the name.

Glaaki is one of the Great Old Ones that came to Earth on a meteor, which crashed in some primal time near the present-day town of Brichester in the Severn Valley. The impact created a large lake, which still exists, and Glaaki is said to dwell there. As with much of the Mythos, this location is disputed and other writers have placed the entity in New Guinea and the highlands of New Britain, as well as in the Adirondacks, the Uwharries, certain lochs in northern Scotland, and in the sewers of London. The being resembles a massive slug with three eyeballs on large stalks and three pyramid-like extensions on Its underside. Added to this, Its back is covered in what look like metal spikes, but are in fact organic growths. In addition, Glaaki can also exude eyes from tentacle-tips, which allow It to peer from below the water and to clandestinely observe what occurs in the world above.

Where Glaaki originally came from is unknown, but it is speculated that Its world was one of acid lakes, corrosive vapors, and constant volcanic activity. It left this world for some unspecified purpose and traveled on a comet to worlds such as Yuggoth, Tond, and Shaggai. In a tiny star-cluster on the fringes of our own galaxy, it became imprisoned behind a crystal trapdoor by a race of vaporous beings that inhabited an asteroid city there. However, It managed to escape by riding a comet that was passing inward through our galaxy, a fragment of which eventually crashed on Earth, bringing Glaaki here. However, this version is disputed and it is suggested that the entity actually comes from a parallel dimension and was accidentally brought into our world by priests in ancient Egypt who misaligned the Reversed Angles of Tagh Clatur. These Angles are a series of geometric shapes and mathematical symbols which, when combined with a certain predefined archway, can create a doorway into another universe. Sometimes, however, the angles can make up the archway itself. The Angles can then be activated in various ways depending on their configuration, either by harmonics, hand gestures, chantings, amulets, and drawings. The Angles can also be used to connect with a corresponding archway in both our own world and one in a corresponding dimension, but a special configuration is called for here. The Angles can also occur naturally, and it is thought that a number of unexplained disappearances throughout history have been due to the accidental transferences of individuals, vehicles, or machinery through spontaneously created archways. It is also thought that certain occultists, sculptors, and artists have sought to either consciously or unwittingly incorporate the Angles in some of their works—such as the paintings of Nikolas Fraken or the works of Justin Le Grand. Some writers have speculated that a miscalculation of the Angles by the ancient Egyptian mages brought Glaaki into our world. Glaaki, it is argued, had been on Earth for many years before Its cult was officially recognized, and has had a profound influence on human history—in fact it was the first of the Great Old Ones to do so.

Glaaki's purposes are largely unknown, but it is thought that the entity was putting together an army of zombie-like followers around Goatswood and Templehill (villages in the Brichester area) in advance of some terrible event. After a certain time (some say 60 years), these bodies start to deteriorate and become susceptible to sunlight through a process known as the Green Decay. It is thought that Glaaki recruits many of Its followers with promises of immortality only to turn them into a kind of Undead who decay after a certain period.

Like many of the Great Old Ones, Glaaki communicates with Its followers by dreams and visions, and uses what some have called a "dream-pull" to draw individuals to the lake. This is not extremely effective, as the creature's power only extends for a limited distance beyond the waters. Nevertheless, the entity still exerts a sinister presence throughout the region, as those who venture too close to the lake will attest.

As with certain other forbidden books within the Mythos, the *Revelations of Glaaki* are concerned with the summoning of the entity, as well as various races, practices, and artifacts associated both with It and Its worship. The *Revelations* consists of a set of 12 books (originally scrolls) that detail some of the history and attributes of the entity. They were originally handwritten and were not meant for consumption outside the cult of worshippers. However, a cult member secretly leaked the text in exchange for an undisclosed substantial payment to the Supremus Press, which published it in a nine-volume leather-bound set in 1865. This is not the full set of the text, however, because either the worshipper did not hand over the complete manuscript or Supremus Press considered parts of it too blasphemous to set in print. Only a small number of books were circulated, and it's thought that a number of Glaaki's followers bought most of these, so it is difficult to find a copy. One complete nine-volume edition was allegedly held by Brichester University, which acquired them from the estate of the late Professor Arnold Hird.

Three other chapters of the work are known to exist, but not much is known of them. Chapters 10 and 11 deal with the dangerous entity M'nagalah (a mass of dark eyes and entrails, which claims to be responsible for the more savage side of human nature and can only be summoned as a growth on the individual's arm, which will quickly destroy the summoner), with the Crystallizers of Dreams (devices for seeing into other dimensions, especially the Dreamworld), and their proper use. The 12th Chapter is by far the most dangerous, because it deals with Y'golonac, one of the Great Old Ones. This entity takes the form of a gigantic headless and flabby corpse covered by small eyeless beings that crawl all over It and act as Its servitors. It has mouths on the palms of Its hands, which continually slobber and ooze a greenish, putrescent liquid. The being spends much of Its time behind a wall in another dimension, which can only be accessed from this world through the Reversed Angles of Tagh Clatur. Furthermore, it can only be summoned by someone who has read a page of the 12th Chapter of the *Revelations* and who runs the danger of being possessed by the entity Itself.

The book also mentions Hydra and Cthulhu and, by implication, several of the other Great Old Ones. Although it exists in printed form, handwritten copies of the text still exist. Even though it is the central text for the Cult of Glaaki, the tome still remains something of an enigma.

The notion of Glaaki is, in part, built around the idea of interdimensional routes along which the being (and those like it) can travel. This idea suggests that there are paths of force that run across the countryside and can transcend our own dimension and allow creatures to cross from one reality into another. The concept is not a new one, and may have its origins in the notion of such things as ley lines and force patterns.

The concept of ley lines as a magical/mystical pattern of occult energy was recently adapted from suggestions by the English amateur archaeologist and geologist Alfred Watkins in a book called *The Old Straight Track* (published in 1925). In his work (coupled with another book *Early British Trackways* published in 1922), Watkins suggested that during Neolithic times, early men had navigated across the countryside by using a set of geographical features (both natural and man-made), which gave lines of sight from one place to the next and more or less created invisible roads and trackways across the landscape. Watkins and others named them "ley" lines, because it was noted that a number of these straight lines passed through areas that ended in the suffix "ley." Other than describing them as navigational aids, no mystical significance was initially attributed to them.

Who knows what ancient forces exist, even in the world today, what effect they may have on us, and what they might bring into our world from the Beyond. Maybe the legend of Glaaki is not so far-fetched after all.

Chaugnar Faugn

Although often counted as a rather peripheral figure in the Mythos, Chaugnar Faugn is still capable of wielding immense powers. The entity was created not by Lovecraft, but by another Mythos writer, Frank Belknap Long, and was featured in his story *The Horror from the Hills* in 1931. It appears as a hyperdimensional creature, resembling a humanoid figure with an elephantine head, webbed ears, and a large disc at the end of Its trunk. It is said to spend much of Its time immobile in a cave on the Plateau of Tsang in Central Asia. It is massive in bulk and only shifts when It moves to consume a sacrifice.

Chaugnar Faugn came to Earth in some dim, primitive time when the only life forms that existed were amphibians. Out of these, It created a servitor race known as the Miri Nigri, which still exist (though not exactly in their original form) today. The Miri Nigri or "strange dark folk" were centralized close to where their Maker actually came down to Earth: in the midst of the present-day Pyrenees. In the early times, they came down to trade with the ancient humans—mainly in the town of Pompelo in Spain, although there was a more sinister motive behind such commerce. From time to time, they would capture certain humans and use them as sacrificial victims to Chaugnar Faugn in their abominable Halloween Rites. Following multiple disappearances, the Roman authorities sent an Army cohort to break up the ceremonies with a great deal of slaughter, during which the Miri Nigri were all but wiped out. Following this, Chaugnar ordered what remained of Its followers to quit the Pyrenees and convey their deity to the Plateau of Tsang. Some anthropologists believe that some Miri Nigri may have mated with some humans to produce the Tcho-Tcho people, who still inhabit some parts of the Far East.

According to Daniel Harms, Chaugnar Faugn did not come to Earth alone but with certain "brothers"—beings that were physically like It, but of lesser power. They may have been the last of an interdimensional species from a vanished world who escaped some cataclysm by leaping between dimensions. However, when Chaugnar was moved to the Plateau of Tsang, Its "brothers" refused to go with It, whereupon Chaugnar cursed them and threatened to devour them when the Time of the Great Old Ones.

Currently, Chaugnar is worshipped in Tsang and in some parts of Tibet and Afghanistan. In fact, some of the rites used in Its worship may correspond to those of the Indian Elephant-god Ganesha, and the two are often mistaken for each other. One may have prompted belief in the other.

Ganesha is often represented as a human being with the head of an elephant. Certain anecdotal legends say that he was born like this, others say that he acquired the elephant head later in life. Some other representations show him with five elephantine heads. The most common story is that Ganesha was beheaded by the Lord Shiva during a dispute. Shiva subsequently relented and replaced Ganesha's head with that of an elephant. Other accounts state that his head was accidentally burned off by a ray from the evil eye of the god Shanni, and that Vishnu replaced it with the elephant's head. Yet another legend says that Ganesha was created by the sarcastic laughter of Shiva who, mocking an elephant, mistakenly created the entity with the head of the animal and with a human pot-belly.

The number of Ganesha's arms also varies, ranging between two or four all the way up to 16. In very early iconography concerning the god, some of these are portrayed as serpents; this vision has sometimes been used by Mythos writers to suggest some sort of connection between Chaugnar Faugn and Yig. In some depictions, Ganesha wears the serpent Vasuki, King of the Nagas, around his neck like a stole, or sometimes around his stomach like a belt. In some traditions, Ganesha's arms contain a deadly poison, which is administered through the form of snakes to punish those who cross him.

Although Chaugnar rarely wakens from what his followers call The Sleep of Ages, it is said that a time will come when It will stir and rage across the world. According to the Tibetan priest and prophet Mu Seng, this time will be heralded by the arrival of the White Acolyte, who will arrive from the distant West and will bear Chaugnar away to a new land where It will reign as a monarch.

One of the several titles that Chaugnar appears to enjoy is that of Magnum Innominandum. The title literally means "Great One Who Is not to Be Named," and it may refer more properly to the entity Hastur. In his correspondences, however, Lovecraft suggested that it might also refer the Chaugnar Faugn.

In Its guise as Chaugnar Faugn, the name of the entity can be used in an invocation to summon a star vampire. These are entities that dwell in the interstellar depths and can be summoned to Earth by a powerful mage. They are transparent, save for a brief period after drinking the blood of their victims and can be commanded by nearly any competent magician. The invocation is laid out in Ludvig Prinn's *De Vermis Mysteriis*.

Ubbo-Sathla

Of all the entities in the Mythos universe, perhaps the most dangerous and fearsome is Ubbo-Sathla, a foul, formless, protoplasmic entity that is supposed to have spawned all life on Earth. Ubbo-Sathla is not a creation of Lovecraft, but of Clark Ashton Smith (although the two may have discussed the entity at some point), who wrote the short story *Ubbo-Sathla* in 1933.

The entity's origins are mysterious and conflicting. According to some traditions, our world was in an alternate universe where the Elder Gods held say. Out of the primal protoplasm, they created both Ubbo-Sathla and Azathoth to be their slaves. In the course of this creation, Ubbo-Sathla acquired great knowledge from Its masters and used it to rebel against them. Using techniques far beyond our comprehension It moved both Itself and Earth into this current dimension. However, the Elder Gods followed Ubbo-Sathla into this Universe, captured It, and completely robbed It of Its senses, leaving It relatively mindless (although some maintain that it was always this way). They are supposed to have done the same with Azathoth, although given this entity's malignancy, this is doubtful.

Others hold that Ubbo-Sathla is the parent of the Great Old Ones who opposed the Elder Gods, and for this It has been punished by them. But most of the Great Old Ones have origins that lie beyond the stars so this seems unlikely. Rather, it is possible that Ubbo-Sathla has a slightly different origin than the Great Old Ones, but has entered into some form of alliance with them and came down from the stars to help them in their various battles. Nevertheless, it may be possible that the entity has produced a few of the Great Old Ones, though it is not absolutely clear as to which of them It has spawned.

Ubbo-Sathla dwells in the gloomy grey-lit caverns of Y'qaa, which may lie far beneath Earth. However, the region is said to be interdimensional and can exist in a number of places at once. Some claim that Y'qaa does not lie on Earth at all, but in some piece of dimensional space, which can be accessed through a number of portals. It is believed that Ubbo-Sathla guards a series of clay tablets that bear the accumulated wisdom of the Elder Gods themselves. Whoever gains access to them will have the power to mold the Universe in whatever fashion he or she pleases, so they have become the goal of many witches and wizards.

According to William Steadman, the tablets that Ubbo-Sathla guards are known as the Elder Key and they can be used for contacting and bringing entities from myriad other dimensions. There are two copies of the Key on this plane of existence, but they are completely inaccessible. The nearest text may be the Tablet of Destinies—a cylindrical artifact possibly of Sumerian or Babylonia origin, which conferred upon the reader the rulership of the Universe and allowed him or her to know all things, even the affairs of other worlds beyond our own.

There is also an idea that Ubbo-Sathla lies in a huge black hole somewhere near the very center of the Universe. This was created by a cosmic explosion, which was perhaps generated by the Elder Gods, which also somehow created Ubbo-Sathla. The entity is formed from the basic protoplasm, but created a malignant, protoplasmic entity that is actually far more intelligent and dangerous than certain texts would have us believe. From this black hole the entity reaches out Its influence to other worlds where It sometimes seeks to shape the affairs there.

Some confusion also exists as just to what Ubbo-Sathla actually *is*. Rumors persist that this entity is actually Abhoth, a being strongly connected with filth and disease. This entity dwells in the Dreamlands, far beneath Mount Voormithadreth in the Grey Barrier Peaks, and reputedly takes the form of a large pool of grey slime. Similar to Azathoth (and perhaps Ubbo-Sathla) It continually spawns offspring of varying physical shapes, most of which It consumes almost immediately. It is also constantly sending out telepathic signals, either calling other beings to it or else driving them away. Such visions often inspire madness in humans. It is mentioned as "Abhoth the Dark" in some early Hittite texts. It is thought that Ubbo-Sathla was worshipped in Its form as Abhoth in Hyperborea, firstly by the Voormis and later by the human Hyperboreans themselves who changed the name of the god to Abhoth and erected a number of temples to It, the locations of which have all been lost. Although such a theory is relatively widespread, many Lovecraftian scholars have discounted it.

Zuchequon

The entity known as Zuchequon (Zulchequon or Zushaquon) is reputedly a child of Ubbo-Sathla. It is also described as "the last scion of Old Night" and "one of the black spirits of the earth" (by Old Castro to Inspector Legrasse in *Call of the Cthulhu*). The being is summoned by worshippers using chants of a particular tone or by very low, droning singing. In this case, It manifests Itself in earthquakes, bringing darkness and cold in their wake.

The inhabitants of Mu worshipped Zuchequon and built small shrines to their god, which they summoned with bells and chants. However, they committed some unspecified offence against It, as It responded with an earthquake that tore the continent in half and caused it to sink beneath the sea. In America, some of the West Coast Native tribes also appear to have known how to summon it, but this knowledge would seem to have been lost for a considerable time. Zuchequon is also served by a mysterious grouping known as the Hidden Ones, who dwell in Tsunth in the Dreamlands. Although a child of Ubbo-Sathla, Zuchequon's relationship with Its parent may be problematical.

Hundun

Early Chinese mythology says the creature Hundun plays a prominent part in proving that Ubbo-Sathla is real. The name means "legendary faceless being," and is the central primordial entity in Chinese cosmology. It is taken that this entity was created in a time before Heaven and Earth separated, and thus may contain elements of both. The *Shuowen Jiezi*—a 2nd-century Chinese dictionary—renders the name *hundun* as meaning "constantly or perpetually flowing," although the older Seal Script, a stylized form of calligraphy dating from the Zhou Dynasty translates the word as meaning "impure" or "angry."

The idea of Hundun seems to come from the Era of the Warring States (roughly 475 B.C.–221 B.C.) and it appears in both philosophical and religious texts (mainly in Daoist and Confucianist writings). This was a period of great confusion in early China, as regional warlords tried to consolidate their power by annexing the smaller states around them. This confusion was often mirrored in the writings that emerged from the period, and perhaps Hundun reflects this. There are Confucian variants of the word, which reflects everything that is opposed to order and to the establishment of a stable civilization—for example, anarchy, barbarianism, and so on.

The being Itself is supposedly a formless mass of energy or matter, which is continually changing and remoulding itself. At times it would appear to be almost liquid, at other times not. It is continually seething. However, other thinking suggests that It is the symbol of fertility and fecundity, and that the "sack" to which the text refers are actually testicles. Out of these springs the Universe and everything that lives in it. Curiously, Hundun is also said to be a physical embodiment of the Yellow Emperor, a mythological figure in Chinese literature. Akin to the faceless sack, the idea of the Yellow Emperor emerged around the Era of the Warring States and was considered to be a patron of magic and dubious arts as well as being the Lord of the Underworld.

Could the Chinese idea of Hundun and the Yellow Emperor, be the prototypes for both Ubbo-Sathla? *And* could they also be the forerunner of the King in Yellow, which features so heavily in Lovecraft's work?

Rhan-Tegoth

More than 3 million years ago, the Great Old One, Rhan-Tegoth, came to Earth from Yuggoth on a massive meteorite that fell into what is now the Arctic. It remained there and was later worshipped by primitive beings in the time before the Great Ice Age. Such worship and sacrifices sustained the being, but later It was forgotten and worship ceased. Rhan-Tegoth lapsed into a kind of hibernation.

In the mid-20th century, the curator of a waxwork museum in London financed an expedition from Fort Morton up to the Noatak River in northwest Alaska to look for the rumored ruins of a mighty city where Rhan-Tegoth might have been worshipped. Finding the ruins, the expedition also found Rhan-Tegoth in Its hibernative state and assuming it to be some sort of statue, they shipped It back to England. The authorities there determined that It was a forgery and It was put on display in the museum. It was later sold to the Royal Ontario Museum where it was put on permanent display. Later, it was sold to an American museum owner, George Rogers, who has an interest in the strange and the occult

It was said that the entity could be "revived" with the following chant:

Wza-y'ei! Wza-y'ei!
Y'kaa haa bho-ii
Rhan-Tegoth—Cthulhu fhatgn
Rhan-Tegoth,
Rhan-Tegoth
Rhan-Tegoth!

These incredibly ancient words of power were uttered accidentally in the museum when Stephen Jones was challenged by Rogers to spend a night in the museum. A revived Rhan-Tegoth destroyed Jones and vanished. Its whereabouts have not been discovered.

It is thought also that the primitive Gnophkeh were the creations or emanations of Rhan-Tegoth, but this is extremely doubtful, as they were active when the entity was in a state of hibernation. Few descriptions remain of the entity, but it would seem that It is vaguely octopoidal with a number of pincers at the end of long tentacles with myriad eyes that search out Its prey. It travels with a scuttling movement that is incredibly fast. Tradition says that Rhan-Tegoth is the only one of the Great Old Ones that can be completely killed or destroyed and that part of Its back is a protective carapace. It also boasts a series of spines through which It can draw up the blood of the victims It captures. The destruction of the entity is probably well beyond the capabilities of humankind.

The being was first mentioned in *The Horror in the Museum*, which was a revision completed by Lovecraft along with Hazel Heald. It was published in *Weird Tales* in November 1932. Since then it has been printed in a number of other anthologies including two recent editions *The Horror in the Museum and Other Revisions* (Caroll and Graf 2007) and Del Ray Books (2007).

Rhan-Tegoth is also mentioned in a number of ancient texts, but the most direct reference is to be found in the *Voormish Tablets*, which are also mentioned in the *Book of Eibon.* They are a set of incised stone tablets that were written by Voormis wizards. It is thought that part of the contents includes the enigmatic Curse of Rhan-Tegoth, but most of the contents are beyond human knowledge.

According to Lovecraft and other Mythos writers, strange beings either from Outer Space or from other dimensions have been lurking among us for thousands of years and may have played their part in shaping human history. We may dismiss all this simply as a work of fiction—even of a writer's rather diseased imagination—but who is to say that there may not be *some* shred of truth in it? For who knows exactly *what* might be moving out there beyond the stars.

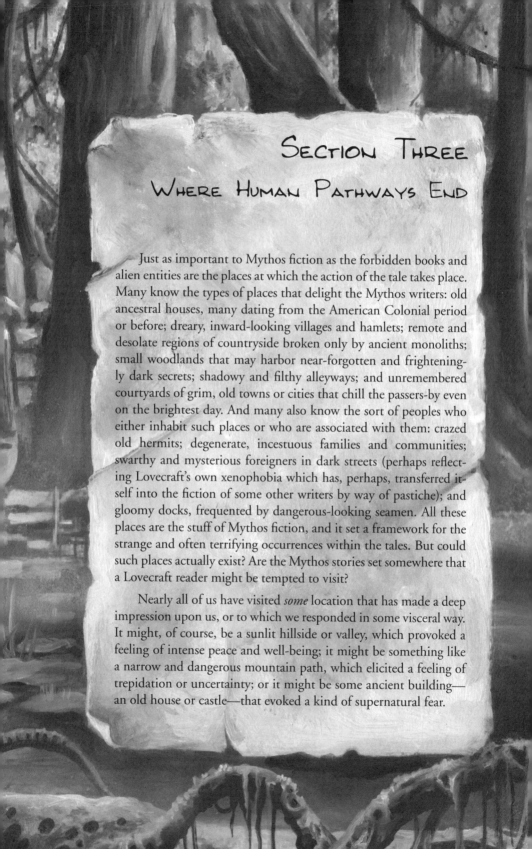

Section Three

Where Human Pathways End

Just as important to Mythos fiction as the forbidden books and alien entities are the places at which the action of the tale takes place. Many know the types of places that delight the Mythos writers: old ancestral houses, many dating from the American Colonial period or before; dreary, inward-looking villages and hamlets; remote and desolate regions of countryside broken only by ancient monoliths; small woodlands that may harbor near-forgotten and frighteningly dark secrets; shadowy and filthy alleyways; and unremembered courtyards of grim, old towns or cities that chill the passers-by even on the brightest day. And many also know the sort of peoples who either inhabit such places or who are associated with them: crazed old hermits; degenerate, incestuous families and communities; swarthy and mysterious foreigners in dark streets (perhaps reflecting Lovecraft's own xenophobia which has, perhaps, transferred itself into the fiction of some other writers by way of pastiche); and gloomy docks, frequented by dangerous-looking seamen. All these places are the stuff of Mythos fiction, and it set a framework for the strange and often terrifying occurrences within the tales. But could such places actually exist? Are the Mythos stories set somewhere that a Lovecraft reader might be tempted to visit?

Nearly all of us have visited *some* location that has made a deep impression upon us, or to which we responded in some visceral way. It might, of course, be a sunlit hillside or valley, which provoked a feeling of intense peace and well-being; it might be something like a narrow and dangerous mountain path, which elicited a feeling of trepidation or uncertainty; or it might be some ancient building—an old house or castle—that evoked a kind of supernatural fear.

Many years ago, I was doing some research around the Ardmore area of County Waterford in Ireland, especially in the vicinity of the ruined shell of the Ardoginna House. When walking across the open fields one evening, I could see one of the ruined towers of the ancient place in the distance over some trees. Halfway across the field I met an old local man coming in the other direction, and the pair of us stopped to look at the distant tower.

"If that place isn't haunted," he said, pointing with his stick, "then it bloody well *should* be!" Even though it was a bright summer's day and the air was very warm, I shivered a little. All the elements were there: the distant, ruined tower rising up over the trees; the strange history of the place; the setting sun; and a flock of crows that had been disturbed, rising up into the evening air. It was all very atmospheric, but in a frightening sort of way. That image still remains with me.

I experienced a similar sensation when, not so long ago, I visited the ruins of St. Katherine's Augustinian convent near Shanagolden in County Limerick. This was an abbey that had been closed on the direct orders of a pope, as the nuns there were said to be practicing witchcraft. Even when the nuns were gone, the Abbess, still known locally as the Black Hag, continued to live in the abandoned building; she was found dead there in what is known as the Black Hag's Cell. The place is now little more than a series of grim stone walls, empty archways, and doorways leading nowhere, but the atmosphere that hangs over the place is extremely claustrophobic. As I made my way along badly overgrown paths and along the wallsteads, I had an uneasy sensation that something was lurking there among the tumbled stones, no more than an arm's length away; the sensation was extremely strong and unsettling. The tombs and memorials of certain local families had been set into the stonework of the walls, and it was not hard to imagine one of these opening and the hands of the dead reaching out to grab me. There was nothing there, of course, but the loneliness of the fallen abbey, the moving shadows in the daylight, the weight of a dubious history, and the sheer claustrophobic *atmosphere* of those enclosed walls all contributed to the sensation. In some bustling cities, I have felt the same chills as I passed long some shadowy side street or alleyway, or passed by the open gate of some half-lit yard or courtyard. These places have played upon my own powers of *suggestion* and probably form part of the reason why I write books in this genre.

Lovecraft clearly experienced the same unsettled feelings in his travels around America, which again found their way into his writings. Perhaps he was suggestive to the atmosphere of certain places as many of us are. His letters to correspondents are filled with sights of neglected and decaying buildings, of near-forgotten churches, of shunned areas occupied only by overgrown and crumbling tumuli, of shadowed entrances into gloomy yards on a deserted street, and of small, isolated communities tucked away from the normal maelstrom of life. However, there was always a sense of *history* to many of these places.

Rhode Island, the place in which Lovecraft grew up, was steeped in Colonial history, and was largely rural. Battles in the Revolutionary War were fought there, and even in Lovecraft's time, areas of the countryside beyond the major towns (particularly in the southern end, which had been known as South County) still held small graveyards (some of them isolated, overgrown, and unmarked) where the bodies of the Revolutionary dead lay. Here, alleyways led across fields to some decaying Colonial house, tucked away behind the trees or shielded by some dip in the land. These were indeed places that could elicit response or stimulate the imagination. But places such as Providence were filled with history too.

The town had been first settled in June 1636 by the English theologian and scholar Roger Williams. Williams had been something of a radical preacher—he had been exiled from the Massachusetts Bay colony because of his views, so Providence Plantation became a focus for many disaffected theological viewpoints. Baptists of various kinds found a ready sanctuary for themselves and their beliefs in the new colony. The Plantation grew steadily and became a center of industry, noted especially for its jewelery and silverware. Williams and his followers also put great emphasis on learning, and encouraged this with the establishment of schools and colleges within the expanding town.

It would be true to say, therefore, that Providence, with its cultural mixture of commerce, education, and religious diversity, was something of a unique (and slightly eccentric) place. Because of the commercial and social interests, the original town grew in a slightly haphazard fashion comprising numerous dwellings of varying architecture. It had also grown out into the surrounding countryside, incorporating a number of outlying farms into its environs, many of which kept their original structures and may have looked slightly odd in an urban setting. A number of these houses had curious histories to them, and this too fired Lovecraft's imagination; some of them were eventually featured in his tales.

For example, there was the Hamilton House at 276 Angell Street (Lovecraft was born at 194 Angell Street, later renumbered as 454) built by the Hamilton family in 1896. The house was brooding and imperious and was designed in the shape of a French chateau. Today, it is a care home and community facility with no trace of anything sinister about it. All the same, Lovecraft was fascinated by the original building, as well as the strange story about a mad woman and incorporated elements of them into his story *The Shunned House*. Not far away at 140 Prospect Street stood the Halsey House, which had been built in 1801 by Captain Thomas Lloyd Halsey. Even in Lovecraft's time the house was believed to be haunted. Strange lights and noises supposedly emanated from its grounds and, although it was lived in, many local people tended to give it a wide berth. Lovecraft used it as the Ward home in *The*

Case of Charles Dexter Ward. He further mentioned the Halsey House and its eerie reputation in a letter to Frank Belknap Long on May 1st, 1926.

And of course there was the Stephen Harris House, which still stands today (much restored since Lovecraft's time) at 135 Benefit Street. This is one of the oldest houses in Providence, and it originally stood on Back Street (the original name for Benefit Street). The houses, which now stand on the street, have been built on the sites of earlier dwellings, some allegedly dating back to the initial establishment of the Plantation.

Because of its religious diversity, the town had no common or recognized municipal burying ground. Therefore, many of the houses had a plot on its own land that would serve as a graveyard for the family who lived there. During the Revolution, Back Street was widened and straightened in order to take on traffic that had built up on Towne Street (now South Main Street), and was renamed Benefit Street—being "a benefit to all." With the widening of the roadway, some of the bodies that had been buried in the gardens were exhumed and removed to the North Burial Ground, which had recently been established for that exact purpose. However, not all the bodies were taken—some lay in unmarked graves, others couldn't be traced—and they were left below the foundations of the new buildings. According to legend, part of Back Street was occupied by Huguenots (Protestants who had fled from France) to avoid persecution and an old couple had lived on the site where the Stephen Harris House now stands. Their bodies were among those that were not recovered.

Stephen Harris was a wealthy Providence merchant whose fortune lay in a fleet of trading vessels and overseas trade. He decided to build his house on Back Street around 1763. No sooner had the house been erected than Harris's fortunes changed; several of his ships were lost at sea, and certain projects in which he had invested failed. The loss of his vessels led to even worse financial problems, and he was threatened with bankruptcy. Even worse, as soon as he moved into the house with his young family, several of his children died from a mysterious disease. It is said that there was never a live birth within the house in its entire history. There was a story that Mrs. Harris went completely insane and had to be confined to an upper room (paralleling a story concerning the Hamilton House). It's said that she would occasionally appear at one of the upper windows, shouting and screaming in French at those passing below—a language of which she seemingly had no knowledge. Many people around Providence declared that she had learned it from the spirits of the dead Huguenots, which continued to haunt the house.

Whether or not these stories were true, they conferred an evil and sinister reputation on the house that lingered for many generations, long after Stephen Harris was dead. The building remained in the family for several generations, as no one would buy it, and it eventually fell into a state of disrepair. The area around it did not prosper either, for gradually Benefit Street became a kind of slum area, with many of the houses falling into a gradual decay. By the 1920s, when Lovecraft was living close by the house, some of those around it were near derelict and run-down.

For Lovecraft, the Stephen Harris House and the legends associated with it held a terrible fascination. It also held a family connection, for the eldest of his two aunts— Lillian Clark—actually lived there briefly between 1919 and 1920. And similar to the Hamilton House, elements of the building and its dread atmosphere featured in his tale *The Shunned House*.

Within walking distance was St. John's Church on 271 North Main Street; the surrounding cemetery was known locally as King's Churchyard. The Church was founded in 1723, but the building that Lovecraft knew was erected in 1809 and designed by John Holden Greene. It had been dedicated in 1811, and then rededicated as the Cathedral of St. John in 1929 when Lovecraft was alive. As with other old buildings around Providence, the Church exercised an influence on Lovecraft, and in a letter to Helen V. Scully dated October 1933, he speaks of roaming around the old churchyard after dark with several friends, exploring the tombs and funeral markers with the aid of a flashlight. What intrigued him about the old place was that the great American horror writer Edgar Allen Poe had also visited the place. In letters to his correspondent Frank Upatel, he tried to imagine himself as the great man of letters, wandering through the shadowed paths between the headstones.

On Thomas Street, behind a fringe of trees, stood a house with a curious bas-relief on its frontage. Known locally as the "Fleur de Lys house," was erected in 1885, and boasted what looked like a French fleur de lys on the front of the building. The design intrigued Lovecraft and he would make mention of the house as the Wilcox home in his *Call of the Cthulhu*:

> HIS CARD BORE THE NAME OF HENRY ANTHONY WILCOX, AND MY UNCLE HAD REC-OGNIZED HIM AS THE YOUNGEST SON OF AN EXCELLENT FAMILY SLIGHTLY KNOWN TO HIM, WHO HAD LATTERLY BEEN STUDYING SCULPTURE AT THE RHODE ISLAND SCHOOL OF DESIGN AND LIVING ALONE IN THE FLEUR DE LYS BUILDING NEAR THAT INSTITUTION.... IT SEEMED TO BE A MONSTER, OR SYMBOL REPRESENTING A MON-STER, OF A FORM WHICH ONLY A DISEASED MIND COULD CONCEIVE.

Judging from his letters it appears that he dreamed of the place on a number of occasions, feeling great apprehension even in his sleep, as images of the house with its curious frontage followed him beyond the waking hours.

Although Providence certainly fed his stories with these buildings, Lovecraft's imagination was piqued by dwellings elsewhere in New England.

For instance, in Salem, Massachusetts, he visited the Witch House in 1922, writing enthusiastically of the experience in a letter to Rheinhardt Kleiner in 1923. The Witch House was the home of Judge Jonathan Curwen, and is actually the only extant building in the town that is related directly to the witch trials of 1692. Curwen was the local presiding magistrate who played a major part in the trials; he investigated the accusations of devilish practice both in the town and in the surrounding countryside. He was a member of the Court of Oyer and Terminer, which sent 19 of the accused to the gallows at the height of the persecutions. The Witch House also had a connection with Providence, as it was occupied at one point by Roger Williams, a fact that seemed to excite Lovecraft. He would feature the building in "The Dreams in the Witch House."

The other celebrated structure in Salem was the old Derby House at 168 Derby Street, reputed to be the first brick house in Salem. It was built in 1762 by Richard Derby for his son Elias Hasket Derby, who would later become America's first millionaire. The Derbys were one of the important families of Salem—Richard Derby was a prosperous merchant in Massachusetts and the family married among the other significant families of the area. Elias's sister Mary married George Crowninshield while Elias himself married Elizabeth, George's sister. The family, however, was wracked by scandal—Elias's eldest daughter Elizabeth eloped (against her father's wishes) with a Captain Nathaniel West, but their marriage ended in an extremely ugly and messy divorce that was gossip long afterward. Her sister, Anstiss Derby, married a prosperous merchant named Benjamin Pickman, thus bringing the Pickman name into the Derby family. It was said that Richard Derby had built the brick house above a system of ancient tunnels and vaults that had existed since pre-Colonial days—some say they had been built by early explorers, others say that they were constructed by more mysterious folk, but the idea appealed to Lovecraft. There were a number of Pickmans who lay not far away in the Charter Street Burying Ground. The Derby House is featured by name in "The Thing on the Doorstep," and the name *Pickman* is used in "Pickman's Model."

Underground tunnels featured in another building that was known to Lovecraft, which he also used in *The Thing on the Doorstep*. This was the Danvers State Lunatic Asylum, a Gothic-looking hospital situated in Danvers built between 1874 and 1878. Sections of the massive building were connected by an underground system of tunnels (designed to make it look less like a hospital), which were self-sustaining during periods of cold weather. Such a labyrinth of intersecting and interconnecting passages and tunnels was immensely confusing, and it was said that individuals could become lost in them and end up wandering for hours and even days. It was also said that there were secret laboratories and underground wards where brutal and inhumane shock therapies were carried on. By the late 1930s and early 1940s, overcrowding in the Institution had reached almost unmanageable proportions with more than 2,000 patients housed in overcrowded conditions. They were kept in underground dormitories and in secured rooms in remote areas of the Institution, which were not designed for that purpose. Stories grew throughout the 1950s regarding the use of straitjackets, lobotomies, and dangerous drugs, sparking controversy all across Massachusetts. In the late 1960s, changes in mental health care meant that numbers within the hospital began to decrease, and by the 1970s the hospital had closed.

By the time Lovecraft was visiting Danvers there were stories that mentally deficient children were being taken there for experimentation and that the place was badly haunted. With his vivid imagination and the eerie impression of the building itself, it was only natural that the Danvers Institution formed a place in his fiction. Indeed, it turns up as the infamous Arkham Sanatorium in *The Thing on the Doorstep* which, in turn, led to the Arkham Asylum, a psychiatric facility within the DC Comics universe. The place is also referenced in "Pickman's Model."

Lovecraft was also taken with the old and picturesque port of Marblehead, situated on a small peninsula that sticks out into the Atlantic. In particular, Marblehead is home to a cemetery, initially known as the Old Burying Hill, which is one of the oldest graveyards in New England, dating from 1638. Early Colonial clergymen are interred there, along with Revolutionary soldiers and sailors. The place was once the haunt of the famous Magician of Marblehead, Edward "John" Dimond, who actually owned a part of the land there. Even in his youth, Dimond was a strange person; he was prone to odd trances during which he could see future events that were happening far away. When his father died, he left John a little money; to the amazement of many people Dimond chose to buy a densely wooded area on the edge of the town's Old Burying Ground. Given his queer disposition and bizarre personality, his neighbors immediately suspected occult motives; it was roughly about 30 years since the Salem witch trials, and the distinct odor of witchcraft was still in the air. There were rumors that the "Wizard Dimond" dug up bodies from the old cemetery for use in occult experiments or magic spells. However, it is true that he walked about the graveyard talking to the occupants who lay beneath the stones and that he sat on grave-markers while going into a number of his trances. From the ancient graveyard, he also telepathically called out to a number of fishing vessels on the seas around Marblehead advising their captains of rocks and reefs in their area. He also called up storms that he could direct against the vessels of those who crossed him.

The atmosphere and strange history of the Old Burying Ground excited Lovecraft. In a letter to Rhinehardt Kleiner in January 1923 he spoke enthusiastically:

> ...WHERE THE DARK HEADSTONES CLAWED UP THRO' THE VIRGIN SNOW LIKE THE DECAY'D FINGERNAILS OF SOME GIGANTICK CORPSE.

An almost similar quotation appears in his story "The Festival." In that story, there are references to a Marblehead church, which was probably St. Michael's Episcopal Church. The church was built in 1714 with materials brought directly from England. It was a meeting place for many of the Massachusetts rebels during Revolutionary times, and when the Declaration of Independence reached Marblehead, the church bell was rung so enthusiastically that it cracked. It was recast by Paul Revere (who was actually a silversmith by trade). Summer Street, formerly known as Frog Lane, runs alongside the church and is a shadowy place that may have appealed to Lovecraft. He writes in a letter to Frank Belknap Long in 1923:

...AND AT ST. MICHAEL'S CHURCHYARD, WHERE AT TWILIGHT HIDEOUS SHADOWS LURK AMONGST THE DENSE WILLOWS OF THE FAR CORNER, AND CAPER A GHOUL- ISH DANSE MACABRE ON THE TOPS OF THE OLD SLATE SLABS AS SOON AS THE MOON GOES DOWN.

In the poem *Fungi from Yuggoth* he warns: "Beware of St. Toad's crack'd chimes!" This could be a reference to the cracked bell in St. Michael's Church, although because of its batrachian connotations, some have tried to link it to the church in Lovecraft's "The Shadow over Innsmouth." Whatever the source of the inspiration, the ancient church of St. Michael's had made a deep impression on him.

Lovecraft also traveled as far as Boston and to Copp's Hill Cemetery to view the tombs of the Mathers family. The cemetery is the second oldest in the city and one of the oldest bury-grounds in New England, and it contains the graves of Cotton Mather (one of the more prominent intellectual figures in the Salem witch trials) and also his father (one of the foremost Puritan preachers of Colonial times). Lovecraft visited the tombs and incorporated the Mathers in his work.

A number of the sites around New England and further afield inspired Lovecraft and found their way, in one guise or another, into his work. But what of the degenerate characters—the reclusive communities and inbred families—that characterized his fiction? Could *they* have existed? And if so where?

Certainly there has been evidence of strange and isolated communities all across Europe since the earliest times. People may have settled, for one reason or another, in strange places, which sometimes barred them from mainstream social contact. Some of these communities were made up of misanthropic individuals who had turned their backs on general mores of a broader society, or who simply found it difficult to "fit in." Others simply found themselves cut off because of natural obstacles, such as bogs, forests, and mountains. In their isolation they turned inward, becoming largely self-sufficient. Lovecraft was correct when he said that although some of them were small communities of differing people, many of them tended to be family groupings. And it was this isolation that often caused these groups to develop their own idiosyncrasies and communal customs and beliefs. Even in the larger towns and cities, immigrants and foreigners came together in certain districts. Many of these groups maintained their own customs, cultural observances, and beliefs, which differentiated them from the main urban areas around them and made them distinct. They also maintained the family lines and occupations of those who had first settled there, again creating a distinctive identity for themselves. These places include Little Italy, Little Warsaw, Chinatown, and Irishtown. People of distinctly colored skins tended to gravitate toward certain areas of the urban conurbations, leading to suggestions of peculiar practices and strange beliefs in various localities (for example, alleged voodoo worship in parts of Charleston, South Carolina, and in New Orleans). This was something that Lovecraft noted and made a part of his tales.

Degenerate and inbred family circles, many living in remote rural areas or in largely inaccessible communities, have played a significant part in Mythos writing. In this age of global communication and enhanced population tracking, it is difficult to imagine that families and communities could evade detection or some form of scrutiny. But there is a long history of such communities dwelling in total isolation in various parts of the Western world.

During the early 17th century, for example, the village of Fence existed in Leicestershire, England, with practically no contact with the outside world. It was surrounded by a forest with no real road access. The village had been established during the reign of King William II as part of a Royal game enclosure, but had gradually become more and more isolated as time went on. It was made up of tightly knit family units, most notably the Devices and the Southerns, and was built around an old ruined tower that may have been used by the monarch's gamekeepers; now it was used as an accommodation by one of the families. The families married among each other—occasionally producing strange and diseased offspring. As Protestantism took hold of the English countryside, the village remained staunchly Catholic. Life centered on two old clan matriarchs (often described as witches) who more or less ruled the village as they saw fit, maintaining control over the village. There was talk of incest and peculiar practices and these featured largely in the Pendle Witch Trials and accusations of 1612. Strange behavior and peculiar family customs became the basis for witchcraft allegations and accusations of occult activity.

Similarly, a number of remote island communities found themselves cut off from mainstream civilization and began to develop their own ways and customs. Most notable was the distant archipelago of St. Kilda in the far North Atlantic. The population of St. Kilda was located on the main island, Hirta, and probably never had more than 180 people at any one time. Until World War I, they had little contact with the outside world. In 1745, following the Battle of Culloden, it was assumed that Prince Charles Edward Stuart had fled to St. Kilda and was hiding there to start another Jacobite uprising. The soldiers dispatched there found the village on Hirta deserted. The people in the island's only village feared pirates and fled to some caves to hide. It emerged that they knew nothing of the outside world, including who the Prince was, and they had never heard of King George II. The same thing happened in 1901 when an official arrived from Scotland to announce the death of Queen Victoria. Once again, the islanders had never heard of her and had no idea who she was.

The islanders were mostly Protestant Christian, although their knowledge of organized religion was very scant. Despite the efforts of an early missionary named

Alexander Buchan, there was no church on Hirta and no regular religious observance, though fragments of older religions did persist. A more organized approach took place in 1822 with the arrival of the zealous Reverend John MacDonald, "the Apostle of the North," a minister in the Church of Scotland known for his fiery sermons and uncompromising attitude. He preached 13 lengthy sermons in 11 days and established an organized religion (though he was privately appalled at their superstition and lack of biblical knowledge). When he left in 1830, the Reverend Neil MacKenzie arrived, and it was he who revived the fortunes of the islanders with new agricultural methods, rebuilding the houses of the village, and building a new church and manse. He also organized a school for them. However, when MacKenzie left in 1844, they changed their allegiance to that of the Free Church of Scotland during the Presbyterian Disruption and invited in the Reverend John MacKay to be their minister. MacKay ruled the island with a fist of iron, insisting on strict religious observance to which no variation could be made. The islanders were to carry Bibles at all times, and each service on Sundays and during the week was to last at least three hours. Attendance was compulsory, and the word of the Minister on all matters was to be regarded as law. Women or small children who made noise in church were to be excluded for a period, lectured, and warned of the horrors of Hell. On Sundays, nothing could be done on the island, which meant that the relief boat bringing supplies had to wait until Monday to land. The islanders had to starve (fast), although the Minister himself, as God's representative, was entitled to eat. John MacKay would remain Minister on St. Kilda for 24 years.

It is also thought that the islanders were physically different from other people. Many had extra, crooked toes, developed over generations to enable them to cling onto the sheer rock faces, which they ventured across to collect fulmar's eggs from their nests. Their immune systems may have been slightly different, making them susceptible to potentially fatal diseases that would not normally affect others. During John MacKay's time as Minister on the island, the population had fallen to about 80, and there was talk of evacuation. But despite outbreaks of "pox" and near starvation, the islanders clung on.

Things changed with the onset of World War I when the Royal Navy erected a signaling station on Hirta and communications with mainland Scotland were established for the first time. On May 15th, 1918, a German submarine entered Village Bay and opened fire. There was no loss of life, but a number of buildings (including houses) were destroyed or damaged. In response to this attack, a manned Mark III QF gun was erected overlooking the Bay, but it never saw action. However, the Navy now had a permanent base on Hirta and the comings and goings of Naval ships had a lasting effect on the islanders. At the end of the War, young men deserted the island and the population fell even further. By 1928, there were only 37 individuals on the island. In January 1930, a young woman named Mary Gilles died of appendicitis, and this proved to be the deciding factor. In August 1930, the island was abandoned and the remaining families were taken to the mainland. However, the military remained, and there is still a base on Hirta today.

There were also such places in certain parts of rural America. Certainly hill or mountain country often held (and continue to hold) tiny communities or family groupings tucked away in hidden hollows or valleys cut off from the rest of the world. These were pioneer families who settled along the deep river courses in mountain areas or families who were not welcome anywhere else and had to move on into the more inaccessible regions of the American countryside.

Such a place would have been Rutherford Mountain country on the Tennessee-Kentucky border. This is a maze of wilderness and mountain intercut by old Indian trails and a number of rivers such as the Rutherford River, the Little Piney Fork, the Bear River, and Honey Creek to name a few. Here and there are cut-offs up into the mountain to hidden places such as Squaw Creek and Coonsfork. These are old pioneer roads carved out in earlier times that peter out into dirt tracks in the upper reaches. Some run all the way across the mountain emerging near Mt. Gilead, in Henderson County, Tennessee, onto blacktop that runs all the way back to Washington.

Up in Rutherford, families have settled in the deep valleys where the trails run out. Many of these have been there since Revolutionary days and have settled in places such as the slopes of the Bear River Valley. In the 1920s and 30s when Lovecraft was writing (according to the often incomplete census of the region that existed at the time), would have been kinfolk such as the Nesbitts, the Panningses, the Baylatches, the Talbots, and the Parrigans—all interrelated and married among each other. Being of pioneer stock they were fiercely independent. From the early 19th century, other families had been moving into the area from places like Virginia and North Carolina and had settled along rivers and creeks in places such as Bingham Branch, Waterfall, Rocky Valley, and Maurley. Names such as Christie, Tunk, North, Billings, Langness, Hardcastle, Faris, Black, Goin, and Tartar appear, living in small communities tucked away in the valleys and folds of Mountain Country, but there were probably many more families whose names are unrecorded. They lived by hunting, fishing, subsistence agriculture, and moonshining, and during the period between 1880 and 1915 they were largely self-sufficient.

The irregular nature of the landscape, coupled with the distance from four local county seats, made administration of any kind extremely difficult. Even in the 1920s and 1930s, there was little law enforcement up along these trails and both schools and medical facilities were few and far between. In the absence of any formal authority, individual codes of behavior, social regulation, and endemic cultures began to develop, some even varying from valley to valley as groups of families began to follow their own traditions and their own ideas of justice and ethics. Early churches in the region tried to establish some sort of generalized order—even going so far as to hand down monetary fines for misdemeanors such as drunkenness and adultery—but they had little influence on the traditions of the hill folk, who paid such institutions a mere lip service.

In these lonely mountains, other social conventions could be disregarded too. It is said that after 1910, one of the most common pieces of legislation to be regarded in the Rutherford area was the Mann Act. This was more formally known as the White Slave Traffic Act, which had been passed by Congressman James Robert Mann. In its original form it prohibited white slavery and the interstate transportation of white females for "immoral purposes." It also addressed immorality and "human trafficking." With relation to remote rural areas, an attempt was made to use the Act to prevent underage sexual relations and marriage between older men and young girls. Local churches also rallied against marriage between near relatives—first cousins or closer—but to no great effect. Localized disputes meant that many families were not all that willing to marry outside their own clan circles and maintained extremely tight networks. Stories concerning strange offspring from such marriages were whispered in the hills but with little effect.

According to William Lynwood Montell in *Killings: Folk Justice in the Upper South,* what emerged in this hill country was a community apart, governed by its own social and religious framework, and community regulation developed in response to the lack of formal authority. As in other isolated communities, social mores lay in the provenance of a few families and mountain patriarchs, and were no less enforced than formal law.

Although the area of Rutherford Mountain Country has been detailed to some extent, it was by no means the only area where such communities existed. In the Great Smokies, for example, clans also existed away from officialdom and similar problems existed. Here, certain branches of the more mainstream clans, such as the Owenbys and the Whaleys, maintained their own forms of justice and social control over their respective regions.

And the same applied to parts of New England. Here, there might have been an added element, for religion may have played a part in the development of isolated communities. Those individuals who found it difficult to fit into the mainstream religious worship or whose views differentiated from that of mainstream preachers, often exempted themselves into distant areas to set up their own communities and to follow their own worship. As in Rutherford Mountain Country many came from old, close-knit families who could trace their ancestry back to the earliest times. And similar to those in the mountain countries, their behavior was governed by custom and tradition, often religiously orientated. Thus, groups of Mother Ann Lee's Shakers, Shadrack Ireland's Brethren of the New Light, the Come-Outers, the Merry Dancers, and the New Lebanon New Lights were found scattered all through remote corners of many of the New English states. Some of these groups performed rituals that might be considered rather bizarre by more conservative worshippers.

Coming from the religious background of Rhode Island, Lovecraft may have been aware of the State's theological history and the various strands of belief, which had made up early New England tradition. The idea of strange, inward-looking societies may have sprung out of this and found its way into the ideas of strange gods and entities that populate the Mythos.

Eerie and isolated places, strange people, and reclusive communities all help to give the Cthulhu Mythos its distinctive color and stir the imaginations of those who read its fiction. And who is to say that somewhere out there among the gathering hill country twilight, there is not a lonely place or a decaying community where such things might lurk. Who knows what might be waiting at the end of that dirt road through the mountains or in the deep and gloomy forest?

Where Human Pathways End

Dreamlands

Although many of the places in both Lovecraft's and Mythos fiction are based on real locations in our world, some of them are not. Lovecraft was a dreamer, and his work reflects that. His fantasy stories often reflect past ages and vanished countries— Hyperborea, Mu, and sea-doomed Atlantis, but these theatres have their limitations. Though he set some of his tales in historical eras, he appears to have no concrete knowledge of archaeology or strict historical interpretation. What he wanted was an entire Universe that he could populate with all manner of creatures, which bore no relation to the real world and where he could let his imagination run.

Thus, he created the Dreamlands, an alternate dimension that lay just *beyond* the real, tangible world; sometimes it impinged upon it, however, it was only accessible to individuals through their dreams. Earlier in life, a person could enter the Dreamlands at will, but as adulthood approached it grew harder and harder. By the time they were in their early 20s, the Dreamlands were closed to all but a few dreamers. Some gateways do exist within the physical world that enable individuals to enter without actually dreaming, but such places are said to be very few and are fraught with danger.

Normally, a journey into the Dreamlands begins with a descent down the Seventy Steps of Light Slumber to the Cavern of Flame. There, two figures await the dreamer, dressed in the robes of ancient Egyptian priests. Nasht and Kaman-Tha, the Guardians of the Dreamlands, determine whether a person is fit to enter their realm or not. Both appear to be identical, although it is thought that Nasht is more familiar with the waking world than his counterpart. It is not known if both Guardians are Great Old Ones or whether they are simply their servitors. They interrogate the individual concerning what he or she knows regarding the Dreamlands, its ways, and its gods. Having passed through the Gate of Deepest Slumber, the dreamer now finds him- or herself in the trackless Enchanted Wood. This region is considered to be relatively safe in Dreamland terms, although dangerous creatures wait deep within the undergrowth and will attack the unwary and those who lose their way.

Native to the Wood are the zoogs. These are creations that resemble large rodents and felines with a row of tentacles between the nose and the mouth. They have a taste for human flesh and will attack travelers during the dark hours as they pass through the woodlands. If the traveler stays on the woodland paths, however, the zoogs should give him or her little trouble, although the shrillness of their high, fluting speech is sometimes hurtful to human eardrums. Those who take the time to learn it can, on occasion, make friends with the creatures.

The zoogs of the Enchanted Wood are ruled by a Council of Sages. These are incredibly ancient zoogs who are well aware of the Dreamlands far beyond the Enchanted Wood, where they have agents who often report to them telepathically from all across the realms of dream. Anyone who befriends them can learn many wonderful things, although one has to be careful. Zoogs, even elderly and venerable ones, are not always trustworthy and sometimes act as agents for other dangerous entities who inhabit the darkest regions of the Dreamlands. Within these woodlands, there are two gateways back to the waking world; no human dreamer knows where they are, but it might be possible for the zoogs to cross into our realm through them. Beyond the Enchanted Wood, the dreamer is free to explore the strange and varied landscape that stretches before him or her.

Having passed through the Wood, there are four ways that dreamers can go. To the west lies Dylath-leen, the largest and most mysterious city in the Dreamlands. Reference to it appears in Lovecraft's *The Dream-Quest of Unknown Kadath* and further references have been made by other Mythos writers including Brian Lumley. Dylath-leen in a port city comprised of curious windowless buildings cut out of black basalt. Little is known about its inhabitants, except that they trade for rubies with dark-skinned turbaned men who arrive in black galleys. In the west also lies the small towns of Ulthar and Ilarnek, desert trading towns that are concealed by high walls.

To the south lies the Southern Sea and the Isle of Oriab. This is the largest island in the Dreamlands and its main port, Baharna, nestled at the foot of snow-capped Mount Ngranek (a dormant volcano), is one of the largest towns in the dream realm. The town is built in tiers with great stone steps arching over bridges and walkways. People here ride on zebras instead of horses, and their main export is statues and statuettes carved from lava that depict improbable beasts and ancient heroes of fable and myth.

At one time, the ancient gods of Earth (the Great Ones) resided on the upper slopes of Mount Ngranek, but later moved further north. The old volcano is also riddled with passageways through the solidified lava, and these connect with an underworld where nightgaunts dwell. The nightgaunts sometimes use these passages to come to the surface and carry off human children for ritualistic purposes far beneath the ground.

Just beyond Baharna's furthest limits lies the Lake of Yali. Around the edges of this lake toward Baharna lie several small towns and villages whose main business is the cultivation and exportation of a fragrant resin, which is prized all over the Dreamlands. On the far side of the Lake, however, lie the ruins of an ancient city, part of which lie under the waters of the Lake itself. No one knows the name, origins, or history of the place, but it seems to be built on a series of graveyards. The ruins are also said to be the home of vampiric wamps. These are creatures with egg-shaped bodies that move on nine pale legs, some of which seem to be splashed with scarlet. The head features two large ears, a long snout, and a blank space where the eyes should be. They generate spontaneously from rotting corpses on which they then feed. They are known to be dangerous and may drink the blood of travelers. Beyond Oriab and the Southern Seas lie the Fantastic Realms, a great landmass about which very little is known; few dreamers have ventured there.

Away to the east lies the city of Celephais, which is a port of the Cerenian Sea. The city is apparently resistant to wear and decay and nothing in it ever changes. It was allegedly created in a dream by King Kuranes, who was a human in the waking world. He was supposedly the greatest of all recorded human dreamers. The city is a large metropolis that trades with the Cloud Kingdom of Serannian. The story of Kuranes have been inspired from Lord Dunsany's tale "The Coronation of Mr. Thomas Shap" (in the *Book of Wonder*, which was published in 1912) in which the protagonist becomes immersed in his own dream world and creates a mythical kingdom for himself. To the west of the city's walls are the Forbidden Lands, where none go.

To the north lies the Plateau of Leng with massive flesh-eating insects and strange beings that inhabit the heights and lower slopes. Beyond this lies Kadath in the Cold Waste and a mountain on the top where the Old Gods of Earth dwell in a closed citadel. These are weak human-like entities with long pointed chins and curious ears. From time to time they will come down from their lofty citadel to mate with men and women in the villages, but in most cases they keep to themselves. If one travels beyond Kadath one enters a zone of dark and cold where nothing seems to move, but the traveler experiences the constant sensation of being watched.

Within these realms, human dreamers can establish themselves; some have even settled in the Dreamlands after their deaths in the real world. Some humans can even travel between the Dreamlands and the world of reality at will, and have become kings and heroes in the former.

The influence of the Great Old Ones is largely peripheral in these lands, although their power is not to be completely ignored. Of all the Mythos entities Nyarlathotep holds the most power here, and there are temples dedicated to It as a deity in all the major human cities scattered across the Dreamlands. It is certainly the being to be venerated if one is to remain safe within this realm. The main gods of the Dreamlands, however, are the old gods of earth or certain Great Old Ones whose power is so weak that they can easily be overcome by an enterprising human. Occasionally these entities will try to strike up an alliance with certain travelers in the hope of gaining more power on the dreamer's return to the waking world, but such agreements are not to be trusted and will inevitably rebound upon the dreamer. From time to time, many of these ancient deities would dance on the peaks of certain mountains within the Dreamlands, but as human dreamers began to scale these peaks, they withdrew to Kadath in the Cold Waste.

Sometimes in Lovecraft's literature it is difficult to know whether some of his tales are set in our own world or in the Dreamlands. In fact, some of his stories seem to refer to continents in the past, such as Hyperborea, Mu, and Atlantis than to the Dreamlands. This would seem to suggest that Lovecraft was not sure exactly what the Dreamlands were, so he integrated them with some of the themes found in adventure stories set in prehistoric times by writers such as Robert E. Howard. The Dreamlands tend to be a fluctuating realm that takes in aspects of bizarre fantasy but also regular sword and sorcery themes.

Other Dreamlands

Although much of Lovecraft's fiction lies in the Dreamlands of Earth, it is well known that other worlds also have their own Dreamlands that their own inhabitants can visit, such as Saturn, Neptune, Jupiter, and Pluto. It is suggested that fungus beings dwelling in the darkness of deep craters on Mercury have their own dream-realms as well. These extraterrestrial Dreamlands are not completely discrete from each other or from that of Earth, but the edges of each can sometimes merge with others and invade the waking world as well. It is sometimes difficult for the traveler to determine whether he or she is in their own Dreamlands or those of another world. Not all creatures dream in the same way, of course, and the bizarre fantasies of beings from other worlds can sometimes influence how we perceive our own dream realms.

Some of these alien Dreamlands can be accessed directly from Earth through gateways and doors hidden in the waking world. The location of many of these portals is usually unknown to all except a select few, but once opened they can lead straight into the dream realms of another planet. The most favored location from Earth are the Dreamlands of Saturn, and it is known that some individuals have inadvertently crossed over there by accidentally opening one of the doors or gates that they have accidentally found. Some Mythos writers have used this to explain certain mysterious disappearances throughout the years, although the evidence still remains unclear. Nevertheless, because some of these doors and gateways are invisible, it is perhaps advisable to be careful even during waking hours.

Lying just below the Plateau of Leng, the city of Sarkomand is one of the foremost of all the Dreamland's metropolises. Of course the name appears to be a corruption of the eastern trading city of Samarkand (the second largest city in modern-day Uzbekistan) with which it shares some characteristics. Similar to Samarkand, Sarkomand lay on a trading route by which the Dreamland humans did business with the other non-human settlements further inland. It also traded with creatures from Leng and this eventually proved to be its downfall. An alliance between these creatures and the moon-beasts led to the city being overthrown and the majority of the humans being driven out. The moon-beasts now use the city as a docking point for their aerial ships and for loading and off-loading human slaves.

The city is the center of a number of roads that radiate out from it like the spokes of a great wheel, giving some indication as to its former trading greatness. Six gates provide entry to the metropolis, each guarded by a stone sphinx, and these lead toward a central plaza where two winged lions made of diorite stand guard over the entrance to the Great Abyss. This is a region where some claim that the edges of all possible worlds come and go, and others claim it is an entrance to the Underworld, which exists far beneath the Dreamlands and is ruled over by Nodens, Lord of the Great Abyss. Occultist Kenneth Grant has alternatively suggested that the Great Abyss is nothing more than a hypothetical concept that separates humans from the true Universe of genuine knowledge.

One of the most spectacular mountains in the Dreamlands is the Peak of Hatheg-Kla. It is said to lie in the Great Stony Desert in the Western Dreamlands, beyond the small town of Hatheg. There is once again a slight confusion here, as some Mythos writers state that the Great Stony Desert is on the top of a great plateau far above sea-level and is interminably flat. Wherever it is located, the mountain is incredibly sacred to all those around it. The Old Gods of Earth sometimes arrive from Kadath in their cloud-ships to gather there and either dance or confer concerning the affairs of men.

Only two humans have ever climbed to the summit of Hatheg-Kla in order to see the gods who have gathered there. One of these, according to the *Pnakotic Manuscripts*, was the tyrant Sansu, also known as the Godstalker. In an attempt to obtain great knowledge from the deities there, he climbed to the very peak of the mountain, but found nothing there except wind and rock. However, he must also have seen something else—a vision perhaps—which maddened his mind and caused him to die insane.

The other person who attempted such a climb was the wise priest Barazai, who was the servant of the Old Gods in the town of Ulthar. Desiring even more knowledge than he already had, he set out for the summit of Hathag-Kla. This, however, was his undoing, for somewhere on the highest slopes he vanished and was never seen again. Many of his handwritten notes were preserved by his servant Atal who still remains as priest in Ulthar though he is more than 300 years old. He has knowledge of the many secrets culled from the pages of the *Manuscripts*, but will not divulge them, except sometimes when drunk. The voice of the holy Barazai is sometimes heard calling helplessly down from the summit of Hatheg-Kla where some say that he had become imprisoned by the gods.

The image of only one of the Great Ones appears in the small towns and villages around Hatheg-Kla, and that is Lobon, who was once worshipped in places such as Sarnath. This entity is usually depicted as an ivy-crowned youth with a spear in one hand, who is thought to have been a god of warriors, although in the Dreamlands he is thought of as a more peaceful deity.

Texts in the Dreamlands

As previously mentioned, certain items and texts coexist in both the waking world and the Dreamlands simultaneously. One such volume is the *Cthaat Aquadingen,* a book penned by an unknown medieval author. It first appeared in Brian Lumley's story *The House of the Temple,* published in *Weird Tales 3* (a paperback revival of the anthology edited by Lin Carter and published by Zebra Books in 1981), and it has appeared in other sections of Lumley's fiction since.

The word *Cthaat* is of unknown origin, although it might have its source in the language of the Kthatans, who inhabited Kadath in the Cold Waste in some former time. It might be a corruption of some word in the language of the Great Old Ones, the meaning of which is uncertain. The word *Aquadingen* is, according to Lumley, a fusion of Latin ("aqua") and Old High German ("dingen") meaning "concerning things of water."

The *Cthaat Aquadingen* has created considerable controversy among Lovecraftian scholars and readers. Some claim that it is one in a series of books of hidden lore, which were collected in Northern Europe around A.D. 400. Portions of it supposedly bear a striking similarity to other occult texts that were in circulation around that time. Others say it is one in a set of volumes that was brought back from the Dreamlands by a traveler to those realms, and that its real antiquity lies there.

The text contained in this book is written in a variety of languages: Gothic, German, R'lyehian, and an unknown script that is specific to the Dreamlands. Certain portions of the book cannot be read by ordinary humans without driving them mad, so they are specially bound within the covers. Some occultists, for example, Lumley's creation Titus Crow, could read part of it, and his library contained a copy bound in covers of human skin. This edition may have been lost in the destruction of Crow's house by wind demons in 1969. The book contains information on Yibb-Tstll, an alien god found in a ruined temple in the jungles of Kled in the Dreamlands. This entity is covered with a kind of green cloak (which may well be part of Its actual body) beneath which lies many breasts that Yibb-Tstll feeds Its nightgaunt servants with. The deity is considered to be omniscient and can be asked any question concerning the Mythos. The book also gives a spell that can be used to dismiss the Small Crawler, which the text claims is an aspect of Nyarlathotep. Here too is a formula for creating the Barrier of Naach-Tith (a protective Barrier that can be erected to protect the chanter when summoning Yibb-Tstll). It has been widely used by wizards in the Dreamlands in the past, but not so much now.

In our own waking world it is said that only five copies of the text exist, but none of them are complete. Recently, the British Museum strenuously denied that it held a copy, though it's been suggested that a copy might be secretly held in its Restricted Section. A partial and extremely limited edition is to be found at the library of the Oakdeene Sanatorium in the South of England. An alleged translation of a small portion of the volume was carried out by an unknown writer named Berkley; some copies of this are said to be in circulation and known as Mad Berkley's Book. Nothing else is known about the author and this text is generally regarded to be a forgery.

Another Dreamland text, fragments of which may exist in our world, is *The Fourth Book of D'harsis*. D'harsis is considered to be one of the greatest and most powerful wizards who ever lived in the Dreamlands. He had access to very ancient text from the early days of that realm, which he painstakingly transcribed in four books, only one of which survives. This is preserved in the library of the Temple of the Elder Gods in Ulthar where only priests may consult it. However, fragments of it appear to have been copied and brought into our own world, and they supposedly lie in a monastery somewhere in a remote part of Italy, although the exact location of this foundation is not known. The text is believed to contain information on an entity known as Fly-the-Light (this is a name for an English goblin that appears among the shadows and in dark places), the evil Dreamlands queen Yath-Lhi and her enchanted court, as well as another formula for the construction of the Barrier of Naach-Tith. Although D'harsis is certainly credited with writing four books of arcane wisdom and occult lore, some authorities say that he actually wrote 11 of them and that other works still lie somewhere out in the Dreamlands.

The stories and locations that are set within Lovecraft's Dreamlands form a series of tales that are usually referred to as the Dream Cycle. Many, he claimed, were based on his own dreams and formed a land that lay on the very edges of his own imagination. Throughout the years, other Mythos writers have written about and expanded on the realm, creating a place that was as full of contrast and color as the actual waking world. The idea of such a place has allowed writers to give their imagination free rein and to devise wonders and ideas that are truly fantastic. But are they, as Lovecraft hinted, writing of a world that may indeed exist—a world that lies just a fraction beyond our own concrete sphere, which we can perhaps visit when we fall asleep? Or is it all simply pure imagination? Maybe it's only the dreamers who truly know.

Where Human Pathways End

Arkham

At the center of Lovecraft's fiction lies the shadowy town of Arkham, located on the Miskatonic River in Essex County, Massachusetts. Although it is an imaginary place, part of Lovecraft's ability as a writer was to blend actual locations with fictional creations to create a geographical locality that has a ring of authenticity about it.

The history of Arkham is, however, rather vague. It was allegedly founded during the latter half of the 17th century by a group of freethinkers and liberals who found the strictures of other religious colonies not to their liking. They settled on the banks of the Miskatonic River in what was to become Essex County, although it was then known as Naumkeag Territory (taking its name from an indigenous Indian tribe). No one knows the origin of the river's name, although Lovecraft admitted that it simply came from a jumble of Algonquin root words that he had put together.

The name of the town might come from the Arkham family, who were among the first to settle on the banks of the fictional Miskatonic and who may have been among the town's first leaders. However, nothing much is known of the family, and they appear to have died out in the region after one or two generations. No memorial to the family survives in the town, although their name appears in several specific landmarks around the area, such as Arkham Hill outside the town of Arkham Woods (part of a virgin forest between Arkham and the Aylesbury Pike, generally known as Billington's Wood). A portion of this land may have been owned by the Arkham family, although the first recorded owners would appear to be Richard and Alijah Billington, who dwelt there in the early part of the 19th century, giving their name to the area. The Arkham Woods form a part of this and lie close to the area where the old Billington house supposedly stood. There is also a stone tower in the area, as well as a stone circle on an island in a dried streambed (this was destroyed in 1924).

There is also a curious tomb that is dedicated to Johannes Aarkhajm. It was built into the wall of the town's burying ground at Lich Street, which runs between Parsonage Street and Peabody Avenue. In an anonymous handwritten pamphlet *Of Evill Sorceries Done in New-England Of Daemons in No Human Shape*, the author deals with reputed sorcerers and necromancers in New England during Colonial times. Reference is made in these pages to a "damned Dutchman" who "brought the curious and diabolick Arts of the Low Countries to the New World." Although the reference is brief, it would appear that this individual fled from Amsterdam to the New World and was out of the New Netherlands "into the wilde where he consorted with heathen Natives." Some local antiquarians have suggested that this sinister figure was actually the founder of the town, however, this is usually disputed.

Records from 1681 also show a Formal Notice of Marriage between Cornelius Aarkhajm and Bertha Van Dekken—both Lutherans—in Ipswich Settlement and a transfer of land from Cornelius to his son Claes in 1709. This could have been the Meadow Hill area just outside present-day Arkham, but what happened to the family or whether they were the founders of the town is unknown.

Not all that far away, another town was founded in Naumkeag Territory. Beverly, which formed part of Salem, may be slightly older than Arkham. It was founded by Roger Conant and named after Beverly in Yorkshire. The early religious differences in the Colonies between the Nonconformists and Separatists drove many more liberal individuals to the settlement at Arkham, which was considered to be more freethinking. Around 1675, part of the town was briefly owned by John Balch, who sold it around 1678 and moved back to Beverly where his house still exists. One of those who stayed was Nathaniel Orne, an erudite and well-read freethinking merchant whose descendants would become one of the more prominent families in the town.

Despite its slightly more liberal attitudes, Arkham was not immune from events in the wider Colonies and, in 1692, the witch-craze swept through neighboring Salem, and Arkham was affected by it. It sent at least one alleged witch, Keziah Mason, to Salem for trial, and Goody Fowler, who brewed potions in a small cottage outside the town, was hanged by an angry mob at Hangman's Hill in 1704. During this time, the rank whiff of witchcraft hung over the town, but although there were whispers, rumors, and accusations, there were no formal witch trials in Arkham.

During the mid-18th century, the town became a bustling port and commercial center. Although never attaining the industrial status of nearby Beverly, Arkham enjoyed reasonable prosperity and gentility. One of the most influential townsmen was the merchant trader Captain Jeremiah Orne, whose liberal bequest coupled with the legacy of an extensive library, led to the extension of Arkham College and laid the foundations for Miskatonic University. By 1861, the College (also known as Miskatonic Liberal College) enjoyed one of the highest reputations as an educational establishment on the eastern seaboard, and was certainly the town's most famous landmark. In that year, it achieved University status, giving a much-needed boost to Arkham.

The town's merchant industries had gone into decline, but many mills sprung up along the banks of the Miskatonic and, although they faced stiff competition from commercial centers in neighboring Beverly, these managed to generate wealth in the town. However, in the spring of 1888, an exceptional period of rain swelled the Miskatonic and severely flooded the areas, including the town itself. In its wake came a serious outbreak of typhoid, which decimated some areas of the town. Typhoid would return again in 1905 and would once more put a blight on Arkham's fortunes, from which it never fully recovered. Pressed hard by the commercial expansion of Beverly (which had been largely untouched by the floods and disease), Arkham began to slide into a genteel decline. Nevertheless, the University continued to generate revenue for the town, although it no longer enjoyed the educational prestige that it had once held. Even though it still maintained a degree of excellence, certain departments had become involved in more dubious areas of academic research, and this tarnished the University's reputation in educational circles. The income from Miskatonic proved to be the salvation of the town and enabled a reasonable recovery during the early to mid-20th century.

In 1969, Arkham experienced another disaster. A major fire at Curwen's Mill—a major textile facility in the town—completely destroyed the building and resulted in the deaths of a number of people, including two firemen. The impact for Arkham was more far-reaching. The Mill had been the last of the great textile centers there as well as a major employer; now that it was no longer in operation, unemployment was widespread. Many moved to find work in the factories of Beverly, leaving Arkham behind. Then in 1980, the Miskatonic burst its banks once more, causing major flooding and destroying many urban areas.

There are now a number of conflicting accounts concerning the present-day condition of the town. Some of them depict it as a rather run-down and squalid place, a network of shadowy streets and gloomy squares framed by antiquated but rather dilapidated buildings. Others describe it as a bustling metropolis, a mixture of old and new structures and a busy commercial center, developed around a state-of-the-art University. All agree, however, that it is a paradise for the scholar of American history or for the serious antiquarian, but actually holds very little for the casual traveler.

There seems little doubt that Lovecraft was unsure of the actual location of Arkham, first locating it on the coast as a seaport, and then depicted it as a mill-town on the Miskatonic and as a university town dependent on neither sea trade nor mill-work. It would appear to lie somewhere between Salem (now a suburb of Danvers) and Beverly in Essex County. However, just to confuse matters, in *The Colour Out of Space,* Lovecraft actually shifts the geographical location of the town. Nahum Gardner's farm (supposedly on the outskirts of Arkham) is frequently passed by tradesmen on their way to the town of Bolton. Bolton is a large Colonial town, incorporated in 1738, lying in Worcester County, Massachusetts, and well away from either Salem or Beverly. Arkham is therefore moving west!

There is also little doubt that Lovecraft incorporated elements of his native Providence into the Massachusetts town, and that some of the descriptions of the quaint streets, old houses, and shadowed courts actually have more in common with the Rhode Island that he knew. However, other New England places are included as well, such as Marblehead, Ipswich, and Gloucester. Like some sort of impressionable magpie, Lovecraft seems to have traveled about, lifting town locations from here and there and piling them together to form an overall idea of Arkham. And for many Mythos readers, Arkham certainly exists as an actual place in the backs of their minds, if not on the map.

Miskatonic University

During the lean years of the early 20th century, it was the revenue from Miskatonic University that enabled Arkham to survive, and the town has always enjoyed a certain reputation for academic study—particularly of the more esoteric kind.

Similar to many other things connected with the Mythos, the origins of the establishment are both obscure and conflicting. Possibly because Arkham's founding fathers were of a liberal and academic persuasion, a number of fledgling educational establishments existed in the area during the town's earlier periods. The first such institution of note would be the Arkham Academy, which was founded around 1690. However, another account states that this establishment was in fact the Salem Academy, which moved to Arkham at that time and took on the town's name. Still, other sources state that Salem Academy did not move to Arkham until 1776 when it merged with the already existing Academy. There are also references to two other colleges in the region: Arkham Liberal Seminary, which was founded in the late 1600s and also named "the College of the Miskatonick Vallye" (although this may have been another name for Arkham Academy). It was to this foundation that Captain Jeremiah Orne granted his bequest and donated his library. The other is mentioned in Reverend Nahum Elliot's *A Historie of Newe-England* (1701) as "The College of the Elder Faith" (later Elder Faith Seminary). This was founded by the Reverend Jabez Creech around 1680, and very little is known about it apart from the fact that it was a fairly strange place. Creech allegedly arrived from Salem as a missionary to a number of native tribes, but took land around Arkham where he founded some sort of religious school that grew into the College. What sort of either religious or educational message was promulgated there is unknown, and the College's student membership is unknown, even today. At some point this College of the Elder Faith became the Elder Faith Seminary when it was been controlled by some sort of shadowy religious Order in the town, which at one time included the mysterious Theron Marks. The Seminary's main discipline was medicine and, in 1861, it merged with the Miskatonic College to form the University, which opened an extensive medical department in 1880.

It's difficult to judge the current status of Miskatonic University. As Arkham College, it grew swiftly after the Revolutionary War and, during the late 1800s/early 1900s, a number of departments benefitted from legacies and endowments to develop their facilities and pursue research. At the turn of the 20th century it was considered one of the foremost universities in America. Both medicine and archaeology are still considered some of the most popular disciplines in American academia; however, certain other departments are slightly less well-regarded. During the 1920s it seems the Department of Anthropology produced a number of questionable texts that were ridiculed by other universities and provoked some controversy in the academic world. Throughout the years, a number of other, more obscure departments had been set up (some allegedly dating from the merger with the Elder Faith Seminary), which raised some conventional academic eyebrows. Questionable research and dubious publications from these departments may have tarnished the name of Miskatonic in some quarters. (Although much Mythos fiction chose to concentrate on the most esoteric aspects of the University, often depicting it as a place where witchcraft and occult studies are taught, it is worth pointing out that Lovecraft described it as a place of rational and scientific learning.)

The University does, however, contain a remarkable library with several Restricted Collections. In fact, it is thought to include the largest collection of rare occult books and materials in the Western world. Scholars may consult some of these books and texts only by express permission of the University authorities. The Exhibit Museum also contains a number of exhibits from very early and pre-human cultures and civilizations and there are some artifacts that are not on display, but that are kept locked away and are only used for the purposes of research by a very small group of academics.

The University is also renowned for financing expeditions to other parts of this world. Of note is the Padbodie Expedition to Antarctica (led by Professor Frank H. Pabodie from the University's engineering faculty) and archaeological explorations in South Africa and Southern Australia in 1933 and 1935 respectively. In many areas of the University world, Miskatonic is an extremely respected center of learning and its motto, *Ex Gnosis Ad Scientia* (From Wisdom to Science), is widely respected as well.

Although he had never been to a university, Lovecraft was fascinated by the notion of disciplined learning. He was extremely well read, and in his fictional world, occult knowledge came through intensive study. It seems natural, therefore, that any imaginary urban setting he created would also contain a learned center of formalized, esoteric knowledge, such as a University. Miskatonic is probably based on Brown University in Providence. Situated on College Hill, the University was only a little way from where he lived, and he could certainly walk to its grounds.

Brown was an established institution founded in 1764, just before the Revolutionary War and, similar to Miskatonic, it was founded to support the social and religious climate of the time. In 1762, The Baptist Church Association of Providence decided that there should be local facilities or the learning of youth and its instruction in Godly ways and pressed for a center of learning in the developing colony. The main proponent of the idea was Morgan Edwards, a prominent Baptist minister, although it was taken forward into documented form by another Baptist clergyman, James Manning. Together with the Congregationalist minister and theologian Ezra Stiles, they prepared a charter for a *College in the English Colony of Rhode Island and Province Plantations*, which would later change its name to Brown University after a substantial request from Nicholas Brown Jr., whose father had been one of the Charter's original signatories.

The historical and religious development of the College may have appealed to Lovecraft (who had been raised as a Baptist), as well as to his attraction toward organized study, and he may have tried to incorporate it into his own fiction under the guise of Miskatonic. The idea of the university has been taken up by a number of Mythos writers and fans who have developed and expanded upon it—even going to far as to publish a prospectus detailing many courses available there.

According to many writers, the University is central to the life of Arkham. Its extensive library of strange and occult materials, coupled with its unique departmental research, makes Miskatonic a place of considerable interest to those who indulge in Lovecraftian studies.

The Theron Marks Society

Extremely little is known about Theron Marks and yet, if some commentators are to be believed, he and his associates have had a profound influence on the later development of the town of Arkham.

As has already been noted, one of the early institutions that flourished in Arkham was the Elder Faith Seminary. Although separate from the town, the Seminary exercised a clandestine influence over the development of the town. Some have suggested that the Seminary was more like a Masonic group that influenced local politics and which maintained links with some of Arkham's more prominent citizens. It has been said that the Seminary controlled some building developments in the area and also regulated trade in the town during the late 1800s. According to some traditions, the Seminary had other, more occult significance and worshipped strange gods as part of its ongoing practice. It also exercised an undue influence over the development of the University, guiding certain departments into areas of research which, according to some academics, were not altogether wholesome.

During the early 1920s, one of the members of the Seminary was a man named Theron Marks. He supposedly formed a clandestine society, which included a number of the leading Town Fathers and several prominent Arkham businessmen, which was dedicated to cementing even closer links between the town and the former faction of the Elder Faith. Others state that it was to keep evidence of the worship of the Great Old Ones from the prying eyes of a wider public. It was a risky thing to do in those times. The U.S. Government was turning its attention toward connections between organized criminal gangs and local authorities, and were investigating groupings that might have been exerting a corrupt influence in some of the more rural areas. Several investigations in Arkham were instigated, but nothing was uncovered. Nevertheless, several of the figures who were associated with the society either died or went mad shortly afterward. Theron Marks mysteriously disappeared without trace. Yet, despite all of this, the Society continued into the 1930s and perhaps there are still some elements of it operating in Arkham, even today. Because of the clandestine nature of both it and its activities, it's difficult to tell.

Randolph Carter

One of Arkham's most famous sons (although he is not immediately associated with the town) was Randolph Carter. He resided in Boston for most of his life, only returning to Arkham sporadically. From the age of 10, he had the gift of prophesy, but more importantly, he could travel to the Dreamlands, visiting places such as Kadath in the Cold Waste. However, as he became older the dream-journeys became less and less until they stopped altogether. Carter began to search for some meaning to his experiences and embarked upon a personal quest for an explanation of his own existence.

During World War I he served in the French Foreign Legion where he made the acquaintance of Etienne-Laurent de Marigny who, like himself, had been a dream-traveler. The two of them traveled to the crypts below the town of Bayonne where they made a pact that would bind them together for years to come. Several months afterward, Carter was nearly killed during an attack on the town of Balloy-en-Santerre and returned home on injury leave.

He went to Arkham where he became a pupil of the Canadian occultist Harley Warren, who had been studying at Miskatonic. Together, the two of them made a trip to the Big Cypress Swamp in Florida for some undisclosed purpose. Here, Warren disappeared and the local police arrested Carter who gave them some rambling and incoherent account. Due to the lack of evidence, the police let him go and he went back to Massachusetts. Here, he became a writer of some note. His most famous work, *A War Come Near*, was published in 1919 and detailed his war experiences in France. It received literary acclaim and established Carter as a serious writer. However, his real interest seemed to lie in stories of the occult and in fantasy. His most celebrated short story was *The Attic Window*, which appeared in the magazine *Whispers* in September 1922. This book contained a number of disturbing passages—so disturbing that several newsstands refused to stock the issue, and the magazine never bought any of his material again. Shortly after that, Carter and a friend were found together on a stretch of waste ground near Arkham's Meadow Hill, suffering from rather bizarre injuries that neither of them could explain, but which Carter insisted were somehow related to the story.

His main writing success, however, came from his fantasy works. He tried to unsuccessfully publish a number of early works related to his dreaming, but several more complex tales received some critical acclaim and made his name known outside Arkham.

On October 7th, 1928, Randolph Carter visited his family's ancestral home just outside Arkham. The place had been long abandoned and was in a serious state of disrepair. When he did not return to his lodgings, a hunt was organized and his car was found near the deserted mansion with a knotted handkerchief on the driver's seat. Carter has never been found and his disappearance has always been considered one of Arkham's most famous mysteries. Some have suggested that he found a way back to the Dreamlands and now reigns in the city of Ilek-Vad, which is set high on a crystal cliff.

Carter was, of course, Lovecraft's fictional alter-ego, displaying some of the characteristics that Lovecraft would have liked to present himself. It is not hard to imagine him walking around the streets of Providence fondly imagining himself to be Randolph Carter strolling along the shadowy laneways of Arkham. And perhaps *that* is how the fictional town of Arkham best functions in the Mythos—as a kind of retreat for the lonely and insecure man who created it.

Where Human Pathways End

Dunwich

Arguably, nothing establishes "Lovecraft country" more than the ruined hamlet of Dunwich. It appears in one of his most famous stories, "The Dunwich Horror" (published in the April 1929 issue of *Weird Tales*), and the location has become a by-word for all things Lovecraftian. According to Lovecraft, the hamlet lies in the Miskatonic Valley.

Although clearly identified with America in Mythos fiction, the name *Dunwich* has firm roots in the English countryside. Originally "New Dunnich," it is the name of a small town and larger civil parish in the English country of Suffolk. It is one of the oldest parishes in the region and, at one time, was much bigger than a whole town. In fact, more than 1,500 years ago it was the capital of East Anglia and the seat of the most senior Anglican bishops. It was taken over by the pagan Norsemen around 870, but seems to have retained its Christian status. The Norman Domesday Book of 1086 states that there were at least three major churches there and a population of more than 3,000.

By the 1280s there were eight churches in the town and the population had grown so much that Dunwich was almost a city. It was also an incredibly prosperous place, boasting a large harbor and a series of waterfront warehouses and dwellings. In 1286, however, the coast of East Anglia experienced a storm of epic proportions and much of the town was lost in the tempest. The inhabitants fought hard to preserve the harbor—even though shipping to the port had declined— but another storm in 1328 caused even more damage and completely destroyed all coastal structures. A further tempest in 1347 completed the town's devastation by sweeping another 400 houses into the sea. Today, Dunwich is no more than a seaside village, although it still retains its status as a town. The ruins of Greyfriars Abbey (a Franciscan Priory) and the Leper Hospital of St. James—both established in the town's heyday—can still be seen.

The story of the rise and decline of Dunwich was documented in a number of history books and it is possible that Lovecraft may have read one of these and been fascinated by the account. A reference to Dunwich also appears in Arthur Machen's novella *The Terror*, which Lovecraft read.

Lovecraft's fictional New England Dunwich was founded in 1692 by a group who fled Salem to avoid the witch persecutions there. There were also members of another group who came along with them from the Merrymount (later Mount Dagon) settlement near what is now Quincy, Massachusetts. Among the arrivals were the Whatley family, who would become one of the foremost families in the new settlement.

For a while, Dunwich prospered. The Whatleys set up a number of mills in the area, which provided the backbone of the growing town's industry throughout the 18th century. However, personal tragedy in 1806 triggered the mental collapse of their owner, George Whatley, which began a downward industrial and social spiral. The name George Whatley may have been "borrowed" from the 18th-century English industrialist and philanthropist George Whatley, who had supported the American Revolution and published the book *Principles of Trade* in 1774. He was also one of the founding members and a guardian (both vice-president and treasurer) of the Foundling Hospital in London.

As if mirroring the decline of the settlement, the Whatley family also degenerated. Some of them left the area and headed off to other parts of New England, and the remainder seemed split up into various branches, some more dissolute than others. There were whispers of insanity and incest amongst certain branches, but nothing was ever proven. With the closure of many mills, the population of Dunwich began to decease as younger folk drifted away to look for jobs elsewhere.

Today, Dunwich is mostly deserted. Much of the population that was left became increasingly degenerate and inbred, so much so that during the First World War, the authorities were unable to get their quota of draft recruits from the area. The inhabitants of the village tried to keep to themselves and to prevent outsiders from seeing what went on there. Throughout the years, Dunwich has sunk further and further into actual decay. Many of the houses are now in an advanced state of dereliction and are barely fit for human habitation. And yet, individuals continue to live there—individuals who are sometimes almost as decrepit as the very buildings themselves. Many are from a branch of the Whatleys who stayed in the area, and some are the Bishops, who were another family that settled close by.

Apart from the rotting village, the surrounding countryside has an eerie reputation. Strange low hills surround the settlement, and it's said that from these strange noises are sometimes heard, the source of which seems to be deep underground. Curiously, these sounds are usually only heard at certain times of the year, for example at May Eve or at Halloween. In the late 1740s, Reverend Abijah Hoadley, a clergyman who took up a post in the Congregational Church at Dunwich in 1747, preached a curious sermon relating to the sounds, which was later published in Springfield, Massachusetts. In the sermon, Hoadley attributes the sounds to demons that were "sleeping beneath those hills." Shortly after delivering the sermon, Abijah Hoadley mysteriously disappeared.

Dunwich's gradual decline continued into the 20th century. Rumors concerning the place and its populace continued unabated; that far from being uneducated, certain individuals were engaging in peculiar study, the populace was practicing peculiar forms of worship and the noises in the hills had grown worse.

According to Lovecraft, Elezer or Noah Whatley (also known as "Old Whatley" or "the Wizard Whatley") featured prominently in the folklore of the region around

Dunwich, and his influence echoes all through "The Dunwich Horror." He was the father of Lavinia Whatley and grandfather to her son Wilbur, who was killed in the Miskatonic University Library. It is said that the Wizard Whatley lived to an immense and uncanny age. Old Whatley's neighbors viewed him with a mixture of fear and loathing, and viewed his interest in the stone circles on some of the hilltops, particularly one on Sentinel Hill, with some suspicion. It was generally agreed that he was a wizard and that he dealt with things that were far older than humanity. None in Dunwich dared question him, and his word was often law in the village.

At some time during his long life, the Wizard Whatley took a wife, although nothing much is known as to who this woman was. She gave birth to a girl, Lavinia, sometime around 1878. Around 1890, his wife disappeared or died, and vanishes from the pages of history. The Wizard Whatley died, apparently from natural causes, in 1924 but, even after all this time, his shadow still hangs over the decaying village like an ominous cloud. There are even some who say that he never died at all.

He left behind his daughter Lavinia who died two years after him. She was an albino and was considered to be mentally slow. In 1913, she gave birth to Wilbur (and apparently another "child") although no one around Dunwich knew who the father might be. Wilbur grew up quickly, both in size and in intelligence, and could even speak quite articulately when only months old. At the time of his death, he was 8 feet tall. He had an extremely dubious reputation among the other folk of the village, and it is said that Lavinia was terrified of him, but like his grandfather, he had a reputation as something of a scholar, particularly of the darker arts. He corresponded with a number of individuals— some in other parts of the world— including Dr. Henry Armitage, the Librarian at Miskatonic University. On Halloween night in 1926, Lavinia simply disappeared and no trace of her was ever found—it was assumed that she had perhaps been murdered by Wilbur, but nobody could prove it. Wilbur died in 1928 trying to steal a copy of the *Necronomicon* from the Miskatonic University Library. His body mysteriously vanished under curious circumstances, however, after his death, cattle and other livestock started to disappear in the countryside around Dunwich and there was some talk of people vanishing as well. Back at Miskatonic University, Armitage began to fear what was actually happening in the hill country and set out for the village with Professors Rice and Morgan. The veil between our own world and the existence of the Great Old Ones had been compromised by Whatley's sorceries. On the top of Sentinel Hill, a lonely promontory outside the village, Armitage performed an exorcism and drove the entities back. Following these events, all signs showing the way to Dunwich were torn down, references to the town disappeared from maps, and the place has been nearly forgotten. And yet, it is still said that *something* still lurks out there in the hills—something connected to that terrible time.

The area is also of passing interest to archaeologists who seem to be fascinated by the queer stone circles and standing monoliths that adorn the tops of some of the strange hills. No real explanation has ever been given for these structures, and they are certainly not artifacts of Native American cultures. Some seem to think that they might come from an extremely ancient prehistoric culture that once controlled the region and that they are somehow linked to the underground noises among the hills. However, what that connection might be is unclear and only adds to the mystery of the district.

The Place of Noises

One of the more significant elements in "The Dunwich Horror" is, of course, the strange noises in the hills around the village, which are suggested as evidence for the activity of the Great Old Ones in their underground lairs. When the Reverend Abijah Hoadley spoke about them in his sermon, he ascribed them to the activities of demons lurking in the depths of the earth; others have suggested that they were something else.

Although such phenomena seem weird and perhaps frightening, they are not altogether unusual. There have been a number of "sound sites" all across America, Europe, and Scandinavia where unexplained noises in the air or from under the ground have sometimes unsettled local communities. Many of these can usually be explained by scientific means or theory: movements in geological formations, collapses in underground workings such as mine shafts, and so forth. However, some areas sometimes defy such rational explanation.

Certainly the area around the former village of East Haddam, Connecticut, is such a place. This is a site where noises are often still heard with surprising regularity. In fact, the old Native American name for the region, according to the New England historian and folklorist Samuel Drake, is Machemoodus, which simply means "the place of noises." Since records have been kept, strange sounds ringing through the air or from below the ground have been heard by a great many people, some of whom have recorded their experiences. Many of these accounts tell of great roaring noises, sometimes accompanied by a distinct quaking of the ground.

One of the earliest accounts of the noises is given in a 1729 letter from Reverend Hosmer, a local minister, to Mr. Prince of Boston, Massachusetts. In it, he states that the area is a very old one, and was formerly used by the Indians for their pow-wows. Allied to the words of the gods was a shaking and trembling of the earth and this continued, together with the peculiar noises, long after the Indians had departed from that particular area. The explanation was that the Indian gods were angry because the settlers' had come to the region and had displaced them, and they were making their displeasure known in a tangible form. Reverend Hosmer claimed to have heard nine or 10 such sounds—thundering roars, screams, groans, and frightful, distant shouting—coupled with a shaking of the earth, which lasted for a full five minutes on one occasion. These sounds were heard, he went on, throughout his parish for at least 20 or 30 years previously, and had occurred at fairly regular intervals. If anything, they were becoming more terrifying.

The sounds, according to Reverend Hosmer, started like "a slow thunder, coming down from the North." They would then take on a noise like a cannon being fired or a continuous round of musket shot, which seemed to pass through the ground, directly under the settlement and the very feet of those who lived there. Houses would shudder and crockery would fall off shelves and break. But even then, things were not finished, for the rumblings would turn into sounds up in the air like screams and voices talking, people shouting a long way off, and unseen explosions that reverberated all around the Haddam area. He went on to state the danger of "shaking ground," but added that recently (around 1729) the noises had become fewer in number and that their effect—the trembling and shaking of the earth—had become slightly less violent. Indeed, he continued, there had only been two occurrences within 1728 and 1729.

Some scientific figures within the community stated that the sounds and vibrations were entirely natural and were due to the movements of air within subterranean caverns far beneath the surface of the earth. Other noises were not voices at all, but were made by wind trapped in underground tunnels. Hosmer, however, was not so sure. In his letter, he dubbed the sounds "the Moodus noises," and suggested that they might be of supernatural origin. Indians, he pointed out, tended to fear and shun the area because they were terrified of the wrath of their own gods. He said an old Indian who dwelt in the place had told him that these gods would take their revenge on anyone who settled in the place, because it was a sacred site and the good Reverend thought that there might indeed be something in this. The vestiges of former paganism, he believed, still lingered in the area and had an effect upon it.

The Reverend Hosmer's romanticised supernatural views seem to have won over scientific investigation as far as the settlers of East Haddam were concerned. Many took to wearing protective charms and amulets against whatever evil the sounds threatened to bring them. In fact, there seemed to be a common consensus that epidemics of disease and other misfortunes coincided with the noises in the hills. To add to the feelings of supernatural terror, lights were sometimes seen flickering along river banks and in the forests, and this stoked ancient fears and tensions.

Around 1731, a certain traveler passed through East Haddam. Several accounts mention him, but the main reference comes from Reverend Hosmer, who gave only a brief account of his activities. The traveler was named Dr. Steele, who came from England. He was intrigued by the Moodus noises and seemingly stopped to investigate them, questioning many inhabitants of the settlement. He heard several old Indian legends and this appears to have piqued the Doctor's curiosity even more. In fact, he took up residency in East Haddam and opened a blacksmith's shop there. Strangely, he worked the forge only at night and turned away people who came to him with legitimate business, which led the people of East Haddam to suspect that he was engaged in some sort of occult enterprise. At the same time, the noises in the hills seemed to grow in frequency and intensity, and the local people approached the doctor and asked him what he was doing. The magician replied that he was engaged in an occult experiment of a momentous nature, and was attempting to grow a massive carbuncle far below the surface, which would draw all the arcane forces of the area into it. There would then be no more noises. Not only this, but Dr. Steele made certain replicas of the carbuncle, which he sold to local people as protection against the Moodus noises and against the quakes and tremors that they created. He enjoyed a large market for his artifacts, although the sceptics stated that he had created the market for himself by preying on the superstitions of the settlers. Steele further declared that the "Place of Noises" was actually the site where a very powerful wizard had been buried, and that the noises were actually the groanings and stirrings of this magician's evil soul. However, he urged the people not to be afraid, as the magical carbuncle that he was creating would draw the poisonous forces into it and render them harmless. Steele immediately gained a wide acceptance of his beliefs around East Haddam, and became something of a major figure in the area.

Shortly after Steele began his work, the noises began to die away and subside completely, so it seemed that the Doctor's experiments were bearing fruit. No sooner had the sounds started to diminish than the doctor suddenly and inexplicably packed up and moved away from East Haddam overnight. In fact, nobody saw him go, but in the morning his forge was deserted. He was never seen or heard from again. After a while, people began to wonder if there truly *had* been a Doctor Steele. Some believed that he'd been an angel sent to help the people of East Haddam, although many others said that he'd been an evil spirit. He left behind a number of ancient books on magic, some of which were written in a language that nobody could read; this was to energize the buried carbuncle should the noises return—which in time, they did. The people patiently waited for Dr. Steele to return and use the books, but he never did.

By the late 1830s, the Moodus noises had returned, together with the trembling of the ground, with renewed ferocity. By the 1840s they were worse than they had ever been. Many in the community remembered Dr. Steele and his allegedly miraculous underground carbuncle, and some speculated that the magical artifact had now worn away and that the dark Indian spirits had returned thirsting for vengeance. Distant and shouting voices were frequently hard, as were strange mutterings from the air, while the ground shook underfoot and it was said that the ghosts of long-dead Indians were holding some kind of Satanic war-dance among the hills.

Once again a mysterious figure showed up to deal with the eerie phenomena— this time in the shape of a traveling hill preacher named Robert Edge. Edge is something of an enigma who appears in the folklore of several New England communities and seems to be a cross between a man of God and a pagan shaman. For a little while, he stayed with a local family in East Haddam organizing a series of tent missions— "days of holying"— at which he preached terrible "hellfire and brimstone" sermons, many concerning the Great Day of Judgement and the end of all things. During his stay in East Haddam, Edge discovered the mysterious books that Dr. Steele had left behind. Taking the books with him, Edge went up into the hill country just as the sounds began again and read out words and phrases in an unintelligible tongue. These were read in an imperious and authoritative tone and, although the sounds did not disappear, they certainly decreased both in frequency and volume.

Shortly after his visit, Robert Edge disappeared in exactly the same way as Dr. Steele had. He simply walked out into the night and vanished. For a while after his disappearance, the noises continued, but they were steadily growing more and more infrequent and had less of an impact on the area. Gradually, they had become so infrequent that they had really become no more than a cultural memory and had passed into regional folklore.

There is one last curious twist in the tale, however. As the War between the states moved toward its bloody conclusion around 1864, the sounds returned with something of a renewed vigor, as did the vibrations in the ground. Although not as strong as they had once been, they were certainly disruptive enough to be noticed. And as before, there were sounds like distant thunder and men shouting, screaming, and chanting, and once again they were associated with the old Indian pow-wows that took place in the region. Others offered the explanation that the wanton spilling of blood across the land during the Civil War had stimulated the appetites of the ancient forces and that they were making their presence known in East Haddam again. Almost as soon as the War ended, however, the noises began to drift away again, and the tremors began to diminish.

Since then, there has been little to report. On occasion, some individuals in the East Haddam area claim to have heard peculiar noises or eerie voices calling to them or to have experienced slight tremors in the ground, but nothing like the 18th and 19th centuries. Many of these accounts are simply ignored or dismissed, and even the name of the "Place of Noises" has been all but forgotten, even in the locality. The Moodus spirits seem to have been stilled at last.

One fragment of the legend can be found in the form of a very long poem by local poet John Brainard, which was later turned into a local ballad. A little East Haddam girl sang the poem in its entity for Samuel Drake when he visited the area in 1883. The last verse states:

THE CARBUNCLE LIES IN THE DEEP, DEEP SEA,
BENEATH THE MIGHTY WAVE,
BUT THE LIGHT SHINES UPWARD SO GLORIOUSLY,
THAT THE SAILOR LOOKS PALE, FORGETS HIS GLEE,
WHEN HE CROSSES THE WIZARD'S GRAVE.

In the late 19th century, variants and sections of this ballad were known and sung all across New England, and were sometimes recited in schools there, often as part of the end of year festivities.

Could it be that Lovecraft knew of the curious events in East Haddam and incorporated them into his tale concerning the ruined village of Dunwich? After all, rural Connecticut is not all that far from his native Rhode Island, so it is *possible* that he might have known of the events in East Haddam. Whether he did or not, such occurrences add to the eerie atmosphere of the decrepit place, and makes us ask what may *truly* be lurking under the remote hills of New England.

WHERE HUMAN PATHWAYS END

INNSMOUTH

No place in Lovecraft's America has been more frequently visited by Mythos writers than Innsmouth. The crumbling, near-abandoned, fishing village on the Massachusetts coastline has inspired the imaginations of those who explore the Lovecraftian world. The story appeared in Lovecraft's 1936 novella "The Shadow Over Innsmouth" and remains the only one of his works published during his lifetime that did not appear in a periodical.

The village was founded as a small town in 1643 and rapidly became a major seaport, mainly due to its position on the coast and its large harbor. From Innsmouth, trading ships sailed all over the world, bringing back goods from places as exotic and as far away as the South Sea Islands. It was the War of 1812 that began to reverse this prosperity and turned the town into the derelict place that it is today. Also, many of the Innsmouth captains turned privateer and started attacking British shipping. Consequently, a British fleet attacked the town, reducing many of the buildings there to rubble. Half the town's sailors perished in subsequent skirmishes with the enemy, greatly reducing Innsmouth's population.

Following the War, most of the town's income came from mills that had been established on the Manuxet and from the ships of Captain Obed Marsh. Much of Marsh's trade was in South America where he had traded in gold among some of the Spanish colonies there. However, around 1840, he lost one of his major gold sources on which he depended, and the town began to steadily decline while Marsh's ships were forced to range much further for trade.

He had already been trading with groups of natives around Ponape, seeking out new gold sources there. His three ships, *The Columbia, The Hetty*, and *The Sumatra Queen* had been dealing with natives who traded with a species of beings who came from a sunken place in the ocean known as the Deep Ones. Marsh had engaged in the rites of some of these natives and was influenced by their religious beliefs. In 1838, however, the group of natives with whom he had been dealing were wiped out by some of the tribes from other islands and Marsh's source of gold was gone.

Things in Innsmouth were in a perilous state as the mills began to fail and there was little trade coming into the port. In 1839/40 Obed Marsh returned from the southern seas and began preaching a new religion based on that of the Ponape Islanders. He set up a church that he called "The Esoteric Order of Dagon." This, he claimed, would be the salvation of Innsmouth and, instead of trading, the town's economy became based on fishing. It was said that Marsh had established some form of relationship with the Deep Ones whom the Ponape Islanders had worshipped. After a time, Marsh's Order was so popular that all other churches in the Innsmouth area were forced to close down.

In 1846, a plague swept through the town. The exact nature of the disease has never been discovered, though it was described as a fever brought in from overseas by one of the few remaining traders in the town. What happened during this time remains a mystery, as no records have survived, but it's thought that much of the town was wiped out by the disease and the remainder resorted to looting and murder. The plague passed, leaving half of Innsmouth's population dead and Obed Marsh and his Esoteric Order of Dagon firmly in control of the town.

Although Innsmouth's wealth now came from fishing and there was still some trading, the place continued in its decline. At this time, some of the newborn babies there began to show physical deformities and abnormalities, which were supposedly linked with poor diet and poverty; some attributed it to the after-effects of the plague, but perhaps the problem ran far deeper. During the Civil War, the town seemed un-able to meet its quota of volunteers because of this now-widespread problem, plus no one would fight alongside anyone who came from a cursed place. During this time, Obed Marsh and his family maintained tight control of the town through the Esoteric Order of Dagon, almost cutting it off from the outside world. When Marsh died in 1878, other members of the family took over leadership of the Order, ensur-ing that his dynasty would continue there. The place was shunned by most people in the communities and few people ventured to Innsmouth unless absolutely necessary.

Legend says that as fishing stocks declined, the town maintained itself through bootlegging and rum-running. As word of these activities began to filter out, they drew the attention of the federal authorities who decided to investigate. This led to a raid on the town in mid-February 1928 in which boatloads of federal agents de-scended on the town and began to search the ramshackle buildings there. What they found remains in sealed government files and no official report has ever been given, but it is known that the agents dynamited many of the decrepit and abandoned build-ings, disbanded the Esoteric Order of Dagon, and took large numbers into military camps never to be released. It's thought that some of the residents were held in these camps until the 1940s when they were transferred to other facilities; some may still be there today.

Although the authorities had been taking an interest in Innsmouth's affairs for several years, the raid was actually instigated by the testimony of Robert Martin Olm-stead, a college student from Toledo, Ohio, who visited the town on July 15th, 1927. Olmstead was a junior at Oberlin College and visited the town in order to ascertain the development of its fish processing business. Instead, he had a rather harrowing ex-perience concerning some of the local townspeople and the Esoteric Order of Dagon. Managing to escape from the town, Olmstead sought out the federal authorities.

Fearful of what might happen to him following the raid, Olmstead sought govern-ment protection, however, late in 1929 it was withdrawn and in 1930 Olmstead and a cousin who had been committed to an insane asylum both vanished without a trace.

Lovecraft never used the name *Olmstead* in his work, but it was certainly found among his notes and papers after his death. Derleth, on the other hand, used the name "Williamson" for this character. Stan Sargent uses the name from Lovecraft's notes in his 2002 Mythos story *Live Bait.*

Since the raid, accounts of Innsmouth's activities became extremely muddled. Some descriptions of the place state that it's little more than a ghost town with only a few inhabitants left; others say the government has set up a business facility there in order to manufacture computer software, and that it is a tourist destination with a number of strange museums and attractions. The most likely outcome of the raid is that the entire area is under government quarantine and that Innsmouth is now populated by both military and scientific personnel. This idea has been given some credence by recent reference to a sub-committee of the U.S. Senate, which is respon-sible for a specific facility on the New England coast. This committee reports directly to the president, however no paperwork appears to exist, there is no record of who sits on it, and its business doesn't appear to be recorded anywhere. Could the "facility" that it oversees be Innsmouth?

Just outside the great bay in which Innsmouth lies is a rocky outcropping, ris-ing just above the waterline, which is known locally as Devil's Reef. During the 19th century, the Reef was visited on a number of occasions by Obed Marsh who claimed he was looking for pirate treasure in one of the many caves that dotted the top of the outcrop, however, others have claimed that he was looking for something *else.* Later, Marsh's Esoteric Order of Dagon frequently visited the Reef for some of their rituals until the cult was closed down in 1928. It was also somewhere off the Reef that the Naval submarine fired its torpedoes just after the 1928 raid, though no record of the action or what the vessel was firing at can be found. Local fishermen still refuse to fish anywhere near the Reef, and it is believed that a Navy vessel still patrols the waters nearby. It has also been suggested that the Reef forms some sort of gateway to another world that is known only to the Deep Ones, which they may use from time to time.

On some maps of the region, Devil's Reef is sometimes shown as Allen's Reef, and this may take its name from Captain Nathan Allen who is reputed to have once lived in the town and was one of its more prominent seafarers. His family hit hard times when the Marsh family came to prominence and their decline was spectacular. He is the ancestor of the town drunk Zadok Allen, who appears in Lovecraft's novella.

A little further along the coastline lies Falcon Point. The name appeared in a story, the notes for which were initially compiled by Lovecraft. The idea originally appeared in his *Commonplace Book* after his death, but was later written up by Au-gust Derleth and called *The Fisherman of Falcon Point.* It was published by Derleth's

Arkham House Press in a collection entitle *The Shuttered Room and Other Pieces* in 1959, and was described by Derleth as "a posthumous collaboration."

There is a rather unsavory legend connected with the Point. It appears that in the past, a local fisherman named Enoch Conger captured a "mermaid" with whom he did some sort of deal. The "mermaid" captured may have been one of the Deep Ones and it inflicted some sort of genetic curse on him. Gradually, he became increasingly aquatic, both in physical form and in his mental yearnings, and eventually seems to have been absorbed by the ocean. It is said that the Deep Ones congregate around the Point at certain times of the year and that those who venture there often leave themselves open to abduction by these sea people. Falcon Point is therefore considered to be a place best avoided, unless those who venture there wish to share the awful fate of Enoch Conger.

Within the Mythos there is another town by the same name. This Innsmouth is located on the Cornish coast and, similar to its New England counterpart, it is a small fishing village. The most famous landmark there is Trevor Towers, which was at one time home to Kuranes, king of the Dreamlands' city of Celephas. He somehow crossed the barrier between the two worlds and took up residence in Innsmouth, but having fallen on hard time, moved to London where he became an author under a variety of names. He was the foremost of all Dreamers and created the mystical city of Celephas from his own dreams, making himself ruler there. While in a dream state, he visited the Court of Azathoth and was the only Dreamer ever to return sane from that experience. Upon his return to Innsmouth, he fell over the cliffs there while on a walk, and his earthly body was destroyed. However, he fled back to the Dreamlands where he now rules, although he often longs to return to our world, something which he cannot ever do. The Cornish Innsmouth, therefore, seems to be some cross-over point between our own world and the Dreamlands.

"The Innsmouth Look"

It has already been noted that a number of babies were born in Innsmouth with either physical deformities or peculiarities. However, many people of the area (prior to the Federal raid of 1928), already exhibited what has been referred to as "the Innsmouth look." This is believed to be a hereditary condition that gradually overtakes the inhabitants of the village as they grow older. Babies seem to be quite normal at the time of birth, but through the years subtle changes start to occur. The main transformation occurs between the subject's 20th birthday and middle age. The affliction is initially characterized by large bulging eyes, loss of hair, and scaly, peeling skin. As the condition develops, the nose tends to flatten, the ears become abnormally small, and there is a slight webbing between the fingers and toes. A wattling occurs on the individual's neck, resembling gills, and in the later stages the bone structure gradually shifts with the shape of the skull and pelvis, forcing the victim to adopt a kind of shuffling gait and hunched position with the entire body thrust slightly forward. Accompanying his physical change there are also several mental abnormalities. The subject may experience continual dreams about the sea, coupled with a certain fixation on the ocean. Eventually, the person involved disappears and it is presumed that they have drowned themselves while answering the obsessive call of the sea.

It is suggested that the "look" did not begin with Captain Obed Marsh, but with his immediate ancestor Obadiah Marsh. Obadiah was a famous Innsmouth sea-captain in his own right, and it was said to have been he who began the trade in the South Seas. One one occasion, Obadiah set sail again, returning with a wife who was seldom seen outside the Marsh house. Those who did glimpse her said that she seemed slightly peculiar, and it was thought that Obadiah Marsh had taken a wife from among the Deep Ones. The mating of a human with the piscine-like woman is though to have altered the genetic makeup of both the Marshes and the Phillips (who married into them), and thus created "the Innsmouth look." The DNA around the town changed through marriage and intermarriage, and this manifested itself in the physical appearance and general demeanor of the people.

The Real Innsmouth

Could such a place as Innsmouth really have existed, and did Lovecraft know of it? Certainly there is no location vaguely resembling the decaying township along the New England coast today. Some scholars have linked Lovecraft's idea to the town of Cohasset, Massachusetts, claiming that it bears some relation to Innsmouth. The suggestion is that Lovecraft knew of the place at a time when their industries were declining, and used it as a template for his fearsome town. Other than perhaps a close geographical location and a slight historical similarity, however, it does not match Innsmouth at all.

The area of Cohasset was first seen by European explorers in 1614 when Captain John Smith sailed up the coast. The town, which was first settled in 1670, took its name from an Algonquin word *Conahasset* meaning "a long rocky place." The area was prominent during the Revolutionary War, providing a hiding place for the Boston Revolutionary leader John Pulling and a base for the Libertarian Pastor John Browne. Several Cohasset men attacked the British shipping that was anchored near the town. Apart from this, there is little to connect Cohasset with decaying Innsmouth.

A much better candidate might be the settlement of Dogtown out on Cape Ann, near the port of Gloucester. Dogtown or Dogtown Commons is known as "Massachusetts' most famous abandoned village" and lies between Gloucester and the town of Rockport. Indeed, during the late 18th century the main road between the two towns ran through Dogtown and all trade had to pass through the settlement. At the peak of its population from 1750 to the beginning of the 19th century, it has been estimated that there were more than 100 families living in Dogtown.

The settlement that would become known as Dogtown was established around 1693 between the colonies of Gloucester and Rockport and it was set well back on the coast, high up on easily defensible ground to protect it from both pirate and Indian attack. The ground on which it was built was rocky, and the soil was sandy and gravely—not very good for agriculture—so the settlers began to look around for other forms of commerce. They found it in the forests that were being cleared away to dispense with the cover for Indian attacks, and soon a large sawmill was established, exporting Cape Ann hardwoods as far away as England from the bay below. By the beginning of the 1700s, the entire area had been completely deforested. Lumber, mainly sturdy cordwood, was flowing through the port of Gloucester at an impressive rate. But there was a downside to this business: Although the forests had been cleared, the harsh soil that was left was not all that good for anything apart from growing weeds.

The Selectmen of Gloucester did not worry too much about this. They didn't see their future in farming, but in merchant commerce and fishing. The Selectmen had hoped to draw new families into the area, but it was some of the Gloucester families who moved beyond the Alewife Brook and took up residence in the developing town. One of the first buildings that they raised was a parish hall and though they didn't know it at the time, such a place would soon prove divisive.

A number of folks wanted to relocate the first Parish Meeting House from the town to the new settlement. In early New England, the Parish Meeting House combined spiritual, political, and practical functions for those who came to it. It was a place where the community gathered to observe both civic and religious matters. Property, sales, announcements concerning Colonial law, and even marriage bans were read there. Sometimes petty criminals were examined and tried there before the community, the heads of predatory wolves were displayed there, and in times of threat, gunpowder was often stored there while religious services were conducted around it. It was certainly central to the life of the community.

Not only was the Hall an important social venue for general and religious meetings, but similar to many New England churches, the seating arrangements within it were extremely important for establishing social status. Seating was laid out so that the community leaders would always sit at the front and a gradual diminution in social status ran all the way to the back of the Hall. There was a pre-specified seating plan drawn up by a Parish Committee that reflected age, wealth, lineage, public service, and Godliness.

However, the new Parish Meeting House proved to be a problem. There was a mixture of old Gloucester folk and newcomers, a number of which owned land in the new settlement and so were to be counted as relatively wealthy. Moreover, some of these newcomers were descendants of old Gloucester families and felt entitled to more prominent seating. Thus, within the new House, seating was being continually rearranged in order to satisfy local egos, but this did not prevent grumblings and disputes.

The newcomers decided that the new House was theirs and that they would assume predominant status there. They had been responsible for building up the new community, so it was only right that they should have full status in the new Hall. The old families whose rank had been assured by their lineage, spirituality, and service to the community suddenly found themselves marginalized, and their place taken by new settlers and a rising merchant class in Gloucester. There was even an idea of actually *selling* the more prominent seats in the new House to the more prosperous merchants, thus ensuring that all construction costs were covered.

The old families fought back, however, and their protest centered around one man: Nathaniel Coit. Coit came from an old Gloucester family and was vehemently opposed to the movement to the new Meeting House where newcomers could sit on Parish Councils. He had several disputes with the harbor leaders who were aligning themselves with the newcomers, and when the new House was built he encouraged people not to attend it.

In 1734, the Parish Council voted to abandon the old Meeting House by Gloucester and move to the new one. Nathaniel Coit redoubled his efforts and for a full year the new Meeting House stood empty. Coit also petitioned to have a new Parish created, which would use the old Hall.

In May 1739, after numerous reconsiderations and resubmissions, Coit's petition was rejected by the Massachusetts legislature leading to great disruption all through the Cape. Undeterred by his setback, Coit filed another petition. In an attempt to reach some form of compromise the Court ruled that meetings could be held in the old Meeting House during the winter months and that those who wished could attend and assume their normal seats. Frustrated beyond words, the Court split the Parish, handing the old Meeting House over to Coit and his followers and the new one to the incomers and harbor folk. Coit had won a hollow victory, but he had split the entire Gloucester colony.

In 1743, Nathaniel Coit passed away at the age of 84, leaving behind a legacy of bitterness and hatred that was almost unimaginable. It was customary in many Puritan communities for local children to come and look into the open grave of the dead person to be reminded of his or her own mortality. Such was the division in Gloucester than only a small handful of children turned up at Coit's graveside. Bile and bitterness rippled through the Cape with a yawning division between many of the Gloucester folk and those in the new settlement. However, this was to change slightly with the dawn of the American Revolution.

One morning in August 1775, a British warship—the *Falcon*—appeared off Gloucester and fired a cannonade into the town. On November 1st, the Massachusetts Legislature granted "Letters of Marque," which sanctioned New England vessels to "harass and plunder" all British merchant vessels coming from the port of Boston and elsewhere. With the War now in full swing, one of Gloucester's most prominent merchants, David Pearce, began building and fitting a ship for the defense of the Mas-sachusetts coast. British warships saw the ports in New England as legitimate targets and Cape Ann was particularly exposed.

On July 1st, 1777, Pearce's ship, *The Gloucester*, sailed off to attack British ship-ping and defend the Massachusetts coast. Six weeks later, the ship's crew sailed into Gloucester harbor in command of a captured British cargo ship *The Two Friends* car-rying liquorice root, balsam, gum, and a supply of much-needed salt. The ship had been captured by the *Gloucester* on the open seas east of New York. There was even greater rejoicing when several weeks later another British trading ship, *The Spark*, sailed into Gloucester. The ship had been bound for Newfoundland, but had been taken by the *Gloucester* just off Grand Banks and sent back to Cape Ann as a prize.

On August 31st, a Captain Fisk, commanding the warship *Massachusetts* out of Boston, recorded that his vessel was leading a squadron of four Massachusetts priva-teers making their way up the New England coast, one of which was the *Gloucester*. The ship seems to have swung north to go raiding off Newfoundland, but Fisk's entry was the last record of it. Somewhere in the ocean, the *Gloucester* disappeared with all her crew.

Back in the town, women waited for news of their husbands and sweethearts. As the days passed, the apprehension grew, and strange stories began to circulate about the vanished crew—many with supernatural overtones. In one, the faces of several sailors had been seen in a well; in another a corposant (a ball of supernatural light) was said to have traveled through the settlement lingering at the door of each seaman's house in turn.

With their men gone, things were hard for the women of the settlement. And the divisions that had been created by Nathaniel Coit meant that they could not turn to some of their most prosperous neighbors in Gloucester for help. But times were hard in Cape Ann as well. English privateers were attacking American shipping and the port of Gloucester was badly hit by their exploits. Cargos were taken and boats sunk, their crews drowned. By 1779, the town had lost more than half its fleet and one sixth of its inhabitants were dependent on charity of one sort or another. There was disease and plague, particularly in the Commons, deepening old divisions even further.

In October 1780, the Revolutionary War was finally over. America had won, but it had been at a grave cost. Cape Ann had been decimated, its people reduced to near-beggary, and the Commons was all but destroyed. The Commons settlement was now living in a state of utter destitution as the poverty created by the War took hold.

To add to all of this, the social split created by Nathaniel Coit still remained as virulent as ever, and few felt inclined to help their neighbors up on higher ground. Indeed, the land beyond the Alewife Brook was considered "evil territory," which was inhabited by witches. As the area deteriorated even further, those who could afford to leave, did. Others built new houses down near the harbor and began to integrate themselves into the developing post-War Gloucester society. Some, however, had no other choice but to stay. And, as the more genteel moved out, more dubious and colorful characters began to move in.

No one knows exactly when the name "Dogtown" was first used in relation to the Commons or what it referred to. Some suggest that it may have originated from the large numbers of feral canines that roamed the area or from the fierce dogs kept by old widows for their protection. Whatever its origins, it gave the place a somewhat seedy air. The name suggests derision and a superior perspective on the part of the Gloucester folk, as well as a reason for keeping the place at arm's length.

For the most part, the people who lived in Dogtown were not foreigners, but descendents of the "Old Commons" people who had originally founded the town back in 1693. Perhaps their relative isolation from mainstream society made them appear colorful and eccentric.

Could a place like Dogtown have somehow served as a template for shadowy, decaying Innsmouth? Could Lovecraft have somehow known about the dismal settlement and used it as the model for several of the gloomy places about which he wrote? After all, places like Dogtown would certainly have exercised a fascination on his imagination.

WHERE HUMAN PATHWAYS END
IREM

Shrouded in myth and legend, the grim walls of Irem, City of a Thousand Pillars, are said to rise above the sands somewhere in the depths of the Arabian deserts. Irem is a hideous and shadowy place, mentioned in both the *Necronomicon* and in a version of the Koran. As with a number of these ancient references, the text states that Irem was destroyed because of its inhabitants' sins. For many centuries, only ghouls and afreets prowled its gloomy streets, so when the scribe Abdul Alhazred visited its haunted precincts, what he saw maddened his mind. Irem is sometimes referred to in other texts as "the Nameless City," although this epithet may also refer to a number of other Mythos cities.

Tales concerning the origins of Irem are conflicting and drift in and out of Arabian myths. One, for example, tells of two brothers, Shaddad and Shaddid, who were joint rulers of the great city of Ad. Shaddid died and was taken up into Heaven by Allah. However, his brother, who was perhaps the more egotistical of the two, decided that he would build a massive palace on earth in order to commemorate him. He gave orders to build a great city and garden complex in the deserts of Aden and named the place Iram, after his grandfather Aram. This, he said, would serve as a memorial both to his brother and his family, and would rival anything that Allah could create.

When the city was completed, Shaddad set out with his entire retinue to view the marvel. However, as they crossed the desert and drew near the city, there was a great noise from Heaven and the city sank beneath the sands, taking Shaddad and all his courtiers with it.

According to Islamic and Semitic beliefs, Shaddad was indeed an ancient king of the city of Ad, during whose reign there was great prosperity. The monarch was said to be a direct descendant of Shem, one of the sons of Noah who had been spared in the Great Flood. During Shaddad's reign, lofty temples and citadels were built and the king began to count himself greater than any god. The prophet Hud warned Shaddad not to become too proud, for Allah could take vengeance on him, but the vain king did not listen.

It is said that in some distant time King Shaddad subdued a number of Adanite tribes and ruled over them, extending his reign on to modern-day Iraq. He commissioned many lavish buildings and the story of Irem can be found in the 277th through the 279th nights of the *One Thousand and One Nights*. The location of the city was given as being in the Rub-el-Kali (the Empty Quarter) down on the Arabian Gulf.

However, just to confuse matters slightly, some variants of the legend describe the actual builders of Irem, the Ahd-al-Jin, as a race of giants and Shaddad as their king.

They then inhabited the city and gave themselves over to wicked practices, which an outraged Allah swiftly punished by destroying the city. This story is gathered from the fragmentary writings of the Muquarrabun (the legendary Ghost Priests of the Bedouin) who date its construction back to before the Flood. The clue, they say, can be found in its name "City of the Pillars." The ancient Arabic word for *pillar* can also be translated as "Old One" giving it a meaning of "city of the Old Ones." Normally this is taken to mean the djinn or the Ahd-al-Jin, but could it also suggest that Lovecraft might have known this and incorporated the idea of the ancient city along with the Mythos notion of the Great Old Ones.

There are, however, other tales concerning the city's destruction. Some describe a descent of creatures from the sky, which killed off or drove away many of the city's inhabitants. Other legends say that Irem was built by the followers of Shudde-M'ell, a Great Old One and leader of a cult of worm entities that dwelt underground The being was worshipped in ancient Stygia under the name of Shuddam-El. Following the end of that age, it is thought that the worship was transferred to Egypt and the Middle East, where it inspired the worship of the serpent-god Apophis. Initially, the entity was trapped by a combination of Elder Signs, but throughout the years, earthquakes and other cataclysms have rendered these useless and Shuddam-El freed Itself. It is possible that a massive city was raised in Its honor on the Arabian Gulf and that it was destroyed by an attack of the sky-creatures, which are opposed to the Great Old One. Other accounts say that the city was destroyed by the being Itself when Its worshippers ignored Its commands.

The most common fable is that Irem was built by the djinn. These were creatures of light and smoke who had great power. Irem, it is thought, was built in the reign of King Solomon around 967 B.C. Solomon, of course, was considered to be an extremely wise king who accumulated a vast amount of arcane and occult lore and, using a combination of signs and magic, was able to control the djinn that lived in the deserts. Many years earlier, however, they built the mighty city of Irem, which they raised against the Israelite king. Here, they worshiped the god Moloch, a barbaric entity that demanded human children as sacrifice.

Solomon was able to defeat the djinn, using a combination of guile and magical powers, and with Yahweh's help, destroyed their mighty citadel. However, some of the beings remained within the city and, according to the writings of the Muquarrabun, the area where Irem stood still forms a gateway to the spirit world of the djinn.

It is said that Abdul Alhazred opened the first gate between the ruins of Irem and the world beyond in order to allow the minions of the Great Old One to inhabit the fallen city. In his writings, Ludvig Prinn placed the beginnings of the worm-entity cult among the tumbled stones. Other texts suggest that an inhuman Supreme One dwelling among the ruins is somehow mystically linked to the Cthulhu and sends out telepathic messages to Its followers across the world.

According to Lovecraft scholars, the gateway into the ruined city bears a curious symbol on its lintel. It supposedly depicts a gigantic open hand reaching for an artifact known as the Silver Key. A legend states that if the hand were ever to clasp that Key, the city would be instantly destroyed. There are some who say that the Key is symbolic and suggests of a much older legend concerning the witch I'thakuah, who is supposedly imprisoned in caverns far beneath the ruined city. The witch possesses a great deal of arcane lore and, in past times, seekers of occult knowledge tried to locate her and release her in order to gain some of that wisdom. However, should she be released and brought to the surface, she will immediately destroy the world. The Key is therefore symbolic of the knowledge that the individual may gain at the hand of destruction wrought by I'thakuah.

A similar symbol can be found on the keystone of the outer and inner arches at the Gate of Justice in Alhambra of Granada, Spain. On the outer arch the likeness of an open hand has been incised into the stone whereas on the inside, just above the inner arch, is a key. The legend states that the Alhambra will not fall until the key has been grasped by the hand. No one knows the source of the legend or who might have carved the hand or the key. A nearby inscription states that the entrance tower was built in 1348 by Yussef I, one of the Nasrid Sultans of Granada. There has been much speculation as to what these two symbols mean. Many have made religious connections—Yussef was a very devout man—speculating that the hand symbolizes the five precepts of Islam, whereas the key is suggestive of the Keys of Paradise given to the Prophet by Allah. No matter what, its symbolism was transferred to the lintel above the main gateway in Irem. Could there possibly be a connection?

Nevertheless, confusion reigns around Irem. Although it is referred to by some writers as the Nameless City, others have suggested that the latter is a completely different site. This city does not lie in the Rub-el-Kali, but still on the Arabian Gulf near Hadramaut. The region is nicknamed Amar bin Qhatan, which means "the court of death" or, more literally, "death has come." It was also a region that was connected with Hazarmarveth (whose name means "court of death") and his tribe. Hazarmarveth was one of the sons of Joktan who was a descendant of Shem in a text known as the *Table of the Sons of Noah*, which listed the various ages of Mankind from the time of the Flood.

It was said that at one time the city lay beneath the sea, but a great buckling of the Earth's crust pushed it to the surface. Amid the ruins, a species of reptilian humanoid—possibly related to the Deep Ones or some of the serpent races—had made it home. Although these beings had great power under the ocean, this power began to dwindle on land and under the sun; the number of the beings decreased significantly. Nevertheless, the civilization that they created among the ruins of the Nameless City was highly advanced, and combined both magical and technological elements. They created a forest atmosphere between the ocean and the desert. However, a second great cataclysm struck the area, destroying the city and forcing the remnants of the civilization to live underground.

Following the great disaster, humans began to appear in the Middle East and built the city of Irem not far away. The reptile creatures emerged from the underground lairs and attacked and fed on some of them, as well as initiating cults among Humankind, which corrupted and debased the human race. The people of Irem rose up and tried to destroy the cults, but had little success. In the end, a massive conflict broke out between the reptile people and the dwellers in Irem with the human city being all but destroyed.

As Irem lay in ruins, the remaining reptiles withdrew further into the earth and down to their deepest temple caverns, thus effectively abandoning the Nameless City. Somewhere down in the dark, they hoped to find the underground Paradise that their gods promised, but found nothing. Only a few of their kind remained in the empty streets of the city, fighting with any survivors from Irem that they came across. Today, the Nameless City is more or less empty, and is largely shunned by all humans including the Bedouin, who sometimes pass through the region.

Some writers state that it was not Irem that Abdul Alhazred visited when he traveled from Sana'a in Yemen, but the Nameless City, and that it is actually the place he writes about in the *Necronomicon*. It is not exactly clear *how* Alhazred actually *visited* the Nameless City since, according to most Mythos writers, it lies *underneath* Irem so he could have visited both at once. However, descriptions from Lovecraft's own work seem to suggest a different location for the Nameless City. Professor Laban Shrewsbury has suggested that Alhazred may not in fact be dead, but still living somewhere in either Irem or the Nameless City; his "death" in Damascus could have been an illusion created by the Great Old Ones. Shrewsbury also suggested that the mad Arab's influence could still be felt in the world today, spreading out from either sunken Irem or the Nameless City like tentacles, especially in the tumultuous affairs of the Middle East.

Part of that baleful influence might be carried out through the dreadful Lamp of Alhazarad. Although very little is known about this particular artifact, it is thought to be a lamp-like object that was created by the Ad-al-Jinn (or by the djinn themselves), who originally built Irem and constructed the Lamp at the same time. For a while, the device was in the hands of Abdul Alhazred, but it has passed through various owners. The last known owner was the Providence author Ward Phillips, who mysteriously disappeared after acquiring it. What became of the Lamp after that is unknown, but it may have been disposed of among the other items at the Phillips estate. According to legend, when filled and lit, the Lamp will act in a somewhat similar fashion to the Glass from Leng. The Lamp will project a scene of a Mythos-related location upon walls and solid surfaces when activated, though the viewer cannot choose which location he or she wishes to see. This may also function as a gateway at various times although the images are so uncertain that it cannot be relied on.

The Lamp of Alhazarad is strongly connected with the ruins of Irem, and it is though that the mad Arab brought it back from somewhere in those shadowed streets.

Too much exposure to its light can, however, drive an individual insane and can distort reality to such an extent that it is difficult to tell dreams from the everyday world.

Irem Inspirations

Certainly there are a number of stories from the Middle East concerning Arab cities that have been overwhelmed by disasters, such as great sandstorms or the sea flooding coastal towns. Two of the most famous ancient cities are Sodom and Gomorrah, which are said to lie somewhere under the Dead Sea. Similar to Irem, they were supposedly destroyed by God because of the intense wickedness and unnatural practices of their inhabitants. For example, in Sodom, it was said that homosexuality was widespread and was openly practiced; this forms the derivation of our modern word *sodomy*. Licentiousness also prevailed and, when God rained down fire and brimstone upon them, it served as a warning to obey God's laws. Only one righteous man named Lot was spared, but his wife was allegedly transformed into a pillar of salt for looking back at the destruction. Although certainly mentioned in the Bible and in certain Islamic traditions, there had been much debate among academics as to whether either Sodom or Gomorrah actually existed. There seems to be little evidence for their existence, and any that has been produced is open to question.

A more concrete suggestion for Irem's model is the ancient Syrian city of Ebla (the name means "white rock," as it is built on a limestone outcropping). The location of this site lies some 34 miles southwest of Aleppo, and the ruined city itself dates from around 1800 to 1650 B.C.). From these ruins, certain cuneiform texts written on clay tablets, known as the Ebla Tablets, have been found; they are written in an unknown language that bares a close resemblance to Sumerian. The tablets give trading receipts and accounts of some of the other races in the area and the king lists for the city of Ebla, which was an important commercial center. Many of the tablets also included Sumerian inscriptions. Among the texts are civil edicts and treaties, and they serve to give a picture of life in the ancient city.

Ebla was excavated around 1964 by Italian archaeologists from the University of Rome La Sapienza under the direction of Paolo Matthiae; apart from the Tablets, they unearthed a number of statuettes and other items that seem to establish Ebla as a trading city and link it strongly with southern Mesopotamia. The city may have been destroyed around 2240 B.C. by the Akkadian armies of Sargon the Great, a conqueror of Mesopotamia. After this physical destruction, Ebla managed to recover slightly, but it could not recover its former grandeur or importance. Its inhabitants were now described as "Amorites," who attached less significance to the site's development and allowed it to dwindle to the status of a village. In 1750 B.C. it was destroyed once again by a Hittite king (either Mursili I or Hattusili I) and it never recovered. It struggled on as a village, but it was eventually abandoned and allowed to sink beneath the desert sands.

The strongest contender as a model for Irem, however, was the vanished city of Ubar, located in the Empty Quarter. Ubar was an extremely wealthy metropolis that lay on a major trading route, the Frankincense Road, between the desert kingdoms and the sea. It was through records found in the Ebla ruins that scholars knew of Ubar as an important trade center. Besides the tablets, Ebla also maintained a large and extensive library relating to trading matters, and there is little doubt that Ebla traded with Ubar along the Frankincense Road, and refers to it from time to time as Iruma. It also refers to it as a City of Pillars—although in this case, the word *pillar* is taken to mean "tower," thus meaning that Ubar was well fortified. It would have to be, as large bands of marauding bandits often attacked the overland caravans bearing spices from other lands—including frankincense. Such groups also attacked desert towns and forts along the road. Such towers were not only there to protect the city, but also to afford protection to incoming camel trains. Altogether, Ubar was regarded as a place of inordinate wealth and culture throughout the Arabic and Asian worlds.

Around A.D. 1,000 all references to Ubar suddenly stopped, as if the city had just disappeared into thin air. Many theories abounded—the most common being that the entire city had been swallowed up in a natural disaster or its population had been slaughtered by bandit armies. There were some legends, however, that Ubar had been swallowed up by the earth and this actually turned out to be true.

For a long time, Ubar remained no more than an intriguing myth and no one actually knew how it fell. In 1984, however, the orbital Challenger satellite, which was monitoring the old Middle East spice routs as part of a historical program, picked out what appeared to be the remnants of an old road system, seemingly designed for the camel trains in southern Oman. X-ray scanning revealed that the surrounding area was actually the roof of a huge underground limestone cavern, filled with a subterranean lake that had acted as a water table for a city that had seemingly been built above it. As the inhabitants from the city above drew water from the lake through a series of wells, the water table in the cavern had lowered considerably. Deprived of its buoyant support, the roof of the cavern had weakened considerably and had collapsed, swallowing the city above. The gaping abyss was eventually covered by the encroaching desert. Challenger also picked out what looked like the ruins of other former cities along the Frankincense Road, some of which dated back to 2800 B.C. The date of Ubar's destruction is estimated at around A.D. 500 or even slightly later, which would appear to tie in with the disappearance of references to it.

According to tradition and legend, the area around where Ubar had once stood was also believed to be the center of a mysterious and secret branch of Islam, which is only to be found in small pockets in Algeria and Libya. This was *Ibadism*, which is a form of Islamic teaching historically distinct from either Sunni or Sh'ia factions. It takes its name from Abdullah Ibn Ibad at Timini who was a prophet less than 50 years after the death of Mohammed. Rumor has it that it is an extremely strict Islamic sect that regards both Sunni and Sh'ia as kuffar (unbelievers or "those who deny God's grace"). It also has a distinct mystical edge to it. It is said that at one time, this Islamic tradition was only to be found in Oman, and that it was centered on the site where

Ubar once stood. There is no doubt that the Frankincense Road into Asia brought teachings and ideas into the city from further East.

However, in the southern deserts of Jordan, the wind blows endlessly across the empty plains, stirring up whirls of sand that can rise into fierce storms. For the Bedouin who live here, this is the breath of the *djinn* and the forces of another world trying to impinge upon ours. The desert lands to the east of Aqaba are perhaps the most mysterious in the Middle East. Bedouin tribes wander across seemingly infinite emptiness, making the same trek as numerous ancient civilizations that have come and gone here. The most eerie and mysterious of all places in these deserts is Wadi Rum, a remote valley boasting a spectacular outcropping of rock, lying about 60 kilometres to the east of Aqaba. Also known as the Valley of the Moon, this depression is the largest in all of Jordan. It has been suggested that the name *Rum* comes from the ancient Aramaic meaning "high or elevated." The highest point in this region is Mount Um Dami which rises 1,800 feet above sea level. One section of its wall, particularly favored by rock-climbers, is the towering Jebel Rum, which is said to be the highest in Jordan.

There is no doubt that Wadi Rum is a special and a mystical place. Local fugara (Bedouin healers and sorcerers) as well as the muquarribun (Ghost Priests) all claim that ancient forces from the very dawn of time are still active there.

The rock formation itself, say the Ghost Priests, is all that is left of an unnamed city that had been built by the djinn. This was a terrible but magnificent place where the very stones were magical and contained formidable powers in their own right.

When and how this monstrous city was destroyed is unclear. Some legends say that the djinn caliphs became so powerful that they rose in rebellion against Allah and, in retaliation, their citadel was turned to stone. Other traditions say that the djinn made war against King Solomon and he called upon Yahweh to destroy their entire city. It is said that carved somewhere within the winding canyons of Wadi Rum are the words that Allah used in order to turn the city to stone. Among certain Middle Eastern Christian traditions of the region it is said that the Antichrist will come to Wadi Rum and supernaturally remove these words of power, and when he does, the djinn city will exist again.

The City of a Thousand Pillars remains an intriguing enigma. Does this dreadful metropolis actually lie somewhere out there in the emptiness of the Rub-el-Kali, perhaps under the drifting sands? And do strange and incredibly ancient energies still crack and fizzle there, driving any visitor to the region insane?

WHERE HUMAN PATHWAYS END

LENG

Leng is a curious place, existing both in our own world and in Lovecraft's Dreamlands. For some Mythos writers, it lies somewhere beyond Kadath in the Cold Waste in the Realms of Dream; for others, its location in the waking world is more problematic. It is possible that the name *Leng* is derived from the Kingdom of Ling, which appears in the *Epic of King Gesar,* a 12th-century Mongolian epic poem scholars occasionally associate Ling with Tibet, and have argued that Gesar (an actual historical figure), was born there around 1027. However, others argue that the epic is even older, and Ling is a remote province on the edge of Tibet, which Gesar ruled during the seventh century.

Like many other locations in the Mythos, the site of Leng can sometimes shift within the real world. Some writers place it in Central Asia (it is even named as a part of China's Xinjiang Province). Others locate it in frozen Antarctica or in a mountain range somewhere in Burma; further references link it to a remote area somewhere in Syria or Yemen. In the *Necronomicon*, Abdul Alhazred speaks of a place where a number of alternate realities come together, so perhaps that explains its shifting location.

The first mention of the dreaded plateau is made in Lovecraft's *The Hound* (written in 1922), which places it in Central Asia as a corpse-eating cult. It appears again in the 1926 tale *The Dream-Quest of Unknown Kadath*, which places it firmly in the Dreamlands. It is inhabited by a Nameless Priest and a race of degenerate beings whom all other men fear. In Lovecraft's novella *At the Mountains of Madness*, the Peabody Expedition to Antarctica found the ruins of the monstrous city somewhere near the South Pole. The story was submitted to *Weird Tales*, but it was rejected by Farnsworth Wright on grounds of length. It was subsequently published in two parts in the March-April 1936 issues of *Astounding Stories*. There is a suggestion in the story—although it is never explicitly stated—that the city actually *is* Leng or that it has a direct connection with it. Other writers and game-players, including Stephen King, Marion Zimmer Bradley, Kim Newman, and Robert Shea have all mentioned Leng, but all give different locations for it or no location at all.

Regarding the description of Leng and what lies there, opinions vary widely, but all of them suggest that it is a place to be avoided by the unprepared traveler. For some writers, a great and bleak monastery of black stone lies at its very heart; for others, there are a number of villages built of curious materials and it is inhabited by a ferocious species with cloven hooves and horns; others describe it as the location of a corpse-eating cult that worship a great, winged hound. For some, it is a bleak and barren place where night reigns continually, inhabited by beings who move in the eternal darkness and wear loose-fitting white robes in order to conceal their true shape. These beings worship in a circle of monoliths that seems to be the only relief on their barren Plateau.

There is also a lighthouse or beacon of some sort on the very edge of the plateau, which sends out a fearful light over the surrounding lands. In some accounts, it is situated close to the dark monastery and is manned by the monks; on the walls of the twisting and interconnecting corridors the ghastly history of the Plateau is displayed. At the heart of the building sits a High Priest who is not human.

The dark stone monastery supposedly lies at the very heart of the Plateau and is both a formidable and forbidding building. It is perhaps based upon the isolated upland Buddhist monasteries of Tibet, such as the Shari and Tsigortang Lamaseries, of the country's Kham region. Some of these were supposedly held by obscure orders of monks. The interior of the Leng monastery was a labyrinth of twisting passages and stone chambers in which a person could get lost and wander for eternity. At the center of this was a large chamber in which the High Priest sat. Its servitors (the monks) may be partially human in nature, but they come from the Plateau and the High Priest communicates with them by playing a series of reedy flutes. No description of the High Priest really exists, except that It wears voluminous robes that conceal Its true shape and a yellow veil over Its face so that It can't be seen. The paws with which It holds Its flutes, however, are furry and look nothing like human hands. To look on the countenance of this High Priest would drive a sane person mad.

However, a number of speculations about this High Priest exist. One is that It is a manifestation of the King in Yellow and an association of Nyarlatothep. Another is that It is some form of Moon Beast.

The Moon Beasts are a species of creature that are specific to the huge moon that hangs over the Dreamlands. They are slippery white toad-like beings whose pink internal organs often protrude through their flat snouts. Akin to the High Priest of Leng, they also communicate with each other by playing flutes. Although they can live on the lighter side of the moon, they prefer to live on the dark side which, unlike our own planet, contains forests and oily oceans, which give them an ideal habitat. Among huge frond-like plants, they built huge metropolises, which they can visit in large black galleons, composed of a mysterious materiel that has the ability to fly through space. Many of these are used for transporting slaves to their moon, although they also maintain a colony in the Dreamlands that serves as a base for their piratical raids.

The people of the Dreamlands find the Moon Beasts abhorrent and will take little to do with them. Therefore, much of the commerce between the Dreamlands and their moon goes through Leng, using other slave races as intermediaries. Most of these can pass for humans by being properly attired or by using magical amulets to transform their appearance to some extent. In the Dreamlands, the Moon Beasts also maintain mines from which they export rubies back to the moon. To do this, they must employ human slaves, as the handling of rubies in their raw state is harmful to them. They are further allied with cat-like beings from Saturn who serve Nyarlatothep and Mnaomquah (a Dreamlands god that takes the form of a large bipedal saurian).

Because It communicates through a series of flutes, the High Priest has been linked with these creatures and may actually be one of them. If It is, then perhaps it is a mutated version, as It clearly displays a subtlety that is beyond the range and intelligence of most of them. Others say It is one of the Tcho-Tcho people who inhabit the lower slopes of the Plateau; indeed, the High Priest is sometimes referred to as the Tcho-Tcho Lama of Leng, or the Elder Hierophant.

The writer and occultist Kenneth Grant has suggested that the High Priest might be a manifestation of Lam, whom he describes as one of the Great Old Ones. Lam, a being with a bulbous forehead, slanted eyes, and a small mouth, is depicted in some of Aleister Crowley's paintings and Grant has linked this not only to the Mythos in the form of the High Priest, but also to the occupants of flying saucers.

There is also a black stone tower that is situated somewhere near the center of Leng, which acts as a kind of lighthouse. It is known as the Pharos of Leng, taking its name from the ancient lighthouse at Alexandria built on the island of Pharos between 280 and 247 B.C. It also contains overtones of the Pharos of Abusir, which was an ancient funerary marker. The Pharos of Leng emits a strange bluish light that can be seen for miles beyond the Plateau. It is said that the Great Old One Nyogtha (a vampiric creature that appears as a dark and amorphous mass and feeds on souls). The *Necronomicon* states that the Pharos will actually give the signal for the Great Old Ones to return to Earth, but that this will only happen when Humankind has been cleared off. In the meantime, its baleful light sweeps our over the darkened land below.

Artifacts of Leng

Also known as the Jade Hound, this talisman made of green jade is the emblem of cannibals and corpse-eaters in Leng. The Amulet of the Hound is supposedly the most tangible connection between the ghastly Plateau of Leng and the outside world.

The Hounds of Tindalos are supposedly interdimensional creatures that prowl the spaces between the various universes and can exist in any form of reality they choose, whether it be the past, the present, or the future. They sometimes resemble large, green, hairless dogs with blue, lolling tongues, but they can also appear as black, formless shadows. They dwell in the city of Tindalos, a place of twisting architecture and corkscrew towers. Sometimes the Hounds can leave the environs of this place in order to hunt down prey, which may be designated to them by their mysterious masters.

The Hounds are the very embodiment of foulness, but they lust after something that is to be found in humans and will hunt them down relentlessly. They are said to be the prototypes of many legends and beliefs concerning demons. An ancient text known as *The Black Tome of Alsophocus* suggests that the Hounds may have been guardians of the Shining Trapezohedron, which may have been in Tindalos. However, Humanity somehow won it away from them and absorbed some of its purer aspects, leaving the Hounds to their own foulness. Therefore, they hate all forms of goodly life and seek to destroy it at any given opportunity.

Motions either in the fabric of space or time invariably attracts the Hounds attention. Once the "scent" of some traveler has been detected the creatures will not give up, but will follow their victim through all worlds and through all ages until they can destroy the unfortunate. They have the ability to *angle* time and space, creating strange corners through which they can pass without too much effort. The occultist Halpin Chalmers was able to measure such angles using some mathematical formula, which he found on some ancient porcelain cylinders. The cylinders supposedly came from Hyperborea, so he changed the angles in order to prevent the creatures from coming through into our world. However, one area of our reality through which they *can* enter is Leng.

When they have been within our own world, the Hounds' leave a bluish slime, which they secrete on entry. An analysis of this slime reveals that the Hounds have no enzymes in their bodies. This may mean that it is impossible to destroy the Hounds; there is certainly no record of one ever being killed.

The Hounds are considered to be the spawn of Noth-Yidik and K'thun, two beings who have a repellent appearance and give off a repulsive odor. Neither has ever been fully described. They are thought, however, to have mated somewhere within the vicinity of Tindalos and produced the Hounds, which may also be somehow linked to Azathoth. There is also some connection to Yog-Sothoth, although this may simply consist of the Hounds' unassuaged enmity toward that entity.

Their main contact with our own world is through the Amulet of the Hound, which has come here through Leng. The cult members who dwell on Leng are powerful magicians who increase their powers through the number of corpses or victims that they devour, hence the cannibalism. Some sources say that the Amulet actually *protects* the individual from the Hounds, as they continually prowl the edges of our reality around the Plateau. Several images of the Amulet exist, and some stories concerning it relate to their acquisition by individuals who are then destroyed by the Hounds.

Like the Plateau of Leng, these ancient artifacts may exist in both our own world and also in the Dreamlands. In our world, The Brick Cylinders of Kadatheron refer to seven circular objects made of a curious material resembling brick, covered in an unknown writing. These were found in the Syrian deserts in 1929 by Norwegian explorer

Per Angstrom. Taken to the British Museum, an attempt was made to translate them using the late Gordon Walmsley's work on ancient cryptograms; the characters were so archaic that only fragments of them could be deciphered. They are currently held within the museum where they are still consulted by academics set on translating them, although another set is held in the Dreamlands city of Kadatheron where they are objects of worship.

What has been translated from the cylinders is a part of history relating to the vanished land of Mnar and the pre-human city of Ib. But mention is also made of of Leng, the monastery there, and the High Priest who dwells there. There seems to be much relating to sigils and dismissal procedures for various entities, and also a fragmentary tale of the wizard Ilathos, who traveled to Leng in order to consult with the High Priest and to learn the secret of the Sarnath-sigil. Part of the translated text seems to be a history of the Dynasties of Kadatheron, and several of these appear to be linked with Leng, although the cylinder-text does not disclose how this linkage might actually occur. Could the rulers of Kadatheron also be the monarchs of Leng?

As mysterious as the Hounds and the Amulet are, more mystery surrounds The Glass From Leng. It is not clear whether it is a single prism of glass or more than one piece. The Glass is a cloudy type that is not found on either Earth or in the Dreamlands, but it came down to the Plateau from the distant Hyades. The Glass is kept in the monastery of dark stone in the very center of the Plateau. To be effective, the Glass must be mounted in either a frame or a window. If the owner desires to use it, he or she should draw a pentagram in red chalk on the ground or floor in front of it and sit within it. He or she must then say the words: "Ph-nglui mglw'nath Cthulhu R'lyeh wgah'nagl fhtagn." At this point, the Glass will become clear and will reveal a scene of special significance to the Mythos, although the meaning of the vision will not always be obvious. However, use of the Glass must be sparing, because it can sometimes form a portal through which the entities can pass through the magical gateway. The Glass From Leng could also be forged into a moon-lens for use in the worship of Shub-Niggurath.

It is said that in the darkness of the monastery atop the Plateau of Leng, the High Priest sits on a dark throne with the Glass From Leng mounted in front of It in a dark onyx frame and views other worlds and other times as It sees fit, meditating on what it sees. Sometimes, It will even supernaturally intervene in some of the events that It witnesses. There is also a fragment of the Glass, mounted on a high pylon-like structure in the very center of the village of Goatswood, England, and this may enable Shub-Niggurath to manifest Itself to Its followers at any time of the year. As it may be surmised, the Glass From Leng is a fabled substance and must be handled carefully. Its use is certainly not for the novice or inept magician.

The Black Lotus

Central to worship on Leng is the ingestion of a powdered black lotus, which is only grown on the Plateau. The name refers to an ebony-hued flower, which was originally grown in Khitai in Hyperborea. In Khitai, only the priests of the mysterious god Yam were allowed to harvest it. Its scent had the ability to induce slumber in the most ferocious beast, but also to madden the human brain. The only ones who used the flower were a cult of black sorcerers and necromancers known as the Black Ring for the purposes of mind control.

At the end of the Hyperborean Age, the flower was taken to the Plateau of Leng where it grew readily. It was harvested by monks of forgotten religious orders, and legend says the dust of the black lotus was used as the basis of a poison used to kill the Buddha. By the rule of the Great Khans (the 12th and 13th centuries) the notion of the Black Lotus had become so powerful that several attempts were made to ban its use, and anyone found with it was executed. However, its use continued throughout the centuries and it may even be in use even today.

The essence of the Black Lotus in modern times takes the form of Liao, also known as the Plutonian Drug. It takes its name from a medieval Chinese chemist named Liao, who discovered a formula for creating the substance. He used it in various forms of worship and eventually the drug traveled into the lands of the Saracens. While being held in a Saracene prison, Ludvig Prinn learned of the substance from his teacher, the magician Emendid Kejir, and subsequently the recipe is found in the pages of Prinn's work *De Vermis Mysteriis*.

The drug allows the person who ingests it to perceive the past, usually from the perspective of someone or something that exists there. The higher the dosage, the further back along the evolutionary path one can go. However, the user should be careful, as entities in the past can sometimes attach themselves to the mind of an individual and return with them to the present.

Monastery Influences

One of the central features of the Plateau of Leng is the dark and labyrinthine monastery, supposedly located somewhere near its center. But could such a place be based on a real place about which Lovecraft might have heard? The candidates for this location must lie in Tibet. Here, scores of small monasteries and Buddhist holy houses lie tucked away in remote valleys and almost-inaccessible peaks.

One monastery in particular is the Lamasery of Paro Taktsang (also known as "the Tiger's Nest"), which stands on the edge of a cliff in the Himalayas within the confines of the Kingdom of Bhutan. This rather elegant structure was built in 1692

around a cave where the great Guru Padmasambhava (the Guru Rimpoche) meditated for three months during the eighth century. It is said that while he meditated,
the Guru was assailed by (and communicated with) the ancient spirits of the air, from
whom he learned many arcane things. The Guru was considered to be a supernatural
figure himself—legend said that he had come to Paro Taktsang riding on the back of
a tiger—hence the name of the monastery.

Another candidate may be an unnamed monastery lying somewhere to the west
of the hamlet of Simiot on the Nepalese-Tibetan border. According to accounts it
was not a Buddhist monastery, but one that followed the older Bon religion of Tibet,
which flourished under the Kingdom of Shang Shung around A.D. 667. This religious
foundation was visited around 1932 by German adventurer Franz Fischer. Fischer
recounts that there were only a small number of monks there and that the High Lama
was never seen, but that he was rumored to be over 280 years old. The monks claimed
that they held secrets that were old when the world was young, written on reed scrolls
and held in a cave library, which they refused to show to the expedition members.
Fischer and his companions stayed there only a few days before being unceremoni-
ously asked to move on.

There is perhaps one other place that might qualify as a template for the dark
monastery, although it is not really a building. In the late 1980s, Bruno Baumann
traversed part of Western Tibet in search of a place that might have been Shangri-la.
Following the guidance of an old monk, Baumann traveled along the Sutlej River to a
great amphitheatre where a number of caves were carved into the cliff and could only
be accessed by ladders. The name of this place was Yungrung Rinchin Barba Drub
Phug—the cave of the gleaming swastika (the swastika is a sacred symbol in the Bon
religion). After a day of rock-climbing, Baumann found himself in a great and ruined
city, which might have been the capital of the legendary Kingdom of Shang Shung.
The city had a "monastic look" about it and may have been some sort of metropolis.
Of course, stories of such a place had been in circulation for years—even in the previous century. Could it be that Lovecraft had heard some of these legends and incorporated them into his Mythos?

Somewhere, whether it be in a remote corner of Asia, the Dreamlands, or even in
some dark corner of the imagination, awful mists wreathe across the darkened Plateau
and lap at the walls of a dark stone monastery. What lurks within? Maybe only the
most fevered nightmares can truly tell.

WHERE HUMAN PATHWAYS END

BRICHESTER

After his death, collections of Lovecraft's stories became increasingly popular, not only all across America, but in other countries as well. Many writers around the world were inspired by the visions of the Mythos—by its arcane books, strange entities and characters, and eerie locations. It seemed natural that some non-American writers would want to create their own Mythos version or at least incorporate their own elements into Lovecraft's universe. Writers such as August Derleth, Lin Carter, and Clark Ashton Smith had already made significant additions to the Lovecraftian cosmos, but other writers also wanted to make their own contributions.

One of the foremost Mythos writers in England is Ramsey Campbell, who, as a young boy in Liverpool, became enamored with Lovecraft's fiction. At the beginning of the 1960s when he was just 15, Campbell sent several Lovecraft pastiches (all set in New England) to Arkham House Publishing, which was then owned by August Derleth. Derleth was impressed, and he wrote back telling Campbell to change the location for his stories and to write about places that he knew. Consequently, Campbell changed the geographical sites of his tales from eastern America to England, setting them in the valley of the River Severn. In many respects, the countryside that he described mirrored much of Lovecraft's own work right down to the layout of the locations. One of the elements that Campbell could draw upon here was the sense of history that pervaded the countryside, for the area had been occupied since before Roman times. Similar to Arthur Machen's Welsh hills, a sense of brooding antiquity, perhaps dating back to pre-human times, hung over the entire area, which suited Mythos fiction well.

The region is also not all that geographically accurate. In the stories, the towns seem to lie on the edge of the Cotswold Hills and the Vale of Berkeley, which are actually in Gloucestershire, well over 60 miles to the south. These, however, contained many villages, some dating back to before medieval times, and could be in with Mythos fiction. They could be adapted to resemble locations such as decaying Dunwich, Aylesbury, and Dean's Corners and, as the land around them was littered with the remnants of former peoples—standing stones, tumuli, and stone circles—they made an excellent addition to the Mythos. Campbell's first story, *The Church in the High Street*, which was published by Derleth in the 1962 Arkham House anthology *Dark Mind, Dark Heart* was, for instance, set in the Cotswold town of Temphill, where accusations of heresy and witch-burnings had been rife for hundreds of years.

Unlike Lovecraft, however, Campbell dated the events of his initial tales not in the 1920s and 1930s, but in the 1960s which was (then) a much more contemporary setting.

Although he was frequently accused of copying Lovecraft in his earlier fiction, Campbell has always argued that the landscapes of his tales probably owed more to post-World War II Merseyside, which he continually explored as a child. The austerity of the post-War period meant that large parts of Liverpool still lay in ruins from German bombing, and that sections of the city were still almost uninhabited. Deserted houses and the fallen shells of buildings, together with struggling villages in the surrounding countryside, all served to create a bleak tapestry in Campbell's mind and certainly fit conveniently into the Mythos.

Campbell followed up his Arkham House short story with a collection of similar tales entitled *The Inhabitant of the Lake and Other Less Welcome Tenants* (1964) in which he developed and expanded on the area around the Severn Valley, creating a series of eerie locations, each with their own particular histories and dangers. Perhaps stung by the criticism that his stories resembled those of Lovecraft, Campbell tried to make an effort, while maintaining Mythos fiction, to distance his own work from that of his literary hero. And yet in his 1973 collection *Demons by Daylight*, the brooding landscapes of the Severn Valley once again showed through. Periodically, Campbell has returned to this region writing tales that draw in the locations that he initially created almost as homage to Lovecraft. It might be fair to say that he has not completely freed himself from the sinister influence of the place.

In his stories, he centered his fictional world around the industrial town of Brichester, a mundane commercial town that takes the place of Lovecraft's Arkham. In a sense, Brichester can be split up into a series of locations depending on the themes in the stories. To the north lies Mercy Hill, one of the older parts of the town, which was built up with tenement housing during the Industrial Revolution. Consequently, it is still regarded as something of a squalid and "rough district" in the town, which most decent people tend to avoid. However, the Hill is characterized by the hospital on its summit, which is well away from the rough dwellings further down. It's said that young children living in the area sometimes experience fearful dreams and, from time to time, some of them vanish. For this reason, few people buy houses in the area and the population remains fairly stable. The mysterious cult leader Roland Franklyn once had his headquarters in Dee Terrace among the squalid and dilapidated houses near the bottom of the Hill. Franklyn is buried in the graveyard near Mercy Hill hospital.

The center of the town holds Brichester's commercial center. This is not a prosperous place, and many of the shops there change hands on a regular basis as local businesses fail quite rapidly. There are several large stores there, but the town center can hardly be called a thriving metropolis.

The southern end of the town is home to Brichester University. Although perhaps not as prestigious as Miskatonic, the University still boasts something of a reputation and does house some interesting artifacts. At one point, it held a partial copy of the *Revelations of Glaaki*, which had been donated there in 1958. This area is usually referred to as Lower Brichester, and parts of it are often described as being "in an advanced state of dereliction." The neighborhood certainly has a run-down feel to it and contains many of the older three-story houses of Brichester's slightly more prosperous days. The area is also the location of the Brichester Arts Lab where courses are run in "interpretative painting," which channels some of the strange dreams that are experienced in the area onto canvas. It was in Lower Brichester than an unknown individual penned the 12th chapter of the *Revelations of Glaaki.*

Lakeside Terrace and the Devil's Steps

There are two places of note just outside Brichester. The first is a large body of water that Campbell refers to in his *Inhabitant of the Lake*. According to geographers, this lake was formed in some prehistoric time by a meteor smashing into the area and may not be all that deep. On its southern shore, however, is a small row of brick houses that are considered part of Brichester Rural District under the name Lakeside Terrace. Most of them are in an advanced state of dereliction, and they were reputedly built in the early 1800s by the followers of Thomas Lee in order to worship an entity that was brought to Earth by the meteor. Although a number of these houses lie almost in ruins, a couple of them are still habitable; it was here that the painter Thomas Cartwright took up residence while he worked on his canvas *The Thing in the Lake.* There is a rumor that Cartwright's voice can still be heard crying from some unknown place on certain nights of the year.

Not far to the east lies a geological feature known as the Devil's Steps. Mentioned in the story *A Mine on Yuggoth,* these are a giant rock formation laid out in a form resembling a gigantic staircase. Local legend states that the Devil carved these out of the indigenous rock in some early time in order to view the surrounding countryside. The top is a plateau, but no one in living memory has ever climbed up to the summit on which three stone towers of unknown origin stand, connected with what appears to be some sort of narrow catwalk. All these towers appear to be windowless and the central one is 30 feet high, apparently accessed by a curiously angled doorway. The towers are surrounded by a curious grey-colored fungus, which seems to writhe and move of its own volition, especially if some creature comes near. There is no wildlife of any kind anywhere near the Devil's Steps. According to Campbell, the top of the stairs form an interdimensional gateway to the planet Yuggoth, and if anyone reaches the plateau on which the towers stand they will instantly disappear.

One other feature of the area to the east of Brichester is a promontory called Sentinel Hill, which rises from a flat area above what was possibly once low-lying bogland. It is capped with a circle of stone monoliths and may have been some sort of ritual site in prehistoric times. There could be some sort of dimensional connection with a similarly named hill near Dunwich, Massachusetts, but the link has never been fully specified.

Goatswood

Sometimes Goatswood is described as a small town with a town square, a number of shops, and a large hotel, and sometimes as little more than a village, although from accounts of the place it could also fit into the category of a hamlet. It lies almost midway between Brichester and Exham and though it can be avoided by road, it is still a regular stop on the train line from Exham.

It is thought that Goatswood grew up around a 14th-century Templar church connected to the neighboring foundation at Temphill. It is a rather gloomy place, cut off from the world by the surrounding forests, and with an air of furtiveness about it. As in Innsmouth, Goatswood's inhabitants are not all that pleasant to look at, having an almost goat-like appearance about them, and a number of them clad in "bizarre and voluminous garments," yet another echo of Lovecraft's Innsmouth. Goatswood is not a welcoming place and very few visitors stop there. In fact, the place has an extremely evil reputation for many miles around and perhaps this is why it isn't marked on some maps.

In the 17th century, a number of individuals from the village met at a clearing in the forest in order to worship a stone that had fallen from the sky. When a number of people in the surrounding countryside mysteriously vanished, nervous local clergymen called in the infamous witch-hunter Matthew Hopkins, who conducted several witch-trials in the vicinity of Goatswood. He sentenced alleged coven members to death, however, Hopkins was not able to eradicate the entire cult and descendants of the original members still reside in the region today.

Goatswood's most significant feature is the peculiar so-called Moon Lens, which is a collection of mirrors made from glass of indeterminate origin. The positioning of the lens, using what is known as the Glass From Leng, concentrates the moons rays on a certain spot, which allows the entity Shub-Niggurath to be summoned at the full of the moon instead of when it is dark.

The name *Goastwood* became famous through an anthology published by Chaosium Inc. Publishing in 1996 entitled *Made in Goastwood*. This was the first collection of tales from this haunted area, written by a number of authors that including Richard Lupoff and Robert M. Price, and it put the name of the abhorred place firmly on the role-playing map.

Temphill

Lying well to the east of Brichester on the edge of Campbell's Cotswolds is the town of Temphill. It appears in the first of Campbell's Severn Valley stories, *The Church on the High Street*, and is described as "a place of ill repute."

The town takes its name from a secret foundation of fleeing Templars, which some say was established in 1307. King Edward II of England did not follow France in arresting individual Templars until 1308, and did not commence trials against the Order until 1310. Around this time, a group of knights traveled to the area bearing certain documents and relics that they had acquired in Palestine. They tried to integrate themselves into local religious foundations, but were unsuccessful. The church in the title of the story is situated in the center of the town built on an incredibly old site, which may have been a temple to Yog-Sothoth in prehistoric times.

During the 19th century, a witchcraft cult existed in the town and, according to tradition, met in these crypts to perform abhorrent rituals. It is said that they disinterred some of the corpses buried in the nearby cemetery where they somehow reanimated them for the purposes of mating. The cult was raided and was disbanded at the beginning of the 20th century (some say that it collapsed of its own volition) although other traditions say that certain citizens of Temphill visit the catacombs below the church on certain nights of the year such as Halloween and that such awful rituals still continue. Temphill was one of the areas frequently visited by the followers of Roland Franklyn in order to take part in the queer rites there. Franklyn's widow, now apparently shut up in an insane asylum, still gibbers concerning the things she saw there when accompanying her former husband to the town.

Temphill was also the home of John Clothier, who was "possessed of incredibly ancient knowledge" and who allegedly kept a formidable library of arcane books who may have been consulted by Albert Young, a young man researching the witchcraft lore of the area. Temphill, then, seems to be the place to go to conduct an investigation into the strange and bizarre.

Clotton

In the mid-to-late 19th century, Clotton was a small but reasonably prosperous town located on the Tone River. It cannot be found on any map, nor does the place even exist beyond a few leaning red brick houses, which are all that remain of the uptown section of Clotton. Of particular interest is a large concrete pillar placed on the banks of the Tone where some of the waterfront houses and shops would have been with an "eldritch sign" crudely drawn on each one of its sides, now blurred by moss and slime. The reason for this construction is never explained to any visitor, nor is there any sign that marks the place of any interest; it is noted that a foul, stagnant, reptilian smell perpetually hangs over the general area and seems to be centered on this concrete pillar.

The story of the town appears in Campbell's Dunwich pastiche *The Horror From the Bridge*, which appeared in the 1964 collection *The Inhabitant of the Lake and Other Less Welcome Tenants*. According to the manuscript, in the early 1800s a strange figure came to Clotton and took up residence in Riverside Alley—one of the place's less-prosperous districts. The street contained few inhabited houses and had a direct view of an old bridge over the Tone. The people of Clotton made some enquiries and found out that he was James Phipps. An unorthodox scientist, he came from nearby Camside because the people there found his so-called "experiments" rather distasteful. He was a gaunt, pallid man with long bony hands who kept to himself. At this time, Clotton had its own witch-hunter, Reverend Jenner, who quickly denounced Phipps and his alleged work. People noticed strange packages and materials being carried into his house by two furtive-looking rustics and were quick to confirm Jenner's opinion. One of the men slipped and the covering of one item fell, revealing a statue of some sort. Word soon spread that it was some sort of pagan idol. Phipps was incandescent with rage at this mishap and stopped short of beating the workman concerned.

Shortly after his arrival, Phipps began to haunt the taverns along the waterfront, although he never drank anything. His purpose was to speak to the more disreputable locals regarding old tales in the area. He listened attentively to stories about witchcraft and strange worship, but seemed particularly interested in legends of a demon lurking somewhere in the neighborhood, and even more so with a tale about number of ancient creatures entombed in a large underground city not far away. He was particularly fascinated by the thought that at least some of these creatures could be released by removing some sort of imprisoning sigil that held them underground. Those who provided him with this information were handsomely rewarded, and some even asked if they might send their children to him for instruction in science; this request was declined.

After a short while, Phipps mysteriously disappeared from Clotton in the spring of 1805, returning at the end of the year. This time he was not alone, for he brought a woman—a strange, silent, pallid being, who walked rather oddly—who he claimed was his wife. He said she was a Temphill woman whom he had met when he went there to procure some extremely rare chemicals. The pair kept to themselves but, late in 1806, a child was born in the dark house. Although the infant boy was born during a thunderstorm, it was noted that many of the thunderings and grumblings associated with the weather seemed to come from *under* the ground.

They named the child Lionel, and he grew up to be a strange boy much given to visions and voices from nowhere. Around 1822, when he would have been around 17 or 18, his father began to instruct him in the strange and occult sciences. Anyone who cared to peer in at the windows often saw them both poring over some ancient tome. In addition to this, both of them seemed to take an undue interest in the ancient bridge that could be seen from their house. They made several nocturnal visits to it and were seen exploring the banks of the river that flowed beneath it. Then, strangers started to call at the house, and they were there for long periods.

While searching Clotton for an escaped inmate of a local prison in 1825, a policeman had occasion to enter Phipps's house and explore the cellar. He found strange things in a glass tank and a door covered in queer symbols, which seemed to open directly onto the river, but *underwater*. He investigated further, but something happened and he became aware of some sort of entity nearby, which tried to attack him. He remembered nothing more until he was found by the roadside by other searchers, covered in some sort of slime. The story only increased local fear of the strange man and his son, and people avoided Riverside Alley as much as they could.

When James Phipps died in 1898, it was the start of the small town's problems. Lionel became extremely wild in his ways, and shouts and screams from the house in the Alley were heard. Curiously, nothing was ever heard of Phipps's funeral and it was assumed that the body might be still in the building. A neighbour named Mary Allen, whose property adjoined the dark building, heard Lionel and his mother arguing and using names and concepts that she could not understand. They seemed to be referring to the *Necronomicon* and the *Book of Eibon*, together with the position of certain stars in relation to Fomalhaut. In the end, the mother left and tried to return to Temphill—although a skeleton resembling her features was found along the road outside Clotton. Now Lionel began showing an even greater interest in the bridge and the stars and made frequent trips to the Library of the British Museum in London in order to consult certain books there. In 1900, he confided in the librarian,

Philip Chesterton, that he was using certain incantations that he had found in their pages, but he wasn't sure if he was using the right one. Alarmed by what he heard, Chesterton decided to make his own investigations. Whatever he discovered during his snooping terrified him so much that he resigned from the British Museum and moved to Bold Street in Brichester, taking up a position as a librarian in Brichester University.

For 30 years, nothing really happened. Then in 1931, Lionel Phipps managed to raise something from beneath the waters of the river, near the position of the old bridge. His incantations awakened at least some of the Great Old ones and brought them forth. Thankfully, Philip Chesterton was on hand to give direction and stop the creatures as they began to emerge from the river. Some of the creatures that emerged were destroyed and the place was sealed off. Most of the houses near the area (this included most of Clotton) were pulled down and destroyed. A great concrete obelisk, marked with a restraining Elder Sign, was placed where they had been, and somehow the horror of that night was wiped from the minds of all those who had taken part. It is thought that many people have moved away from Clotton and are now living in Brichester but, although the village is now more or less non-existent, the horror of the period still lingers in the air and the place is better avoided by all sane people.

Warrendown

The village of Warrendown lies just off a major road that runs between Brichester and Birmingham. Although it is close to an arterial road, the village maintains an air of dereliction and remoteness about it. Many of the buildings (including the church) are in a ruinous state, and most look as if they are uninhabited. Both the ruined church, with a falling tower, and a rotting moss-covered school, lie on the very edge of the village; under the alter-stone (which can be levered up) there exists a system of tunnels and catacombs in which things are aid to dwell. The ghastly village first appears in Campbell's own contribution to the anthology, *Made in Goatswood* (1996), which was entitled *The Horror Under Warrendown*. The Horror is never given a name, but it is said to resemble one of the great heads of Easter Island, which is covered in a fungal growth. However, the growth is not external to the head, but is a part of the entity Itself. It can extend tentacles in order to grab a victim or to grant communion to a worshipper. Essentially a vegetable being, It can replicate Itself through offering pieces of Its own body as food, which is consumed by Its worshippers.

According to Campbell, the stench of a "rotten vegetable sweetness" hangs over the entire village and the people of the locality share a "look," which is slightly similar to Lovecraft's "Innsmouth look." In this respect, the people of Warrendown resemble rabbits more than anything else.

Although the Horror is unnamed, the *Call of the Cthulhu* role-playing game has named It "The Green God" perhaps because of Its plant-like origins. It (or some similar entity) has been given the name E'ilor in the story *Correlated Contents* by James Ambuehl and dwells in a vast cavern beneah a farming community in the Severn Valley where I attempts to garner worshippers by polluting the crops and vegetables which are grown there. Like neighbouring Clotton, this village is best avoided.

Severnford

The town of Severnford lies to the northwest of Brichester, well past its prime and gradually sliding into an era of dereliction and decay. Although the center of town is still reasonably busy, the further one travels out into the suburbs, the more the evidences of dilapidation and abandonment increase.

There is very little for the tourist to see in Severnford, although the town is said boasts one of the oldest inns in England in its central square. However, in 1958, the owner was declared bankrupt and the inn was closed for good. It has suffered vandalism throughout the years and is now in such an advanced state of dereliction that there is little chance of it ever being a working hostelry again.

On the outskirts of the town are a ruined castle and an Anglican Church. The latter is famous for a celebrated stone carving of an angel holding up what looks like a star in front of a cowering toad-like creature. This is said to refer to a local legend concerning the adjoining castle. The Castle was the home of Sir Gilbert Morley, an 18th-century warlock. It is the location of Campbell's *A Room in the Castle* in his *Cold Print* collection (1969). The story says Morley captured Byatis as a small toad-like creature and imprisoned the entity in Severnfod Castle where It grew so big that the warlock could barely control It. He was forced to let It out each night to feed upon the local populace; even today, long after Morley's death, It may still lurk there.

About 2 or 3 miles out of Severnford the traveler will come to an area of small rounded hills and twisting valleys, one of which forms the basis for another Campbell story, *The Plain of Sound*, which appeared in *The Inhabitant of the Lake* in 1964. Among these low hills, queer sounds come and go. A house in the area was once owned by Professor Arnold Hird of Brichester University, who did some research into the phenomenon and found that such sounds might be used to access the Gulf of S'glhuo from our world.

Beyond Severnford is a peculiar river island. It is reference in the Campbell story *The Stone on the Island*, which also appeared in *The Inhabitant of the Lake*. The island is roughly 200 feet across and circular. Little grows on this island except a short tank grass, which sweeps up a little rise to some Roman ruins on the summit of a small hill, which is possibly all that remains of a temple to an unknown deity. On the opposite side of the hill from Severnford is a small depression that descends about 10 feet; in this lies the stone. The stone is said to predate Roman occupation, as it may be associated with some ancient prehistoric cult. According to local tradition, a witch supposedly lived on the island, but very little is known about this occupation. However, in the 17th century it was the center of a witch-cult, which reputedly invoked water-elementals, but this was disbanded around 1790—although some say that stray cultists still continue to visit the site sporadically.

During the 19th century, there are a series of mutilations connected to the island—and the stone on it. The victims include a local cultist Joseph Norton in 1803, followed by a clergyman Nevill Rayner in 1826, an unnamed prostitute in 1866, a folk collector and amateur anthropologist named Alan Thorpe in 1870, and a Brichester University student in 1930. In 1962, the paranormal investigator Dr. Stanley Nash and his son Michael decided to investigate. Something terrible happened on the island, which Nash survives, but Michael does not. On his return, Nash begins experiencing strange visions and hallucinations, and gradually the distinction between reality and dream begins to break down under the influence of the peculiar stone. The tale contains a number of psychological elements, which foreshadow Campbell's later work in *Demons by Daylight*, begun the following year.

The island beyond Severnford appears in a piece of work known as "the Franklyn Paragraphs" (attributed by Campbell to the cult-leader Roland Franklyn), which form a section of the overall *Demons by Daylight*. They were described by T.E.D. Klein as "highly important" within the context of the Mythos. The paragraphs give fearful hints at what might be lurking out in the Severn Valley, particularly below the river waters and who knows what may be lurking out there on the island, waiting to attack anyone who approaches the curious stone?

Camside

The small village of Camside lies between Severnford and Berkley, and may have some legendary connections with both towns. The Berkley Toad, which prowled the area there, has a labyrinth beneath the village, which stretches for miles around, and is somehow sacred to the entity known as Eihort.

On the outskirts of Camside lies a large mental hospital in which a number of inmates from the surrounding countryside have been placed. One of its most celebrated patients was Edward Taylor who in 1924 attempted to climb The Devil's Steps; his experiences are recounted in Campbell's story *A Mine on Yuggoth*. In his story *The Render of the Veils*, Campbell also gives Camside as the home of Henry Fisher, a famed occultist who managed to summon the entity Daoloth from beyond the veil of space and time.

In Campbell's mind The Valley of the River Severn is a place of great antiquity. Certainly there are ancient ruins along its length, some dating back to the Roman period, and the river formed a significant thoroughfare through the west of England, particularly during the time of the Industrial Revolution when small villages grew up along its length to service the transportation of goods and materials to the larger cities. What better place then for ancient entities to lurk? What better setting for brooding Mythos tales? Campbell's Severn Country—the haunted countryside of his own imagination—mirrors Lovecraft's own dark New England regions and perhaps it is none the worse for that.

Where Human Pathways End

Other Places

Although some places such as Innsmouth and Dunwich have assumed a greater significance with many Mythos writers, other locations lie tucked away in the pages of Lovecraft's fiction. Some perhaps only appear in one story, others in two or three, and some are only mentioned in reference, but each one holds a special significance within the Mythos, and a few deserve to be looked at in their own right.

Sarnath

Lovecraft described Sarnath as "the doomed city." The name has, of course, a particular significance to Buddhists as a place of pilgrimage for the faith, lying about 13 kilometers northeast of Varanasi, India. This was the place where the Buddha taught the Natural Order of things, or Dharma, and it holds a special place in Buddhist philosophy. The village of Singhpur, about 1 kilometer away, also holds a special place in the Jain religion of India, as it is the birthplace of Shreyansanath, one of the Tirthankara of the religion. Although he certainly knew of this place, Lovecraft always maintained that it had come to him in a dream.

In the Mythos, however, Sarnath is a city near a great lake in the land of Mnar in the Dreamlands, which had been initially built by a band of human nomads. Reference to it can be found in Lovecraft's story, "The Doom That Came to Sarnath," written in 1919 and first published in a magazine entitled the *Scot* in 1920, which was a publication of mainly Scottish amateur fiction. The tale was also used as the title-story of a collection of Lovecraft's short stories published in 1971, and has appeared in collections of Dream Cycle stories ever since. References within the story may well have been inspired by Lord Dunsany's story "Idle Days on the Yann," which seems to have been one of Lovecraft's favorite stories.

In the tale, a group of shepherd-kings (perhaps loosely based on the Hyksos in Egyptian history) establish a series of trading cities, of which Sarnath is one, on the banks of the River Ai in Mnar. Through the years, these cities grew, forming the basis of a great trading culture on the shores of a lonely lake in the heart of Mnar, of which Sarnath is the center. However, the city is not alone in its location.

Further along the lakeshore was the ancient grey-stone city of Ib, which was inhabited by a race of pre-human, semi-aquatic creatures known as (according to Lin Carter) the Thuum'ha. These beings had descended from the moon in some former time and had built their city half in the lake and half on the land. They were repulsive to look upon, having green-tinged skins, flabby lips, bulging eyes, and curious ears, and were without any voice (communicating by a kind of croaking). They could live within the water and out of it, and some have suggested that these were the forerunners of the Deep Ones in some of Lovecraft's later stories. They worshipped an amphibian god named Bokrug, also known as the Great Water Lizard, who dwelled at the bottom of the lake and whose idol stood within the main temple of their city.

The men of Sarnath, however, passionately hated their neighbors. They turned on them, entered their city, and slaughtered most of the inhabitants there. They stole the idol of Bokrug from its temple and carried it back to Sarnath as a prize. They placed it in their temple as subservient to their own gods. On the first night, the idol disappeared mysteriously and the High Priest of Sarnath, the Venerable Taran-Ish, was found dead in the main temple. Before he died, he had written the word *doom* in his own blood. It was seen as an evil threat and the men of Sarnath were fearful.

And yet the curse (if it was a curse) did not seem to materialize. For the next thousand years Sarnath flourished, becoming a commercial capital and conquering several of the small kingdoms around it. It became one of the wealthiest and most important cities in all Mnar. At the height of its power, a great feast was held in the city to celebrate the destruction of Ib a thousand years earlier. Several days before this, however, the lake had appeared to mysteriously bubble, and a dank and eerie mist hovered above its surface. On the very night of the revelry, strange lights were seen in the sky over Sarnath and a heavy fog seemed to creep in from the lake, completely enveloping the city. The lake rose so much that the tidal marker, the granite pillar Akurion, was all but submerged. With the fog came figures, and some said that these were the lurching bodied of the frog-like Thuum'ha. Maddened by fear many people fled the city, others in their panic ran toward the lake.

In the morning, the fog had lifted and the lake was quiet once more. Some of the survivors of Sarnath who had fled to the neighboring city of Ilarnek returned, bringing soldiers from that city with them. Of Sarnath they found nothing—it was as if the city had completely disappeared, leaving only a few ruins covered in slime. Chillingly, in the ruins of the temple they found the intact idol of the god Bokrug while all the effigies of other gods had been destroyed. Other things were also discovered, but those who found them refused to say what they were. Ever since then, however, Bokrug has been the primary god in Ilarnek. No attempt was made to rebuild the city of Sarnath and the area where it stood was abandoned, eventually becoming a reedy marsh.

In another Dream Cycle story *The Quest of Iranon* (written in 1921 but not published until 1935 in an amateur magazine *The Galleon*) the title-character notes that he has seen the marshes where Sarnath once stood. In *The Nameless City* (written in 1921 and published that year in *The Wolverine*) the narrator states that he beheld the massive ruins of a fallen city and "thought of Doomed Sarnath."

In some variants of the story, Sarnath was built by the Great Old Ones, and the priests of the Sumerian civilization, who could magically transport themselves back through time, traveled back in order to study in a fabulously ancient library that was held in its temple. Most writers, however, agree that Sarnath was a human settlement, and that it may have been overwhelmed by the lake near which it was built. As a powerful city, it dominated part of Lovecraft's Dreamlands where its ruins still lie.

Ulthar

Sarnath is, of course, not the only human settlement that is named in the Dream Cycle. The town of Ulthar lies in the Western Dreamlands just beyond the River Skai. Unlike Sarnath, Ulthar is not a city, but a small town or village of peaked medieval cottages and cobbled streets. Reference to it appears in Lovecraft's *The Cats of Ulthar* (written in 1920 and originally published in *The Tryout* magazine of amateur fiction in that year). It is also mentioned in *The Dream-Quest of Unknown Kadath* and in *The Other Gods*. The story may have been influenced by the works of Lord Dunsany.

Ulthar has an unusual law that forbids anyone to kill a cat within the confines of the town. There is a story that tells of an old couple who took great delight in killing many of the cats that they found; one was the kitten of a small boy with a traveling group of strange wanderers who passed through Ulthar. The child called upon a mysterious deity who caused all the cats in the locality to rise up and turn upon the old couple and kill them. Having witnessed this, the town authorities passed a law protecting felines. Lovecraft expanded on the theme making the cats of Ulthar highly intelligent and able to converse with each others. Individuals could do so too, if they took time to learn the cat-language. The cats around Ulthar were very ancient and very wise, and held great knowledge that had been passed down since earliest times. They also are often spiteful creatures and can sometimes take vengeance even on the descendants of those who have wronged them in some way.

According to the dream traveler Randolph Carter (thought by many to be Lovecraft's fictional alter-ego) the Elder Ones had a small temple in Ulthar. The priest there was Atal, who had lived for a considerably long time; he was originally a shepherd-boy in the town, but had become a disciple of Barzai the Wise who succeeded him as priest. And according to tradition (and the wisdom of the zoogs) a copy of the *Pnakotic Manuscripts* is held somewhere within the confines of this temple.

Just to confuse matters, the name *Ulthar* is also that of an Elder God who is mentioned in the *Sussex Manuscript* (also known as the *Sussex Fragments*), which was found in Northern Europe and also in parts of Britain. This entity has been sent to Earth to keep a watch over the Great Old Ones who lie there in suspended slumber. However, It is to be treated as a deity and requires constant worship and frequent ritual if It is to maintain Its vigilance. This entity may be summoned by a practitioner of the occult arts by using a ritual that can be found in the *Pnakotic Manuscripts*.

As a location, however, Ulthar is to be counted as something of an idyllic place as long as one stays well clear of cats!

Averoigne

Although both Sarnath and Ulthar lie in the Dreamlands, Averoigne lies in our own world and has a specific geographical location there. It is not really a creation of Lovecraft, but of his collaborator Clark Ashton Smith.

Averoigne lies in south-central France, though it is not clear whether it exists somewhere in the past or if it still to be found there today. It is based on the Province of Auvergne, which is a historical area in central France. According to Smith, it is the most witch-ridden area in all of the country, where vampires and ghouls walk the roads and where evil is practiced in remote rural regions.

The *Annales* of Flavius Alesius (written around A.D. 300) state that the area was settled in the time of the Gauls by a tribe named the Averone who gave the location its name. They were the surviving descendants of the race that had inhabited a land that sank beneath the Western Sea (possibly Atlantis). The venerable scribe also states that they carried with them a series of stone tablets on which a text was written; it may have been the original of the *Book of Eibon*. Of course, neither Alesius nor his Gallic tribe existed but there were movements of ancient peoples around the year A.D. 100 right across France, as many of the tribes there began to consolidate themselves.

During the Roman period two main towns began to emerge and develop—Simaesis and Avionium, later known as Ximes and Voynes—where a cult belonging to the god Sadoqua flourished. One of the most famous of all the figures in Averoigne's history is unquestionably Gaspard du Nord of Voynes. He was a reputed wizard who translated the *Book of Eibon* into a form of French (as was spoken in the area) around the 13th or 14th centuries. The book underwent a series of copies in various other French dialects and led to a resurgence of witchcraft in the country, especially in Averoigne.

Much of the landscape of the region is composed of deep, dark forest. The walled city of Voynes, with its massive fortifications and its impressive cathedral, dominates the northern half of the province with the smaller town of Ximes to the south. A single road runs between them through the depths of the dark forest. The main river through the region is the Isoile, which rises in the mountains in the north and flows down into a great swamp that dominates much of the southern area. All along the road—or just off it—lie other small towns and villages such as Moulins, Touraine, Sainte Zenobie, Les Hiboux, Le Frenaie, and Perigon (with its famous abbey). Other settlements lie tucked away in the forest depths. Scattered throughout the woodlands and hilltops are the ruins of former castles and strongholds, which have been held in former times by the powerful families who dominated the region. The most impressive are said to be the ruins of the stronghold of Ylourgne about which very little is known, except that it was a military fortification during some of the wars in the region. Around 1281, it was home to a sorcerer who constructed a great colossus, which briefly rampaged around the country before being destroyed.

The land, then, is a place where time passes slowly, if at all, and change scarcely comes. When passing through Averoige, one has only to reach out to touch the past. What better place for Lovecraftian mystery?

Chateau des Faussesflames

Not far from the Abbey at Perigon, a rounded hill rises out of the forests, on top of which lie the ruins of an old chateau. The gateway into the ruins boasts on its archway the family crest of an ancient family, together with a representation of a salamander, the medieval symbol of alchemy. During medieval times, the place was a spectacular manor house and also the residence of the Sieur Hugh de Malinbous and his wife, both widely suspected of being witches. There was reputedly a great library, crammed with diabolical books of various sorts, together with a bizarre and diabolic workshop in the cellars beneath the chateau, but after the deaths of both the Sieur and his wife, these were allegedly sealed up by order of the Abbots of Perigon. Tales of disputes between de Malinbous and Abbot Bernard of Perigon are legion in the surrounding countryside, and it was said that the Sieur tried to place the Abbey under a curse of some kind. Even after the evil couple's death, the sinister reputation of the place lingered on and it is said that the new master, de Malinbous's son (the new Sieur) went mad within its walls and tried to destroy the place. It was later left to deteriorate and is now a ruin, although its dark reputation is still legendary in Averoigne and even further afield. Some of those who have visited the place do not return and it is said to be the haunt of vampires, werewolves, and even worse things. Somewhere deep in the ruin there is a double tomb in which Sieur High and his dark wife still lie, though locals will say that they are not dead and often rise to roam about the surrounding countryside in a ghastly state, killing and devouring those whom they meet. Most curiosity-seekers try to avoid the chateau's shattered walls. In 1932, however, the Cabot Museum in Boston put on a brief display of some curious mummies and attendant artifacts, which had been found in the crypts beneath the old chateau. Some of these were so terrible and disturbing that they had to be withdrawn and the exhibition was closed. Nevertheless, the old ruin still stands brooding on its hill in the center of Averoigne.

Zothique

The land of Zothique does not exist as of yet. It is an imagined future continent—the last land on Earth—on which Mankind will live in the final days. It features in a collection of tales by Clark Ashton Smith and falls into the Dying Earth classification of fantasy fiction, which contains writers such as Jack Vance. The continent corresponds to Northern Africa, the Middle East, and some parts of Southern Asia, and it will rise when the world is flooded and all other continents have sunk beneath the waves.

Although there are many alleged maps of Zothique, they are often contradictory or contain omissions and have very little to do with the stories themselves. Many have derived from the artist's own imagination about what the continent should look like. There is nothing to suggest, in either the stories or the maps, as to what lies in the north of the continent, which seems to be simply an unexplored waste. The continent is, however, bounded by the sea to the west, south, and east with a number of islands lying off the landmass.

To the West lies the Island of Iribos, also known as the Island of Crabs, and further West lies the larger Island of Naat, which is famous for its necromancers and magicians. Just beyond that is a strong oceanic current known as the Black River, which sweeps travelers away to the darkness at the World's Edge. Many notable sorcerers have come from Naat, including the kings of some of the other realms in Zothique, and the very air there hums with their magical energies.

South of the continent lies the Indaskian Sea, with the islands of Cyntrom and Uccastrog, the Island of Torturers. Uccastrog's king Ildrac, and many of the nobles at his court, are well known all across the final Earth, for their sadistic torture practices on all those who land on their island. Many competed with each other as to who could inflict the most pain on their visitors until they were unexpectedly visited by a plague known as the Silver Death, which reduced much of their island to a graveyard.

East of Zorthique lies the island kingdom of Sotar with its capital of Loithe, and beyond that lie only atolls and tiny islands known as Yumatot. The largest of these islands is Tosk about which not very much is known, and beyond this are the scattered islands of the Ilozian Sea, all of which are unnamed except for Omava, the Island of Birds.

The mainland of Zothique comprises four great realms: Xylac, Yoros, Ustaim, and Tasuun. Xylac is an empire in the northwest of the continent and there is little to the north, save for the kingdoms of Ilcar and Dooza Thom with its capital of Avandas. Most of the north is taken up by the great desert of Nooth-Kemmor beyond which nothing is known. Xylac is governed by an emperor whose principal seat is the city of Ummaos. Its principal trading port on the north-western coast is the city of Mirouane, with the town of Oroth a little further along the coastline. Both these ports trade with Yoros and galleys frequently travel the coast around them. Over land one can travel through the Celotian Waste to the city-state of Zul-Bha-Sair.

Zul-Bha-Sair is a dreadful place; here is the ornate temple of Mordiggian, god of the dead to whom all who die within the walls of the city are given so that the god may feast on their corpses. Beyond this and far to the south lies Tasuun, which is famous for the number of its mummies. The valleys throughout this region are lined with tombs. The capital here is Miraab, beyond which lie the mysterious ruins of an ancient city known as Chaon Gacca, reputedly destroyed by a great earthquake.

Yoros is famed for its fine wines, which are exported all over Zothique. Its chief city is Faraad, which lies on a crossing on the River Voum, which flows into the Indaskian Sea. The city is famous for an ornate bridge—a wonder of construction—that spans this river. Roads connect Faraad to the cities of Silpon and Siloar and lead on to the River Vos, on the other side of which is the demon-haunted wasteland of Izdrel.

The land of Tinarath lies far to the east of Xylac and north of the kingdom of Cincor—described as "a grey and dead" country where only a few people, who live in fear of witches, dwell. Ustaim is the easternmost realm of Zothique and its ports trade with Sotar, the island kingdom. From here one can journey to the dead lands of Calyz.

Although these are the main realms of Zothique, they have been added through time and the country has been greatly expanded and developed by a number of writers. Within the final continent are the remnants of lost kingdoms that have existed in previous aeons. Foremost among these is the ancient kingdom of Ossaru, which once ruled half of Zothique. Its monarchs were wizards who ruled with the aid of an extraterrestrial monster named Nioth Karghai. The wizards were eventually overthrown and the monster destroyed. Now the very name of the ancient realm is all but forgotten, and where its capital stood (on the borders of Yoros) is a desolate waste, inhabited only by the cannibal Ghorii.

The Empire of Cincor followed on and established itself over a quarter of the continent and was ruled by the Nimboth Dynasty. However, its monarchs and many of its people were wiped out in a great plague that swept part of Zothique (the ruins that can be seen today are still thought to be plague-ridden). After 200 years, necromancers from Naat tried to raise those that had died in the plague to a kind of half-life in order to over-run the continent, but before they could do so, the Undead kings turned on them, killing them and driving themselves into oblivion.

The next Empire to emerge was that of Tasuun, founded by King Tnepreez at Chaon Gacca. The dynasty which Tnepreez founded was, however, an unstable one, and it led to internecine fighting, murder, and intrigue. Son rose against father and wives slew husbands. Nevertheless, the Empire was well known for its opulence and decadence and for its dark experiments in sorcery.

Almost contemporaneous with the rise of Tasuun was the emergence of the Empire of Xylac. A number of emperors came and went, the last being Zotulla who was a despot who enslaved most of his people. His battles with the sorcerer Namirrha are the stuff of legend. Namirrha's vengeance would bring about the utter destruction of Xylac's capital Ummaos, but out of the ruins a new city grew where the astrologer and necromancer Nushain is said to have dwelt.

Little is known regarding the Empire of Yoros. Even its date is uncertain. The last king is thought to have been Fulbra, whose realm was devastated by the Silver Death, which also decimated Tasuun. Fulbra is supposed to have kept himself alive by magic, but is also said to have fled to Uccastrog, the Island of Torturers, taking the plague with him and wiping out much of the island population.

Gods and deities abound in Zothique—many are specific to certain realms and kingdoms. Some, however, transcend the boundaries of the various countries. One of the most common is Vargama or "Destiny," a god who has no temple but is frequently invoked by all peoples across the continent. It is depicted as a muffled and cowled being seated on a marble throne. Its power is questionable, but many sages agree that It is probably omnipotent. Basatan is a sea god that is worshipped by all mariners and has power to control the mighty Kraken, which lie off the coast of Zothique and are the symbol of this capricious deity. Also widely worshipped (and feared) is Thasaidon, "Lord of the Seven Hells beneath the earth" and "black god of evil," who is said to be seated on a throne of "ever-burning brass." The deity's female counterpart is Aila, "queen of perdition and all iniquities," who was reputedly worshipped with a number of unspeakable rituals in Tasuun.

During the age of Zothique some of the most powerful wizards who have ever lived on earth have come to the fore. Their magical energies have charged the entire continent like an electrical force and this has allowed some sorcerers to experiment with time-travel back into their past. The magical energies have been harnessed to form interdimensional gateways, which might appear randomly (owing to the fluctuations in the energy-flow) and in which the unwary in other times, such as our own, might become caught. At least one intertemporal portal between our own time and Zothique is known to exist, but there might be others.

Zothique then, successfully fuses fantasy with sorcery and science. It is Mankind's final place on this planet and its limits only seem to be those of the imaginations of Mythos writers. Perhaps there is more of its geography and its history waiting to be explored.

All through the Mythos, uncanny places lie, both within our own world and in other realms. Some are known only by reference and some by vague description, but they are part of the Lovecraftian nightmare world nonetheless. And who knows where else might lie out there waiting to be discovered and to terrify us all with its horrors and strangeness? One has simply to turn the pages of new Mythos fiction to find out!

Conclusion

Behind the Pallid Mask

This has been a difficult book to write; it has also been great fun. It has opened the pages of arcane and forbidden books; it has taken me to fantastic places of wonder and terror, and it has allowed me to glimpse entities that lurk just outside the realm of human consciousness. It has allowed me into the dark and eerie world of H.P. Lovecraft.

Lovecraft's world is like no other, and perhaps that's why it has remained so popular through the years and why so many writers have tried to imitate and add to it. It's an inspirational world that tugs at the edges of our imagination and leads us toward dark and labyrinthine paths. But curiously, Lovecraft was not a particularly colorful (or overly sinister) character. He was strange, but it was the kind of strangeness that people tended to avoid rather than be frightened of. His world was incredibly narrow and yet the universe that he created was huge, vibrant, and seething with myriad forms of life.

Although it is true that Lovecraft was well read on a number of topics—including Egyptology and mythology—it is doubtful that he had actually probed too deeply into occult books or had explored texts of terrible lore in any great detail. His was the interest of an inquisitive student rather than as an exponent of the Darker Arts. Nor did he appear to study them from an academic perspective—he may have heard of them, of course, and incorporated them into his tales but, apart from the eldritch books that he created, there is no real attempt at any deep analysis of the sorcerous and occult material. Nevertheless, his letters to his numerous correspondents reveal him to be "a man of letters" and an erudite scholar. It is perhaps his greatest disappointment that he was not an "academic" in the conventional sense.

It was possibly the narrowness and isolation of his life that provided the impetus for his vision. Appalled and perhaps slightly overwhelmed by the pace and the harshness of the life around him, he had the ability to withdraw from it and to immerse himself in his own world. This world was drawn from a combination of what he had read in his books and how he imagined and interpreted the worlds about which he read. Into this universe he could place his own inner fears and prejudices, and these too would lend depth and color to that cosmos. Thus, the fears of foreigners, the constant fear of hereditary insanity, and the fears of having to face the horrors of actual life manifested themselves in the strange characters and terrifying monsters, which stalk the pages of his fiction. These fears served to give a sharpness and imminence to his vision. Writing about the strange foreign characters or the crazed hermits who inhabited falling, near-derelict buildings in remote areas or mad women confined to locked rooms in gloomy garrets, Lovecraft tasted his own personal terror regarding such individuals and conveyed that fear to his readership.

And in much of his work, the terror derives from a sense of history—not the wholesome histories that might be taught in a school or college—but a shadowed history that contained both dubious and sinister overtones. Part of it was the darker history of Colonial America, from a time when the Founding Fathers believed in witchcraft and in ancient things still lurking in the dark forests of a new country. As we know, he had read about many aspects of Eastern, Middle Eastern, and European history. What may have appealed to him and given his own conservative background, was the sheer *alienness* of some of the things—the events and beliefs—about which he was reading. Some of what he read must have also dealt with the darker side of some of these cultures—druidism in Europe, and ancient mystery religions in Egypt and the Middle East—which also compounded the sense of strangeness. Some of these elements may have been easy to incorporate into stories of primal horror. Thus, we find references to ancient gods worshipped in groves in Roman times; ancient serpent mounds from the time of the Native Americans; and old and decayed families who harbor ghastly secrets dating back to the time of the American Colonies.

And with this eye to the past, Lovecraft's imaginative sensitivities had the ability to fasten on some old building or geographical feature of the landscape and to invest it with some terrible history. And there were many such sites around Providence and in rural Rhode Island. These were sites that sometimes dated back to the very earliest days surrounding the foundation of the town or the state, and they held that same sense of history that so appealed to Lovecraft. Remote buildings tucked away in the rural landscapes, small rural hamlets that the train passed by on its way to somewhere else, and ivy-covered dwellings on some back street all provoked his imagination and often found their way into his stories. The strange rounded hills around Rhode Island, the small rural villages, the tracks seeming to lead nowhere across the fields, and the remote hollows, some containing cemeteries dating back to the Revolutionary Wars, were obvious fuel for his imagination and were suggestive of things just outside of human sight or cognisance. These may have affected him just as much as the decaying, gambrel, slope-roofed Colonial buildings that he sometimes saw around Providence.

Lovecraft viewed all of these with the sense of perspective of an outsider. He had always considered himself outside the mainstream of society—perhaps as a creature apart. Raised as an only child, pampered and cosseted, and later as an individual who found relationships difficult though not impossible, Lovecraft thought of himself as someone who hung around the very periphery of society. In other circumstances, he would have found a job and developed a life of his own, but he did not. Even when forced to look for work in New York, his attempts to find work and to hold it down were ultimately unsuccessful largely because he was content to live off Sonia, and earn whatever pittance he could writing for small magazines. The rush and demands of the modern world were not for him. At night he wandered the streets, peering at the night-life like some detached observer. He was by his own admission the quintessential "outsider" and, even by his own standards, Lovecraft was a man who didn't readily "fit in."

And because of this feeling, it was easy to build up a separate world in which he could lose himself and from which he could keep the real world at a distance. As a child, growing up largely in isolation, he had already experienced such a world—playing alone and creating personal (if lonely) environments for himself. And of course, in such a sensitive child (and in an emotionally stunted adult) such make-believe environments took on a kind of impetus of their own and became more and more complex. Like many writers, Lovecraft could withdraw into his own world, but it was the intensity and vibrancy of that world—right down to its rewriting of human history and the history of our planet—that made it unique. Some commentators have claimed that Lovecraft's stories are sometimes contradictory, but this was because the world that he was creating for himself (as a possible retreat from reality) was constantly shifting and realigning itself. It is possible that Lovecraft's world was originally a "supernatural" one, but then it changed slightly to a more "scientific" one to meet with what may have been perceived as market demands from the publishers. Also, this allowed him to develop the fantasy side of his work as his correspondence with fantasy writers such as Robert E. Howard developed. In fact, it was his voluminous correspondence that provided his main "bridge" with the outside rational world. Some of his critics have commented that he spent far more time on his letters to other people than he did on his stories, but this was his way of reaching out to the world beyond his room or his house. Finding face-to-face relationships difficult, Lovecraft poured most of his emotional (and often creative) energies into the letters to correspondents. In doing so, he sharpened, refined, and developed the fantastic world in which he lived.

And into this make-believe world he could channel all his innermost fears and prejudices—things such as the fear of insanity and the implicit dislike of foreigners, the underlying fear of the unknown, or something that could disrupt his "normal" world.

It's not clear whether Lovecraft actually saw himself as a ground-breaker of horror fiction. It's probably doubtful that he did. And although his fiction has certainly inspired generations of both writers and fans after him, it is not masterly work in the way of some writers such as Poe. For example, there is little (and sometimes no) characterization in the stories. The characters who appear in them are largely one dimensional, lacking any real depth, and simply exist as ciphers for a sense of "evil history" or for Lovecraft's own latent fears and disquiet. Some only exist in hints and references. Of course, this allows the reader to "fill in the blanks"—and there are just enough hints to allow him or her to do so. And it is certainly possible to argue that this is indeed the mark of a good writer—that he allows the reader to engage with his text and create his or her own horror from the references that he has given.

And where Lovecraft went into the eldritch dark, others followed. He seems to have had the power not only to put his own terrors into fear fiction, but to inspire other writers with them. Indeed, much of his writing became the foundations of a genre into which others were drawn: the Cthulhu Mythos. Other writers—not only his friends and correspondents—seemed somehow drawn toward this strange Universe that he had created out of his own uncertainties and began to write their own stories which were set in the eerie New England landscape or in the infinite fantasy world of the Dreamlands. And in doing so, they brought their own perspectives and both expanded and developed Lovecraft's original vision. Thus, writers such as Clark Ashton Smith, Brian Lumley, Lin Carter, and Ramsey Campbell began to create their own worlds and universes within the general parameters of the Mythos. They have also interpreted the work through their personal viewpoint, changing and amending it as they saw fit. This has invariably led to some confusion and contradiction within many of the stories, but it does not detract from the initial horror, eeriness, and utter strangeness of Lovecraft's nightmare world. They simply added their own layers to the overall Mythos, and it is all the stronger for that. Many became absorbed in developing pseudonyms for themselves within a Mythos context—for example, the High Priest Klarkesh-Ton (Clark Aston Smith). Since then gamers and role-playing designers have taken elements of Lovecraft's work and developed them to fit into their own entertainment products. Filmmakers too have offered their own interpretations, many of which have paid little more than lip service to Lovecraft's work, although some have been quite passable and done quite well, such as David Greene's *The Shuttered Room* (1967), Daniel Haller's *The Dunwich Horror* (1970), Christophe Gan's *Necronomicon* (1993), and C. Courtney Joyner's *Lurking Fear*. All of these took the Mythos in slightly different directions and added to its complexity and diversity.

Since then, Lovecraftian themes have turned up in many different formats. They have appeared in comics—in Marvel's *Dr. Strange* and in D.C.'s *Batman*, for example—and in computer games such as the cross-over with Batman and Arkham Asylum. Recently, Lovecraft has become bigger and bigger, and has touched more and more people.

So where now for the Mythos? Already some stories are starting to appear, set in some near-future world and in the strictly science-fiction genre. In fact, much of the Mythos lends itself to these interpretations and settings. Does its future then not lie in queer, partly boarded up gambrel houses in remote areas or in dark parts of town, where crazed inhabitants come and go, but in the infinite spaces overhead and in the darkness between worlds? Or will the sinister world of decaying hamlets and eerie hermits who know things that are beyond the knowledge of decent human folk still have a place somewhere within the Mythos? One would like to think so.

Howard Phillips Lovecraft has been called one of the founding fathers of modern horror fiction and there is no doubt that he inspired many of today's horror and fantasy writers. And he has inspired many authors, from the dedicated professional to the enthusiastic amateur. That is his true legacy. On top of this, he has inspired an industry that is centered on his creations, and creatures that continue to grow, expand, and develop. And so perhaps it is true, with little fear of exaggeration, that his impact on the world of fear fiction has been immeasurable. However we may think of him as a person, perhaps he genuinely *was* the true Outsider. And perhaps he, like no other, could see some of the dreadful things and some of the fearful places that lurked out there in the eldritch gloom, just beyond the furthest edges of the rational human mind.